W9-CBJ-049

"METICULOUSLY RESEARCHED . . . Under Andersen's pen, Jagger is the personification of sex, drugs, and rock 'n' roll."

—*Detroit Free Press*

"SCINTILLATING!"—*Time*

"[Pulls] back every bedcover in Jagger's life. . . . Dish-wise, this leaves no stone unturned."—*Booklist*

"Offers enough steamy anecdotes, titillation and voyeurism to satisfy those with inquiring minds."—*Palm Beach Post*

Find Out the Shocking Secrets Mick Doesn't Want You to Know . . .

- Why "Satisfaction" almost landed on the scrap heap before it ever got released . . .
- Why Marianne Faithfull's biggest mistake might have been introducing Mick to Rudolf Nureyev . . .
- Why Mick wanted to dump Brian Jones . . . and the real deal about Jones's mysterious death . . .
- Who Mick dresses up as, and we mean "dresses" . . . and what he learned from his mum, the Avon lady . . .
- What Mick's wife, Jerry Hall, told Andy Warhol about how she keeps her husband happy . . .

"OBVIOUSLY, I'M NO PARAGON OF VIRTUE."
—Mick Jagger in . . .
JAGGER UNAUTHORIZED

JAGGER
UNAUTHORIZED

CHRISTOPHER ANDERSEN

A DELL BOOK

Published by
Dell Publishing
a division of
Bantam Doubleday Dell Publishing Group, Inc.
1540 Broadway
New York, New York 10036

ISBN: 0-440-21417-3

Reprinted by arrangement with Delacorte Press

Printed in the United States of America

Published simultaneously in Canada

August 1994

10 9 8 7 6 5 4 3 2 1

OPM

For Valerie,
who was there when

"I'd rather die than be forty-five and still singing 'Satisfaction.' "

Three weeks remained in the decade, but for those of us who were there, the sixties came to an end December 6, 1969, at the Altamont.
—The Author

Tie dyed and leather fringed, they swarmed over the naked, crescent moonlit hillsides like pilgrims to Mecca—and in a way they were. Only four months before a half million of their spiritual brethren had assembled peaceably at Woodstock to celebrate the budding promise of rock's first generation to the sounds of such seminal groups as Crosby, Stills, Nash, and Young and the Who. Now they gathered at the remote Altamont Speedway some forty miles east of San Francisco to pay homage to the greatest rock and roll band of them all. The same day the Rolling Stones released their fourteenth album. Its hauntingly fitting title: *Let It Bleed*.

Why Altamont? On the spur of the moment Mick Jagger had decided that the Rolling Stones would culminate their triumphant eighteen-city United States tour with a free concert—largely to squelch criticism concerning the Stones' routinely stratospheric ticket prices. Since San

Francisco's Haight-Ashbury district was the birthplace of "Flower Power" and, by extension, the counterculture itself, Jagger thought it fitting to hold the concert in the city's Elysian Golden Gate Park. When the San Francisco Parks Department refused to issue a permit because of drug use at previous park concerts, the Stones management turned its attention to the thousand-acre Sears Point raceway, an hour's drive to the north. A stage was constructed, the lighting towers erected—but then the raceway's owners suddenly demanded a $125,000 cash payment for use of the site. A furious Jagger refused.

The Stones brought in legal heavyweight Melvin Belli, the "King of Torts," to sort through the legal problems and field offers. Using the colorful lawyer's turn-of-the-century San Francisco office as their unlikely headquarters, the group's tour manager stood anxiously by as Belli massaged and cajoled zoning officials and law-enforcement officers.

When race-car promoter Dick Carter called Belli to offer his eighty-acre Altamont Raceway gratis, Jagger jumped. Nothing more than a clapboard announcer's booth and some weathered bleachers overlooking a dusty ellipse, the raceway itself sat at the bottom of a natural bowl—accessible only by dirt road and hidden from civilization. Technically, it was within the city limits of Livermore, a town best known as the home of the Lawrence nuclear weapons laboratory. "Father of the H-bomb" Dr. Edward Teller, the laboratory's director and the model for Dr. Strangelove, watched with interest as Jagger prepared to drop a megaton device of his own.

In those predawn hours of December 6, 1969, early arrivals parked their cars alongside one of the narrow country roads that led to the raceway's perimeter. Then, hauling mattresses, bedrolls, and ice chests full of beer and wine, they hiked the remaining half mile to the concert site itself. Shivering in the bone-chilling California night air, some crawled into the rusted wrecked hulks of abandoned stock cars to stay warm; others ripped apart the racetrack fence to fuel bonfires or huddled beneath blankets, fortifying themselves against the cold with hearty swigs of jug wine. While workers perched precariously on scaffolding and hammered away overhead, many chose to generate body heat by making love in their sleeping bags.

Throughout the night the Stones' advance men tore across the countryside in jeeps and pickups. At one point shortly after two A.M., a helicopter churned up eerie blue-white clouds of dust as it landed in the center of the raceway. Out jumped Jagger, wearing an oversized red beret and matching red velvet cloak, followed by a bedraggled Keith Richards and the rest of the Stones. After checking out the stage, Jagger and Richards—rock's legendary "Glimmer Twins"—moved among the faithful like generals visiting troops on the eve of battle.

The whole scene was captured on film by San Francisco filmmakers Albert and David Maysles, who had been hired to make a movie about the concert. Mick intended for his film to upstage the highly anticipated Woodstock documentary from Warner Bros., the film company that at the time was holding up Jagger's feature film debut by refusing to release the sexually explicit *Performance*. The Maysles Brothers film would indeed overshadow the competing film, but for reasons Jagger could not have anticipated.

For the most part the mood was upbeat. Diesel-powered floodlights that had been trucked in from San Francisco now provided illumination for games of Frisbee and touch football. These diehard fans, who were willing to brave near-freezing temperatures for a ringside seat, seemed stunned by the sudden appearance of the two rock deities in their midst.

Around one bonfire Jagger encountered several young women huddled around a single man. Impressed with any man who could boast of his own personal harem—much less one that would follow him into this wasteland—Jagger tried to strike up a conversation. The gaunt, bearded figure with wild eyes leaned out of the shadows, declared himself the Stones' greatest fan and offered Mick a joint. Jagger drew back, partly because of the stench emanating from the stranger and partly because of the swastika painted on his forehead.

Jagger had good reason to be nervous. Five months earlier the wild-eyed stranger, Charles Manson, had led his drug-crazed followers on one of the most heinous murder sprees in U.S. history. Soon Manson and his notorious "family," the objects of a fevered national manhunt, would be arraigned on homicide charges.

Their tour of the concert site complete, Jagger and Richards returned to the safety and comfort of their San Francisco hotel. Meanwhile, tens of thousands heeded the repeated calls from San Francisco Bay Area radio stations throughout the morning to attend the "Greatest Free Concert in Rock and Roll History." As cars began backing up on Highway 50, disc jockeys warned listeners they would not be able to drive within miles of the site itself. Undaunted, they simply abandoned their cars by the side of the road and trekked across the corduroy-textured hillsides on foot.

Landowners who had tried but failed to obtain an eleventh-hour court order prohibiting the concert did what little they could to protect their property from these unwelcome intruders. Several isolated residents, unable to prevent the trespassers from knocking down their fences and frightening their livestock, stood guard on their front porches, shotguns at the ready.

By noon the crowd had swelled to nearly 350,000, and there were ample indications that this would not be a repeat of Woodstock. Enterprising drug pushers, some of whom flew in from as far away as New York, made sure that the crowd was amply supplied with everything from marijuana and speed to LSD and heroin.

The resulting spectacle was nothing short of macabre. A naked woman, her hands bloodied like some modern-day Lady Macbeth, wandered about in a drug-induced daze, finally collapsing at the feet of a stunned reporter. She would be only one of hundreds of overdose cases treated by emergency medical personnel on the scene, then sped by ambulance to Livermore Hospital fifteen miles away.

A couple tried out various positions of the Kama Sutra, with their nervous-looking Doberman chained to the woman's ankle. Orange-robed Hari Krishnas moved among the throng chanting and waving bowls of incense. Meanwhile, only a dozen portable toilets were trucked in to accommodate a crowd more than half the population of San Francisco. Not surprisingly, fistfights broke out among the hundreds who waited in line for hours to use the facilities. Others who were less fastidious merely relieved themselves where they sat.

By midmorning Altamont had claimed its first victim. A stoned seventeen-year-old from a neighboring town had wandered off alone and plunged into the concrete aqueduct that sliced through a nearby valley, carrying water from the north to the San Joaquin Valley and beyond. His screams for help went unnoticed by the throng, which by now was in the throes of a communal acid trip. The boy's body, carried off by the rushing current, would be recovered nearly a mile downstream.

Meanwhile the raceway owner, Dick Carter, proudly announced over the public address system that a baby had been born to a woman in the crowd—the first of Altamont's four hysteria-induced deliveries.

The fuse to this explosive situation was lit by the noisy arrival of the Hell's Angels. Members of the notorious motorcycle gang had policed several concerts in northern California, and the Grateful Dead enthusiastically recommended them to the Stones. Six months earlier Jagger had allowed the gang's decidedly more sedate British chapter to keep order at a Stones free concert in Hyde Park, and that event had gone off without incident. Now, promised all the cold beer they could drink and a ringside seat, the Hell's Angels agreed to keep fans from breaching security and climbing onto the stage.

On the surface the Stones and the Angels were an obvious mismatch—to everyone but Jagger. The Stones' counterculture following was clearly at odds with the brazen thuggery of the notorious Angels. On the other hand, Jagger was not unaware that the presence of the menacing Hell's Angels only added to his own satanic mystique. Over six years on the world stage, he had reveled in his role as the very personification of sex, drugs, and rock and roll. It seemed only fitting now that the pop world's bad boy emeritus be surrounded by the baddest boys of all.

Just how bad surprised Lucifer himself. The Hell's Angels, boasting tattoos, plenty of leather, and the occasional tough-as-nails biker chick, made their entrance merely by gunning their engines and steering their Harleys directly into the crowd. People screamed as bodies flew in every direction. When someone was brazen enough to object, the bikers would simply dismount, then wildly swing the lead-tipped pool cues they carried with them until their path was cleared. Behind them followed a yellow school bus loaded down with liquor, drugs, and enough weapons to arm a third-world country.

The mounting aura of danger led credence to repeated warnings from astrologers and professional concert organizers alike that this event would dissolve into bloodshed. Legendary rock promoter Bill Graham, whose Fillmore auditoriums in New York and San Francisco had showcased the greatest acts of the decade, blasted Jagger as a "selfish prick" who was willing to risk injury to others to satisfy his hunger for glory.

In America's most psychically attuned city warnings from mystics and seers were taken seriously. Astrologers noted that on the day the concert was scheduled, Mercury, Venus, and the sun were all in Sagittarius, and that the moon was in Scorpio—all unmistakable signs of impending chaos. Jagger, who for years had dabbled in the occult, nonetheless decided to ignore the doomsayers. He was intent on beating Woodstock to the theaters with his own rock documentary, and that could only be accomplished if there were no delays.

By the time San Francisco's brassy Latin band Santana

struck up the first chords of "Black Magic Woman," a platoon of chain-twirling Hell's Angels were positioned toward the front of the stage—a solid wall of leather that blocked the field of vision between the performers and their audience.

The driving beat of Carlos Santana ignited a new wave of violence. Once the crowd began to push forward to get a better look at the band, the Hell's Angels responded by kicking at them with steel-tipped boots, lashing at them with hunting knives, beating them into unconsciousness with pieces of lead pipe and brass knuckles.

The Rolling Stones could see none of this from the air as their helicopter returned in midafternoon—only a faceless, shapeless sea of humanity. "Jesus," said Jagger. "Have you ever seen so many people in one place in your whole life?"

While one group of Hell's Angels indulged their passion for violence on the stage, another used their blood-stained pool cues to clear a landing spot for the Stones' chopper. No sooner had Jagger emerged than someone leapt out from the crowd shrieking "I hate you! I hate you!" and punched the Stones' lead singer in the face. While the Angels wrestled the man to the ground and kicked him senseless, the stunned Jagger was hustled off to the Stones' backstage trailer.

Things were no less unruly onstage, where the Jefferson Airplane was struggling to perform its psychedelic repertoire while a battle raged around them. At one point in the middle of the group's somewhat ironically titled hit "Somebody to Love," singer Marty Balin jumped down off the stage and rushed to the defense of a bloodied young black man who had been singled out by the Angels. Within moments a sullen-faced biker swung around and brought his pool cue down across Balin's head, knocking him cold.

While Balin lay unconscious in the dirt, another band member, Paul Kantner, halted the music and demanded to know why his fellow musician had been brutally attacked. A menacing, bearded, beer-swilling Hell's Angel grabbed the open microphone and threatened to do even more to Kantner if he didn't shut up.

Grace Slick tried to calm both sides down. "People get weird, so you need people like the Angels in charge," she tried to explain as the scuffling continued. "But you don't bust people in the head for nothing. So both sides are fucking up temporarily. Let's not keep fucking up!" Slick's appeal quieted the crowd down just long enough for Jagger to emerge from his trailer to sign a few autographs, then return confident that everything was under control.

It wasn't. The lilting harmonies of Crosby, Stills, Nash, and Young might have been expected to soothe any other audience. But in this surreal setting it had the opposite effect, causing the long-haired peace-and-love crowd to surge forward and the surly Angels to ruthlessly beat them back. Stretchers carrying the wounded were lifted over the heads of the crowd to the overwhelmed medical personnel behind the stage. After a half hour CSN & Y, clearly terrified by the mounting mayhem, cut short their performance and dashed to a waiting helicopter.

Still, Jagger remained in his trailer with the other Stones, nibbling canapés, smoking pot, and drinking champagne. He was an expert at the waiting game, knowing how to let the anticipation build into a crescendo. At all the Stones concerts the crowd was whipped into a veritable frenzy of expectation even before the band played those first, driving chords.

Jagger shrugged off the reports of violence, confident that his Hell's Angels would protect him. At this point, however, the gang members themselves were fed up with waiting, and "suggested" that he take the stage rather than continue to "fuck around" with the fans that had made him. Jagger would not be budged. His stage makeup, he insisted, always looked better at night.

Ninety minutes after the last act had departed, the Stones took the stage. Wrapped in his trademark Lucifer getup—a black-and-red satin Harlequin outfit designed by London couturier Ossie Clark—Jagger launched into "Jumpin' Jack Flash" behind a phalanx of Angel thugs. A young boy ripped off his clothes and tried to crawl onstage, only to have his jaw shattered with a biker's single kick. Jagger halted the song, not because of the boy who was being savagely beaten a few feet in front of him, but because the crush of 150 people onstage made it impossible for him to make his trademark moves.

Jagger then launched into his paean to Satan (and a particular favorite of Charlie Manson), "Sympathy for the Devil." Another naked fan, this time a woman, was pummeled and pitched back into the crowd. This time Jagger reacted. He stopped singing and asked the Angels if it was really necessary for six of them to gang up on a single woman.

"People, please cool out," Jagger pleaded, "Please just cool out." Then, almost guilelessly, he allowed that "something very funny always happens when we start that number."

The group started up again, but from this point on it was clear that Jagger was no longer in control. While the visibly shaken superstar sang and strutted meekly in what little space was allotted him, a German shepherd prowled the stage. Hell's Angels felt perfectly free to walk up to Mick in midverse and whisper in his ear. Under normal circumstances burly bodyguards would prevent anyone from coming near the Stones while they were performing. These were not normal circumstances. Mick, fearing that any minute he might be torn apart by the tattooed demons he had unleashed, gamely complied.

Suddenly, the glint from a gun under the bright stage lights caught Jagger's eye. "Fuck, man," Jagger said to guitarist Mick Taylor, "there's a cat out there pointing a gun at us!" Taylor and Richards saw a tall black man wearing a green suit and a large hat waving a pistol in Mick's direction. Jagger retreated to the rear of the stage.

What Jagger could not see were the final agonizing moments of eighteen-year-old Meredith Hunter. One Hell's Angel, displeased by the sight of this young black man with an attractive blond girlfriend, had tried to provoke a fight with Hunter, chasing him through the crowd and pulling at his hair.

Suddenly, just a few feet from the edge of the stage, Hunter pulled out a gun in a desperate act of self-defense and waved it in the air. His girlfriend begged him not to shoot, but before Hunter could do anything, one of the Hell's Angels thrust a knife in his back. Another stabbed him in the face. Then they chased Hunter through the crowd, stabbing him again and again until he collapsed at the edge of some scaffolding. "I wasn't going to shoot you," Hunter told his pursuer. "Why did you have gun?" the Hell's Angel demanded. Before Hunter could answer, his attacker grabbed a garbage can and bashed it over his head. Then a half-dozen hulks descended on what remained of Meredith Hunter, stomping him mercilessly. When they were finished, the Hell's Angel who had taunted Hunter in the first place walked over and gave him a final kick in the face. He then stood on his head for two minutes before walking away.

Two witnesses to the whole sickening episode tore off his shirt to reveal one fist-sized hole in Hunter's side and another in his back. Brain matter was clearly visible through the gaping wound in Hunter's temple. They screamed for the Stones to stop playing, but Jagger, straining to hear what they were saying, continued for several minutes. It was not until he actually saw the litter bearing Hunter being hoisted over the heads of the crowd that Jagger interrupted the song. He called for an ambulance and a doctor, and then tried once again to calm the crowd.

"This could be the most beautiful evening—I beg you to get it together," Jagger pleaded. "Hell's Angels, everybody—let's keep it all together. . . . Let's relax, get into a groove. . . . Come on, we can get it together. Come on."

Keith Richards, who had wanted to stop the show earlier but deferred to Jagger, was more to the point: "If you don't cool it, you ain't gonna hear no music!" A bearlike Hell's Angel rushed Richards and grabbed the mike from his hand. "Fuck you!" Richards, glassy eyed from a steady diet of LSD, marijuana, cocaine, and opium, wisely chose not to fight.

Jagger then launched into "Under My Thumb," followed by "Brown Sugar" and "Midnight Rambler," Jagger's own tribute to a modern-day Jack the Ripper. If these songs were somehow intended to pacify the crowd, they failed miserably.

The bedlam persisted. Another drugged fan, this one an obese woman stripped to the waist, tried to claw her way onstage only to be kicked in the face and hurled back into the crowd. Again Jagger sprang somewhat limply to the fan's defense. "Hey hey hey hey hey hey!" Jagger yelled. "One cat can control that chick. Hey, fellows, hey, fellows, one of you can control her, man."

Without a hint of irony Jagger then belted out the refrain to "Gimme Shelter": "Rape, murder, it's just a shot away." The group was pelted with roses during "Satisfaction." Mick took a swig of Jack Daniels before launching into "Honky Tonk Women," finally ending with the all-too-appropriate "Street Fighting Man."

"We're gonna kiss you good-bye," said Mick, blowing kisses into the darkness as if they had just finished a show at the Palladium. "And we leave you to kiss each other good-bye. You have been so groovy. Good night."

The Stones then dashed from the stage and ran up a hill to a waiting helicopter—the last one out. In a scene reminiscent of the fall of Saigon, the Stones and their entourage ran up a hillside and climbed rope ladders up into the helicopter as the rotor blades whirred overhead. Then, straining under nearly twice its normal passenger load, the chopper veered sideways before finally lifting off. "Shit, that was close," sighed a shaking Jagger, looking down at the hundreds of thousands who now, in the blackness and in the middle of nowhere, would somehow have to find their way home. "But it's going to make one fucking terrific film."

Meredith Hunter's corpse lay on a table in a small room

behind the raceway announcer's booth, his muddy boot sticking out from beneath a blood-spattered sheet. Stones staffers who had been left behind passed around a joint and laughed while they waited for an ambulance to pick up the body.

Incredibly, Altamont had not yet claimed its last victim. Shortly after midnight a 1964 Plymouth sedan plowed into a group of people camped around a bonfire, crushing two young men to death in their sleeping bags and critically injuring two others.

Altamont's final toll: four dead, scores seriously hurt, and an estimated two thousand overdoses and freak-outs. In his lavish suite at Nob Hill's Huntington Hotel, Jagger rehashed the day's events. When groupie Pamela Des Barres, who had had the good sense to leave Altamont after a Hell's Angel spit on her, called, Jagger begged her to come to his hotel room.

When Des Barres arrived, she found Jagger, Richards, and their musician friend Gram Parsons lounging about in their costumes and running stage makeup, very stoned. "Mick kept saying he felt like it was his fault," recalled Des Barres, "and maybe he should quit rock and roll forever."

Jagger's despair vanished with the arrival of the Mamas and the Papas' Michelle Phillips (who in the 1980s and '90s went on to star in the *Knots Landing* television series). Jagger proposed a ménage à trois to help him forget the day's unsettling events. Des Barres opted out, but Phillips eagerly complied. The next day, refreshed, Jagger ordered his secretary to book him a first-class seat on the first available flight for London.

On the way to the airport he passed a billboard advertising the Stones' new album, released the day of the free concert. Its appropriate title: *Let It Bleed*.

Bill Graham wasted no time laying the blame squarely at the feet of the Stones' flamboyant leader. "I'll ask you what right you had, Mick Jagger, to go through with this free festival," demanded Graham. "And don't tell me you didn't know the way it would have come off. What right did you have to leave the way you did, thanking everybody for a wonderful time and the Angels for helping out? What right does this god have to descend on this country this way? But you know what is the greatest tragedy to me?" Graham added, shaking his head. "That cunt is a great entertainer."

"I am not important. I was just an invention of journalists."

"I was born in a crossfire hurricane."
—"Jumpin' Jack Flash"

The banshee wail of the air-raid sirens filled the night, soon followed by the drone of Hitler's unmanned V-1 rockets as they flew just below the level detectable by radar. What terrified Britons even more than these familiar sounds of the Blitz were the inevitable moments of silence—the few breathless seconds between the time a rocket's engines cut out and the moment it rained death on its target.

During World War II more than seventy thousand British civilians would be killed by these crude but deadly "doodlebugs." Most of the casualties were either residents of London or of one or another of the small industrial towns unfortunate enough to be situated along the V-1's flight path. Aptly called "the Graveyard," this narrow swath between the southeastern coast of Kent and London was pummeled mercilessly by German forces.

None of these dreary communities in harm's way was harder hit than Dartford, where Mick Jagger spent his childhood years. Exploding bombs, the thunder of antiaircraft guns, dogfights between the Luftwaffe and the RAF in the skies overhead, showers of shrapnel, the house next door that vanished (along with its inhabitants) in a blinding flash—these were the sounds and images that would make up Mick's earliest memories.

The situation was frenzied and at times utterly terrifying, but not so terrifying that Eva Jagger ever stopped being a meticulous British housewife. Of all the Dartford women who strove in the face of imminent death to lead a passably normal suburban existence, Eva seemed most concerned with maintaining appearances. She was breezily charming and outgoing, but she possessed an undeniable aura of pretentiousness. Eva Jagger was determined to be thought of as the very epitome of ladylike grace.

Eva's acute social insecurity stemmed from the fact that she had been born and raised in Australia. She was quite convinced that her neighbors looked down on her as the product of a race of loutish, boomerang-throwing redneck ex-convicts.

Eva Scutts may have inherited this inferiority complex from her own British-born mother, who had migrated with Eva's boat-builder father to Sydney shortly after the turn of the century. Born in 1913, Eva often spent time with her father and brothers on the Sydney docks, much to her mother's consternation.

Wilting under what she considered to be the oppressive Australian heat and longing to return to a more "civilized" environment, Eva's mother finally delivered an ultimatum to her husband: Either the family returned to England, or she made the voyage alone.

In truth, Eva's mother harbored her own dreams of glory. To stand out among her twelve siblings she had become the family show-off, singing selections from Gilbert and Sullivan classics like *The Mikado* or *The Pirates of Penzance* for anyone who deigned to listen.

Once the Scuttses were firmly ensconced behind the hedgerows of Dartford, Eva and the rest of the family would make the thirty-five-minute train trip to London to catch the occasional variety show at the famed Palladium, or to see a play like *Cinderella* performed at the Coliseum.

At home Eva would either listen to her favorite singer,

Bing Crosby, on the BBC, or borrow records from her eldest brother's extensive collection of Broadway musical scores. She even studied piano for four years.

But it was the escapist fare Hollywood had to offer that really thrilled Eva. She had a particular passion for shoot-'em-ups; two of her favorite Western heroes were Tom Mix and Gary Cooper. As for romantic leads, Eva fantasized with every other girl in England about being swept up into the arms of Ronald Coleman, Robert Taylor—and especially Rhett Butler himself, Clark Gable.

Eva also imagined what it would be like to be in Ginger Rogers's shoes, gliding across the polished marble dance floor with Fred Astaire in *The Gay Divorcée*. In fact, Eva did more than just dream; as a schoolgirl she performed country dances in local talent shows, and at seventeen was accomplished at the demanding art of ballroom dancing.

The Great Depression hit London's working-class suburbs with a particular ferocity, but Eva managed to find work as a hairdresser in 1934. Then twenty-one, she vividly recalls being chastised by her fortyish employer for having the audacity to listen to music by the upstart Bing Crosby over the radio while she worked. "That's not music," shouted Eva's boss, bitterly dressing down her new employee before a shop full of customers. "You don't call that singing!" It was an experience she would remember nearly thirty years later, when her son was confronted by the same criticism.

Not long after taking the hairdresser's job she began dating Basil ("Joe") Jagger, a young physical-education teacher at a local school. Although the pretty, extroverted Eva customarily dated Dartford's most roguish bachelors, she regarded the lanky, unassuming Joe as a good catch. He was college educated, gentlemanly, and, most important, came from a family that was regarded a full step up the social ladder from her own. "My mum is very working class," said Mick, "and my father is bourgeois, because he had a reasonably good education, so I come from somewhere in between that. Neither one thing or the other."

At the age of twenty-seven, older than most brides of the era, Eva Scutts married Joe Jagger precisely one year to the day before the Japanese attack on Pearl Harbor—December 7, 1940. The bride wore a blue silk dress, and was given away by her eldest brother. The groom was distinguished, if frightened looking, in waistcoat and tails; his more garrulous elder brother Albert was his best man. Because of strict wartime rationing the reception was modest—fifty relatives and friends gathered at Dartford's marginally shabby Conybeare Hall to drink beer and nibble cucumber sandwiches.

Joe Jagger soon proved himself to be more than a run-of-the-mill gym teacher. A serious student of exercise, he rose to become a lecturer in physical education at Strawberry Hill, the distinguished Catholic teachers' college in nearby Twickenham. Over the next fifteen years he would also establish himself as Britain's leading expert on the sport of basketball, a distinctly American pastime that left most Britons feeling baffled and confused. Jagger senior went on to write a successful book on the sport, and further established his credentials as a leading physical-fitness expert with his appointment to the British Sports Council.

Eva was no less diligent in her pursuit of a career as the suburban housewife nonpareil. A meticulous housekeeper, she worked feverishly cleaning and dusting to insure that her home would be nothing less than a local showplace. "You might call her a compulsive cleaner today," recalled one neighbor. "She was very sensitive to criticism of any kind, but most of all she seemed eager to have people think that she was, well, refined."

The Jaggers' first child was born July 26, 1943, and christened Michael Philip. That week the RAF responded to Hitler's blitz by pounding Cologne, Hamburg, and Essen. With British and U.S. aid the Russians had halted the Nazi advance on the Eastern Front and were slowly driving them out of Eastern Europe. Mussolini stepped down just as U.S. troops led by George Patton were encountering their heaviest resistance from German forces entrenched on Sicily.

That was also the year audiences stood in line to watch

Humphrey Bogart and Ingrid Bergman rekindle their romance in a new film called *Casablanca.*

Indulged to the hilt by his adoring mum, Michael, as he was called, was four when his parents informed him that he would be the lucky recipient of a very special Christmas present. On December 19, 1947, Michael's new baby brother, Christopher, was born.

If Mike, as he was called, resented the arrival of his only sibling, there was but a single manifestation of it, in a small incident that summer. "We were on holiday at a seaside resort," Eva Jagger remembered, "and all of a sudden Michael broke away from me and bolted down the beach, just knocking over all the other children's sand castles as he ran. He was clearly angry about something."

Rising out of the lush green English countryside that had once inspired the likes of Dickens and Kipling, Dartford and the surrounding towns—dreary little communities with names like Bexley, Woolwich, Plumstead, Sidcup, and Abbey Wood—came to symbolize a kind of British Babbittry during the postwar years. Brick row houses with tiny courtyards and wash flapping on the line flanked the tracks leading from Charing Cross Station in the heart of London through the Kent countryside.

Not far beyond, Dartford took on a different, marginally more affluent appearance. The town center, bustling with activity like any London suburb, boasted a supermarket (which would be taken over a decade later by America's Safeway chain), several coffee bars, and numerous taverns with names like the Jolly Miller, the Plough Pub, and the Fox and Hounds.

Jagger's first home was just around the corner from a Laundromat and the Dart Pub, at 39 Denver Road. The family occupied the right half of a two-story duplex, part of a large working-class subdivision that had been built in the late 1920s. To add a much-needed touch of class, the walls were covered with something called pebbledash, a pearly mixture of rock and cement designed to conceal the rough stucco-and-brick exterior. In front was a small courtyard garden surrounded by a brick fence with a wooden gate. The house itself was no more than twenty-five feet wide.

Mike's second-floor bedroom overlooked the family's small garden in the rear, where for the first decade of his life he would be drilled in a variety of physical endeavors by his fitness-obsessed dad. By the time his son was three, Joe Jagger was leading the boy in calisthenics and teaching him how to grip a barbell.

The strict exercise regimen fit right in with the spare-the-rod-spoil-the-child philosophy of Joe and Eva. Grace was always said at meals, and both boys were assigned chores around the house. Stern punishment was meted out for any infraction of house rules, however minor. Mike seldom misbehaved. To do so would have meant a slap or a spanking.

The cherub-cheeked lad with the oversized smile showed an early interest in music—and the sound of his own piercing voice. "Give us a couple of nursery rhymes to sing," he recalled, "and I'd be loudest hollering out the words. Even if I forgot the lyrics, I'd still keep right on going. Boy, I must have been a noisy one. . . ."

Although the Jaggers did not own a record player at the time, Mike was glued from the time he was a toddler to the BBC and to the more avant-garde, jazz-oriented Radio Luxembourg. Eva remembered him prancing and gyrating to the swing of Glenn Miller and Artie Shaw—a portent of things to come.

In fact, the boy was a veritable blur of activity; he seemed to be in a constant state of motion, throwing rocks, scaling fences, never walking when he could sprint. At times his exuberance left him bruised, bloodied—and worse. While chasing a playmate through his backyard Jagger tripped and, to his mother's horror, impaled his hand on a spiked fence.

At Maypole Infants School, which he attended from the ages of five through seven, Mike was considerably more restrained. The school itself, a brick-walled, tile-roofed Dickensian monstrosity situated directly across from Bexley

Hospital, inspired a feeling of dread that permeated the lives of most students who went there. Not so Jagger. He was universally regarded as a prize pupil with a sunny, upbeat demeanor and a clear eagerness to please his teachers. "He was bright, cheerful, always volunteering to help out in the classroom," recalled Ken Llewellyn, one of Jagger's teachers at Maypole. "Almost too good, really. . . ."

Mike's sterling reputation followed him to another bleak house of learning, albeit one of more recent architectural vintage: Wentworth County Primary, a sterile, flat-roofed, single-story yellow brick-and-glass structure surrounded by hedges and located just two blocks from the Jagger homestead at 39 Denver Road. For all its fifties blandness it was at Wentworth that young Jagger experienced a fleeting encounter with destiny in the form of a cherub-cheeked schoolmate. His name was Keith Richards. "We weren't great friends then, but we knew each other," Jagger would later remember. "He used to dress in a cowboy outfit, with holsters and a hat, and he had these big ears that stuck out. . . . I asked him what he wanted to do when he grew up. He said he wanted to be like Roy Rogers and play guitar. I wasn't that impressed by Roy Rogers, but the bit about the guitar did interest me."

Richards lived just two blocks away from Michael at 33 Chastillian Road, yet he might as well have lived on another planet. In contrast to the upwardly mobile Jaggers, the Richardses were mired in poverty. His father, a foreman at an electrical plant, barely earned enough to pay the rent and provide the bare necessities. The Richardses could afford neither a refrigerator nor a telephone, and Keith was resigned early to a future no less hopeful than his present.

Unbeknownst to either at the time, Jagger and Richards had already exhibited an innate musical faculty. As early as age two Keith sang along in perfect pitch whenever the likes of Frank Sinatra or Nat King Cole came over the radio. At the age of seven he was given a small saxophone that he dragged everywhere with him, despite the fact that it was almost as big as Keith was.

Mike Jagger, meantime, was lugging around the guitar his mother had brought back from a vacation in Spain. He had a particular passion for Latin music, and was not about to let the fact that he did not speak the language stop him; Jagger, strumming away, just made up his own nonsensical but Spanish-sounding lyrics and sang along—in pitch that was less than perfect.

They had something else in common: like Jagger the too-willing-to-please Keith was considered by the rest of the neighborhood to be something of a mama's boy. The staff at Wentworth viewed him as open and cooperative; his peers pegged him as a teacher's pet. For the most part he would keep to himself, retreating to a tent he had pitched in the backyard.

In 1954 both families moved—the Richardses to, in Keith's words, "a fucking soul-destroying housing project at the other end of town," the Jaggers to a leafy, upper-middle-class neighborhood known only as The Close. Like the spacious homes of the physicians and solicitors that surrounded it, the Jaggers' new brick-walled abode with its leaded windows, circular drive, rose garden, and quarter-acre of manicured lawn offered mute testimony to the vaunted social standing of its inhabitants.

In the best tradition of grand English homes, this house even had a name—"Newlands," carved on a sign hanging from the apple tree that shaded their front entrance. Eva strictly forbade Chris and his older brother to climb the tree, or the towering pines just outside their bedroom windows in the back. But they did anyway. Jagger "nearly broke his neck" falling out of one, recalled a childhood playmate, "but I don't think that bothered his mother nearly as much as the broken branches that littered the driveway." Eva remembered that her son "was cricket mad when we lived there." Jagger played the game in the front drive with his brother, though their early relationship could hardly have been called close. "As far as I was concerned he was nothing more than a punching bag," Jagger said later, "and I used to beat him up regularly."

For anyone hoping to somehow break through the seemingly impenetrable barriers of Britain's rigid class system, the only real chance came after they turned eleven years old. In their final year at Wentworth Primary each student took the all-important "eleven-plus" exams—a single battery of tests that, in essence, determined a British child's academic (and in all likelihood economic) future. Those who passed were then admitted into the elite grammar-school system, which inevitably led to a university education and ultimately entree into one of the more lucrative professions. Those who failed the dreaded eleven-plus were relegated to the more basic state-run "secondary modern" schools—destined, almost inevitably, to remain working class forever.

Not surprisingly, Jagger, urged on by his overweeningly status-conscious mother, passed the eleven-plus and proudly donned Dartford Grammar's crimson with the brass buttons. Richards did only well enough to qualify for Dartford Technical School, where strapping classmates from neighborhoods tougher than his promptly labeled Keith the school "pansy." For the next six years Jagger would only catch an occasional glimpse of Richards flying by on his bicycle, his tormentors in hot pursuit.

In sharp contrast to Richards's rough-and-tumble existence among the bully boys at Dartford Technical, Jagger and his well-heeled classmates were learning how to be proper English gentlemen. Founded in 1576, Dartford Grammar was an ivy-covered upper-class bastion smack in the middle of a beer-drinking, blue-collar town. The school itself—Tudor style, with arched Gothic windows and imposing chimneys—was partially hidden behind a curved brick wall. Even the emerald-green playing fields were surrounded by a forbidding spiked iron fence.

Not long after enrolling at Dartford Grammar, Mike got his first delectable taste of celebrity. Joe Jagger, hired on as a consultant to a BBC television series called *Seeing Sport*, enlisted his eldest son and some of Mike's friends to demonstrate the finer points of canoeing and rock-climbing. "I was a star already," Jagger would later recall, "I was think-ing, *Never mind the bloody canoe—how does my hair look?*"

The television appearances set Jagger apart from his con-temporaries, and he reveled in the attention. Yet even this modicum of fame exacted a price. "Mick's father was a very demanding, unyielding person," said Dick Taylor, a school-mate at Dartford Grammar. "I remember going over to the Jaggers' house to see him, but he'd only be a few feet out the door before his father shouted, 'Don't go out until you do your weights.' Joe also made sure his son did a set num-ber of sit-ups and push-ups every day, and that he ran at least twenty laps around their back garden each afternoon. However tyrannical Joe Jagger may have seemed to those outside the family, Taylor claimed his friend Mike "always did what he was told, without complaint. He wanted more than anything to please his parents, particularly his father. I think he was afraid of him."

Because of the demands his father made on him, Jagger was amply qualified to take a job at the age of twelve teach-ing physical education to the children of GIs at a nearby U.S. Army base. There Mike learned the rules of American football and baseball and, more importantly, all about rhythm and blues from a black cook named Jose. Listening to Jose's records, a whole new world opened up to young Jagger. "This was the first time I heard black music," he recalled. "In fact, it was my first encounter with American thought."

Part-time employment and fitness aside, Jagger was equally determined to live up to his mother's expectations. Even in this suffocating suburban environment Jagger har-bored dreams of becoming a man of wealth and taste. "As far back as I can remember," said brother Chris, "he said the thing he wanted most was to be rich."

During his early teen years Mike remained the dutiful son. At school he studied hard, competed in cricket and rugger, and was constantly volunteering to assist his teach-ers. One of them, William Wilkinson, remembered Jagger volunteering to take on the daunting task of doing a stock inventory of every book in the school. "It took days," said Wilkinson, "and we were completely exhausted when it was all over. More than any other student he went out of his way to be helpful."

Jagger, like all the other Dartford students, also belonged to Britain's ROTC, the Combined Cadet Force. With the draft still in effect these young cadets were expected to go on to become officers in the British military. Jagger marched and drilled with a zeal that was deemed commendable by Dartford Grammar's faculty.

Unaccountably, Jagger began to slack off shortly after he turned fourteen. He had never really been a joiner; with the exception of working as a stagehand on one school play, Jagger belonged to no societies or clubs, edited no school publications, nor sought any school office. He did not sing in the choir, play a musical instrument, or learn to read music. Thanks in part to his father's fascination with the game, Jagger did eventually join the basketball team, eventually becoming captain even though he was far from the team's best player. "You could always," said former teammate Keith Hawkins, "reckon to get the ball off of him."

Jagger began to enjoy bending, if not breaking, the rules. "Every week there was a five-mile run over Dartford Heath," said Jagger's friend Clive Robson. "Nobody liked doing it, but you could get out of it. Jagger worked out that if you broke off at a certain point you could hide in the dunes, have an illicit smoke, and rejoin the homeward run half an hour later. No wonder he looked so relaxed afterwards."

Jagger also began to chafe under the school's strict dress code. He would wait until a faculty member turned his back to whip open his maroon blazer, revealing a purple mohair sweater beneath. Jagger's "house master," the British equivalent of a homeroom teacher or guidance counselor, recalled that young Michael frequently challenged authority when it came to matters of dress. "He would wear those tight pants even then, and his hair began to spill over the ears," said Walter Bennett. At one school event to which students from a neighboring girls' school were invited, Jagger showed up out of uniform altogether. He arrived wearing a "bright blue jacket with these shimmering silver threads. The girls swarmed around him."

These incidents seemed minor to everyone except the school's martinet headmaster, Loftus ("Lofty") Hudson. A diminutive disciplinarian, Mr. Hudson was not, in the words of one of his teachers, "averse to caning pupils from time to time. Boys used to sit on these hard wooden chairs in the hallway waiting to be called into Mr. Hudson's office. They'd jump three feet off the chair every time they heard the crack of the cane on some other poor wretch's backside." Hudson cast a watchful eye on young Master Jagger.

At one point Mr. Hudson became so enraged over the issue of students in increasingly tight pants that he called an assembly to discuss the matter. "Since we were all told how angry Mr. Hudson was, everybody showed up at the assembly wearing the regulation loose-fitting trousers," recalled David Herrington, a student who was two years younger than Jagger. "In the middle of the lecture, in walks Jagger—wearing the tightest jeans I'd ever seen. Hudson stopped everything and sent him home on the spot. Jagger just smiled and walked out. It was a deliberate sort of rebellion."

Biology may have been behind Mike's newfound defiance. A steaming cauldron of hormones, he now found it almost impossible to concentrate on his studies, even if he had wanted to. "When I was thirteen, all I wanted to do was have sex," said Jagger, "I just desperately want to. . . . I didn't know much about it. I was repressed. It was never discussed with me. And it wasn't just a question of being repressed. There wasn't that much sex around when I was thirteen."

Jagger coped with these sexual anxieties against the all-male backdrop of Dartford, with its menacingly brawny upper classmen and faculty members who seemed to take pleasure in meting out corporal punishment. In his book *Eton Voices*, Danny Danziger notes that English boys' schools are fraught with "adolescent eroticism, expressed (and sometimes fulfilled) in homosexual liaisons, sometimes amorous, sometimes lustful, sometimes innocent."

So it was with Jagger. "I had my first sexual experience with boys at school," Jagger admitted. "I think that's true of almost every boy." According to one contemporary a typical such encounter might start with towel-flinging in the shower room, then escalate to wrestling and sometimes oral sex. One "wanking" contest involved several boys standing in a wide circle and masturbating to see who could ejaculate the farthest.

"It's hard for Americans to understand," explains writer Victor Bockris, "but this sort of early homosexual activity is very, very common in England. Most males go through it, but it doesn't mean they're gay at all—it's just sort of a rite of passage. The vast majority go on to become lifelong heterosexuals with wives and children." Jagger's early homoerotic experiences would clearly influence the evolution of one of the most sexually ambiguous personae of the age.

Meantime, Mike was commencing his first real love affair—with American culture and American pop music. By 1957 Jagger and many of his contemporaries were besotted with the America they read about in magazines and saw depicted on screen in teenage rebel films starring Marlon Brando, Natalie Wood, and James Dean. The pastel-colored cars guzzled gas and sprouted tail fins. Waitresses at drive-ins wore roller skates, poodle skirts, and ponytails.

And at the heart of it all was an entirely new form of music being called rock and roll. Jagger was not particularly fond of the then twenty-two-year-old Elvis ("He just seemed so *ancient* to me at the time") or Bill Haley and the Comets. Instead, he first latched on to the raucous, no-holds-barred sounds of Little Richard, Chuck Berry, and Jerry Lee Lewis.

At about the same time they were learning about these American artists, Britons were suddenly swept up in a national craze known as "skiffle" music. Played on tin cans, washboards, and the like, it mimicked the rollicking sounds of hillbilly music. Skiffle bands popped up everywhere, and ultimately Jagger would belong to a number of them.

Emboldened by the success of skiffle music, British record companies began to release the works of such blues legends as Big Bill Broonzy, Robert Johnson, and Leadbelly. These were quickly followed by the grittier sounds of Bo Diddley, Muddy Waters, and Howlin' Wolf.

Jagger found kindred spirits in classmates Dick Taylor, Bob Beckwith, and Allen Etherington. "We all liked rock, of course," recalled Taylor. "But what interested me most about Jagger was his interest in the blues. So few people in England knew about it, and here was this guy who knew everything there was to know about Muddy Waters and Bo Diddley."

By this time Mike had begun to amass a sizable record collection, paid for by a series of odd jobs that ranged from pedaling an ice cream wagon around the neighborhood (wearing a white jacket and paper cap) to delivering holiday mail at Christmastime. Joe Jagger dismissed his son's musical tastes, which now embraced the likes of Fats Domino and Chuck Berry, as "jungle music." Mike liked the phrase. "I used to say, 'Yeah, that's right, jungle music, that's a very good description.'"

Jagger and his three blues-loving pals got together to form Little Boy Blue and the Blue Boys—Mike picked the name to emphasize their allegiance to the blues as opposed to pop—with Taylor on drums ("I had a grotty set which my grandfather had given me"), Etherington on maracas, Beckwith on guitar, and Jagger singing. A convincing mimic, Jagger's first attempts at sounding like a soulful black from the Deep South struck his parents as nothing less than hysterical. Eva would spy on the Blue Boys as they practiced downstairs, "trying hard not to laugh."

Within a matter of weeks the pasty-faced schoolboys from Kent were belting out a startlingly authentic-sounding version of raw urban blues. From that point on, said Joe

Jagger, "his mother and I never interfered because it used to sound quite good." (Mick remembers things differently: "My father was bloody awful, he was so disciplinarian. He was a schoolteacher. . . . I mean, they're not known for their libertarianism. I wanted to be a musician—it was so obvious, you know—and he just didn't want me to be.")

It was more than just the sound Jagger and his friends were making that began attracting attention. Whenever performers like Chuck Berry and Little Richard appeared on popular British *American Bandstand*-type shows like *Cool for Cats* or *Oh Boy*, Jagger was glued to his television set, studying every gesture. "We'd practice at my house a lot," recalled Dick Taylor, "and my mother would drop everything to sit on the couch and be our audience. She loved to watch Mick move." Added Taylor's mother: "We used to sit in the next room and crease up with laughter. It was lovely, but so loud! I didn't dream they were serious."

In the fall of 1958 Taylor and Jagger had gone to the Woolwich Odeon Theater to see Buddy Holly perform. At that time English rock and roll fans were "split into two camps," Keith Richards would later observe. "It was either Elvis or Buddy. The Elvis fans were the heavy-leather boys and the Buddy Holly ones all somehow looked like Buddy Holly."

Although he lacked the thick, black-rimmed glasses, Mick was squarely in the Buddy Holly camp. At the concert he attended with Taylor, Mick was "absolutely trans-fixed—you could see the little wheels going round in his head, trying to learn as much as he could," said Taylor. "It was great, terrific—the first time we heard the Buddy Holly classic "Not Fade Away." From that night on, Mick and I played it all the time."

A spunkier Mike Jagger began to emerge. Unfortunately, Dartford's Mr. Hudson hated spunk. Jagger got into trouble for drinking at a local pub, and on a dare drove a motorbike across the school lawn. But these incidents paled in comparison to the Combined Cadet Force debacle. As England moved toward an all-volunteer military, Jagger led a whole-

sale withdrawal from Hudson's cherished Combined Cadet
Force. Fewer and fewer showed up on the field for drills,
until the unit was completely disbanded. For the rest of his
life Hudson would hold the upstart Jagger accountable for
what he perceived to be an overt act of dishonor and betrayal.

Mike began casting himself, albeit surreptitiously, in the
role of campus rabble-rouser. Gone was the eager-to-please
trouper, replaced by a sulking, heavy-lidded, somewhat
whiny adolescent shirker. Those trademark lips, already
much commented upon by superiors and classmates alike,
contributed to the overall demeanor that could now best
be described as sullen. He still did what he was told, but
now only after driving teachers to distraction with unend-
ing questions and complaints.

Mike was having less success at home, where his parents
were in a virtual state of panic over the length of their son's
hair. This was still the fifties, after all. "I was shocked,"
insisted Eva. "Even though it wasn't really long by today's
standards, I held up my hands in horror when it started
growing over his ears." Joe Jagger's constant refrain to Eva
was "Get him to have his hair cut!" Sighed Eva: "I used to
get so fed up with it. I'd say, 'Look, I can't *make* him.' " But
she did, sitting him down in a chair and doing the deed
herself. "Please don't cut too much off," he pleaded. "Don't
take too much off! That's enough!" Mike then burst into
tears.

At school the rebellion gained momentum. Now Jagger
was adopting a political stance designed to raise faculty
hackles. He began questioning the then-conservative government's Cold War policies, as well as the basic tenets of
the capitalist system itself. "He was definitely a bit left
wing," recalled teacher William Wilkinson. "It was enough
to infuriate Hudson and make some of the other teachers
uncomfortable, but not enough to get him into real trouble.
He was very careful not to cross that line."

Not that he squandered his time at school. According to
Wilkinson, Jagger "had a fondness for historical biogra-

phies—particularly of nineteenth-century political figures."
He was also reading the classics—the works of Baudelaire,
Rimbaud, and Blake—and, not unexpectedly, brushing up
on his knowledge of American music. "He ordered a book
through the library called *Blues Fall This Morning*," said
Wilkinson, who also served as Dartford's librarian at the
time. "When the book arrived, he sort of fondled it and
then walked off to a back table. He sat there for hours,
totally immersed in what he was reading. A bomb could
have gone off in the room, and I don't think he'd have
noticed."

Jagger's interests may have broadened, but school records
show that his grades started to slide once he turned fifteen.
In 1955, after he'd completed his first year at Dartford,
teachers were uniform in their praise of Jagger's academic
performance: "A good term," scrawled one faculty member.
"Good work," concurred another.

As reflected in his teacher's written comments on Jagger's report card, this high level of performance continued
until 1957, when the decline began. What had once been
"good work" was now described as "generally satisfactory,"
with a "determined effort needed." In 1958 it was noted
that Jagger's performance was "better, but [he] is too easily
distracted." But later in the term Jagger's faculty advisor
penned, "Must not throw away his chances! Not a consis-
tent effort. Must settle down next year."

He didn't. William Wilkinson wrote, "Attitude rather
unsatisfactory," on Jagger's report card, noting that the boy
had now developed a pattern of missing exams altogether.
On the basketball court he was also turning in a lackluster
performance. "Jagger was an average player," said team
coach Arthur Page. "He wanted to succeed in everything
he did. If he didn't right away, then he gave up and moved
on to something else."

His lackluster performance notwithstanding, a momentous event in Jagger's life did occur on the basketball court.
At the height of one game he slammed into an opposing
player with his jaw—and bit off the tip of his tongue. Blood

gushed down the front of his jersey, and before Jagger realized what had happened, he swallowed the bit of tongue.

"He didn't talk for days," recalled Dick Taylor. "Of course, the Blue Boys didn't play either; we'd lost our singer. We all wondered if that was it—if Mick's singing days were over." But Jagger did come back, and when he did the other boys were amazed at what they heard. It was as if the once seemingly indelible British veneer had come off with that tiny piece of Jagger's tongue. The result was a coarser, more hard-edged, grittier sound. "We were shocked," marveled Taylor. "He sounded so *weird*—the way he sounds now, actually. That accident just changed his voice completely. Biting off the tip of his tongue might have been the best thing that ever happened to Mick Jagger."

By this time, at age sixteen, Jagger was finally starting to experience a bit of luck with the opposite sex—although not nearly as much as he would have his friends believe. As in any all-male environment Jagger and his friends attempted to top one another with tales of their sexual conquests. For his part Jagger claimed to have talked a few girls out onto the dunes for some adolescent fumbling. He also halfheartedly joined the school photo club so he could lure his unsuspecting prey into the darkroom. "We used to talk a lot about girls," allowed Robson, "and Jagger had quite a reputation."

At the time, the reputation as a ladykiller was less than legitimate. "There were some good-looking boys around that we all kind of drooled over," said one student from the local girls' school. "But Mike Jagger certainly wasn't one of them. We all thought he was kind of ugly, really. He had this sort of scraggly dark hair, he was too skinny, and he was very spotty—he had lots of pimples."

Jagger did have a gimmick, however. Roughly the same time he began dating girls, Mick's mother took a job selling cosmetics door-to-door as an Avon lady. Using Eva's sample case to lure a girl to his house when his parents were out, Jagger would generally invite her into his mother's room. There they would sit at a dressing table, giggling as they tried on makeup together. By all accounts these encounters were platonic. "He just seemed happy letting me put lipstick and mascara on him," said one of his dates. "Then he'd do the same for me. It did strike me as very strange at the time, but it was all in fun. Dating Mick was more like being with one of the girls."

While he enjoyed jamming with his friends and bragging about his spurious sexual conquests, Jagger still clung to dreams of becoming a wealthy and powerful businessman. He planned to pursue an economics degree at the prestigious London School of Economics. Toward that end Jagger applied himself during his last few months at Dartford Grammar. Although his schoolwork remained mediocre, he managed to sail by on the strength of his exams—graduating twelfth in a class of twenty-five. Of this group five would go on to Oxford or Cambridge, and three more to London University. Three would eventually become solicitors, one the librarian of Oxford University, and one a leading psychiatrist.

In recommending that Jagger be accepted at the London School of Economics, the implacable Mr. Hudson was grudging in his praise. After writing that Jagger had shown "a greater intellectual determination than we had expected," Hudson added that "Jagger is a lad of good general character, though he has been rather slow to mature. The pleasing quality which is now emerging is that of persistence when he makes up his mind to tackle something. . . . He should be successful in his subjects, though he is unlikely to do brilliantly in any of them." Despite this egregiously halfhearted endorsement Jagger won admission to LSE on a state scholarship.

A decade later, when Dartford Grammar invited its "old boys" to return for a reunion, Jagger was pointedly left off the guest list. Even after it was suggested that Jagger might be willing to perform at a fund-raiser to benefit the school, Mr. Hudson nixed the plan. "The more famous the Rolling Stones became, the more Hudson hated him," explained

Wilkinson. "He thought Jagger was just this bad lot, and he didn't want the school's name attached to him in any way. The rest of the faculty and staff agreed with him." Added Dick Taylor: "Hudson thought Mick was leading young people astray. It was crazy. The school should have been proud of him." Another of Jagger's teachers, Eric Brandon, had a more accurate view of how his former pupil was regarded by youth at large. "Yes, I did teach Mick Jagger," Brandon would tell newcomers to the school, "and I haven't washed since. You may kiss my hand."

"Mick? He's a lovely bunch of guys."
—Keith Richards

Few institutions of high learning could boast such a stellar reputation. John Fitzgerald Kennedy had studied at the London School of Economics. So had many of England's celebrated statesmen and business leaders. To Jagger, LSE offered not so much an opportunity to learn from some of the finest minds in academia as a broad avenue to power and riches in the world of finance. Despite his professed interest in European history and literature, Jagger's eye was on a career that thrust him foursquare into the bosom of Britain's moneyed elite.

Jagger's government grant was just enough to cover tuition, which meant that he would have to live at home and commute to central London by train. For Mike this was enough. For the first time in his eighteen years he would be sampling life outside the suffocating confines of Dartford. "The overwhelming thing about life in the suburbs is the envy, the gossip and pettiness," he later recalled. "I hated it, and I was glad to escape—even if it was for only a few hours a day."

If he truly regarded Dartford as a sort of suburban prison, he certainly did not share those feelings with his family. He still played the role of dutiful son, helping his mother out with chores around the house—Mike's room was as orderly and spotless as any found in a decorating magazine—and slavishly submitting himself to the grueling exercise regimen mapped out by his fitness-expert father. "He still couldn't go anywhere without his father shouting behind him that he needed to do his weights or push-ups," said Dick Taylor. "And he would drop right to his knees and do them! It seemed very odd at his age to never complain or rebel. Here he was a grown man, and not once did I ever see him even hesitate to do exactly what his parents wanted."

Another acquaintance was also perplexed by Jagger's behavior at home: "He had been this sort of seditious character at school, but a robot at home. I think he was afraid of his father, really. He used to get whacked if he misbehaved. I never saw any real affection between them."

Before he began his studies at LSE, Mike Jagger took a fifteen-dollar-a-week orderly's job at Bexley Mental Hospital. The place was filled, by Jagger's own recollection, with "nymphomaniac nurses and nymphomaniac patients." On numerous occasions women patients tried to seduce the young orderlies. Alerted that any fraternization with the patients would result in immediate dismissal, Jagger managed to fend off these attempts—in one case a deceptively demure-looking patient simply threw open her blouse and placed his hand on her breast. It was not so easy to resist the more aggressive members of the nursing staff, however. One raven-haired nurse who had emigrated to England from Rome pulled Jagger into a linen closet where, amidst the mops and bedpans, he lost his virginity in an upright position.

In typical fashion most first-year students at LSE were instantly swept up in the campus social whirl, which essentially consisted of getting drunk at least twice a week. Jagger did not allow himself that luxury at first; most of his free time was still devoted to practicing with the Blue Boys. Basically considered a loner by his fellow university students, Mick shied away from social interaction for over a month, and only then began making tentative overtures to other students. "He was almost reclusive," said a fellow LSE student. "Most of us who commuted to school would make arrangements to stay with friends in the city, but he always declined. He was kind of standoffish, even antisocial."

Gradually, as he became more comfortable in his new environment, Jagger began to cultivate friends with interests in the arts. He seemed particularly fond of student actors, and began staying over with friends in the city to discuss Olivier and Gielgud over the requisite half-dozen pints of ale. This period gave Jagger a singular opportunity to reinvent himself, and he seized it. Michael Philip Jagger ceased to exist. From this point on the pimply-faced lad with the big lips introduced himself simply as "Mick."

Jagger's new persona included a wildly exaggerated sexual past. He continued to boast of his conquests, and remained adept at enticing young coeds without ever actually following through and bedding them. "He was a complete fraud," said Jill, one of the attractive University of London coeds who moved in similar circles. "He was all over me in public, and my friends always said they assumed we were 'doing it.' But whenever I got near him in private, he'd back away." At one point Jill invited him point blank to spend the night with her. "He hemmed and hawed like a schoolboy, making all sorts of ridiculous excuses. I just think he was terribly inexperienced and insecure at the time. But I understand," she added in a masterpiece of understatement, "that eventually he got over this problem."

Before the year was out, in fact, Jagger overcame his insecurities with the help of a plump Dartford shopgirl named Bridget. She was less than plain—"ugly, with a face like a pudding," according to one acquaintance—but at nineteen it was enough for Mick that she satisfied his animal urges.

By this time Jagger had all but forgotten his childhood friend Keith Richards. In a sense Richards had begun his own musical career years before Jagger ever picked up a microphone. At twelve Richards was singing Handel's "Hallelujah" chorus for Queen Elizabeth as a Westminster Abbey choirboy. Two years later, in the middle of another royal performance, Richards's voice cracked. The next day Richards was summarily kicked out of the choir. His dismissal left him bitter and angry. "I think that's when I stopped being a good boy," conceded Richards, "and started to be a yob."

Keith had never shown any aptitude for carpentry, welding, or any of the other skills taught at Dartford Technical School. No longer able to express himself through his music, he spent the next year cast in the role of troublemaker. Richards was finally expelled without a diploma less than thirty minutes before graduation. His crime: taking a celebratory last-minute joyride on a friend's motorcycle.

By way of a last chance to make something of himself, Dartford Tech's headmaster recommended that Richards be admitted to Sidcup Art College. In a postwar Britain where even the sons and daughters of working-class families were demanding some sort of higher education, art schools proliferated to offer an alternative to college. Anyone with even the slightest artistic bent was a candidate for admission.

Ironically, Sidcup and the scores of other art schools strewn around Britain can claim more celebrated musicians than accomplished painters and sculptors among their alumni. Veritable hotbeds of musical talent, these schools spawned dozens of rock superstars, including John Lennon, Ron Wood, David Bowie, Pete Townshend, Eric Clapton, and Jimmy Page.

By the time he reached art school, Richards had already been introduced to the glories of the guitar by his eccentric grandfather, Gus Dupree. His mother, Doris, whose indulgent attitude toward her only son contrasted sharply with Jagger's upbringing, bought him a guitar of his own—a Rosetti acoustic for seven pounds (then about twenty-five dollars). Eschewing lessons that Richards felt would undermine his natural style, Keith taught himself to play by ear, listening hour upon endless hour to John Lee Hooker and Muddy Waters and mimicking what he heard on the guitar.

At Sidcup, Richards met another self-taught musician— Jagger's Dartford Grammar schoolmate and fellow Blue Boy Dick Taylor. The two hit it off instantly. Although he had started out playing drums, Taylor found that he now shared Richards's passion for aping Hooker and Johnson and other blues legends on acoustic guitar. Between classes Taylor and Richards would sneak into the cloakroom adjoining the principal's office to practice. "The principal would come in yelling at the top of his lungs for us to shut up," recalled Taylor, "but Keith didn't care. . . . He was a real hooligan, and I used to really like him for that." If nothing else, he dressed the part. "Keith always wore tight jeans, purple shirt, and blue denim jacket, no matter what the weather," said Taylor. "He never wore anything else, ever, in all the time I knew him. And he never changed."

Richards reveled in playing the part of unrepentant bad boy. To the delight of his friends Richards unabashedly lifted ashtrays, silverware, even china, whenever he had the opportunity. During a school field trip to a pricey furniture store, Richards made himself right at home while his teacher lectured on the finer points of interior design. "Keith was sitting on this really nice sofa worth hundreds of pounds," remembered Taylor, "and quite casually dropping his cigarette on it and burning a hole in it and not giving a monkey's ass about it."

Surprisingly, Taylor—not Richards—was the superior musician. At least for the time being. Richards was a sponge, eagerly soaking up all he could from his more polished classmate. To fuel their late-night sessions and still be able to attend art classes the next day, the two aspiring guitar players began taking drugs—diet pills, even nasal sprays and the British equivalent of Midol. "It seemed relatively harmless at the time," said Taylor, "until you look at what it ultimately led to for Keith. . . ."

All this time Keith knew about Little Boy Blue and the Blue Boys, but Taylor never invited Richards to become part of it. "Keith really was the school's rocker. It just never occurred to me that he'd be interested in joining our group," shrugged Taylor, "and Keith was too shy to ask."

That changed one fateful morning in December of 1961 when Jagger and Richards, who hadn't spoken in seven years, bumped into each other at the Dartford train station on the way to their respective schools.

Keith, his guitar hanging from his shoulder, noticed that Jagger was holding several albums under his arm. "We recognized each other straight off," recalled Richards. " 'Hi, man,' I say. 'Where are you going?' he says. And under his arms he's got Chuck Berry and Little Walter, Muddy Waters."

One of the albums was actually the newest release by Keith's favorite artist: Chuck Berry's *Rockin' at the Hops*. "Chuck Berry!?" wailed Richards, who assumed that he was the only person in Dartford who had ever heard of Berry. "You're into Chuck Berry, man, really?" Jagger told Richards that he had written to Chess Records in Chicago, and that the LPs had just arrived. If nothing else, Keith was greatly impressed with Jagger's initiative in sending away for the LPs, none of which had been distributed on their side of the Atlantic.

On the train Richards showed Jagger his guitar and asked him if he played as well. Mick sheepishly replied that he sang with a local band, just for fun. As the train pulled into the Sidcup station, Richards turned to Jagger and invited him to tea—"and bring your records," he shouted as the train doors closed behind him. Later that day, recalled Taylor, "Keith came up to me and said 'I've met Mick.' " Taylor finally asked Keith if he'd be interested in playing with the Blue Boys. "It seemed logical for us all to get together," said Taylor, "which we did."

There was an instant bond between Jagger and Richards, a bond that transcended the similarity in their musical tastes. "We were born brothers by different parents by accident," said Keith. Yet, despite the fact that they grew up in the same town, there were major differences. A full step up the social ladder from Richards, Jagger was an obedient, industrious son who was perfectly willing to play by the rules if that was what it took to get ahead. Richards was an unapologetic delinquent—"a real lout," in Taylor's words—and a loner.

Keith respected Mick from the outset. "Keith was attracted to his intelligence, his dramatic flair, his streak of ambition," said Taylor. But it was Mick's obsession with Keith that formed the bedrock on which the reputation of rock's greatest rock and roll band would be built. "Keith is a much freer person than Mick," contended Taylor. "The only thing he is obsessed about is his guitar, the music—Mick valued and nurtured that from the very beginning." Another friend from that time puts it more bluntly: "Keith had the balls to tell everybody to fuck off while he did what he wanted to do, period. Mick is too calculating, too ambitious, for that. He is *always* sizing people up, analyzing them, deciding which of his masks to put on. Keith's honesty was a counterbalance to his own Machiavellian personality."

For all Mick's unalloyed ambition, the Blue Boys remained little more than a ragtag gang of barely semiprofessionals. Another Sidcup student who started out jamming with Keith after class in the boys washroom was Phil May, who went on to form his own group called the Pretty Things. He would occasionally sit in with Jagger, Richards, and the other Blue Boys during their practice sessions. "They would just sit on Mrs. Taylor's floor, listening to records and trying to play along on their guitars," said May. "They were all very amateurish at this stage of the game, but Mick was quite unique even then. He could get inside a blues lyric and give it expression; he acted out a lyric instead of just performing it."

In March of 1962, while Mick, Keith, and the other Blue Boys were dreaming of actually performing blues before an audience, Alexis Korner was getting ready to open a club in the West London suburb of Ealing to showcase just such talent. Korner was a flamboyant and popular character on London's jazz scene. For nearly twenty years he had played banjo and guitar with Chris Barber's Jazz Band, eventually striking out on his own to form an all–R & B group, Blues Incorporated. Korner occasionally called on a Harrow Art

School student, a melancholy-looking truck driver's son named Charlie Watts, to fill in on drums.

Jagger was leafing through *The New Musical Express* when he came upon a small advertisement announcing the March 17 opening of Alexis Korner's Ealing Jazz Club. The club, according to the ad, would specialize in blues. Thrilled to find that there were enough like-minded souls around to justify the opening of a blues club—not to mention the remote possibility that it might offer them a place to perform before a paying audience—Mick and the other Blue Boys headed for Ealing that weekend.

The basement club, located across from the train station and beneath a jeweler's shop and a bakery, was dank and fetid. Water dripped constantly from the ceiling and, Jagger would later recall, "we had to put a thing over the stage, a sort of horrible sheet which was revoltingly dirty, and we put it up above the bandstand so the condensation didn't drip directly on you, it just dripped through the dirty sheet on you." Comfort aside, there was also the very real risk of electrocution: water dripped onto amplifiers that occasionally sent a shower of sparks into the crowd, wires snaking through puddles of water sputtered and cracked. "It was damn amazing that no one was killed there," said one musician.

Jagger and his friends were more than willing to take the risk. Squinting through a layered haze of blue cigarette smoke, they were mesmerized by the sounds of Korner on guitar, the two-hundred-pound Cyril "Squirrel" Davies playing blues harmonica, and goateed saxophonist Dick Heckstall-Smith and, of course, the doleful drummer, Charlie Watts. "When you walked into that club," said Taylor, "it was like being on Chicago's South Side—or at least the way we all *imagined* it to be."

Every Saturday they piled into Allen Etherington's car and sped to the club. "By week three," said Taylor, "we said 'we can do this. We can do *better* than this.' We wanted to be more electric and more loud."

Over the next few weeks the crowd that filed into Korner's squalid establishment would include the likes of Eric Clapton, Eric Burdon, and Jeff Beck. These and other musicians, in addition to shaping successful solo careers for themselves, would go on to form such groups as the Animals, the Kinks, Cream, the Yardbirds—and, of course, the Stones. By the age of thirty-two, Korner, credited with opening the ears of jazz purists to the raw, soul-wrenching sound of R & B, was rightly described as the father of England's R & B movement.

Another pilgrim to the Ealing Jazz Club was a short, square-jawed towhead who played the saxophone with a rock and roll band called the Ramrods. His name was Brian Jones, and, like the boys from Dartford, he had been raised in a relatively comfortable suburb. Actually, Jones's hometown of Cheltenham was considerably more affluent than most other bedroom communities encircling London. Featuring massive, columned Regency manor houses and broad, tree-lined boulevards, Cheltenham was, in Keith Richards's words, "a very genteel old ladies' resting place; very pretty in its way, but dullsville."

Jones's heritage virtually insured that he would possess some form of musical talent. His mother taught piano and his aeronautical-engineer father played organ at church. By the time he was fourteen he had discovered Charlie Parker. At sixteen he was kicked out of school for impregnating his fourteen-year-old girlfriend.

Over the next three years Jones held down a series of jobs from conductor on a double-decker bus to truck driver to architect's trainee, sales clerk, conductor, and optician's assistant. All along he hung out with beatniks in coffee bars and played alto sax with a series of more traditional, or "trad," jazz bands until he hooked up with the Ramrods.

In 1961 another girlfriend, Pat Andrews, gave birth to Brian's second child. They called him Julian (after Julian "Cannonball" Adderley) Mark. Pat had every reason to believe Jones intended to marry her. He visited her at the hospital when the baby was born, and spoke enthusiastically about his plans for the boy's upbringing. When he left to pursue a career as a musician in London, she managed to convince herself that he would send for her. News that he was seeing other women—several other women—prompted her to pack up their son and set out in search of Brian.

Back at the Ealing club, where every Saturday night aspiring blues singers were encouraged to audition for Alexis Korner's Blues Incorporated, Jagger and Richards were about to make their debut. They had sent a demo tape to Korner containing three songs—"Bright Lights, Big City," "Reelin' and Rockin'," and Chuck Berry's "Around and Around"—but it hardly mattered; anyone fearless enough to face the Ealing's famously unforgiving audience was more than welcome to try.

Looking every centimeter the London School of Economics student in white shirt, blue cardigan, and striped tie, Jagger downed several beers before working up enough courage to sing in public for the very first time. With Korner, Richards, and the basset Charlie Watts behind him, Jagger fumbled with the microphone, then, weaving a bit under the influence of alcohol, launched into "Around and Around." When it was all over, the audience burst into applause. The normally taciturn Squirrel Davis congratulated Mick, and Korner invited him back. Although his phrasing was impeccable, Korner and his fellow veteran musicians were more impressed with young Jagger's undeniable stage presence. They liked the way he "threw his hair around . . . for a kid in a cardigan, he moved quite excessively."

Unfortunately, they did not share the same high opinion of Richards. Davies had pushed him aside to pat Mick on the back and it was clear that Korner viewed Richards's high-voltage playing as little more than cacophony.

Jagger's next gig would be his first paid singing job—a few shillings and free beer to substitute for Korner's six-foot-seven-inch regular vocalist, "Long John" Baldry. That May, Jagger quit the Blue Boys and joined Blues Incorporated as permanent backup singer, stepping in for Baldry whenever he was unavailable. Richards and the other Blue Boys understood that this was an opportunity Mick could not pass up, though there would be lingering resentment over the apparent ease with which Jagger dumped his friends.

Hiring Jagger was a bold move for Korner, who was warned by some patrons of his club that his new young singer's stage mannerisms were a bit fey for a hard-drinking crowd of blues aficionados. Even though he was nowhere near as flamboyant as he would eventually become, Jagger was already making sweeping feminine gestures with his hands, writhing suggestively, and prancing about the stage. "I think you can imagine just how shocking Mick was in the early days," Korner later remembered. "Frankly, it was wildly embarrassing first time around with it."

Jagger was inspired in this not so much by Chuck Berry or even Little Richard as he was by Marilyn Monroe. What he offered was a sort of wicked parody of the female sex symbol. He consciously mimicked her style—the elegant hand movements, the swiveling walk, pouty lips, the playful toss of the head.

Jagger actually respected Monroe, and according to one friend saw in the star-crossed screen goddess a kindred spirit. When Marilyn died that August, Jagger was visibly distraught. "Monroe was a seductress," said Korner, "and that's the way he saw himself . . . he's helped to alter the whole idea of what it is to be male."

Mick still had a few moves to learn. When he and Keith walked into the Ealing club one night, a young singer named P. P. Pond was belting out "Dust My Blues." Yet their eyes were riveted not to Pond, but to the slide guitarist backing him, a ruddy-faced blond in a sharp Italian suit and Bond Street shoes who called himself Elmo Lewis.

Richards was astonished by his technique, his fingering, the unbridled passion of his playing. Jagger watched as the newcomer would lean into the crowd, taunting them, and then retreat. Jagger sensed in this Elmo Lewis a latent cruelty that was both sensual and exciting. Mick made the decision that night to adopt the young man's deliciously sullen expression.

As soon as Elmo Lewis stepped down off the stage, Mick rushed forward to introduce himself and offer to buy Lewis a drink. He accepted, on the condition that Jagger call him by his real name: Brian Jones.

Mick and Keith were in awe of Jones. They, after all, still lived at home and relied on their mothers to cook their meals and do their laundry. Jones had already fathered two illegitimate children, had played with two bands, and was on his own in London. In truth, Jones spent his days selling toasters and vacuum cleaners at Whiteley's department store while Pat worked as a laundress. Their combined income was forty dollars a week.

On those torrid nights when he was too drunk to make it home, Brian was welcome to crash on the kitchen floor of Alexis Korner's Moscow Road house. Another frequent guest to Korner's home was Mick. Arriving with Keith in tow, Jagger would sit for hours at Korner's feet, soaking up all the musical knowledge he could from England's unchallenged blues guru.

During these relaxed evenings Mick was a dervish of nervous energy. An endless fidget, every so often he would bound to his feet and race to the kitchen under the pretext of making tea.

Even with Korner the normally courteous Mick showed a capacity for sarcasm that would become a hallmark of his career. More than once Jagger snidely accused Korner of coopting "our working-class music." Korner replied that, given Mick's own bourgeois background, such criticism rang hollow: "Mick! You're at the London School of Economics! What could be more middle class than that?"

In a curious way Jagger did feel a strong emotional bond with the Chicago bluesmen and rock and roll pioneers he now blatantly imitated. "We were white suburban boys," recalled Phil May, "so of course we could have nothing in common with suffering blacks. But we felt there *were* similarities. We were looked down upon because of our long hair, the way we dressed. People on the street would look at you and you saw hate in their faces—they hated you solely for the way you looked, nothing more. So we could really relate in terms of oppression. We weren't on a chain gang, but the music brought our own pain to the surface."

That spring Jagger showed up religiously every Thursday night to sing at the Ealing—even though the only way he could find the courage to go was to drink himself into a near stupor. Keith had more reason to drown his sorrows. Korner and the other middle-aged members of Blues Incorporated did not appreciate Richards's megalomaniacal guitar playing; whenever Mick was asked to sing, Keith was physically barred from joining him onstage. He could only sit in the audience and clap while his best friend and soul mate took his bows.

Now that Jagger had abandoned the Blue Boys to sing with Korner's Blues Incorporated, Keith felt free to accept Brian Jones's invitation to sign on with the band he was forming. Jones had already put an ad in *Jazz News* announcing auditions for the group to be held in a storeroom above a seedy Soho pub, the Bricklayer's Arms. Ian Stewart, a lantern-jawed shipping clerk, had been the first to turn up. Looking more like a bouncer or a stevedore than a polished musician, the burly "Stu" sat down at the battered upright Jones had commandeered from the pub and effortlessly banged out several ragtime numbers, instantly earning Jones's respect—and a spot in the band. Next on the board was vocalist Brian Knight, quickly followed by guitarist Geoff Bradford.

All were consummately talented musicians, but in Jones Richards found a kindred spirit. "At the point where Mick and I met Brian, Brian's version of the blues was Muddy Waters, Elmore James, Sonny Boy Williamson, Howlin' Wolf, and John Lee Hooker. Whereas Mick and I were pushing Chuck Berry, Jimmy Reed, Bo Diddley. And Brian never *heard* of Chuck Berry."

If Brian was unabashed in his admiration for Keith's musicianship, it was a feeling not shared by all the other members of the group. "Richards came in basically wanting to play the *Chuck Berry Songbook* and nothing else," said Bradford. "Brian Knight and I were less interested in rock and more interested in jazz. We fought about it constantly."

In Mick's absence Brian and Keith grew closer. The musical bond evolved into a deep friendship that began to cause friction within the as-yet-unnamed band. As tensions mounted between Richards and Bradford, everyone turned to the embattled Jones to chart the band's musical course. Only Stu appeared unfazed by it all; sitting at the piano in his customary uniform of leather shorts and workshirt, intermittently taking a bite of his lunch, he kept staring out the window to make certain no one would snatch his motorbike.

After one shouting match between Richards and Bradford that nearly came to blows, there seemed little doubt that Jones would fire Keith to placate the more seasoned Bradford. Instead, Jones stood by his friend and, in typically blunt fashion, told Bradford and Knight they could "fuck off." To the dismay of both Keith and Bryan, the others returned for rehearsal the following week.

Mick was not oblivious to Keith's pain; occasionally he sat in with Keith, Brian, and the others upstairs at the Bricklayer's Arms. But Jagger's first priority (at least musically) was Blues Incorporated. To Alexis Korner's delight the crowds at the Ealing club were getting larger and larger—though it never occurred to him that Jagger might have something to do with the group's growing popularity.

One sticky July night Harold Pendleton, who managed the popular Marquee jazz club on Oxford Street, popped into the Ealing club to check out his new competition. Blues had grown so much in popularity that at the Marquee, a bastion of traditional jazz, Thursday night was now R & B Night. Pendleton invited Blues Incorporated to be the regular R & B band, and Korner eagerly accepted.

Blues Incorporated enjoyed a newfound respectability, and as the group's semiregular vocalist, Mick basked in Korner's reflected glory. He was by no means convinced, however, that he was cut out for a career in show business. Still pursuing his studies at the London School of Economics, Jagger toyed for a time with the notion of becoming a journalist. "But it seemed too much like hard work," he confessed. Then he seriously considered a career in politics. "But I believe it is harder initially to get into politics and then get to the top than it is in the pop world. There are parallels one can draw between the two fields. In selling yourself as a politician, like selling records, not so much depends on what you have to say but on how you say it."

A turning point came July 12, when Blues Incorporated was booked to make its nationwide debut on the BBC show *Jazz Club*. Trouble was, the program's producer insisted that he would pay for only six band members; he demanded that the shaggy-haired vocalist with the strange moves be cut from the show. Mick, not wanting to spoil the group's chances for national exposure, graciously stepped aside.

The BBC engagement brought with it a host of problems, and opportunities. With Blues Incorporated unable to play the Marquee July 12, the club's intermission band fronted by Long John Baldry moved up to star attraction. That, in turn, left Harold Pendleton without a band to play during intermissions.

In stepped Elmo Lewis, aka Brian Jones, and his as-yet-unnamed, ragtag little group. Although he knew them as fixtures at the Ealing, Korner was unaware that they had been rehearsing for weeks at the Bricklayer's Arms. Largely on the strength of Mick's vocal talents Korner persuaded Pendleton to give the group a chance. At this point it made sense for elements of the Blue Boys and Bryan's band to merge. Allen Etherington and Bob Beckwith peeled off, as did Brian Knight and Geoff Bradford. "There really wasn't much choice for me," said Bradford, whose shouting matches with Richards now stopped just short of violence. "In came Mick Jagger and Keith Richards, and out went Geoff. Simple as that." Dick Taylor stayed on; Mick Avory, who would later become the drummer for the Kinks, rounded out the band.

So, one question remained: What would they call themselves? During their weeks of rehearsals Brian had, according to Taylor, "always been amusing and relaxed—he never pushed himself as the boss." But now he took charge. Since Brian had formed the band and with justification considered himself its leader, he decided unilaterally that they would be called the Rolling Stones, after the Muddy Waters song "Rollin' Stone." Everyone, including Mick, hated the name. But Brian was firm, and no one challenged the fact that, at the moment at least, this was his group.

That word had apparently not gotten to the editors of *Jazz News*, who ran an item on July 11 trumpeting the band's debut:

> Mick Jagger, R & B vocalist, is taking a rhythm and blues group into the Marquee tomorrow night while Blues Inc. is doing its Jazz Club gig. Called "The Rolling Stones" ("I hope they don't think we're a rock and roll outfit," says Mick), the lineup is: Jagger (vocals), Keith Richards, Elmo Lewis (guitars), Dick Taylor (bass), "Stu" (piano), and Mick Avory (drums).

Even before they took to the stage for the first time, the Rolling Stones knew they could not possibly top the previous act. John Baldry had just begun to sing when he popped a button and his pants slid toward the floor. The audience went wild and a woman in the audience ran up to the stage and handed Baldry a safety pin. He fastened his pants and the show went on.

After Baldry strolled offstage, still holding up his trousers with one hand, the Rolling Stones faced their first paying audience. Visually, the group's members seemed oddly mismatched. Mick, fortified by several pints of ale, sported his customary bright blue pullover, while Keith wore a tight-fitting black business suit and Brian a corduroy jacket. What Dick Taylor wore made less of an impression than his instrument—an oversized bass guitar that seemed only slightly smaller than a cello.

Once Richards began ferociously attacking his instrument and Jagger started shaking his mane, a large segment of the crowd turned overtly hostile. "It was a case of instant dislike," recalled Dick Taylor. "The jazz purists who frequented the Marquee barely tolerated Alexis Korner's brand of blues one night a week. The sight of us—and particularly Mick—was more than they could handle."

Watching from the wings, the Marquee's manager wondered if he had made a mistake booking them in the first place. "Our regulars weren't ready for Jagger," said Pendleton, "and if I'd known he was going to sing the way he did and that the rest of them were going to play the way they did, there was no way I would have hired them."

Not that everyone was offended. The Rolling Stones' defenders in the audience may have been smaller in number at first, but they were more vocal than the groups detractors. Each number ended in a din of boos and cheers, the palpable tension between the two factions generating a degree of excitement Pendleton had never before witnessed. He grudgingly decided to keep them on Thursday nights, though he left no doubt about his personal disdain for their brand of music.

The Stones were well aware that they lacked an essential ingredient for any successful rock band: a good drummer. The best around was Charlie Watts, but he belonged to Alexis Korner and Blues Incorporated. Besides, explained Richards, "we couldn't afford him."

But even with a succession of less-than-polished drummers, word of mouth was pulling larger and rowdier crowds into the Marquee Thursday nights. (Pendleton was sufficiently impressed with the Rolling Stones' box office power that he soon began sponsoring other up-and-coming blues bands, albeit groups whose sound was more to his liking. One of these, which alternated on Tuesday nights, was called the High Numbers. They later changed their name to the Who.)

Jagger was not yet convinced that he should drop out of the London School of Economics to pursue a career in show business. He did not want to disappoint his parents—

particularly his taskmaster father—and he was not about to forgo the modest government grant that was affording him a first-class education.

Yet Brian and Keith managed at least to shame Mick into leaving home. As a half step toward independence Mick moved with Bryan and Keith into a flat at 102 Edith Grove in Chelsea. The two-room apartment was basically unheated, with a bathtub in the kitchen and a communal toilet two flights up. A single light bulb dangled from the ceiling. Paint and plaster flaked off the smoke-smudged ceilings; the walls and floors were green with mildew.

The tenants made themselves right at home. Before long the rooms were strewn with putrid, half-eaten sandwiches, grimy clothes, and shards of glass and smashed crockery. Rats skittered across the floor, which was covered by a carpet of cigarette butts. By way of decoration Jagger, Richards, and Jones smeared excrement on the walls and signed it. "If somebody had thrown a bomb in the place," Keith's mother, Doris, said, "it couldn't have been worse."

"The atmosphere was fetid," recalled Dick Taylor. "I thought, *Do people really live like this?*" Although Jones and Richards never were particularly conscientious when it came to household chores, Jagger had always been almost compulsively neat. Now he was clearly rebelling against his mother's oppressive orderliness. "It was quite amusing to see Mick in this pigsty," said Taylor. "The others had no idea of housekeeping. But Mick came from a very nice middle-class home where he did quite a lot of the cleaning himself. And here he was wallowing in absolute filth."

This was only part of Mick's transformation from dutiful bourgeois son to working-class street-fighting man. Virtually overnight he exchanged his proper upper-class accent for a cockney patois. Ironically, over the years Keith would shed his lower-class dialect for the more polished speech pattern that came to Mick naturally. "We switched accents," Jagger would privately acknowledge.

By way of immersing himself in the low life Mick paid an occasional visit to his downstairs neighbors. "Allo, dahlin', 'ow are ya? All right?" they would ask each time Mick made his way up the rickety stairs. Keith described them as "real old boots," but in reality they were probably in their mid-thirties. More nursemaids than hookers, they brought barley soup and blankets when the boys were suffering through hangovers or the flu. Appalled at the conditions under which these young musicians were living, they even volunteered to do the cleaning. By way of compensation Mick, Keith, and Brian would take turns having sex with the women.

The two male student teachers who lived upstairs also contributed, unknowingly, to the welfare of their fellow tenants. They were the antithesis of the Stones in appearance—neat, well groomed, and nattily attired—yet they managed to throw several parties a week. Mick, Keith, and Brian would listen to their neighbors dancing to the music of Duke Ellington, and when the music finally died down in the early morning hours, they crept upstairs and let themselves in.

While the students and their dates slept, their neighbors tiptoed around the living room collecting half-eaten sandwiches, half-smoked cigarettes, and empty bottles that they would return for the deposit. At other times they would crash parties in the neighborhood and, when the host wasn't looking, snatch as many edible items as possible from the refrigerator.

Brian, who had already been fired for stealing from the department store, soon became more brazen; whenever he was short on cash, he would break into the students' flat and rifle drawers and pants pockets in search of spare change.

To help make the rent Jones invited his old Cheltenham pal Richard Hattrell to join them at Edith Grove. Mick was aware that Brian was capable of cruelty—that was painfully evident in his offhand treatment of Pat and their son Julian Mark—but just how much pleasure Brian derived from sadistic acts only became evident after Hattrell's arrival.

Slavishly devoted to his old friend, Hattrell, a short, rotund young man with thick black hair and even thicker glasses, would simply do whatever Brian asked of him. When they walked down the street, Brian ordered Hattrell to walk twenty yards behind them. That winter was the harshest in a century, yet when Jones instructed Hattrell to give him his army coat, Hattrell unhesitatingly whipped off the coat and wrapped it around Brian. "Now," said Brian, "give Keith your sweater." Keith continued, "So I put the sweater on, and off we'd walk to the local hamburger place. 'Ah, stay there. No, you can't come in. Give us two quid.' We'd be inside eating, and this cat would stand outside in the freezing cold. Then we'd let him in and stick him with the bill."

The breaking point for Hattrell came one snowy night in December, when Jones arrived home to find his friend sound asleep in Brian's bed. Jones pulled him out of bed, then stripped him. Then Jones grabbed a cable from behind an amplifier and, wild eyed and laughing maniacally, began chasing Hattrell around the room. "This end is plugged in, baby, and I'm coming after you." Sparks flew as Jones pursued his roommate around the flat. Mick collapsed with laughter as Hattrell fled outside, shrieking "They're trying to electrocute me!" into the night air. Brian locked the door behind him, then leaned out the window and, brandishing the wires, threatened to "fry" his friend if he dared come inside. Hattrell sat on the front steps, naked and shivering in the snow for four hours before he could be persuaded by Mick to return. "By then, the poor guy was blue." Hattrell left the next morning, for good.

These incidents only hinted at the breadth of Brian's cruel streak. Over the ensuing years he would increasingly direct his anger at women. Beyond the savage beatings he inflicted on the women in his life were those episodes that separated the bully from the true sadist. He would make a habit of pointing to his bloody, rumpled sheets and brag to Mick that he had deflowered another virgin. In one instance he covered a hole in the floor of his flat with carpeting and coaxed a woman friend to it; Jones laughed as she injured herself plunging to the floor below.

After Hattrell's abrupt but entirely understandable departure, the tables were turned when a new roommate, Jimmy Phelge, arrived on the scene. If possible, Phelge's personal habits were even more revolting than the full-time inhabitants of 102 Edith Grove. When Mick returned home from school, he would encounter Phelge standing on the front steps wearing nothing but his feces-streaked and urine-stained underpants on his head. "Unfortunately, I haven't made enough money this week to help chip in with the rent," Phelge said, "so instead I'll entertain you and be as disgusting as possible for the whole week." That included hiding microphones in toilets to secretly record neighboring tenants' bowel movements, and inexplicably spitting at his roommates. "It wasn't a thing to get mad about," shrugged Keith. "Covered in spit, you'd collapse laughing." Mick was less charmed by this than were Keith and Brian, and after a few weeks Phelge moved mercifully on.

During that bleak winter of 1962 Jagger and his remaining roommates were less concerned with their music than they were with sheer survival. They seldom had money to feed the coin-operated electric heater in their room, so the three men slept each night in the same double bed, huddled together for warmth.

This curious sleeping arrangement underscored the Rolling Stones' homoerotic nexus. Jagger took it upon himself to adopt a feminine role. Wearing scarlet lipstick, heavy mascara, and pancake makeup, Mick Jagger began flouncing around the house in a lavender hairnet and powder-blue linen housecoat. He painted his fingernails and toenails red to match his lipstick, and even took to wearing the stockings and high heels left behind by one of Brian's girlfriends.

According to Richards, Mick was "wavin' his hands everywhere—'Oh! *Don't*'—a real King's Road queen. Brian and I immediately went enormously butch, sort of laughing at Mick. That terrible switching-around confusion of roles that still goes on. Brian and I used to kid the piss out of him. But Mick stayed on that queen kick for about six months."

Jagger was not only exploring the bisexual aspects of his own personality, but the power such gender-bending gave him over others. By shedding his cloak of masculinity he was able to make Jones and Richards seriously doubt their own. What resulted was an atmosphere of confusion, anger, and lust that Mick found strangely exhilarating. If he could provoke such a strong reaction from his friends what, he wondered, would be the effects on an audience? Inside the seedy Edith Grove flat with the excrement-smeared walls and the stench of rotting vegetation, Jagger was consciously conducting his own experiment in androgyny that would have powerful implications not only for popular music, but for society at large. He was taking the first steps toward redefining what it means to be male.

Not that he was indiscriminate in his tastes. In fact, Mick appeared to be infatuated with only one man: Keith. "Long John Baldry was notoriously, famously gay," recalled Dick Taylor. "He had a hankering for Mick." Long John, whose name did not refer merely to his height, stayed over at the Edith Grove flat one night, and Mick awoke to find Baldry's tongue in his ear. "Mick was most upset about that," added Taylor. "He kicked Long John out, but he didn't have any lasting resentment about the incident. They remained friends."

In the short run Mick's queenly demeanor scarcely concealed the fact that he was jealous of Brian for having stolen Keith away from him. Indeed, while Jagger was away at class, his roommates stayed in the flat all day, incessantly practicing their music, leaving only to scrounge or steal enough money for booze and cigarettes. When the thermometer plunged, they spent whole afternoons together in bed sans Jagger, telling dirty jokes and practicing funny faces. Jones could reduce Keith to tears by pushing his nose up and lower eyelids down—a face he called the "Nanker."

Mick began to feel odd man out, and he was. The bond

forged by constant mutual struggle far transcended any relationship Mick and Keith had had up until now. Mick was not entirely without fault in this. He had refused to leave school and had not committed himself wholly to the cause. Nor was he generous with his partners. Jagger still received his government stipend and a regular allowance from his parents, and his dates singing for Blues Incorporated netted him two pounds (about seven dollars at the time) each week. But rather than share any of his comparative good fortune with the others, Mick sneaked off to dine alone at restaurants while Keith and Brian foraged for scraps.

Mick was justified in his suspicion of Brian as a spoiler. Behind Jagger's back Brian was lobbying hard to replace him with his former singer, P. P. Pond, alias Paul Jones. "Brian would smile and pat Mick on the back and tell him what a great singer he was," says a Marquee Club regular, "then as soon as Mick was out of earshot he'd call his singing a piece of shit and tell Keith he wanted Mick out of the group. Everybody told him he was crazy, and he'd shut up for a while."

What ensued would be the first round in a lifetime of sex games for Jagger. Although Brian was anything but faithful to Pat Andrews, every now and then she and Julian would stay over at the Edith Grove flat. One afternoon Mick arrived home to find Pat alone, waiting for Brian. Jagger charmed and disarmed her, eventually talking her into bed in the hope that Brian would catch them in flagrante. Brian did not walk in at the opportune moment, but it hardly mattered; Mick made sure Brian got wind of the affair. "I figure the only reason he balled Pat, who was certainly not very attractive," Ian Stewart suggested, "was to get at Brian."

In that Mick was successful. Brian definitely was not in love with Pat, but his fragile ego could not withstand the shame of being cuckolded—particularly by a mincing, flouncing "King's Road queen."

But Jagger was far from finished. While he had inflicted psychic pain on his nemesis, Brian's relationship with

Keith was stronger than ever. To drive a wedge between them once and for all, Mick, according to Anita Pallenberg, seduced Brian. Yet by presumably conducting a short-term sexual relationship with Brian, Mick wound up feeling exposed, vulnerable. "Brian did break up a lot of things by actually going to bed with Mick," said Pallenberg, who at various times became sexually involved with Keith, Brian, and Mick. Brian told her of his relationship with Jagger. "And I think Mick always resented him for having fallen for it. In later years there have always been rumors about Mick being gay, but then it was as if Brian violated Mick's privacy by revealing his weak side."

This bizarre triangle would ultimately result in the destruction of a Stone. Meantime, all three were inexorably linked emotionally, physically, and professionally—infusing them with an energy and creative power they could never have summoned as individuals. Mick knew that together, they were infinitely greater than the sum of their parts. Jagger also knew that, from this point on, he would be first among equals.

"I am not a Judy Garland or a Frank Sinatra. I can live without adulation quite comfortably."

The fortune-teller's long red fingernails traced the lines in Mick's palm for only a few seconds before she rendered her verdict. "You've got the star of fame!" she proclaimed. "It's all there!" Since this particular mystic was actually one of the downstairs neighbors who had taken up palmistry as a hobby, everyone at the flat laughed that night. Everyone but Mick.

He had little apparent reason to believe that success might be on the horizon. On the verge of starvation, Mick and Keith were now shoplifting food from the local grocer. But, given the response he was getting at the Ealing and Marquee clubs, Jagger was beginning to convince himself that he had the potential to become a successful musician, if not a household name.

He continued to agonize about dropping out of the London School of Economics. Mick turned to his blues mentor Alexis Korner, whom he and Richards had taken to fondly calling "the Guv'nor," for advice. What if they failed, Mick asked Korner. Was it worth throwing away a very real chance to enter one of the professions? Give it a year, Korner suggested. "If we flopped, would it matter?" Brian added. "At least we'd have tried. No regrets, no 'what ifs.'" It was better, Jagger decided, to have made the effort and failed than to live with a lifetime of recriminations. Still, it would be months before Jagger made the total commitment and dropped out of school altogether.

Group members were reshuffled again that December of 1962. Dick Taylor left to enroll in the Royal College of Art (eventually he would return to the music world to play bass with the Pretty Things). Tony Chapman, their drummer-of-the-moment, recommended a friend of his, Bill Wyman, to replace Taylor on bass. Wyman, a married storage clerk who had played part-time with bands in the area, had showed up for his audition on December 7 hauling an enormous speaker and a Vox AC 30 amplifier—both pieces of equipment the band needed but could not afford. The amp, he informed them, was merely his spare. Brian and Keith went back to drinking their beer, leaving Mick the only member of the group to feign interest during the audition. It scarcely mattered if Wyman could play or not; he had already been hired for his speakers and his amps.

Jagger then asked drummer Carlo Little, a member of the popular Cyril Davies's Rhythm and Blues All-Stars, to join the Stones. He was doubtful at first, but Little relented. "They were pretty pathetic," recalled Little, who was six years Jagger's senior. "They didn't know where their next penny was coming from, and their personal habits were, well, disgusting. They drank out of these dirty cups, and their clothes looked and smelled like they hadn't been washed in months."

Little was impressed by Jagger's unbridled ambition, but he was also struck by his lingering insecurities: "Mick would ask me, 'What should we do? What should we play?' He would get frantic, like a little kid. He wanted *stardom* much more than the others, that was obvious. He just wasn't completely sure how to get it."

Little felt at the time that the Stones "copied American stuff better than anyone else," but had no idea that they would end up "capturing the whole world the way they did." Even then, however, it was obvious to Little that if the group made it, it would be because of Jagger's magnetism. "You couldn't put your finger on it, but there was something very weird about him even in those days. It made you uncomfortable to look at him jerking around, but you couldn't help it. He was just damn exciting." As for the rest of the band: "I thought they were just another nice, semipro band. And they still are."

Behind the scenes Mick had already begun to subtly stake his claim to leadership. To the outside world, however, the Rolling Stones was Brian's band. He worked the phones, relentlessly hustling for work in clubs throughout Greater London. It was a daunting task. Managers of traditional jazz spots had a stranglehold on the nightclub industry. They grudgingly tolerated Alexis Korner because there was clearly big money to be made on the R & B craze. They were not about to extend this same courtesy to scruffy young upstarts who, in their opinion, made noise rather than music. The jazz establishment was so threatened that it occasionally reverted to sabotage, hiring the Stones and, once they showed up, mysteriously canceling.

All of which merely made them that much more determined to succeed. Against formidable odds Jones managed to land dates at seedy outposts like the Red Lion Pub in Sutton and Windsor's Ricky Tick Club. "There was no doubt about who ran the show when it came to the business side," said the Marquee's Harold Pendleton. "At that time Brian ran the show. It was Brian's band." Unfortunately for the others, that meant that Brian also collected the money and, without restraint, pilfered from the till. "He conned us and we knew it," Bill Wyman would later admit. "But he was such an energetic leader no one cared much about Brian's extra few pounds."

With the arrival of the New Year the Stones were more convinced than ever that they needed a new drummer. They had long had their collective eye on Charlie Watts of Blues Incorporated. He was not only a superb drummer, but a snappy dresser. Jagger in particular felt Watts's zoot suits and expensive shoes made him the perfect foil for the rest of the group, which, to put it charitably, could be described as unkempt. But Watts was fiercely loyal to Alexis Korner. Watts also had serious doubts about ever making it in the music business; he was reluctant to quit his day job as a graphic designer at a London advertising agency. He was still hemming and hawing when Mick finally said, "Look, you're in this band. That's it, end of story." Watts relented, though it was a toss-up as to whether he or Wyman hated the band's name more.

Mick, Brian, and Keith were now faced with the messy task of firing Tony Chapman. As they packed up the equipment after a show at the Ricky Tick Club, Brian and Keith abruptly fired Chapman. When Wyman, whom he had brought into the band, refused to go with him, Chapman stormed off in a rage. In what would be the start of a life-long pattern of avoiding such unpleasantness, Mick—who had actually orchestrated the ousting—stood silently on the sidelines.

The newly reconstituted Stones—consisting now of Jagger, Richards, Jones, Watts, Wyman, and Stewart—debuted at Soho's Flamingo Club on January 14, 1963. The reception was cool. The white jazz buffs still dismissed them as amateurs, and the blacks in the audience, who were there to see the club's regular singer Georgie Fame, resented Mick's obvious attempt to sound like one of them.

At the Marquee Club, though, the Rollin' Stones (they would not formally restore the g until March) were drawing bigger and bigger crowds as the Thursday-night intermission band for Cyril Davies's R & B All Stars. By mid-January more than six hundred people were packing the club Thursday nights. Watching enviously from the sidelines as the Stones did encore after encore, the hard-drinking Davies began heckling them, then ordered the band off the stage. When Keith spotted Harold Pendleton grinning from the sidelines, he picked up his guitar and swung it at Pendleton's head. Mick, thinking more about holding on to this lucrative gig than Pendleton's well-being, pulled Richards back. Richards missed striking Pendleton, but the damage to the band's fortunes was done—they were banned on the spot from playing the most influential jazz club in London.

The wet snow and bone-chilling temperatures did little

to boost spirits back at Edith Grove. Despondent, Mick, Brian, and Keith veered over the thin line between eccentric behavior and the truly bizarre. One afternoon a new neighbor dropped by to introduce himself. Mick threw open the door and stood there, nude, scanning the visitor with a puzzled look. He then screamed "Fuck off!" before slamming the door. On another occasion Richards locked himself out and, unable to wake his roommates, smashed his guitar case through a window and let himself in. The window was never fixed.

Rather than clean their linens, which hadn't been laundered in months, they threw their soiled blankets and sheets out the window and burned them on the front lawn. After trying to fix Brian's record player they plugged it into a soggy wall outlet and it exploded in a fountain of sparks. For amusement in the predawn hours Mick and Keith liked to terrorize the other tenants. They tied a frying pan to a string, then swung it down along the side of the building in an effort to shatter their downstairs neighbors' bedroom window. Luckily, no one was injured in the resulting shower of broken glass.

The boys at 102 Edith Grove, in what amounted to a mad science experiment, would return from posting flyers around town and pour the excess glue into the bathtub. As time went on and the glue level rose, Mick tossed cigarette butts, holey socks, used toilet paper, and even leftover food into this homemade bog. "Everything was in there," recalled a visitor. "This glue was kind of growing out of the bathroom into the kitchen and everywhere, it was crazy."

Amid this escalating insanity Mick managed to fall in love—with a black sixteen-year-old schoolgirl named Cleo Sylvestre. The daughter of a Trinidadian who disappeared when she was born, Sylvestre harbored dreams of becoming a singer. She was a devout fan of Blues Incorporated and a regular at the Marquee, where she hoped to learn all she could about American music.

At first, Mick was shy and tentative. He invited Sylvestre to the Edith Grove flat for tea, and once the shock subsided, she brought several girlfriends to help "tidy up. We made the place barely livable," recalled one, "but within a day it went right back to being a filthy hole." Added Wyman: "They lived like rats. They'd sit in bed with hundreds of half-empty bottles with fungus growing out of them. They looked right at home."

Jagger and Sylvestre soon began dating; a loyal fan, she showed up at every Stones club date, including one at the Ealing when only six people showed up in the middle of a snowstorm and the boys wound up playing in their overcoats. Yet, as far as she was concerned, there was scant chemistry between them. "Mick was no heartthrob in those days," Cleo recalled. "None of my friends were jealous or thought he was a great catch. But we were really on the same wavelength, although we came from very different worlds. I had a real cockney accent, so I could tell that his was put on."

In an unexpected display of adolescent ardor Jagger began writing love letters to Cleo in hopes of coaxing her into bed:

> Dearest Cleo,
> I want somebody to share everything with, someone to respect, not just someone to sleep with. I feel that in you I've found that something that I've been looking for a long time.
> Cleo, what have you done to me! I've got to the stage where I just want to cry because I won't have you.
> I really do want to see you desperately. I don't care about much else at the moment.
> Don't forget that I love you and don't hurt me too much. Cleo, please make me happy, it's the one thing missing from my life now.

The letter was signed simply, "Michael."
In another letter to Sylvestre, Jagger gushed:

> Darling Cleo, I want to share my life with you. I don't just want to sleep with you. . . .

"I was shocked Mick liked me so much," said Cleo. "Even in those days it was unusual for a boy to send so many love letters, especially since we saw each other twice a week. But he wanted things to go much further, and that's why sometimes I was scared to see him almost—because I knew he'd expect something from me. All I wanted was a quick kiss and a cuddle on my mother's balcony when he said good-night, but he wanted sex."

It was then that Mick stunned her with an offer she found impossible to refuse. The Stones were toying with the idea of hiring backup singers à la Ike Turner's Ikettes. Would she be interested? Cleo instantly forgot about Mick's untoward advances and leapt at the chance. He had already selected a name for the backup group—the Honeybees—and had very definite ideas about their sound. If they were going to sound as authentically American as the Ikettes or any of the other girl groups that were now proliferating in the U.S., Jagger figured that the next best thing to actual Yankees were English girls—no one with a West Indian lilt need apply (Jagger believed English girls could mimic American singers more convincingly than could Caribbean women).

The next day Sylvestre showed up for rehearsals with another young woman who called herself a singer. Mick was convinced that he had stumbled upon a gimmick that would enable the Stones to break away from the pack. Keith, Brian, and the rest believed him—until they began singing. Although he did not know the lyrics to the Richie Valens hit "La Bamba," Mick insisted on trying to get by using Spanish-sounding "words" of his own creation. The result was hysterical; the band would only get halfway through the tune before both women dissolved in laughter. Between the backup singers' unremitting giggles and the new girl's blatant inability to carry a tune, the experiment ended in disaster.

Sylvestre returned to her studies, but continued dating Jagger over the next eighteen months. The stream of letters continued unabated. On Valentine's Day, Mick sent Cleo a card. The front of the card read, "Let's Spend the Night Together," and inside, ". . . Before I Fall Apart." At one point he proposed marriage, then jokingly suggested that her other serious boyfriend be best man.

While Mick seemed obsessed with bedding Sylvestre, Brian was making a professional connection that would change their lives forever. After the Stones were banished from the Marquee Club, a fiery White Russian impresario named Giorgio Gomelski told Brian that he had just opened a new blues club at the Station Hotel in suburban Richmond. Gomelski invited the Stones to play there—as soon as there was an opening. Meantime, the garrulous, bearded part-time filmmaker agreed to arrange dates for the Stones at other clubs so they literally would not starve in the interim.

At places like Ken Colyer's Club and Eel Pie Island in Surrey, Jagger worked on his signature prance. "I thought it took real guts," said Wyman, "to stand up in front of a local Saturday-night crowd and sing and dance that way. I mean, if I were in the audience, I would have thought he was a little queer."

When Giorgio Gomelski's regular group failed to show during a snowstorm, Jagger raced to a pay phone to beg for the job. Before he could begin, Gomelski invited them to play at the club's Sunday-afternoon dances. They jumped at the chance.

Located thirty minutes from London by train, Richmond was an affluent, bucolic hamlet on the Thames. Not on a par with the centrally located Marquee, perhaps, but not so remote as to discourage the diehard blues-lover.

True to his Russian soul Gomelski was passionately committed to the Stones—and particularly to Mick—from the start. He willingly took on the role of paterfamilias, at first forgoing his own cut of the profits so that they would at least have enough to survive. A master of hyperbole, Gomelski ran ads in *Melody Maker* hailing the arrival of "the inimitable, incomparable, exhilarating Rolling Stones!"

Such unalloyed enthusiasm proved infectious. The size

of the crowds grew geometrically with each new ad—from thirty the first weekend to one hundred the second to three hundred the next. The Stones always ended each forty-five-minute set with Bo Diddley's "Doing the Crawdaddy." As more and more patrons—many of them art students from Kingston College—flocked to Richmond, Gomelski decided to name his club the Crawdaddy.

At first patrons at the club stood motionless, awed by the music but uncertain as to how to react to it. Gomelski urged them to cut loose of their inhibitions, and they did—with a vengeance. While the sleet fell outside, temperatures soared inside the Crawdaddy, where customers ripped off their shirts and danced on tabletops. The crowds, said Gomelski at the time, "simply went berserk."

Phil May, Keith Richards's old friend from the early days back at Sidcup Art School, knew who they were coming to see. "Mick was their secret weapon from the beginning," recalled May. "He was incredible, electrifying—a complete original. Before Mick the girls would hug the stage while the guys would hang back at the bar trying to look as disinterested as possible. For the first time it was mainly guys who fought their way to the front—they literally shoved women and punched other guys to get close to Mick. Jagger was the first performer to appeal to *both* sexes—heterosexual males as well as females and gays. He could arouse both sexes like no one before, or since."

Mick's ability to electrify audiences was irrefutable, but mercurial Brian was still battling behind the scenes on behalf of the group. Through his friend Glyn Johns, who worked as a recording engineer at IBC Studios, Jones arranged for the boys to cut a demo. In a single three-hour session they recorded five songs. When seven record companies rejected their demo point-blank, Brian was crushed.

It took a story in the April 13, 1963, edition of the *Richmond and Twickenham Times*—the first newspaper story ever written about the Stones—to boost the band's spirits. "A musical magnet is drawing the jazz beatniks to Richmond," wrote music journalist Barry May. "The attraction is the

Crawdaddy Club at the Station Hotel, the first of its kind in an area of flourishing modern and traditional jazz haunts. R & B is replacing traddy-pop. The deep earthy sound is typical of the best R & B, and gives all who hear it an irresistible urge to stand up and move. . . ."

The piece went on to call Mick "the driving force behind the group," but Jones was thrilled anyway. He carried the clipping with him in the "group wallet" at all times, and whipped it out at the slightest provocation. His group, he told anyone who cared to listen, was winning the war against the hidebound jazz establishment.

Brian was certain the group had found its manager in Gomelski, and told Mick that he was going to have a contract drawn up formally giving Giorgio the job. Jagger argued that, for all that he had so quickly accomplished on their behalf, Gomelski was still small-time—an imaginative promoter, true, but someone with limited vision and no major contacts in the music business. Jagger, who still attended classes at the London School of Economics and harbored a social agenda of his own, also found the bear hugs and bravos of the affable Russian annoying.

For his part Gomelski did not concern himself with such trifling details. He felt he had a verbal agreement with Mick and Brian, and their word was enough for him.

It can be argued that the period of broad social and cultural upheaval that falls under the rubric of "the sixties" actually began in 1963, as the world emerged from its collective shock over John F. Kennedy's assassination that November. England was in the throes of a cultural renaissance that would soon become its greatest export. That year suave James Bond was the screen's reigning adventure hero, *Tom Jones* won the Academy Award, and such exciting young stars as Albert Finney, Julie Christie, Vanessa and Lynn Redgrave, Alan Bates, and Peter O'Toole seemed to dominate the film world. The satirical *Beyond the Fringe* was an enormous stage hit, and David Frost's bitingly satirical *That Was the Week That Was* was an overnight favorite with American as well as British television audiences.

Royal College of Art alumni David Hockney, Richard Smith, and Peter Blake followed close behind Andy Warhol, Jasper Johns, and Robert Rauschenberg as pioneers of something called "pop art." Mary Quant was crowned the new queen of a fashion mecca called Carnaby Street, and Edwardian jackets, Cuban-heeled boots, black leotards, and string vests became the uniform of the young. Trendsetting models like Jean Shrimpton and Twiggy sported startling wedge-cuts by an innovative young hairdresser named Vidal Sassoon, while more and more men were forgoing haircuts in favor of the bowl-shaped "Mod" look.

Nowhere were things moving faster than in the world of pop music, and no figures in the music world were having greater impact than the Beatles. Unlike the comparatively well-off Stones, all four members of the Beatles had come from grinding poverty in Liverpool, where they, too, played down-and-dirty clubs before finally attracting notice in a basement dive called the Cavern.

"Love Me Do" was actually their first hit, having climbed to No. 17 the previous November. But by the time the Beatles hit No. 1 with "Please Please Me" in late February of 1963, they had established themselves not only as musical trailblazers but as mainstream artists—and commercially the most promising group in England.

Everybody was thrilled by the Liverpool group's success, with one exception. Jagger vomited when he heard that the Beatles had a hit record before they did. After so much struggle Mick wondered now if there was a big enough market out there to support two major pop groups. Would the Stones be left in the Beatles' dust? This would mark the beginning of a complex love-hate, ally-adversary relationship between the two supergroups of the era.

On April 14 Mick was belting out Bo Diddley's "Road-Runner" at the Crawdaddy when four men in matching ankle-length black leather overcoats walked into the club and were led to a table by Gomelski. Giorgio, who was acquainted with George, John, Paul, and Ringo, had invited them earlier that day to catch the "inimitable, incomparable, exhilarating Rolling Stones" at his club. As Gomelski winked at Jagger, the blood drained from Mick's face. Richards's mouth was agape, and Wyman kept thinking *Shit, that's the* Beatles.

They needn't have worried. The Beatles were thunderstruck at what they saw that night. They knew that, among hip young Londoners, it was now very fashionable to spend Sunday afternoons at the Crawdaddy—even if it meant standing for an hour or more in a line that stretched around the building. What they could not have anticipated was a singer whose movements verged on the spastic but who at the same time generated a raw sex appeal that drove men as well as women wild.

The Beatles hung around at the bar, and then accepted Mick's invitation to return with them to Edith Grove for a drink. Like everyone else who entered this squalid inner sanctum, these guests were plainly horrified. Yet the nine men who would collectively shape a generation sat for hours swigging beer and talking about their hopes and dreams.

Mick reserved judgment, but Brian was unabashedly in awe of his guests, even though John Lennon haughtily dismissed the music of their beloved Jimmy Reed as "crap." Before they left, he wangled an autographed eight-by-ten glossy from the Beatles, then taped it on the dirt-streaked wall next to the signed nose pickings.

Four days later Mick, Keith, and Brian accepted the Beatles' invitation to their concert at Royal Albert Hall. To avoid paying, the three grabbed the Beatles' guitars from a van and pretended they were crew members. As Mick headed for the stage door, someone shouted, "There they are!" and a screaming crowd rushed the hapless imposters. Once they realized these weren't the Beatles, the fans turned away in mild disgust. No matter. Keith was mildly amused by the adulation, however short-lived. Both Mick and Brian were instantly, hopelessly hooked.

Their friendship with the Beatles blossomed that spring, but only Mick and John Lennon would go on to form a close relationship. Lennon, who had reportedly slept with the Beatles' gay manager, Brian Epstein, dropped in unannounced at Edith Grove one afternoon and found Jagger and Richards naked in bed together. "I'm not sure about those two, you know," he told Paul McCartney later. "What do you think?" According to McCartney it was a question they never resolved.

Mick had formed other intimate relationships with musicians outside the group, most notably with a quiet, struggling young guitarist named Eric Clapton. They met before Clapton formed the Yardbirds, when it was simply enough for the shy teenager to work up the courage to mumble his own awkward version of Chuck Berry's "Roll Over Beethoven." Offstage they had both been somewhat diffident, and surprisingly ill at ease with the women who swarmed around them after each performance. Their friendship would grow even more after the two achieved stardom, causing some to speculate on the nature of their feelings for each other.

When Giorgio Gomelski called Peter Jones, editor of the influential *Record Mirror* music magazine, Jones balked at spending his one day off watching another so-so band in the suburbs. But Gomelski was insistent. He had telephoned Jones to tell him that he was filming the Stones for an R & B documentary the next Sunday, and that the film and the group might make an intriguing piece. "I did not want to waste my Sunday," said Jones, "but Giorgio is a very persuasive man. I went there very much under pressure, but I went."

When Jones arrived at the club, he was surprised to see no one in the audience—just the band onstage, performing while Gomelski lined up camera angles. "They were playing a song called "Pretty Thing," and it was so explosive that even without an audience you were sort of lifted right out of your seat," the journalist recalled. "Afterward, Brian and Mick came over to chat." Mick began to talk, but Brian butted in and took over the conversation. "Brian was eager to let everyone know that he was the spokesman—

that was obvious," said Jones. "It was equally obvious that this rubbed Mick the wrong way."

Brian pulled his tattered press clipping from *The Richmond and Twickenham Times* and proudly showed it to Jones. "It seemed odd, but Mick went out of his way to tell me that Gomelski was *not* their manager, as I had assumed. They went so far as to say Giorgio had 'nothing to do' with them."

Mick and Brian also knew that Decca Records owned the magazine Peter Jones worked for. "When Mick said they were looking for some kind of advice and guidance," said Jones, "I thought it would be a nice challenge. I knew they certainly weren't your ordinary sort of blokes, and for some reason I felt compelled to help."

Jones went back to the *Record Mirror* offices and persuaded another reporter, Norman Jopling, to size the group up for him. The resulting article ran in the April 1963 issue:

> THE ROLLING STONES—GENUINE R AND B
> At the Station Hotel, Kew Road, the hip kids throw themselves about to the new jungle music like they never did in the more restrained days of trad.
> And the combo they writhe and twist to is called the Rolling Stones. Maybe you've never heard of them—if you live far from London, the odds are you haven't."
> But by gad you will! The Stones are destined to be the biggest group in the R and B scene—if that scene continues to flourish. . . . The fans quickly lose their inhibitions and contort themselves to the truly exciting music.

The piece went on to point out that "unlike all the other R and B groups worthy of the name, the Rolling Stones have a definite visual appeal. . . . They sing and play in a way that one would have expected more from a coloured U.S. group than a bunch of wild, exciting white boys who have the fans screaming and listening to them."

Ironically, Norman Jopling declared that the Stones' music bore only a "superficial resemblance to rock 'n' roll." He then quoted Mick as saying they would only play American-written material: "After all, can you imagine, a British-composed R and B number? It just wouldn't make it."

The same day he sent Jopling to Richmond to cover the Stones, Peter Jones bumped into a "skinny young maniac" named Andrew Loog Oldham. At nineteen Oldham was a year younger than Jagger, but he already boasted a colorful past. The illegitimate son of a U.S. Air Force officer who was shot down over Germany the year he was born, Andrew took both his parents' surnames—Loog and Oldham. He was kicked out of private school at sixteen, went to work for Mary Quant as a window dresser, and moonlighted as a doorman at one jazz club and a waiter at another. Oldham was also a part-time press agent, but he confided in Peter Jones that he really wanted to be a disc jockey, or a rock journalist, or a singer. Or maybe a comedian. At various times he went under the names "Sandy Beach" and "Chancery Lane."

By the time Jones approached him about the Stones, Oldham had already worked briefly for legendary manager Brian Epstein, doing the publicity for Epstein's clients the Beatles. With an eye on becoming "a teenage tycoon shit," Oldham had recently begun renting office space from Eric Easton, a highly regarded agent and manager.

Peter Jones zeroed in on Oldham for one other important reason. "My point was to get someone who had the ear of Decca Records Chairman Sir Edward Lewis," said Jones, "and that was Andrew. Sir Edward had a strong gay streak, and Andrew would have been a good catch. Whatever Sir Edward's motives, I knew he'd listen carefully to what Andrew had to say."

"Andrew was 105-percent confident all the time. The moment I told him about this group that was looking for a manager," said Jones, "he lit up. That was the thing about Andrew. If he was in a pub, his eyes would be open wide, scanning the room. He was always hustling—a smooth operator." But before he could make the trip to Richmond to see the Stones, Oldham had to convince the button-down

Easton to even consider handling an act as over-the-top as the Rolling Stones.

While Oldham cajoled Easton, a comely seventeen-year-old secretarial student was betting her date at the Maidenhead International Club in Windsor that she could get the Stones' shy lead singer to kiss her. Chrissie Shrimpton, whose sister Jean was starting to pop up on the covers of leading fashion magazines, had had her eye on the gangly vocalist since he sang his first song with Alexis Korner's band at the Ealing Jazz Club. And though he often seemed to be singing to her, he had never approached her. This time with cash at stake the leggy, auburn-haired beauty pranced straight up to Jagger and asked him for a kiss. He obliged, and her date paid up.

Shrimpton was surprised at how small Jagger was. Mick would always seem larger than life onstage, but up close he was surprisingly diminutive—five feet nine inches tall, barely 130 pounds, but with a head that seemed too large for his body. She was also shocked by his almost feminine demeanor. "He was very giggly, very pretty, very camp," she said, and though he suffered from severe acne, she found him somehow physically appealing. Shrimpton was particularly impressed with the wedge of brown in one of his blue eyes. It was just one of the things, she observed, that "made him different from everybody else."

Two days later Andrew Oldham and Eric Easton walked into the Crawdaddy and witnessed the pandemonium that Peter Jones had described. "They blew me away immediately," said Oldham. "They made the Beatles look like choirboys. The instant I saw Mick on that stage, I knew what they were all about. Sex, pure and simple. Sex—and magic." Although Oldham recognized from the start that Jagger was the sexual sorcerer of the group, all the Stones fit his ideal of the new generation of pop star. All were lean, long haired, and sullen looking—much like Oldham himself.

Except for one. During intermission Oldham wandered into a side alley, lit up a cigarette, and wondered what to do about Ian Stewart. Stu's close-cropped hair, burly build, and distinctive jut-jaw, a congenital abnormality, clashed with the rest of the band.

As Oldham grappled with this problem, he noticed an attractive couple silhouetted against an amber streetlamp at the other end of the alley. They were arguing bitterly. As the quarrel escalated, the woman slapped the man hard across the face. They were arguing, apparently, over his demands for sex. As they moved closer, a startled Oldham realized that the man was Jagger, and the woman Chrissie Shrimpton. Just forty-eight hours after their first meeting they were already literally at each other's throats. "That should have given everyone a pretty clear idea," said Oldham, "of what their relationship was going to be like."

The following day Oldham proposed to Easton that they sign up the group that was creating havoc each Sunday at the Crawdaddy. The conservative theatrical agent hesitated. His biggest reservation: that Mick couldn't sing. Oldham managed to convince him otherwise, however, and the two agreed to divide up responsibilities for handling the group. "It was decided," said Peter Jones, "that Andrew would make all the artistic decisions, and that Eric would take care of the business side." Easton would also supply the much-needed start-up money to give the group a proper launch.

"There was no doubt about who to deal with in the negotiations," said Oldham. "Brian acted like he ran the whole show, and the others just sort of tolerated it." During the negotiations, conducted while Giorgio Gomelski was out of the country, Brian went along with Easton's suggestion that Mick be dropped from the group. Oldham dismissed the notion as "insane." Jones also secretly arranged to be paid five pounds a week more than the others.

The ink on the three-year contract was barely dry when Oldham took his first official action as manager: firing Ian Stewart from live performances. "He just didn't have the right look. He didn't fit," said Oldham. "It had to be done." Stu waited for his friends to leap to his defense, but they didn't. "Brian was a total jerk—he could have been expected to go along with it," said one colleague. "They would've kept Stu if Mick had insisted. But he didn't." By way of consolation Stu was allowed to play in Stones recording sessions (where he couldn't be seen), and was offered a job as the group's road manager. Reluctantly, he agreed.

"They listened to me," said Oldham of those first days managing the Stones, "because we identified with each other. Mick especially. He was only twenty, but I was even younger, more arrogant—and he really liked that."

At about this time Giorgio Gomelski returned from his father's funeral in Switzerland to find that while he was out of the country he had been ousted in a palace coup. Actually, he had to learn the truth himself. Brian introduced Oldham to Gomelski not as the group's new manager, but as an old school friend. Mick said nothing.

"Giorgio was angry and deeply hurt," recalled Peter Jones. "He had done everything for these boys, and he thought their verbal agreement was enough. Since I was the one who put Andrew onto them in the first place, Giorgio blamed me for a while. He estimated that I cost him at least two million dollars in future management fees."

If Gomelski justifiably felt betrayed, Mick was unimpressed. He had never taken the affable Russian seriously, and was not about to let any misguided sense of loyalty stand in the way of stardom.

For Jagger a lifelong pattern of relying on people and then callously discarding them in absentia was already taking shape. Not long after Alexis Korner gave him his first singing job, Mick privately dismissed him as second rate. Each time someone had to be jettisoned—drummer Tony Chapman, Stu, and now Gomelski—Mick conveniently avoided confrontation.

Events were moving too swiftly now for recriminations. Oldham invited Dick Rowe, the Decca Records executive who was trying to live down his reputation as "the man who turned down the Beatles," to catch the Stones' act at the Crawdaddy. He signed up their first single ("I didn't want to make the same mistake again"), and within days the group was in Olympic Studios recording Chuck Berry's "Come On." (And on the B side Muddy Waters's "I Want to Be Loved.")

Oldham had never been in a recording studio, and told the sound engineer so. "I'm entirely new at this," he said, "so let's just play it by ear." The result was a serviceable tune, but one that didn't sound at all like the Stones. Mick thought "Come On" was "real shit," and refused to sing it onstage. Oldham was enraged. "Come On" was the Rolling Stones' debut effort; not to perform it live was tantamount to disowning their own record. After nearly coming to blows with Oldham, Mick backed down.

Jagger was rebelling in other, smaller ways. In the beginning Oldham had viewed the Stones not as the bad boys of rock, but as a sexier version of the squeaky-clean Beatles. He dressed them head to toe in matching black outfits— black Cuban-heeled boots, black turtlenecks, black sweaters. Mick wore a brown suede jacket instead, and traded in the high-heeled boots for loafers.

"Andrew tried to turn them into the Beatles," said a former publicist. "He put them in leather suits with black shirts and ties. The Stones got pissed off. Eventually, their uniforms disintegrated, and they became more disheveled."

On June 7, 1963, the Rolling Stones made their first TV appearance lip-synching "Come On" on the pop music program *Thank Your Lucky Stars*. Because it was a national television broadcast, they relented and donned black-and-white houndstooth blazers with black velvet collars. A world away in Brian's hometown of Cheltenham, their hapless friend Richard Hattrell was watching the show with his conservative, rock-and-roll-hating father. When the Stones came on, Hattrell senior retrieved his World War I Army pistol from a back closet, aimed it at the set, and fired into the TV screen.

As soon as they went off the air, the Stones agreed with

Mick that the uniforms looked "bloody terrible"; they shed the jackets on the spot and tossed them into a waste bin. But even in their matching outfits the Stones had infuriated parents as much as they delighted fans.

That summer "Come On" made its inexorable climb to No. 18 on the charts. "God knows how it ever got on the charts," said Jagger. "It was such a hype." This was by no definition a major hit—certainly not big enough to warrant the kind of press they were receiving. What they offered to the teenagers of Britain—both boys and girls—was raw sex appeal. Soon the Rolling Stones, always focusing on Mick as the main attraction, were splashed across the pages of every fan magazine in the country, from *Boyfriend* and *Valentine* to *Rave*.

None of which sat particularly well with the possessive Chrissie Shrimpton. Barely two weeks after their first argument in the alleyway next to the Crawdaddy, Shrimpton's parents took a weekend trip to celebrate their twenty-fifth wedding anniversary. She invited Mick to spend the night at the family's farm in Burnham, west of London.

For the next several months Mick would make the trip to Burnham, wait in the bushes until her parents fell asleep, then sneak into Chrissie's bedroom for nights of furtive lovemaking; the recent invention of the birth-control pill now made it possible for him to dispense with his condoms and, as Brian Jones would often say, "ride bareback." In the predawn hours before her parents stirred awake, Jagger would crawl out her bedroom window and head back to London.

Mick halted his nocturnal visits in September, when at last they abandoned Edith Grove for more civilized quarters on Mapesbury Road, in West Hampstead. The move dramatically shifted the balance within the group. Brian, who still clung to the belief that he was the de facto leader of the Rolling Stones, now left to live with his current girlfriend, Linda Lawrence, at her family's home in Windsor. Meantime, Mick, Keith, and Andrew Oldham moved into the Mapesbury Road apartment. They were joined by

Chrissie, who through Mick now had a clerical job at
Decca. All four were crammed into two rooms, and shared
a single bathroom. Compared to their previous habitat it
was Buckingham Palace.

With Brian removed from the scene, Jagger, Richards,
and Oldham formed a sort of unholy alliance, deciding in
Jones's absence what direction the group would take. Mick
and Keith, who had already formed an intense personal
bond, were in awe of Oldham's energy. Keith called him
"an incredible bullshitter, a fantastic hustler." Mick envied
his vision for the Stones.

Oldham had supplanted Jones as the third point in the
Stones' creative triangle, but that was only part of the original Stones' undoing. As Eric Easton usurped more and
more authority on the business front—arranging concert
dates, collecting and monitoring the group's funds—Brian
had already seen much of his control over the group slip
away. Onstage he was also having to come to grips with the
simple fact that, despite his firm belief that anyone could
sing better than Jagger, it would be virtually impossible for
any guitarist to wrest the spotlight from a lead vocalist.

Now that momentum was building, it was imperative
that the group find its next hit song. That problem was
solved when Oldham spotted Paul McCartney and John
Lennon leaving a Variety Club luncheon at the Dorchester
Hotel. They had just written a new tune, "I Wanna Be
Your Man" and thought it would be perfect for the Stones'
second single. From their meeting with Oldham, Lennon
and McCartney drove straight to the Stones' rehearsal studio and taught them the song. Again, Mick was in awe of
Lennon's skill as a lyricist; the Beatles' tune "She Loves
You" was, after all, the No. 1 record in the nation. Lennon,
in turn, was envious of Jagger's gritty drawl.

Socializing on the nightclub circuit, Lennon and Jagger
often frequented one of the hottest spots in London, the
Ad Lib. Among other Ad Lib regulars: Roman Polanski,
Michael Caine, Elizabeth Taylor, and Richard Burton. "All
the Beatles and the Stones came," said Brian Morris, who

co-owned the club with author Jackie Collins's husband, Oscar Lerman. "Keith and Brian Jones and Mick would come in together, but before long Lennon and Jagger would be in the corner, wrapped up in intense conversation."

The Stones thought they were returning the Beatles' generosity by opening for the Beatles (along with Adam Faith and Cliff Richards) a week later at London's Royal Albert Hall. Instead, the Beatles watched anxiously from the wings as their young friends whipped the audience into a writhing frenzy.

After the concert there was a press reception in the elegant Sir Henry Cole Room of the Royal Albert Hall. It was there that Keith Altham, a writer for *Fabulous* magazine, who would later become their friend and publicist, first met the Stones. "We were in these auspicious surroundings," recalled Altham, "and Mick and I watched Keith as he stood over the buffet table, picking his nose and flicking it across the room."

Altham turned to Mick and said, "Well, that was certainly distasteful."

"You're lucky it wasn't a green one," Mick replied matter-of-factly, and much to the abject horror of several guests. "He *eats* those."

Altham viewed that revolting episode as another bit of theater calculated to bolster the Stones' loutish image. "They were *not* working class the way the Beatles were. They were solidly middle class. Mick was particularly adroit at playing the guttersnipe."

At this backstage gathering it was clear to Altham that the schism between Brian and Mick was widening. "Jagger was a detached figure even then," Altham observed. "Brian regarded himself as spokesman for the band, so Mick just sat back and let Brian be spokesman. He watched Brian from the sidelines with this slightly contemptuous look, just biding his time. . . ."

He may have seemed aloof around the press, but the torrent of publicity intoxicated Mick. "We were always hustling to get our picture on the cover of *Fab* or *Rave* or

Teen," Jagger later conceded. "As soon as the teenyboppers caught on, we were in for the Big Scream."

Oldham, for one, did not take this for granted. At all the Stones' live performances he stood near the rear and let out high-pitched, girlish screams that instantly caught on. He often paid a few teenage boys to push their way past the girls to the front, encouraging other young males to follow suit. "Fakery, hype, hustle," said Oldham. "It's all part of the music business."

He followed up by throwing the fan-club machinery into high gear. The membership shot from three hundred to tens of thousands in a matter of weeks. Valerie Watson Dunn was an awestruck girl of fifteen when she first met Mick and the Stones after a concert at the British Legion Hall in South Harrow in mid-September of 1963. "They were walking to the train station," she recalled, "and when I asked for their autograph, Mick was by far the friendliest. We girls all felt the same about Mick. His face was sort of ugly, but he had those narrow hips, and you'd look at that wonderful little bum and sigh. . . ." The woman who was actually hand-picked by the Stones to run the fan club, Shirley Arnold, knew firsthand about the kind of hysteria they could inspire: Arnold met the Stones after she fainted at a concert. Her limp body was passed over the heads of the audience so she could be revived backstage.

Oldham made a quick succession of cosmetic changes. He knocked five years off Bill Wyman's official age (teens would never swoon over a creaky twenty-seven-year-old). Keith was ordered to drop the s from Richards because it was too pedestrian sounding. Jagger took it upon himself to order Charlie Watts to grow his hair longer.

Most important, each member of the group had to appear unattached, so that the fans could freely fantasize about being with them. Brian Epstein was desperately trying to keep secret the existence of John's wife, Cynthia, and their infant son, Julian Lennon; despite his precautions the news leaked. Female fans were crestfallen at the news of Lennon's state of domestic bliss, and for a moment it looked as if it might seriously cut into Beatles record sales.

Jagger not only agreed with Oldham that the women in their lives should be relegated to the shadows, he once again assumed an active role in enforcing this rule. He ordered Wyman not to refer to his wife and child in interviews, period. Brian was also told to be quiet about his pregnant girlfriend, Linda Lawrence—not to mention his illegitimate children and their mothers. None of the Stones were to admit to being anything but freewheeling bachelors.

Jagger went so far as to instruct Watts not to marry his longtime love, Shirley, at this delicate juncture. At Mick's insistence they canceled their wedding plans.

Mick made no exception for himself. He told Oldham he firmly believed that a serious girlfriend for a rock star was only so much excessive baggage. Chrissie, understandably, thought otherwise. Privately, he professed his undying love to her. In his early interviews Mick sarcastically waved off any suggestion that he had a girlfriend.

"Mick really doesn't respect women," said Shrimpton, who was, with the other Stones girlfriends, banned from the recording studio. Whenever Shrimpton and the others did see Mick, they saluted him with "Heil, Jagger!" Said Chrissie: "It made him furious, but that *is* how we all felt."

Shrimpton was not content to remain a cipher. Her sister Jean ("The Shrimp") was, with the aid of fashion photographer David Bailey, already fast becoming one of the most celebrated beauties of the decade. Chrissie was too strong a personality to settle for this phantomlike existence.

Jagger and Shrimpton quarreled bitterly and often about the intrigue surrounding their affair, and he reassured her that it was a temporary situation. Once they were established superstars, this need to placate the fans would pass. Then they could declare their love to the world.

As 1963 wore on and their fame grew, Jagger became more callous in his treatment of Shrimpton. He never displayed affection in public; the minute a group of fans appeared he put as much distance between himself and Chrissie as he could. "If we were holding hands and someone was coming," she recalled, "he'd drop my hand and turn away. Of course I was hurt and humiliated. But he said it was necessary."

One evening, when a mob of fans jumped out of the bushes to accost him on the street, Jagger literally shoved her away from him and began signing autographs. Once the fans were gone, she repaid him with a stinging slap in the face and a kick square to the groin.

These matches were not entirely one-sided. When she struck him, he sometimes hit her back. "We were very passionate from the beginning," said Shrimpton. "It was First Love for both of us, so everything about our relationship was intense." Their turbulent affair would be punctuated with scenes in restaurants, slammed doors, and shouting matches. They concealed their scratches, bruises, and black eyes behind dark glasses and shovelsful of pancake makeup.

Jagger's wounds would have been more serious, no doubt, had Chrissie known that he was still romancing high-schooler Cleo Sylvestre—and still writing Sylvestre love letters:

My dear Cleo,

I was half expecting to see you at the Ken Colyer club on Sunday . . . and wondered why you didn't come. I had my usual row and breakup with Christine instead which I suppose will be patched up this week.

I really would like to see you this week, could you write and say when—anytime day or night. OK?

By the way, this may all be stale by the time you get it as I am thinking of coming round tonight. Bad Boy.

Be careful with this letter, don't let him [her other boyfriend] see it.

Don't forget I love you Cleo.

Write soon,
Mick.

Also behind Shrimpton's back he wrote:

> My dearest Cleo . . . Seeing you on Sunday gave me a big nervous kick. I don't know what it is you do but I could hardly sing a note. I was shaking like a leaf!! That doesn't mean that you shouldn't come again though. . . .

"I wasn't jealous," insisted Sylvestre of Jagger's open affair with Shrimpton, "because I thought they had a completely different sort of relationship from ours."

What neither Sylvestre or Shrimpton knew was that Jagger the nouveau celebrity was beginning to sample from a sexual smorgasbord. "Jagger was only twenty," said a friend from that time, "but he was just starting to realize that he was a sex symbol. Girls wanted Mick Jagger. Boys wanted Mick Jagger. He loved Chrissie, but for the first time he was wondering why he should limit himself—to any one woman or any one person, for that matter."

No matter. Oldham was fast coming to the realization that his original vision of the Rolling Stones as an updated alternative to the Beatles was flawed. Parents had quickly come to accept the Beatles as somewhat asexual creatures who posed no threat to their daughters' virtue. But the Stones were shaggier, more unkempt, and more overtly sexual, both musically and visually.

Oldham seized on the difference. Instead of being cast in the image of the Beatles, the Stones would be the flip side of the Beatles—the Bad Boys of rock. He told Jagger & Co. to grow their hair even longer, and to dress any way they pleased. In interviews they were to be rude, sullen, as offensive as possible. That meant blowing smoke in interviewers' faces (all the Stones chain-smoked), chewing gum, spitting, being generally as nasty as possible.

Meantime, Oldham, who was now convinced the best publicity for the Stones was bad publicity, played the press like a concert virtuoso. He spoon-fed them copy that newspapers and magazines printed verbatim: "They look like boys any self-suspecting mum would lock in the bathroom.

But the Rolling Stones—five tough young London-based music-makers with doorstep mouths, pallid cheeks, and unkempt hair—are not worried what mums think."

Oldham's most successful line would be picked up in headline after headline, caption after caption: WOULD YOU LET YOUR DAUGHTER GO WITH A ROLLING STONE? which quickly graduated to WOULD YOU LET YOUR DAUGHTER MARRY A ROLLING STONE?

Oldham didn't exactly "invent" their negative image. "I can't take credit for something that was already there," he explained. "They were all bad boys when I found them. I just brought out the worst in them. By the time I was finished, every parent in England was disgusted by the Rolling Stones." Which made their children love the Stones even more.

"Long haired and ugly and anarchic as they were," said rock critic Nik Cohn, "Oldham made them more so; he turned them into everything that parents would hate most. It was good basic psychology: kids might see them the first time and not be sure about them, but then they'd hear their parents whining about those animals, those filthy long-haired morons, and suddenly they'd be converted. They'd identify like mad."

"We were pitched as the black version of the Beatles," recalled Jagger. "Actually, they were every bit as cynical as we were, they just wore suits." Oldham was, Jagger thought, the logical architect of their rebel image. "Andrew had a real talent for creating a splash and a fuss," he allowed. "He was younger than us, and he had a very irrelevant attitude. We needed someone like Andrew. It would have taken a lot longer without him."

In late September 1963 the Stones embarked on their first national tour of England. Topping the bill were the Everly Brothers and Bo Diddley. Five days into the tour they were joined by Little Richard. While Keith and Brian sat at Bo Diddley's feet, paying homage to their idol, Mick studied Little Richard's piano-pounding antics and sweaty striptease.

Little Richard was still years away from donning sequined Liberace costumes and white satin capes. But his heavy mascara, exaggerated pompadour, and wildly effeminate stage manner still raised eyebrows in the post-Eisenhower era. Mick responded by becoming even more coquettish in his performances. Jagger also wore makeup even when he wasn't working. "His stage makeup was already pretty extreme," recalled a fellow musician. "Jagger was tarted up like some transvestite. It wasn't that jarring when you saw him from the tenth row of Albert Hall. But up close in the afternoon, it was pretty shocking."

Thousands of hysterical teenage girls greeted them in every city, but Jagger also had a growing following of gay men. "At the time most gays didn't dare appear too obvious," recalled a friend. "The stigma was just too great. But even then there were drag queens, and they were all over Mick. It didn't make him uncomfortable at all. He enjoyed the attention, as much as he did from the women."

Chrissie had always known that life on the road forged intense personal relationships. Watching Mick and the rest exhausting themselves onstage, then scrambling to escape mobs of hysterical teenagers, she realized strong bonds had to develop between the band members—if only in the interest of self-preservation. She was surprised in those last weeks of 1963, however, that Mick seemed to have grown even closer to Andrew Oldham than he had been to Keith.

The turbocharged Oldham often seemed quirkier and more flamboyant than the people he managed. Whereas none of the Stones could be remotely described as conventionally handsome, the blond, tousle-haired, pink-cheeked Oldham had the deceptive good looks of an English choirboy. He had always dressed like the Stones—skin-gripping black jeans, black turtlenecks, and dark glasses were standard—but now he had, like Jagger, taken to wearing makeup.

Shrimpton knew of the rumors that swirled about concerning Mick's sexual preferences. She often saw Mick with his gay friends, tossing his head back and giggling uncontrollably as he had the first night she had dared him to kiss her. But she remained convinced for the time being that, despite outward appearances, he was completely heterosexual.

Her confidence was shaken when Andrew Oldham's girl-friend (and later his wife), Sheila Klein, approached Shrimpton and asked her what the sleeping arrangements were at the new flat on Mapesbury road. "Do Mick and Andrew sleep in the same bed?" Klein asked point-blank.

Shrimpton was stunned. "Not when I'm there," she answered defensively, "because I sleep with Mick." Klein accepted the answer matter-of-factly. In fact, when their women were not there, Jagger and Andrew Oldham did sleep in the same bed.

"Later," said Shrimpton, "I did see Mick and Andrew in bed together. They were undressed, asleep—and I was so naive at the time I thought they looked very innocent and sweet together. But it's obvious Mick was bisexual even then."

Oldham shrugged off the rumors. He conceded that he had indeed grown closer to Mick as they worked in tandem to shape the group's bad-boy image. But theirs was strictly a platonic relationship, he insisted, nothing more.

To the public at large the length of Jagger's hair alone was enough to put his manhood in question. The pouty lips and eye shadow added to the confusion. "Mick was very masculine-minded; he was very strong and very aggressive, for example. But physically he was very feminine," said Shrimpton. "Even to me, he seemed outrageously camp."

Jagger and interior designer Nick Haslam were dining at a King Road restaurant when an older man seated at the next table leaned over and, shoving his face at Mick, loudly asked Mick, "Are you a man or a woman?"

The restaurant fell silent as Mick stared at the man, expressionless. Without saying a word Jagger stood up, unzipped his pants, and produced the evidence.

"He's a smart little motherfucker,
I'll give him that."
—*Keith Richards*

"Oh, *Mr. Shampoo*," Jagger gushed, tousling Brian Jones's hair playfully. Jones pulled away, annoyed. "Your coiffure," Jagger went on, "is looking especially *luuuvly* today." Reacting to press reports that the Stones were dirty, Brian shampooed twice a day. This compulsion was only one of the things about Jones that Jagger and Richards delighted in making fun of. The pair, egged on by Andrew Oldham, now took obvious pleasure in ganging up on Jones, teasing about everything from the bags under his eyes to his stubby legs. "You had to be strong to join the Stones," recalled Bill Wyman. "The fainthearted or ultrasensitive would not have stood the gibes that poured from Mick and Keith." Their comments, according to Wyman, were often "spiteful and hurtful."

This unremittent needling, coupled with Jones's growing sense of powerlessness within the group and his own hard-drinking, womanizing life-style, took its toll. A lifelong asthmatic, Brian now relied more and more on a medication to keep from going into respiratory arrest. "There'd be this terrible gasping, wheezing sound," recalled Ian Stewart. "Sometimes he'd turn this horrible shade of gray-blue while he was searching for his inhaler. It always scared the hell out of us."

Asthma was only one of an array of maladies that began to cause Brian to miss rehearsals and performances. The others became inured to Jones's excuses and chalked his absenteeism up to hypochondria. In truth, Jones probably suffered from an undiagnosed form of temporal-lobe epilepsy—a condition that was passed on to one of the many illegitimate children he never met.

In January of 1964 the Stones toured Britain again, this time sharing top billing with the hugely popular American girl group the Ronettes. Ronnie Bennett, whose rendition of "Be My Baby" would become a pop classic, was engaged to the legendary songwriter-producer Phil Spector at the time.

That hardly mattered to Mick, who openly made a play for the sultry singer. In interviews Ronnie proclaimed Mick was "sexy, provocative, and gorgeous." But in private she politely rejected his advances. Though Keith later bragged that he had succeeded where Mick had failed, Ronnie insisted that she never slept with Richards. "He was very into himself, in his own room, in his own world," Ronnie later said. "He was a bit of a softie."

Unlike Keith, Mick did not retreat to his room to lick his wounds. No sooner had Ronnie turned Jagger down than he zeroed in on another Ronette, Ronnie's sister Estelle. Their affair lasted the duration of the tour.

Their heterosexual prowess notwithstanding, all the Stones were now targeted for ridicule wherever they went. After one of the concerts with the Ronettes the Stones stopped in at a cafeteria and were instantly showered with insults from a nearby table. Mick ignored the shouts of "queer" and "homo" for a time, then leapt to his feet and defiantly confronted the hecklers. Within seconds Jagger lay sprawled on the floor, unconscious. It was the first time Jagger had ever been punched, and the blow had come from an American tourist. Richards rushed to his friend's defense, and wound up sprawled on the floor beside him.

That barely matched the mayhem that occurred at nearly every one of their concerts that spring. Gripped by mass hysteria, screaming fans would surge toward the stage, threatening to pull their idols down into the roiling sea of humanity. Fistfights broke out, chairs were hurled, girls overcome by it all were passed overhead and taken to waiting ambulances. Bedlam.

Such chaos was gratifying to Oldham; after all, he had engineered much of it. But Oldham also realized that, if they were to challenge the Beatles, the Stones would have to produce their own material. The changes Jagger and Richards made to Buddy Holly's "Not Fade Away," their third single, convinced Oldham that they had latent ability as songwriters. Those alterations were so extensive, in fact, that Oldham would consider "Not Fade Away" the first Jagger-Richards collaboration.

Neither Jagger nor Richards had ever even considered becoming songwriters; it was a completely alien notion to both men, and an intimidating one. But Oldham was insistent. He told them they could be the next Lennon and McCartney. When they balked, he locked them in a tiny room and refused to let them out until they had written a song.

They emerged with two songs, which Oldham conceded were "bloody awful." One, "Tell Me," made it onto their first album, released by Decca on April 17, 1964. Months earlier Brian had anticipated that individual group members might start writing their own material, and convinced the others that songwriting royalties should be shared. Toward that end Andrew and Mick formed Nanker Phelge Music, Ltd.—Nanker from the funny faces they used to make at one another back in Edith Grove, and Phelge after their ill-mannered former roommate Jimmy Phelge.

The debut LP featured another Oldham masterstroke: He insisted that there be no writing on the jacket whatsoever—just an arresting shot of the Stones themselves, staring directly into the camera. It was a daring maneuver, and an effective one. Within days the debut album of the Rolling Stones had skyrocketed to No. 1.

Amid the chaos the indefatigable Oldham pursued his dream of becoming another Phil Spector. He convinced Jagger and Richards to write a song for another of his discoveries, a young woman named Adrienne Posta. To promote her debut single, Oldham threw a sixteenth birthday party for Posta on April 9, Good Friday.

This innocuous affair would come to mark an important turning point in Jagger's life and, by extension, something of a milestone for the sixties. Paul McCartney and his girlfriend Jane Asher were among the guests; they in turn invited Cambridge art student John Dunbar and his date to tag along.

Marianne Faithfull was only seventeen years old and still attending a convent school when she walked into the party on Dunbar's arm. She was the daughter of philology professor Glyn Faithfull and baroness cum ballet dancer Eva Sacher-Masoch; appropriately enough, considering the life Marianne was to lead, one of her ancestors had lent his name to the word *masochism*. Faithfull's porcelain complexion, enormous cobalt-blue eyes, cornsilk hair, and—most important—her aristocratic bearing contrasted sharply with the brittle hangers-on who crowded the room. A childhood case of tuberculosis had shaped her outlook on life, and left her with a translucent beauty.

"She had this remarkable quality—ethereal and at the same time very modern," said Oldham, who spotted her from across the room and wasted no time introducing himself. Faithfull hardly knew what to make of Oldham. Beneath the hexagonal pink shades she could make out the traces of eyeliner and mascara. He also wore face powder, lipstick—and a flowing lavender blouse.

When the bizarre-looking character offered her a record contract on the spot, Faithfull was taken aback. Oldham didn't ask her to sing; he didn't care. "It was her *look* that interested me," said Oldham. "That virginal, angelic, *pure* look was gold as far as I was concerned. Oh, yes, she also had a terrific body." Her name was another plus; it would have been hard to make up a stage name that had more potential marquee value than Marianne Faithfull. (Ironically, while fantasizing about a career on the stage, Marianne would sit at her desk at the convent scribbling down dozens of possible pseudonyms—it never occurred to her that she already had the perfect stage name).

"Marianne thought it was all kind of amusing," recalled Dunbar. "She was this convent girl—classically trained, the farthest thing you can imagine from a rock star. These people all seemed very odd to her; she didn't know what to make of them."

At the party Jagger and Chrissie Shrimpton were experiencing another frisson. He had asked her to marry him, and she had accepted. But much to Shrimpton's consternation Jagger was still telling the press that he had no intention of ever marrying. Aside from an intermittent icy glare they were now making a show of ignoring one another.

While Chrissie watched him out of the corner of her eye, Jagger walked up to Faithfull and introduced himself in his forced cockney accent. Marianne was not a follower of the rock scene, but it was hard to imagine that there was anyone left in England who had not heard of Mick Jagger. Before she could say a word, Jagger, quite intentionally, spilled a full glass of Dom Perignon down the front of Marianne's blouse. He reached over and wiped her breasts with his hand, and she ran to the kitchen, furious. *What an arrogant, ill-mannered bore*, she thought. Mick shrugged and went back to the party.

"Marianne was really disgusted by them at first," said Barry Miles, a friend of Faithfull's who later joined the Stones' inner circle. "She told me, 'What horrible, ugly, dirty, pimply people.' She thought they looked greasy and sort of disgusting."

Nevertheless, Oldham sent over a contract the next day. Ever since her parents' separation ten years earlier, Marianne's mother, the baroness, had been forced to eke out a modest existence in a tiny house in the middle-class suburb of Reading. The prospect of adding to the family coffers—not to mention escaping the suffocating confines of the convent—appealed to her tremendously.

Oldham had asked Jagger and Richards to write a song

for her—"something a convent girl would sing, no sex"—and they came up with "As Tears Go By." Marianne would always suspect that the song was just a Stones reject, but Jagger insisted it was inspired by her. To be sure, it seemed nothing short of miraculous that these two men could, after only a few months as collaborators, create this gentle ballad destined to become a pop classic.

After the half-hour session was over, Faithfull was very pleased with the results. So were Oldham and Jagger, though they failed to tell her. "It was very strange because they didn't speak to me," she recalled. "There was Andrew and Mick and Keith and friends and I just went in there and did it. I was quite staggered that they wouldn't give me a lift to the train station. After the session I thought *Now, I'm entitled to some sort of star treatment.* I didn't say it but I really felt . . . you know . . . where's the car? And when I actually had to walk out of that scene and get a taxi back to Paddington Station I felt very pissed off."

While Mick and the others celebrated, Faithfull spent that night back at the convent. "They saw me," she recalled, "as a commodity . . . a hunk of matter to be used and discarded." She would forgive Oldham and Jagger when "As Tears Go By" became a worldwide hit late that summer.

The Stones juggernaut rolled on across the United Kingdom. Full-scale rioting was now par for the course. Cars were stoned, windows smashed, buses overturned. One promoter in Scotland complained that the "fans were like animals. The girls were the worst."

The Stones were ready to export their patented brand of pandemonium to the United States. To pave the way they released their third single—the gritty remake of Buddy Holly's "Not Fade Away"—in the U.S. in April. The record made it to No. 2 in the U.K., but fizzled in America.

On home turf the Stones were surpassing the Beatles in popularity. Their debut album toppled the Beatles from the No. 1 spot, and one poll now rated Jagger as the most popular male singer in England—ahead of all the Beatles.

Eric Easton had been dispatched to New York to personally arrange the upcoming U.S. tour. Still, Jagger was having second thoughts. Without a hit record there, what were the chances of anyone knowing who they were? Not one to leave such matters to chance, Oldham had already generated a mountain of breathless publicity. *Vogue* warned American audiences that "for the British the Stones have a perverse, unsettling sex appeal, with Jagger out in front. . . . To women Jagger looks fascinating, to men, a scare." The Stones were not, proclaimed Oldham, "just a band, but a way of life."

One British MP apologized to America in advance. "Our relations with America," he said, "are bound to deteriorate. The Americans will assume that British youth have reached a new low of degradation."

In America the Stones, the Beatles, and the lesser groups spearheading the so-called British Invasion—among them the Animals, the Yardbirds, the Kinks, Gerry and the Pacemakers, Peter and Gordon, Herman's Hermits, the Dave Clark Five—were still better known for their manes than their music.

No lesser publication than *The New York Times* ran several breathless pieces on this topic, warning Americans that the trend toward longer hair for men was about to sweep across the Atlantic. Under the front-page headline BRITISH 'HIS AND HER' HAIRDOS BLUR 'HIM-HER' LINE, the *Times* described the plight of a tourist from Kansas who "stopped a youngster in the Kensington area of London to ask about the nearest post office. The person she had politely addressed as 'Miss' turned out to be a sixteen-year-old lad in a bright pink shirt and tight trousers. He had long brown hair that skimmed his collar. The tourist was the more embarrassed of the two."

"We have become a very shaggy lot in England," wrote British journalist Anthony Carthew in a *New York Times Magazine* piece. "Foreheads have disappeared beneath hedgelike fringes and can only be glimpsed in a high wind. Ears and collars are similarly buried." Carthew went on to proclaim that the Stones had unseated the Beatles as champions of the new tonsorial style.

As silly as it would seem three decades later, the issue of hair length obviously struck a collective nerve. Symbolizing both youthful rebellion and a redefining of sexual stereotypes, it triggered confrontations between student and teacher, child and parent. Why all the fuss? "Adults seem to have a sort of personal anxiety because we are getting away with something they never dared to do," answered Jagger. "It's a sexual, personal, vain thing. They've always been taught that being masculine means looking clean, cropped, and ugly."

The Stones were, of course, profoundly aware that their untamed look had much to do with their success—though Mick struck a characteristically blasé pose for the press. "We just like our hair the way it is," Jagger told the *Times* reporter. "I suppose it gave us our chance. But it doesn't represent anything special to us." Brian was more candid: "My own mother thought I was ridiculous at first. But I told her about all this money we're earning and she saw the point."

Later that year, while defending Jagger for a minor traffic infraction, lawyer Dale Parkinson waxed eloquent on the subject of his client's hair:

"Put out of your mind the nonsense talked about this young man. He is not a long-haired idiot, but a highly intelligent university man.

"The duke of Marlborough had much longer hair than my client," Parkinson continued, "and he won some famous battles. He powdered his hair, too, because of fleas. But my client has no fleas. Caesar Augustus also had long hair and he won many great victories. Long hair, curled up at the ends, is worn by barristers in court." Jagger was fined just forty dollars.

Mick's concern that the Stones were not yet well enough known in the United States vanished—for the time being—when they were mobbed by hundreds of screaming fans upon their arrival at New York's Kennedy Airport.

Their confidence evaporated three days later in Los Angeles, as they taped ABC's popular TV variety show *The Hollywood Palace*.

The host of *Hollywood Palace*, Dean Martin, made no secret of the fact that he had taken an instant dislike to these scruffy, hirsute invaders. Holding his nose, Martin introduced them as "the latest rage from England," then wasted no time cracking, "Their hair isn't that long. They just have high foreheads and low eyebrows."

After their first number, "I Just Wanna Make Love to You," Martin came out and gestured to the group. "Aren't they great?" he sniped, eyes rolling skyward. As he broke for a commercial, Martin added, "Don't go away, anybody. You wouldn't leave me with these Rolling Stones, now, would you?" As the audience broke up, he added, "Actually, the boys are going back to England to have a hair-pulling contest with the Beatles." Mick finished singing "Not Fade Away," and the group took a bow. The next act—an acrobat bouncing on a trampoline—provided Martin with more ammunition for his sarcastic fusilade. "This is the father of the Rolling Stones," said Martin. "He's been trying to kill himself ever since!"

Since they could only make out fragments of Martin's comments from backstage, the Stones were satisfied with their performance and moved on. Their first American concert, at the Swing Auditorium in the small southern California city of San Bernardino, was an unqualified triumph. Nearly five thousand fans waved banners, rushed the stage, broke through police barricades—they may as well have been in England.

Their confidence was soon shattered, however, as they moved farther into America's heartland. In city after city they played to as few as six hundred people in arenas that seated fifteen thousand. They were also encountering outright hostility wherever they went. They could not walk through an airport terminal or hotel lobby without hearing someone yell, "Fag," "Homo," or the ever-popular "Get a haircut."

In Omaha a policeman wandering backstage noticed a few bottles of Coca-Cola and some Scotch in the Stones' dressing room. He ordered them to pour the bottles into the sink, and then turned to Keith Richards, who was sipping a plain Coke. "Pour it into the toilet," he said. When Richards asked why, the officer drew his revolver and pointed it at Keith's head. Richards obliged.

Things were more pleasant in Chicago, where they decided to record a few tracks in the legendary Chess Studios, home to Jagger's childhood idols Muddy Waters and Chuck Berry. Mick's spirits soared when Waters himself showed up to help them carry their instruments into the building and Berry popped in with words of encouragement. Among the songs they recorded that day was Bobby Womack's "It's All Over Now." It would go on later that year to be the Stones first No. 1 record in the U.K.

The emotional rollercoaster ride continued. Backstage in Minneapolis, Jagger watched the broadcast of *Hollywood Palace* and for the first time clearly heard Martin's relentlessly snide remarks. Purple with rage, Jagger phoned Easton in England and blasted him for having booked the show in the first place. "Fuck you, Eric," he screamed, "for doing this to us! Never, ever *again*. Got that?"

Their last stop before returning home: New York's Carnegie Hall. At least here the Stones were accorded what they had come to regard as a proper welcome. Oldham made sure of that this time, planting people in the audience to "stir things up a bit."

It worked. Hundreds of fans stood up on their seats and screamed throughout the show; others rushed the stage before being carried off by security guards. Outside the Hall on Seventh Avenue, police held back a mob as the Stones made their escape after the concert. Following the near-riot, shaken Carnegie Hall officials banned all rock bands from performing there in the future.

The Carnegie Hall hysteria momentarily buoyed Mick's spirits, but it was too little too late. Their all-important first U.S. tour was a major disappointment, and no one felt the sting of rejection more deeply than Mick. As the front man for the group he was more frequently singled out for insults and abuse. What frustrated him even more was the knowledge that he had been right all along: Contrary to what his management had been telling him, the Stones could not crack the huge and diverse American market without a major hit record.

Mick returned to England to find that a new star had exploded on the pop scene. "As Tears Go By"—" 'Greensleeves' goes pop," quipped the *Daily Mirror*—was in the Top Ten, making Oldham's favorite convent girl one of the hottest properties in the music industry.

Even before the Stones' plane touched down at Heathrow, Oldham was planning a European tour to rebuild their shattered self-image. But before they headed out, Mick and Chrissie flew off to unwind on the Spanish resort island of Ibiza. For the first time Mick realized that there was no escape from crazed fans and hungry paparazzi. He and Chrissie were virtual prisoners inside Ibiza's exclusive Palmyra Hotel.

The situation was no better at home. Teenage girls and boys kept vigil outside the Mapesbury Road house. Some managed to get inside; once Mick found a fan crouched beneath a table. Mick, Chrissie, and Keith decided to relocate to a more spacious apartment at 10a Holly Hill in Hampstead, leaving Andrew behind. The move helped allay Shrimpton's concerns over Mick's relationship with Oldham, but they had not eluded the fans. Less than a week later they awakened in the middle of the night to find one cowering in their bedroom closet.

For the remainder of the summer the Stones wreaked havoc and grabbed headlines throughout Europe. POLICE RIOT SQUADS READY FOR ACTION shouted a front page headline in Britain's *Melody Maker,* and the precautions were justified. Wherever the Stones visited, Jagger whipped the throng into a destructive frenzy. Scores of hysterical fans in Belfast, Northern Ireland, were carried out in straitjackets, while another four hundred fainted and were carried away on stretchers.

On July 24, 1964, the Stones ignited the biggest rock and roll riot to date. In Blackpool a mob of inebriated Scotsmen on holiday began spitting at the rockers, and Keith responded by sinking the toe of his boot into one drunk's forehead. In the ensuing chaos the red velvet stage curtains were pulled down and shredded, a Steinway grand piano was pushed off the stage, and Watts's drums were smashed to bits. Later, Ian Stewart walked up with a few bits of wood and said, "Here's your amp . . . here's your guitar. . . ."

In Paris the Stones were ferried to the Olympia Theater in a riot van and guarded by helmet-wearing gendarmes toting submachine guns. After the concert thousands of fans poured into the streets, waving banners, smashing windows, and attacking patrons at sidewalk cafés. What distinguished these rampaging mobs from those in other countries was the fact that they were made up mostly of young males. "Mick stirred up some incredibly intense feelings in many males," said Oldham. "Sex, rage, rebellion—he brought it all to the surface."

Mick understood. "I get a strange feeling onstage," he explained. "I feel all this energy coming from an audience. They need something from life and are trying to get it from us. What I'm doing is a sexual thing. What really upsets people is that I'm a man and not a woman. I don't do anything more than a lot of girl dancers, but they're accepted because it's a man's world. What I do is a striptease. I take my jacket off, and I loosen my shirt, but I don't stand in front of a mirror practicing how to be sexy, you know."

But, as Chrissie could attest, that is exactly what he did. Sometimes for hours Jagger stood before their bedroom mirror, staring at himself, posing, *practicing how to be sexy*. She could tolerate his narcissism, but not his desire to exert control over everyone he knew.

Jagger's prohibition of marriage for the Stones continued to be a sore point. That autumn Charlie Watts finally defied Mick by clandestinely eloping with his longtime girl-friend, Shirley. Shrimpton gladly kept their secret. When he later found out, Jagger was furious—at Watts for jeopardizing the band's sexy image, but even more so at Chrissie for taking part in their little conspiracy. This sparked another of the couple's celebrated brawls. Jagger grabbed her, leaving purple bruises on her arm. She kicked, bit, and scratched him in return. That night, as usual, they made up in bed.

Behind the scenes Jagger and Oldham still pulled all the strings. When one of Brian Jones's many girlfriends announced that she was pregnant with his fifth illegitimate child, Mick and Andrew sprang into action. Without telling Brian they met with the young woman and convinced her to sign over any claim on Brian's earnings for £700 (then the equivalent of about $2,000). Frightened and without any legal representation, the pregnant girl signed the paper, promising never to mention the child's existence to anyone. Mick then told Oldham to deduct the £700 from Brian's earnings. Jones was never aware of the deal, or of the deduction.

Increasingly, Jones was being relegated to a secondary role in the band. Peter Jones, who had initially introduced Oldham to the Stones, recalled that Brian "tried to write songs, but he was too insecure to let anybody see them. Mick and Keith would just burst right into my office with a tape recorder and say, 'Listen to this.' Brian never had the courage."

As Jones gobbled amphetamines and washed them down with Jack Daniel's, he became more and more paranoid. "He was a brilliant musician, but a complete asshole," said fellow rocker Phil May. Concurred longtime Stones associate Keith Altham: "Brian would do something to provoke everyone, like not show up at a concert or beat up a woman, and then do this pathetic routine. 'Why does everyone hate me? Why is everybody against me?' He said that a lot."

Of course, even paranoids have enemies. Brian feared

that Mick was talking about him behind his back, and he was right. Mick was completely fed up with Brian's antics. Once, while leaving a concert, Jones complained so bitterly about his treatment that Mick ordered the driver of their van to pull over. To the delight of the other Stones Jagger kicked Jones out, forcing him to find his own transportation home.

Buoyed by the success of their European tour, they made another stab at the U.S.—this time to promote their second album there, *12 X 5*. (Both their debut album and two singles, "Time Is on My Side" and "It's All Over Now," were already modest hits in America. At Kennedy Airport one fan stopped screaming long enough to tell a television reporter why she liked the Stones: "Because they're so ugly, they're attractive!"

It was a feeling shared by New York's cognoscenti even before British high society embraced Jagger as one of their own. The Stones, along with woman-of-the-moment "Baby" Jane Holzer, were guests of honor at a "Mods and Rockers Ball" thrown at the spectacular Central Park South loft of society photographer–nightclub owner Jerry Schatzberg. Holtzer, another discovery of Mick's friend David Bailey, had been immortalized as the "Girl of the Year" in an article by Tom Wolfe. She had starred in Warhol's underground films, had been splashed across the cover of *Vogue* and in the pages of *Life*. But mostly, as was first said of Gertrude Stein, Baby Jane was famous for being famous.

The party was something of a milestone in Mick's life, for no other reason than that it marked his first meeting with Andy Warhol. Jagger regarded the enigmatic painter of soup cans and Coke bottles as a bona fide genius—perhaps even one of the giants of twentieth-century art. Warhol, in turn, was bedazzled by Jagger's sexually ambiguous glamor. Later, they would form a personal and professional bond that would stretch across two decades.

For now, Mick was busy winning over the Holzer crowd by being rude and obnoxious. "Come on, luv," he told Holzer, squeezing her behind. "Give us a kiss." It was a line repeated to half the other women in the room, and in each case the lucky girl was eager to oblige. "This boy has exceptional lips," Holzer wrote of the experience, "particularly gross and extraordinary red lips. They hang off his face like giblets . . . the lips start spreading into the most languid, confidential, wettest, most labial, concupiscent grin imaginable. Nirvana!"

Yawning with feigned boredom, Jagger got up in the middle of this party in his honor and vanished into Schaztberg's bachelor-pad boudoir. There, he held court like a visiting pasha. At three A.M. Mick, along with Brian and Keith, left the party altogether to spend the rest of the night with the Ronettes.

At the time, all manner of illicit drugs—including marijuana, LSD, cocaine, heroin, and morphine—were inaccessible in England, even to wealthy rock stars. Wherever they went in the U.S., however, outstretched hands offered a variety of mind-altering substances. Watts and Wyman dabbled, but for Oldham, Richards, and Jones this exposure was the first step on a steep road to self-destruction.

Jagger fell somewhere in between these two extremes; initially, he contented himself with the occasional joint. But he would soon graduate to harder stuff. Contrary to his later assertions Mick Jagger was far more than just a symbol of the psychedelic sixties. Drugs would become an important part of Jagger's life, and remain so for decades.

On October 25, 1964, the Rolling Stones made their debut on *The Ed Sullivan Show* singing "Around and Around" and "Time Is on My Side." Sullivan had scored major coups broadcasting the first national TV appearances of Elvis Presley and the Beatles. Judging by the audience packed with screaming teenagers, Sullivan was confident that once again he had stumbled on a group destined for pop greatness. After the show he shook Mick's hand and congratulated the Stones for getting the most frenzied reception ever accorded an act in the show's history.

After an avalanche of letters and thousands of phone calls from angry parents, Sullivan changed his mind. "I had not met the Stones until the day before they were due to appear," he said in an interview. "They were recommended to me by my agents in England. I was shocked when I saw them; I promise you they'll never be back on the show. Now the Dave Clark Five are nice fellows. They are gentlemen and they perform well. It took me seventeen years to build up this show and I'm not going to have it destroyed in a matter of weeks." As the Stones' popularity grew and it became clear they would be around for some time, Sullivan did have them back, of course. Five more times.

Before they departed for home, the Stones did some recording at RCA studios in Los Angeles, then headlined an all-star show at the Santa Monica Civic Auditorium. They were given top billing over Marvin Gaye, the Beach Boys, Smokey Robinson and the Miracles, Gerry and the Pacemakers, and Jan and Dean. Only one star objected. When James Brown was told he would not get top billing, he had one response: "I'm going to make the Rolling Stones wish they never set foot in America."

Mick, terrified that Brown would steal the show, watched in awe as the "Godfather of Soul" tore up the auditorium with his guttural howl and mind-spinning moves. Jagger was especially impressed with Brown's trademark finale in which, glistening with sweat, he is enveloped in a satin cape and led offstage by solemn-faced bodyguards—only to throw off the cape and return to the microphone.

Brown was no less impressed with the white Britons who dared to tackle R & B. When the Stones left the stage, Brown was there with an outstretched hand to congratulate them. Once he was back home, Jagger spent hours practicing Brown's moves before a full-length mirror. He had no trouble incorporating the preening, prancing, and even the James Brown slide across the stage into his repertoire, but try as he might, Jagger's bony frame just wasn't suited to the splits.

Mick picked up something else on the second U.S. tour. He seemed to genuinely miss Chrissie, sending her love notes daily. But that did not prevent Mick from sleeping with several of the groupies who swarmed over Manhattan's Park Sheraton Hotel. "That tour," recalled one member of the Stones' retinue, "opened my eyes to everything—men with men, girls with girls. I walked into this room and all these people were fornicating, right out in the open. I was knocked out." According to Oldham the Stones came back with "lots of clap—the price they paid for their indiscriminate fucking."

"I'm living out my adolescent dreams
perpetually."

**"From when I first met him, I saw Mick was in love
with Keith. It is still that way."
—Anita Pallenberg**

By 1965 Jagger had settled comfortably into his role as the
world's number-one rock and roll antihero. "It seemed a
natural progression," observed Jagger's old friend Phil May.
"Jagger's not slow at picking up trends. More than any
other pop star of his generation he is most conscious of his
image and what it represents. Mick has always been keenly
aware of where he is in time and space and how he is perceived—of his place in the universe and what it means.
He's always seen himself as a symbol, and if he could push
it further, he'd push it further."

Andrew Oldham continued to champion the Stones'
negative image. "The Beatles were touted as the sweet boys
next door," said photographer Gered Mankowitz, "but the
basic philosophy of the Stones was that they just didn't
give a shit. Andrew encouraged them to be as nasty as they
possibly could be."

Oldham, whose shameless imitation of Phil Spector now
extended to hiring a menacing bodyguard (nicknamed
"Reg the Butcher"), was also an ardent fan of writer An-

thony Burgess. Oldham viewed the Stones as present-day "droogs"—the sociopathic, Teddy Boy–like thugs who terrorized the innocent in Burgess's futuristic novel *A Clockwork Orange*. Oldham borrowed heavily from Burgess in creating the jacket copy for the next album, *The Rolling Stones, Now!*:

> It is the summer of the night London's eyes be shut tight all but twelve peepers and six hip malchicks who prance the street. . . .
>
> This is The Stones new disc within. Cast deep in your pockets for loot to buy this disc of groovies and fancy words. If you don't have bread, see that blind man—knock him on the head, steal his wallet and lo and behold you have the loot if you put in the boot, good. Another one sold!

Once they realized that the pretentious, Burgess-inspired prose was actually urging people to mug a blind man for the money to buy the album, British officials pressured Decca to remove the copy from later editions.

Even as he acquired a global reputation as an anarchist and despoiler of the public morals, Jagger was being courted by England's pedigreed elite. As "Swinging London" reached its apotheosis, social barriers were breached. Loose-cannon scions of the nation's oldest and most revered families now hobnobbed with the artists, writers, actors, and designers—many from working-class backgrounds—who breathed new vitality into Britain's cultural life.

"It was suddenly very chic to be seen chatting with a rock star, especially a Beatle or a Stone," recalled Ad Lib nightclub owner Brian Morris. "The aristocrats were falling over one another to invite them into their homes. In a way, Mick was probably the most sought-after socially, since he was thought to be the most dangerous."

Fashion photographer David Bailey, a darling of the "aristos" perhaps because of his solidly working-class roots, got Mick's foot in the door. An added nudge came from art-gallery owner Robert Fraser. A handsome adventure-seeker with a taste for high-stakes gambling and high-quality cocaine, Fraser had been introduced to the Stones by American actor (and fellow drug-user) Dennis Hopper.

It remained for Chelsea antique dealer Christopher Gibbs to throw the door wide open, allowing Mick entrée into the rarefied world of refinement and breeding that he had aspired to since his Dartford boyhood. A classmate of Fraser's at Eton, Gibbs journeyed to North Africa in 1958 and returned brimming with ideas that would literally change the look and texture of the 1960s. He introduced the Moroccan print drapes, carpeting and pillows, painted furniture, brass lamps and fixtures that would come to epitomize the classic ethnic "hippie" look.

Gibbs took it upon himself to school Mick in the ways of café society—and vice versa. Jagger seemed an eager pupil. Gibbs invited his new protégé to a dinner party at his sprawling flat on London's Cheyne Walk. Jagger sat down and leaned over to trendsetting tailor Michael Fish. "I'm here," Mick whispered, "to learn how to be a gentleman."

Gibbs's exclusive circle included the designers Fish and Ossie Clark, and Sir Mark Palmer, who owned a modeling agency, English Boy. Adding luster to the crowd were the comely daughters of Great Britain's onetime ambassador to the U.S. Sir David Ormsby-Gore—Victoria, Alice, and Jane.

The witty repartee at these gatherings was fueled with copious quantities of champagne—and marijuana. Bob Dylan had introduced the Beatles to pot in 1964. Since it had long been supposed "reefer madness" was a vice restricted to jazz musicians, no one suspected that it was behind the Beatles' unremitting giggle fits on the set of their second film, *Help!*

At first Jagger warned Chrissie never to go near pot, or use any drug, for that matter. It was the one thing he would not tolerate. That changed when Oldham told her Jagger frequently lit up when he came into his office, and in fact had just left "stoned out of his head." Stung by his hypocrisy, Chrissie once again flew into a rage. They settled the argument over a joint, and began smoking grass on a regular basis at home.

The Rolling Stones may have been the world's top-selling hard rock band, but because of some creative accounting procedures at Decca, they were not yet millionaires. Money problems beset Oldham, who found that on several occasions he had to twist the arms of promoters—or rather, have Reg the butcher twist the arms of promoters—to get them to pay up.

Australian entertainment mogul Robert Stigwood, who had copromoted several of the concerts in Britain, supposedly owed the Stones in the vicinity of £12,000—about $30,000 at the time. Stigwood, later known for his association with the Bee Gees at the height of the disco era, refused to pay up. According to Keith Altham, Richards and he spotted Stigwood at a posh restaurant and demanded the money. Stigwood said nothing, so, without warning, "Richards began hammering away at him. Stigwood hit the floor, got up, and wham—down he'd go again. When I tried to stop it, he almost flattened me. I asked Keith why he kept hitting Stiggy and he said, ' 'Cause the bastard keeps getting up!' " Later, Richards told Altham his vicious attack on Stigwood was "nothing personal. Biz-ness," smiled Richards, "is wot biz-ness about."

The Stones solidified their reputation as irredeemable delinquents immediately after a concert with the Hollies in Essex. At 11:30 P.M. Mick's black Daimler pulled into the Francis Service Station in east London so Bill Wyman could use the rest room. The attendant told Wyman the rest room was closed for renovations (it would later be revealed that this was not the case) and that he could not use the staff washroom either.

When Mick got out of the car and pressed the issue, the attendant began screaming, "Get off my forecourt!" Jones then joined in, making faces and dancing around as he chanted "Get off my foreskin!" With that Mick, still smeared with mascara and trailing billowing silk scarves behind him, relieved himself on the service station wall. Wyman and Richards followed suit. A few giggling girls waited until Mick zipped up to ask for his autograph.

Not all the bystanders were amused. An outraged customer named Eric Lavender admonished them for being nothing less than "disgusting." The Stones shot back with somewhat more colorful language and tossed a few obscene gestures his way as they sped away in the Daimler. Incensed, Lavender and the station's mechanic called the police.

The papers had a field day with the incident. Three months later the three offending Stones were hauled before a magistrate and forced to defend themselves against charges of "insulting behavior." Mick brushed away the suggestion that he physically threatened the garage owner. "I think we were top of the hit parade at the time," Jagger testified before a courtroom packed with dozens of fans and ringed by hundreds more. "We had every reason to be happy. I've never been in a bad enough mood to want to hit anyone."

Nevertheless, they were found guilty and fined five pounds apiece. "Whether it is the Rolling Stones, the Beatles, or anyone else, we will not tolerate conduct of this character," said the magistrate. "Because you have reached the exalted heights in your profession, it does not mean you have the right to act like this. On the contrary, you should set a standard of behavior which should be a moral pattern for your large number of supporters. You have been found guilty of behavior not becoming young gentlemen." That, the magistrate clearly did not comprehend, was the very secret of their success.

Gered Mankowitz had already photographed Mariane Faithfull for Oldham, so when Andrew asked him to shoot the cover for the Stones' *December's Children* album, he "jumped at the chance. Andrew had used David Bailey for the previous covers," said Mankowitz, "but now he felt Bailey was too slick for the Stones' image." Over the next several years Mankowitz would accompany the Stones on tour and become, for a time, a member of their tight inner circle.

Arriving at Mankowitz's West End studio for the afternoon shoot, the Stones were surprisingly ebullient. "Mick was laughing and full of fun," recalled Mankowitz, "and here Oldham was standing in the background, telling me he wanted stark and gritty." When he saw the results, the young photographer was surprised that "Mick didn't stand out at all. It was Brian who was striking in the picture; he sort of leapt out at you."

Even during that first brief encounter it was clear to Mankowitz that Jones "could be very charming. But he could turn very quickly. Brian was quite strange—complicated, moody, difficult to read. He had a cruel streak—he liked to laugh at other people's mistakes. If someone stubbed his toe, he took pleasure in watching that person's pain."

Jones's naughty-boy act extended to sabotaging Mankowitz's efforts. "Brian loved to make these grotesque faces, or hide behind his hands at the last minute. Once or twice, fine. But he kept it up. Very amusing for him, but hell for me." Frustrated, Mankowitz would often let Jones have his way. The final glossies, used for posters and press releases, often showed Brian hiding behind a newspaper or making a silly face. "I think it was all," recalled Mankowitz, "a desperate play for attention."

Aggravating the situation was Jones's increased dependence on amphetamines. "Someone would walk up to him at a party," recalled a friend, "and hand him a pill and he'd take it. At any given time he would reach into his pocket and pull out all kinds of capsules—blue ones, yellow ones, red ones. Oval pills and round pills and pills with stripes. He'd take them without knowing what they were." The pills had the effect of heightening Jones's paranoid delusions—so much so that those around him suggested that he smoke more pot, just to calm him down.

Brian's anxieties were not entirely ill-founded. Although he remained one of the group's most charismatic members and probably its most talented musician, Jagger had eclipsed him. When the Stones launched their third U.S. tour in April of 1965, everywhere posters and marquees heralded the arrival of "Mick Jagger and the Rolling Stones." The band Jones had founded was slipping through his fingers.

For Brian it was the beginning of a long slide to oblivion. Over the next several years, while Mick would miss not a single performance, Brian racked up more than fifty absences. His offstage behavior was no easier to stomach; Brian's treatment of women rankled even the flagrantly misognynist Stones.

Although he maintained relatively long-term relationships with several women, he did not hesitate to pick up groupies nearly every night on the road. "I used to run with him, basically," recalled Wyman. "He used to pick a girl up in Birmingham or Manchester and say, 'Come with me to London for the weekend.' So this girl of seventeen or eighteen would jump in the van with us and come home." After dropping the other band members off at their homes, the van would drop Brian off "and he would leave the girl in the van . . . just desert her."

Often, that was best for the girl. Brian beat many women so savagely that, on several occasions, disgusted tour personnel returned the favor. After a teenage girl ran, bloody and screaming, from Brian's Florida hotel room, one outraged roadie responded by cracking two of Jones's ribs—an act applauded by the other Stones.

Oldham made no effort to conceal his contempt for Brian. Unaware that he, too, would fall victim to drug abuse and be forced out of the Stones organization, Oldham pressed hard to replace Brian. In this he had allies in Mick and Keith. Without the total support of the others, however, Mick was unwilling to force the issue.

That spring turned out to be momentous for several reasons—the least of which was the fact that, after his previous vow to ban the Stones from his show forever, Ed Sullivan welcomed them back with open arms.

In 1965 the Stones chalked up a number of major hits, including "The Last Time," "Play with Fire," and "Get Off of My Cloud." All would pale in comparison to the 1965 Rolling Stones release that many would consider the greatest rock and roll song ever written—and the anthem of an era.

"Satisfaction"—at least the melody—came to Keith Richards in a dream on the night of May 9. He woke up in his Clearwater, Florida, hotel room, grabbed his guitar, and recorded the riff. Then he dropped his guitar pick and fell back to sleep—all of which was audible on the tape.

When he brought the tune to Jagger, Keith said, "The words that go with this are 'I can't get no satisfaction.' That was just a working title. It could just as well have been 'Auntie Millie's Caught Her Left Tit in the Mangle.' I thought of it as just a little riff, an album filler. I never thought it was anything like commercial enough to be a single."

Mick sat on the edge of his bed and poured out the frustrations he was experiencing on the road—and to which everyone at some time in their lives could relate. Several days later they recorded the song at Chess studios in Chicago.

Richards was unhappy with the results. "If I had my way, 'Satisfaction' would never have been released," conceded Keith, whose judgment may have been clouded by the amphetamines and cocaine he was now taking to keep awake. A hyper, insistent Richards even forced a vote of the band members. Incredibly, Jagger, who shared Keith's misgivings about "Satisfaction" and trusted his musical intuition, sided with Richards and voted not to release it (Jagger would later deny that he ever had any doubts about the song). The others, thankfully, overruled the pair. When it was released later that year, "Satisfaction" became the Stones' first No. 1 hit—and the anthem for an era.

There was no question that Mick, more than his Beatles counterpart John Lennon, had tapped into the angst of his contemporaries just as the Vietnam War and the advent of the drug-fueled counterculture was about to polarize the generations.

Jagger's nihilist lyrics to "Satisfaction" dripped with libidinous innuendo: "She says, 'Baby, better come back, maybe next week, 'cause you see I'm on a losin' streak. I can't get no . . .'" The record had been lounging at No. 1 for weeks before someone actually decoded the lyrics, but once they did, it ignited a fire storm of controversy. Seduction and menstruation were not exactly considered acceptable topics for discussion over the airwaves.

Reacting to pressure, some radio stations went so far as to ban the record altogether, while others—following the lead of *The Ed Sullivan Show*—merely culled the offending stanza. The controversy provoked widespread outrage, just as Jagger had intended.

On the other side of the Atlantic the Stones' rivals and friends the Beatles showed up on the Queen's Birthday Honors List, drawn up annually by Britain's prime minister. Each of the four lads from Liverpool was made a Member of the Most Excellent Order of the British Empire—a step short of knighthood, but a great honor nonetheless. Clearly designed to win over young voters, this was a canny political move on the part of Harold Wilson's Socialist government. Just the same, it acknowledged the fact that pop music in general and the Beatles in particular had become one of the nation's biggest exports.

At one of New York's more popular nightspots, Trude Heller's, a woman asked Mick if he was one of the Beatles. "No, ducky," he responded. "I'm one of the Andrews Sisters. What group are you with?"

Jagger laughed when he heard the news of the Beatles' vaunted MMEOBE status. Less amusing to Mick, who was still infatuated with Marianne Faithfull, was the news that she was pregnant and had wed John Dunbar in May.

"I didn't want to anymore than Marianne did," said Dunbar. "We were far, far too young. But we both wanted the baby, and she wanted to be respectable. And at the time I was very much in love with her."

Dunbar was studying natural science at Cambridge University when he met Marianne. In January 1966 he teamed with journalist Barry Miles (known simply as "Miles") and Peter Asher of Peter and Gordon to open London's Indica Gallery, an underground bookstore that quickly became a favorite hangout for sculptors, painters, and artists of every stripe. It was there that Dunbar introduced his friend John Lennon to avant-garde artist Yoko Ono.

Marianne, meantime, was riding the crest of her own successful pop career. She had been courted by Gene ("Town Without Pity") Pitney and was even lured by Bob Dylan into his Savoy Hotel suite. There, scribbling poetry in a notebook, he grilled her about her background, her aspirations. When Marianne blurted out that she was marrying a Cambridge undergraduate in one week, Dylan angrily lectured her on the "stupidity" of student "assholes."

For the first time in her young life Faithfull also had a substantial amount of money at her disposal—though not enough to fund her lavish tastes. She became a compulsive shopper, spending thousands of pounds on dresses, shoes, handbags. Oldham fueled these fantasies, phoning Faithfull one day and telling her to look out her window. There, parked on the street, was a sleek, jet-black Mini with smoked-glass windows.

Dunbar, no longer able to finance his wife's luxurious life-style, gravitated toward his Beatle friends, John Lennon and Paul McCartney. Marianne felt more comfortable with the scruffier, more iconoclastic Stones and their expanding coterie of sycophants and friends.

"It was a crazed, frenetic time," explained Dunbar. "We lived our separate lives, in separate worlds." As for their infant son, Nicholas: "There were loads and loads of nannies and baby-sitters," recalled Miles. "Marianne wasn't about to let that stop her."

Jagger eased his pain after the taping of the popular ABC television series *Shindig* in Los Angeles. He brought two dancers back to his pink Ambassador Hotel bungalow. According to Jagger's friend, veteran Los Angeles music promoter Rodney Bingenheimer, "Mick said it was a wild party—mattresses on the floors, bouncing off the walls, an incredible night." One of the women went on to movie stardom and was nominated for an Academy Award. The other recorded a number-one record; Jagger even found his way into the song's title.

In addition to the girls picked up on the road, there were the regulars who were often enlisted to fend off the more persistent female fans. Flo, a lanky black woman who was a particular favorite of Mick's, wore a switchblade around her neck. Jagger's indelicate sobriquet for Flo: "the Grand Canyon."

Despite such diversions Jagger moaned to anyone within earshot that he desperately missed Chrissie. She was the quintessential mid-sixties woman—a statuesque, auburn-maned flesh-and-blood Barbarella in Courrèges boots and a lime-green plastic minidress. As stunning as she was in her own right, Shrimpton complained bitterly that she existed only as a pale reflection of her famous sister and even more famous lover.

To bolster her confidence Mick arranged for Chrissie to write a regular column for an American teen magazine, *Mod*. "Mick and I went down to visit George and Patti Harrison last week," she wrote. "We sat in John's private cinema, had hot chocolate, and watched a film called *Citizen Kane* . . . I think Steve Winwood is the best singer we have. (Ouch! Mick has just hit me.)"

When he was out of town, Mick arranged for a £20 (equivalent to about $50 at the time) weekly allowance to be paid to Chrissie so that she could afford to buy her own drinks when she went to her usual hangout, the Scotch bar in London. He also sent her roses when he would be gone for more than a day or two.

For the time being Jagger succeeded in concealing from Chrissie and the world that Richards, Jones, and other members of the Stones entourage were dropping acid. Mick worried about the effect on his musicians, as well as the legal repercussions.

Brian's antics, often carried on in full public view, were of special concern. At Los Angeles's Ambassador Hotel, Brian, tripping on LSD, ran through the lobby screaming that the floors were crawling with snakes. Later, in the middle of a recording session, he ran screaming from the millions of beetles he said were filling the studio.

Jagger was less concerned, however, about the band's use of marijuana. By mid-1965 Mick was a heavy pot smoker, and he and Keith jealously guarded their supply. Friction over drugs grew, and once Mick and Keith barricaded themselves in Mick's hotel room rather than share their marijuana. Other members of the Stones' party broke the door down, and after a shouting match Mick was knocked against a wall and relieved of his stash.

Life back home in London was equally manic. One night Mick arrived at his home in Bryanston Mews East to see Shrimpton battling a fifteen-year-old Beatles fan who had been waiting to catch Ringo Starr outside Starr's house nearby. "I got really annoyed," recalled Jagger. "The fans had had an argument with Chrissie the previous evening and she was very upset."

According to the teenager, Shrimpton had been knocking the Beatles "and I won't let anyone get away with that." Said Jagger: "I pulled the girl off and gave her a kick in the bottom. I was only wearing plimsolls so I didn't hurt her much. In fact I got the worst of it, because she gave me a few clouts." Did he really kick a girl? the papers wanted to know. "She was laying into my girl and using filthy language," replied Mick without hesitation. "Sure I kicked her."

Chrissie was well aware that there were legions of young women out there who were just as passionately devoted to Mick. The one-night stands did not bother her, but when Shrimpton discovered that he had an American girlfriend and that she had followed him to London, she retaliated. Once Jagger learned that Chrissie was secretly dating singer P. J. Broby, he snapped. After hiding his tears behind dark glasses during a press conference, Mick broke down in front of Chrissie and promised to break off his affair if she would do the same. "Whenever he'd stray," said Shrimpton, "I'd just go out with somebody else and Mick would be back like a shot. He would never let the woman be the one to call things off. Mick *has* to be the one in control—giving the orders, calling the shots."

Jagger was now a fixture in the world of privilege, and he invited Chrissie to bask in the reflected glory of his new-found social status. At the sixteenth birthday party of Lady Victoria Ormsby-Gore, they were announced as "Michael Jagger and Christine Shrimpton," and all heads turned to see Mick decked out in an Edwardian-cut suit.

Shrimpton watched in amazement at the ease with which Jagger moved in this circle of titled aristocrats. In this company he abandoned his fake cockney accent for a higher-pitched pseudoaristocratic slur, complete with lisp. Jagger had fashioned himself into a modern-day Scarlet Pimpernel. Or Jekyll and Hyde.

No sooner were they seated than Princess Margaret, wearing a low-cut gown that revealed ample cleavage, beckoned Jagger to her table. He walked over dutifully, leaving a fuming Chrissie behind. Shrimpton watched Jagger and the queen's younger sister cozying up to each other for nearly a half hour before finally making her exit. When Mick spotted Chrissie leaving, he leapt to his feet, knocking over Princess Margaret's table and sending wineglasses flying. "He came after me," said Chrissie, "and we ran down the street together." It was the last time Jagger would choose Chrissie over his born-to-the-purple friends.

Meantime, gossip ran rampant about the unlikely pairing of Princess Margaret and Jagger. Since she was still years away from divorcing Lord Snowdon, the British press was scrupulously careful not to offend Buckingham Palace by implying that the princess and the scruffy rock star were anything more than good friends.

Not everyone was convinced. "There was a flirtation going on there, definitely," said an observer of London's social scene. "Princess Margaret was only in her thirties at the time, and quite attractive. And, as everybody knows, she was attracted to younger men."

In upper-class company Jagger was unfailingly charming, courtly, almost fey in his mannerisms; he could play the English gentleman to the hilt. But these people had also seen him perform, and the aura of raw sex mingled with power surrounding Jagger was even more compelling.

Princess Margaret was an early convert. "They spoke on the phone constantly," said one London partygoer, "and Margaret invited him to social events. Like many other women she found him sexy and exciting. If you saw them laughing together, dancing, the way she'd put her hand on his knee and giggled at his stories like a schoolgirl—you'd have thought there was something going on. . . ."

Princess Margaret's feelings for Jagger were apparently not shared by her sister. "The queen could tolerate the Beatles because they were clean cut and sort of sweet—at least that was their reputation at the time," said one palace-watcher. "But the Stones were an entirely different matter. Princess Margaret had always been a free spirit and caused more than her share of scandal. The last the queen wanted was her sister running off with Mick Jagger!" (Over the years the friendship between Princess Margaret and Jagger deepened. He would eventually build a home not far from hers on the remote Caribbean island of Mustique.)

Jagger thrived in this rarified atmosphere, but Chrissie found it increasingly difficult to breathe. After he returned from yet another social function, she flew at Mick in a rage. Her ring, a gift from Jagger, slashed across his face. Blood gushed from the deep wound, and he ran out of their apartment, shrieking in pain. The scar is still visible today.

Returning a few minutes after the attack, Jagger apologized. That made the temperamental Shrimpton even more furious. She went berserk yet again, smashing glassware, ranting, beating on Jagger's chest. When the dust had settled, they agreed to get married as soon as he returned from his fourth U.S. tour in October.

Before this could happen, the Stones were entering into

a business marriage that would prove nothing short of disastrous. Even though he had engineered the rise of the world's biggest-selling rock group, Andrew Oldham was not yet a millionaire. Nor were any of the Stones. So when Allen Klein promised to make him one, Oldham was receptive to the idea.

The pudgy, oleagenous New York accountant with slicked-back hair numbered among his show-business clients Bobby Vinton, Steve Lawrence and Eydie Gorme, Bobby Darin, and Sam Cooke. After he tried and failed to wrestle the Beatles away from the canny Brian Epstein in 1964, he zeroed in on the Dave Clark Five, Herman's Hermits, the Animals, and Donovan.

All that remained were the Stones, and Klein was determined to have them. Meeting at the Hilton Hotel on Hyde Park, Klein asked Oldham point-blank:

"How would you like to be a millionaire?"

"I'd like that," he replied cautiously.

"How about now?"

Oldham didn't hesitate. "A Rolls-Royce—just like John Lennon's."

"No problem," nodded Klein. "You got it."

On Mick's twenty-second birthday Oldham and the Stones met with Klein at his Hilton Hotel suite and listened to his plans for negotiating deals and squeezing every last penny out of the record companies. That afternoon they signed a deal effectively handing over control of the Stones' business affairs to Klein. Theoretically, this was to leave Oldham, who was never adept at business affairs, free to pursue more creative pursuits.

Lost in the shuffle was Oldham's partner and mentor Eric Easton, the stalwart business manager who had put the money up to launch the Stones in the first place. Oldham apparently had no qualms about firing Easton, and neither did Mick. Again Jagger, de facto leader of the group, left it to Andrew to fire Easton in the most offhand way possible.

Had Oldham not been strung out on speed, barbituates, LSD, and an endless list of other disorienting substances, it is doubtful if he would have succumbed to Klein's blandishments. "Klein was obviously out to grab the Stones away from me," said Oldham, "but I was just too fucked up to notice."

It was, in the words of Gered Mankowitz, a "weird little scene." And no one seemed better suited to it than Anita Pallenberg. She had been born in Italy of Swiss, Swedish, and German descent, her father an erstwhile composer who owned a travel agency in Rome. After being expelled from school in Munich, she sailed to Manhattan in 1963 and hobnobbed with Andy Warhol, Larry Rivers, Jasper Johns, and the poet Allen Ginsberg while trying to get her modeling career off the ground.

Leggy, blond, and only eighteen, she was in Munich for Oktoberfest when a friend took her to see the Stones. Armed with amyl nitrite and hashish, she elbowed her way backstage and offered Mick a smoke. "Oh, no," he said, pushing her hand away, "we can't smoke before we go on-stage."

Afterward, Brian walked up to her and blurted out, "I don't know who you are, but I need you." He begged her to spend the night with him, and of course, she did. That night he gave her an instant course in the dynamics of the group, the plots he perceived were being hatched against him by Mick and Oldham, the hopelessness of his situation. "He basically needed comforting," she recalled. "Someone to hold and be there for him." Jones could not have known that she would prove his undoing.

Perhaps the omens were there the following night when, in a Berlin amphitheater where Hitler once presided over Nazi rallies, Jagger goose-stepped his way through "Satisfaction." Afterward, marauding crowds overturned subway trains and smashed store windows, sending more than a hundred people to the hospital. To make their escape the Stones raced to their hotel through a series of underground tunnels and bunkers that had served as Hitler's nerve center during World War Two.

Pallenberg moved in with Brian as soon as they returned

to London. From that point on Pallenberg's life would be inexorably intertwined with that of the group. Before her association with the Stones was over, she would descend into a hell of drugs, madness, and Satanism.

The Stones got their first glimpse of Klein's promotional handiwork when they arrived in Manhattan and saw themselves staring down from a ten-story-high Times Square billboard. The black-and-white David Bailey photograph announced the release of their new album, *December's Children*.

The photograph was grainy, but not nearly so indistinct as the words plastered over the photo: "The sound, face, and mind of today is more relative to the hope of tomorrow and the reality of destruction than the blind who cannot see their children for fear and division. Something that grew and related. Five reflections of today's children. The Rolling Stones."

If Oldham's message seemed infinitely more puzzling than profound, the liner notes for *December's Children* offered mute testimony to his growing dependence on mind-altering substances:

> Twelve new blackbands, six in each hand december's children, children of stone that in the words of that folk singer whose name I forget contemplate, and meditate and speculate for you and bring new weapons for your washing machine to show where you've been and where you're at . . .

Floating on the success of their new, grass-touting single "Get Off of My Cloud," the Stones again rolled across the American countryside, this time in the company of Patti LaBelle and the Blue Belles, Nona Hendryx, future Supreme Cindy Birdsong, and the Vibrations.

"I was amazed by the hordes of girls, the cavalcade of police cars—it was all like a movie," recalled photographer Gered Mankowitz, who traveled with the Stones on their autumn 1965 U.S. tour. Mankowitz rode with them from

JFK Airport into the city, and when they arrived at the Stones' hotel hundreds of hysterical girls swarmed over the car. "It was terrifying," said Mankowitz. "Fans pounded on the windows, rocked the car back and forth. Then they climbed up onto the roof and it started to collapse. We had to hold it up with our hands." (A similar scene would occur four years later in Long Beach, California. Then, when the roof of the Stones' limousine began to buckle, blood from injured fans streamed down the windshield—an image indelibly etched in Jagger's mind.)

Mankowitz's overall impression of the tour was that it was "disorienting and rather sad for the guys. We lived a totally reversed life—right after a concert you'd fly straight to the next city and get there at four or five in the morning and collapse in your hotel room. Then you'd sleep until three P.M. or four P.M., head for the concert, then off to the next city and so on. It was grueling, and it took an emotional toll. There was tremendous frustration, alienation. The loneliness was oppressive. I was acutely aware of Mick missing Chrissie. He would nearly be in tears when he hung up the phone."

It did not show in Mick's performing. "Mick teased outrageously, wiggled his bum, emanated a sexuality that for the period was quite over the top," said Mankowitz. So, too, was the atmosphere at New York's City Squire Hotel. There dozens of groupies performed oral sex on doormen and bellhops in elevators and stairwells in exchange for access to the Stones' floor.

One young fan carried a stick of butter in her purse, offering to smear it over Mick's body and lick it off. Kathy and Mary were legendary groupies who had slept with dozens of rock stars, and now set their sights on Mick. They managed to land Brian Jones, and when they were finished they said he was "great, but he's no Mick Jagger." They then slept with Keith Richards. Again, they determined he was "great. But he's no Mick Jagger." Finally, Kathy and Mary, fraught with anticipation, bedded Jagger. "He's great, but," they sighed, "he's no Mick Jagger."

Drugs, even more than sex, became their chief form of recreation. "Brian spent a lot of time with Bob Dylan—they smoked a lot of pot and hashish together," recalled Mankowitz. "Once he just freaked out during a concert, and just sort of spun offstage." At that point, said Mankowitz, "Ian Stewart grabbed Brian by the collar and slammed him against the wall and said 'Why?! Why are you doing this? You are letting everybody down.' "

The famous November 9, 1965, blackout occurred while the Stones were in New York, plunging the entire city into darkness. Mankowitz, who had been in Greenwich Village shopping with history buff Charlie Watts for Civil War memorabilia, returned to his room to find Bob Dylan and Brian Jones surrounded by pretty girls, jamming, drinking, and smoking dope.

"All the guests at the hotel were issued these little candles in the lobby," said Mankowitz, "and, because the elevators weren't working, we were shown how to walk up the stairs to our rooms. On the Stones' floor, all these giggling, naked girls were holding their candles, running from room to room and party to party. It was wild.

"I put my candle on a little glass ashtray on the bed. The heat from the candle shattered the ashtray, spewing flaming wax all over the bed and it started burning. Everybody panicked until two of the girls rushed in with an ice bucket and put the fire out."

The Stones left the next day, but only after going through the normal ritual of trashing their hotel. "They felt so much like prisoners in these hotels," added Mankowitz, "that whenever they left they'd vent their frustrations by running through the halls on every floor, turning over tables, lamps, wastebins, anything they could find. Another favorite pastime was peeing in the sinks."

The tour had its amusing moments. At a coffee shop in Shreveport, Louisiana, a grizzled granny who didn't like the length of the Stones' hair began beating them over the head with her umbrella.

The mood in other parts of the South was similarly hostile. In several cities black performers on the tour were forced to stay at separate, black hotels. This particularly angered Mick, who now spent most nights in the company of Patti LaBelle.

LaBelle and Jagger kept their distance when Chrissie Shrimpton joined Mick in Los Angeles and checked into the old-guard Bel-Air Hotel. There he was informed that his vocal rendition of Marianne Faithfull's hit "As Tears Go By" was about to hit the U.S. (it would eventually reach No. 3).

At a party in Los Angeles thrown by *One Flew over the Cuckoo's Nest* author Ken Kesey, Brian and Keith both dropped acid. Mick, still wary about consuming drugs in public, declined.

Brian was less cautious, in public and in private. He had become obsessed with the hallucinatory effects of LSD. "Once he handed me one of two tabs and told me to trip with him," remembered Mankowitz. "When I told him I wasn't interested, he said, 'Okay, then watch me, and take down everything I say.'" Mankowitz declined. "LSD scared me. I wasn't interested in the loss of control, and I didn't want to be party to any of his experiments. The whole scene was just too weird."

Pallenberg joined Brian on the road, and there was general agreement that her presence aggravated an already dicey situation. "Anita was an exotic, ambitious, sexy, decadent, *dangerous* woman," observed Mankowitz. "In a word, she was trouble."

Jagger made no effort to hide his resentment of Anita. "Mick resented me," she said, "because I was this positive force in Brian's life." Convoluted as it may seem, there is an element of truth to Pallenberg's logic. Pallenberg had allied herself with Jones, and was determined that he wrest control of the group back from Jagger.

Toward that end Brian and Anita competed with Mick for the limelight. They were both extraordinarily dressed— all huge hats, feather boas, white pointy boots, tight velvet pants, and flowing scarves. Sometimes they wore identical outfits, had the same hairdos. "We caught the eye of everybody," she reminisced. "We were invited everywhere. We were both kind of clowns, really."

No one was laughing when Anita convinced Brian to dress up in a Nazi SS uniform and be photographed with his foot on the throat of a doll supposedly depicting a Jew. The shocking photo, published in newspapers around the world, lent credence to the growing feeling that there was something truly evil at the core of a group that spawned so much senseless violence.

Jagger himself was hardly without blame for this. It was Mick, after all, whose goose-stepping imitation of a Hitler youth sent mobs into the streets of Berlin. Yet Brian's Gestapo photo, which Pallenberg insisted was somehow meant to be amusing, strengthened his resolve to rein in Brian—if not dispense with him altogether.

Pallenberg would pay a heavy price for her two-year affair with Jones. Although she was a head taller than Brian, he was infused with Herculean strength when he was angry—which was often. He beat Pallenberg savagely, and at various times hurled everything from a pot of hot coffee to an end table at her, leaving Anita covered with massive welts and bruises. Later, overcome with remorse and sobbing, he would beg her to forgive him.

"I think Brian was a terrible person, really," Pallenberg later conceded. "And I put up with a lot. He was a tortured personality, insecure as hell. He was ill very early on—totally paranoid."

Certainly, LSD only fed Jones's paranoia. Even more distressing was a potentially lethal new "game" that was fast becoming popular with the London's in crowd—spiking the drinks of the unsuspecting with acid and then watching their reaction. No one enjoyed this game more than Brian and Anita.

"Spiking drinks went on at one club practically every night, and it scared the hell out of me," admitted Mankowitz. "Some of those people ended up being carted off to mental hospitals. That's why I tried to stay away from Brian and Anita even during the daytime, so they wouldn't find a way to slip something into my coffee."

Jagger had warned Shrimpton away from LSD just as he had earlier demanded she never smoke grass. Now that they were smoking pot together constantly, she began to wonder if Mick was concealing this from her as well. There were times when he sat, lost in his own world, describing visions and feelings in language she could not hope to comprehend. Since these episodes invariably took place while she was high on marijuana, Shrimpton doubted her own judgment.

When Brian told her that Mick had been experimenting with LSD for months, Shrimpton felt angry and betrayed. Earlier, when she was at home with Jagger, she had become violently ill and frighteningly disoriented. Now Chrissie wondered if someone had slipped her LSD without her knowing it.

An answer of sorts came with the release in February of 1966 of "19th Nervous Breakdown." "On our first trip I tried so hard to rearrange your mind," went Jagger's telling lyrics, "But after a while I realize you were disarranging mine."

Jagger told Shrimpton he had written his subsequent hit single, the medieval-sounding "Lady Jane," about her—even though the official record-company line was that the song dealt with one of Henry VIII's doomed wives, Lady Jane Seymour. Jagger also led Lady Jane Ormsby-Gore to believe she was the inspiration for the song. In truth, Lady Jane comes from one of Jagger's favorite novels, D. H. Lawrence's *Lady Chatterley's Lover*. "Lady Jane" is what the protagonist called his mistress's vagina.

Reflecting Mick's growing hostility toward Shrimpton and women in general, the Stones' new album, *Aftermath*, was a litmus test for misogynists everywhere. After one of his frequent rows with Chrissie, Jagger sat down and wrote what would become the wife-beater's anthem, "Under My Thumb": "Under my thumb's a squirming dog who's just had her day/Under my thumb's a girl who's just changed her ways." "Stupid Girl" is nothing short of an antifemale diatribe: "I'm not talkin' about the way she digs for gold/ Look at that stupid girl."

"Mother's Little Helper" was a searing indictment of middle-class prescription-drug abuse, but there was more than a hint of malice in Jagger's words: "Doctor please some more of these. . . . What a drag it is getting old." In "Out of Time," still working out his tangled feelings for Shrimpton, he finally dismisses the woman in the song as simply "obsolete."

A European tour in the spring of 1966 left Jagger emotionally drained and physically battered. At a concert in Marseilles, Mick was closing the show with "Satisfaction" when a chunk of wood came flying out of the audience, bloodying him above the eye. He finished the number, then rushed to a hospital emergency room, where he received six stitches—but not before shrieking at a cat-sized rat that scuttered down a hospital hallway.

That June, Jagger suffered his own nervous breakdown. He was pronounced unfit for work by his doctor and ordered to take ten days' rest. Overwork was not the sole cause of Jagger's frayed nerves; his turbulent affair with the hot-tempered Shrimpton had left him limp—and looking for a new love.

Marianne Faithfull would later offer a tongue-in-cheek account of how she came to be involved with Jagger. "My first move was to get a Rolling Stone as a boyfriend," she insisted. "I slept with three and then I decided the lead singer was the best."

Jagger was not Faithfull's first choice, to be sure. She regarded Mick as cockey, and arrogant. When he drank, she said, he was "obnoxious, belligerent. A cliché drunk." Besides, Jagger already had his hands full with Chrissie.

Beginning in late 1965 Brian and Keith both spent time with Marianne. She slept with Brian after he introduced her to LSD, but it was Keith who most intrigued her. After Faithfull and Richards spent their first night together, she hoped it would be the start of a long-term affair. Instead, she told writer A. E. Hotchner, Keith informed Marianne that Mick had fallen for her: "There Keith was in the sheets explaining to me that nobody had to know about this night because Mick was in love with me and all, blah, blah, blah. I just thought, *Oh, dear, well it's a shame.*"

Gered Mankowitz, who had known Faithfull before she met Mick, understood Jagger's fascination with her. "Jagger loved her," said Mankowitz. "What man didn't? She was this exquisitely beautiful, dangerous combination of convent girl, English rose, and pop star all in a very sexy body. Marianne looked at Mick and he just fell apart."

There was another reason Mick coveted Faithfull. Chrissie was a bit common for his new circle of friends. A bona fide aristocrat, Marianne glided effortlessly among the likes of Princess Margaret, the Ormsby-Gores, the Lambtons, and the Guinnesses. She was, in short, a more suitable consort for His Satanic Majesty.

"Marianne was truly classy," said Mankowitz. "She never, ever said anything remotely about her social standing or her family background. But her bearing was regal, and certainly fit Mick's purposes socially. But I think lust was more important," he added. "Love and lust and animal magnetism that make for a really magnificent love affair, because that's what it was. From the beginning it just sort of had to be."

In midsummer Marianne was desperate to end her marriage to Dunbar. He stirred methedrine in his morning coffee, smoked dope, and dropped acid. But these were not the reasons she left him. Dunbar simply didn't make enough money to enable her to quit her career and live in style.

"It was over before she left me for Mick, really," said Dunbar, who added that Faithfull was already heavily into drugs by this time. "When she had her first hit, I was very protective of her. But it was a starry scene where everybody around you wanted to give you anything you want. Soon she was stoned all the time. We couldn't live together. It was very difficult."

Marianne fled to the Italian coastal resort of Positano

with their son, Nicholas, that summer to try and sort things out. Jagger besieged her with love letters and phone calls. In the end she relented, leaving Dunbar in October of 1966. "I went with the one," she later confessed, "who had the most money. And that was Mick."

"All women are groupies," Jagger often said. And, said Dunbar, "to him they were—and are. It has always been a self-fulfilling prophecy. That's the way he ended up treating Marianne and Bianca and Jerry Hall and all the others." Dunbar remained friends with both Marianne and Jagger, and in fact worked as a crew member on the Stones' 1967 European tour.

When Jagger and Marianne met at a private screening for Roman Polanski's film *Repulsion*, starring Catherine Deneuve, it was obvious to everyone in the room that something was going on between them. But Mick could only imagine how Chrissie would react when she heard the news. He insisted on keeping the affair under wraps until some way could be found to deal with her.

During the first few tentative months of their affair, Faithfull did not entirely live up to her name. Jagger had once turned down an unknown guitarist named Jimmy James. After he became a star as Jimi Hendrix, he set out to seduce Marianne. Twice they went to see Hendrix in concert, and both times Jagger fumed as Hendrix made an egregious play for Marianne. Once Mick was out of town, Faithfull took Hendrix up on his offer. So did Richards's girlfriend, Linda Keith; she eventually left Keith and moved in with Hendrix.

Faithfull had her fling with Hendrix while the Stones were in New York promoting their new single, "Have You Seen Your Mother, Baby, Standing in the Shadow?" The picture used on the record sleeve made millions of fans shudder, and—since Jagger was now perceived as the one calling the shots—once again raised questions about Mick's sexual orientation.

Photographer Jerry Schatzberg had dolled all five Stones up in drag, then shot them in a Manhattan side street. Bill

Wyman, aka "Penelope," wore a WACS uniform and sat cross-legged in a wheelchair. Brian ("Flossie") had a purse slung over his/her shoulder and puffed jauntily on a cigarette, while Watts ("Millicent") looked on glumly in a fur-collared coat and "Molly" (Keith) checked her makeup. As "Sarah," Jagger, wearing white gloves, cloche hat, and a diamond circle pin, rested his/her bejeweled hand on Wyman's shoulder. Mick, wearing more lipstick than he ever had before, was the only one smiling.

After the shoot these "mothers" all headed for the nearest bar in full drag. No heads turned. Why would they? These were, by any standards, five exceptionally homely women. "What? Nobody wants to make a pass?" joked Jagger. "How insulting!"

Once he'd had a few drinks, Jagger beckoned the others to a back room. One of the crew had brought along a movie camera to record the photo session, and Brian suggested a few more shots of the group in drag.

While the camera was rolling, Brian raised up his skirt to reveal he wasn't wearing anything underneath. Then, grinning widely, he began to masturbate. The cameraman kept shooting, right through Jones's orgasm. For years after Jones's untimely death Jagger would screen this rather shocking footage for the amusement of his guests.

Ike and Tina Turner's "River Deep" had just begun its climb up the charts when they toured Britain with the Stones that autumn. The first night of the tour, at London's Albert Hall, Tina was dancing up a storm before a thundering crowd when she noticed someone staring at her from the wings. "God," she said, "who's that boy with the big lips?" Recalled Tina: "He would just stand behind the speakers and all you could see was this white face and these eyes and this mouth."

Later, Ike Turner brought Mick to Tina's dressing room. After brief pleasantries Jagger asked which of her background singers, the Ikettes, he should "go for." She recommended Pat (P. P.) Arnold, according to Jagger. That's not quite the way Turner remembered it: He said hello and "then immediately—*doinnng!* he had his eye on P. P. Arnold, and he zoomed in on her." Jagger's affair with P. P. Arnold continued for months, even as he professed his undying love for Marianne.

Mick made a habit of bursting into the women's dressing room. "He never knocked," said Tina, "so you always had to stay kind of dressed." It was on this tour that Jagger insisted Turner teach him the new dance called the Pony. "I said, 'Look at the rhythm on this guy! God, Mick, come on!' I mean, we *laughed*. Because Mick was *serious*—he wanted to get it."

It was more than that. Jagger was mesmerized by Tina Turner's animal moves onstage. He studied every nuance, every gesture, every strut and bump and grind. Then he spent hours mimicking Tina's moves in front of a mirror. These moves may have come naturally to Turner, but for Jagger they were the result of painstaking practice. "Mick wanted to *be* Tina Turner," said a friend. "He told me that when he's performing that's the image he has of himself. He *sees* himself as Tina Turner."

At long last Jagger made the decision to end his two-year relationship with Chrissie. The day he and Shrimpton were to fly to the Caribbean for Christmas vacation, he canceled the tickets and went to lunch with Faithfull instead. Once he returned to the flat Chrissie and he shared, she flew at him like a banshee.

That night—Sunday, December 18—Shrimpton took an overdose of sleeping pills. After she narrowly survived the suicide attempt, Jagger refused to pay her hospital bill. Jagger waited until Christmas Eve to have a moving van pull up in front of Harley House and remove all Shrimpton's personal possessions from the apartment they'd shared.

"Mick completely broke me in the end," Chrissie conceded. "But until he did, I was always stronger than him." Shrimpton believed that his treatment of her was symptomatic of a "fundamental animosity" toward the opposite sex. "He can be sweet and caring," she said, "but he is also manipulative and possessive and extremely controlling.

Mick is a master of verbal abuse. He has a vicious, vicious mouth. The fact is that Mick doesn't like women. He never has."

After four years of breaking up and making up and endless promises of marriage, she had collected no fewer than five engagement rings from Jagger—and an astonishing six hundred love letters. Years later, when a women's magazine approached Shrimpton with an offer to publish the love letters, Jagger successfully filed suit to prevent her from selling them. "I had no intention of selling them in the first place," she said. "But Mick made me so furious, I stuffed all six hundred in a box and sent them back to him."

In a bizarre coincidence, the same day Chrissie Shrimpton had tried to take her life, a close friend of both Mick's and Brian's was killed in a tragic accident. Guinness scion and playboy Tara Browne, apparently under the influence of drugs, ran a red light and was killed. The incident was immortalized by John Lennon in the Beatles' "Day in the Life":

He blew his mind out in a car/he didn't notice that the lights had changed.

"I'm one of the best things England's got. Me and the queen."

7

"Mick Jagger wishes to deny that he is dead," read the official statement, paraphrasing Mark Twain, "and says that rumors of his death have been grossly exaggerated." The rumor, reported on both sides of the Atlantic, had veteran publicist Les Perrin working overtime to reassure millions of shocked fans that Jagger was in excellent health.

That January of 1967 the Stones arrived in New York to once again appear on *Ed Sullivan*. This time Sullivan was insistent: he would not allow them to sing their blatantly sexual new song "Let's Spend the Night Together" on the air.

A compromise resulted in the famous tape that would be shown countless times over the years to illustrate the prudishness of the times. After singing the other Rolling Stone hit-of-the-moment, "Ruby Tuesday," Jagger, dressed in a gold brocade tuxedo jacket and ruffled skirt, rolls his eyes skyward every time he sings the Sullivan-mandated line "Let's spend some TIME together."

Sullivan may have worried that Jagger's lyrics would corrupt the morals of a generation (and, more importantly, turn off parents and offend key sponsors). But the world press now regarded Jagger as nothing less than a spokesman for his generation.

At a time when John Lennon was being pilloried for saying the Beatles were more popular than Jesus, Jagger showed a remarkable willingness to pontificate. "After the destruction of the Christian ideal," Jagger told *Time* magazine, "kids have to figure it for themselves. It's easy to throw Christianity at anybody and say that's how you've gotta live. But now, that's what's hanging people up, there's nothing for anybody to believe in."

Jagger was equally candid about the royal family. "The queen is the chief witch," Jagger proclaimed, explaining that black magic was the only thing that could account for the royal family lasting so long.

On then-president Lyndon Johnson: "There are a lot of good politicians around; they don't necessarily make good presidents." And the Vietnam War: "There's no point in fighting for any country. It's not worth it. If they took over in South Vietnam I don't think it would be the end for America. The cops would still be trying to run us in." Jagger had no idea just how prescient that last statement would turn out to be.

On January 22 the Rolling Stones appeared on *Sunday Night at the Palladium*, Britain's answer to *Ed Sullivan* and *The Hollywood Palace*. Although the show's audience was considerably more staid than the usual Stones crowd, everyone connected with the program claimed to be delighted with the group's lip-synched performances of "Ruby Tuesday" and "Let's Spent the Night Together"—until the finale.

At the end of each *Sunday Night at the Palladium* spectacular, all the performers were to stand on a revolving stage and take a bow. No one—not Frank Sinatra or Judy Garland or Sammy Davis or, indeed, the Beatles—had ever refused. Jagger, however, did.

Even Oldham tried to persuade Mick to change his mind, but all the Stones agreed with Mick that this gesture was not only corny but demeaning. Many Britons considered Jagger's refusal to ride around on the *Sunday Night at the Palladium* carousel an affront to the national honor. The tempest in an English teapot raged in the press for weeks, having the hoped-for effect on record sales. In a single week their new album shot up ten positions—to No. 4.

"What the fuck is this?" asked Jagger, sweeping half the newspapers that covered his bed onto the floor. Marianne, lying at his side, stirred awake. "I'll sue the fucking bastards!"

Jagger was clutching the February 5, 1967, edition of *News of the World,* the Fleet Street tabloid with the singular distinction of being the most widely read newspaper in the world. In the second of a five-part series headlined "The Secrets of the Pop Stars' Hideaway," it was divulged that Mick Jagger had attended an LSD party at a house shared by members of the Moody Blues. Incredulous, Mick went on to read that he had been cornered at a club called Blases, and confirmed the story. "I remember the first time I took it," Jagger was quoted as saying. "It was on tour with Bo Diddley and Little Richard. . . ."

The article went on to report that, during the interview at Blases, "Jagger took about six Benzedrine tablets. . . . Later at Blases, Jagger showed a companion and two girls a piece of hashish and asked them to his flat for a 'smoke.' "

Instead of Mick Jagger the befuddled *News of the World* reporters had been talking to a different Stone—Brian Jones.

Jagger was livid. Of course, he did smoke hashish and pot, he did take pills, and he did use LSD. But as far as he was concerned, none of this mattered. Above all else Jagger wanted to maintain his superstar mystique—and that meant keeping the press and the public guessing about his private habits. He had already become a master at talking endlessly to interviewers while revealing nothing. Now, the largest paper in the world showed him popping bennies and blabbing like an idiot.

That evening Mick went on a British talk show and announced that he intended to sue the *News of the World* for libel.

For the next several days a mysterious van was parked outside Harley House. Then a stranger called to warn Mick that his line was tapped. For some inexplicable reason Jagger sought to ignore these signs and accepted an invitation from Keith Richards to spend a weekend in the country.

The following Saturday night, after a brief recording session in London, a motorcade of Bentleys, Minis, and Aston Martins pulled up to Keith Richards's moat-encircled estate, Redlands, for a weekend get-together. Jagger and Faithfull were among the guests, as were Beatle George Harrison and his then-wife, Patti, the redoubtable Christopher Gibbs, photographer Michael Cooper, a Chelsea flower child named Nicky Cramer, and gallery owner Robert Fraser (who brought along his Moroccan manservant, Ali Mohammed).

The newest member of this exclusive little group, Californian David Schneiderman, would be the weekend's most sought-after companion. Schneiderman, better known as Acid King David, arrived carrying a monogrammed briefcase packed with an astonishing assortment of drugs. It was his job to dispense Sunshine—orange tablets laced with premium-quality LSD—with the guests' morning tea.

That night, while Keith's guests partied, an anonymous informant walked into the *News of the World* and tipped them off to a wild drug party in progress at Redlands. The party, according to the obviously well-placed source, was to last until Monday.

The next morning Keith and his guests bundled themselves into their respective cars and tooled around the countryside. Later, Michael Cooper photographed Richards strolling on the beach, the collar of his Afghan fur coat turned up against the February chill.

That evening everyone gathered in Redlands's cavernous living room to watch television while the Who blasted over the stereo. Marianne, the only female remaining in the house, had gone upstairs to take a bath. Emerging still wet on the landing, she tiptoed down clad only in a tawny fur rug, then stretched out languorously on a sofa. Jagger sat at her feet, running his hand up her naked thigh. The air was heavy with hashish and incense. Fraser's caftan-clad manservant, Ali, served tea. Strobe lights flickered. The stage was set.

Only the mystery man in their midst, David Schneiderman, heard the first heavy rap on the door at a little before eight P.M. He told Keith, who peered out the window and saw what he thought was "a little old lady" rapping on the window for an autograph.

When Richards opened the door, he realized the "little old lady" was one of nineteen police officers who had descended upon them with a warrant to search the premises for drugs. "It just so happened," Keith later admitted, "that we had all taken acid and were in a completely freaked-out state when the police arrived. . . . Everybody was just sort of gliding down from the whole day of freaking about."

It was later widely alleged that the police encountered an incredible sight when they entered Redlands: Mick Jagger with his head between Marianne's legs, nibbling on a strategically placed Mars bar. (No mention of this bizarre incident was made in court testimony, but the Stones' own lawyer, Sir Michael Havers, paid a visit to Redlands shortly after the raid and did find several Mars bars that had been left on a countertop).

Sergeant Stanley Cudmore later testified that Marianne, pleading to be left alone, intentionally let her rug slip to reveal "parts of her nude body." One of the three policewomen took Marianne, who had not yet touched ground from her twelve-hour acid trip, upstairs to be searched. During the search she reportedly loudly objected to being searched by "a dyke."

The men were quickly sized up and divided by appearance into two categories: long-haired hedonist or British gentleman. Gibbs, Cooper, and Fraser all fell into the latter category, and were treated with the respect befitting their station. "I'm so very sorry, sir" one policeman whispered to Fraser as he searched him, "you're obviously a cut above this lot, but we must do this." Fraser had managed to empty his antique pillbox of several heroin tablets. When the officer found the pillbox in his pocket, Fraser explained that he was a diabetic, and that the pillbox had contained his insulin. The heroin tablets were then shaken out of the lining of his coat, and handed back to Fraser. But at the last minute the officer changed his mind: Better take these for tests. Fraser's heart sank.

Police inspected David Schneiderman's briefcase, and were surprised to find it stuffed with aluminum-wrapped packets. "Film," he explained, asking the police to shut the briefcase before it was ruined by the light. They quickly latched it shut and, apologizing for the inconvenience, handed it back to Schneiderman. (Seeing this was a remarkable stroke of good fortune, everyone urged Schneiderman to leave the country as soon as possible. He did. Acid King David, in fact, vanished forever.)

Slung over the back of a chair in an upstairs bedroom, police found Jagger's green jacket. Fishing around the one inside pocket, Detective-Constable John Challen pulled out a vial containing four amphetamine tablets—"pep pills" that Jagger said had been legally prescribed for him. In truth, they were Marianne's. Later, she offered to volunteer this information, but Jagger gallantly took the rap.

The police then conducted a thorough search of the premises, rifling drawers, opening cupboards, peering into closets and under beds. They opened the miniature hotel soaps that Richards had begun collecting even before he was a Stone, though they managed to overlook a vial of heroin hurriedly stuffed under the seat cushions of a living-room sofa.

Richards maintained a lord-of-the-manor haughtiness throughout. "Would you mind stepping off that Moroccan cushion," he told one female officer, "because you're ruining the tapestries." Richards was then told that if drugs were found and they could not assign blame to anyone else, he would be held legally responsible. "I see," said Richards, "then blame it all on me."

The police had asked Richards to turn down the music, and Keith refused. Now, someone put on Dylan's "Rainy Day Women." As the officers filed out the door, Dylan's words blared over the speakers: *"Everybody must get stoned."*

Jagger awoke the next morning to find no mention of the raid in the papers—a clear sign that corrupt police officials were waiting for a payoff. "Spanish Tony" Sanchez, the drug dealer who supplied both Fraser and Richards, informed Keith that for $12,000 the case would be dropped. Several hours later Jagger sent a messenger with the cash. Sanchez delivered the bribe at a pub in the London suburb of Kilburn.

Mick woke up early each day to check the morning papers, and each day breathed a sigh of relief. For an entire week not a word concerning the incident had appeared in the press. Then, one week after the raid, the *News of the World* struck again. In a story that mentioned no names, the paper provided every lurid detail about the confiscation of pep pills from a "nationally known star." It was as if, Jagger marveled, "they had a reporter in the room." And whatever happened, he began to wonder, to Acid King David Schneiderman?

Mick decided that there were only two people present that night who might have set them up. Nicky Kramer, the prototypical English hippie, was eliminated as a suspect after Jagger's friend David Litvinoff, a colleague of Britain's most notorious gangsters, the Kray brothers, tried and failed to pummel an admission of guilt out of him.

Suspicion then fell squarely on Schneiderman. Why did the police let him leave with his drug-filled briefcase while confiscating joss sticks and miniature hotel soaps? How did he manage to leave the country so quickly, and why had no one heard from him since? And why did he carry two U.S. passports—one under the alias "David Edwards"? Jagger raised the possibility that Schneiderman was a CIA agent out to destroy the Stones. But there was another, more obvious theory that Jagger would eventually come to accept: The *News of the World* had set them up to thwart Jagger's pending libel action.

A month passed, and no charges had been filed. Assuming that the $12,000 bribe had found its way into the right hands, Jagger agreed to a holiday in Morocco. Mick planned to fly from Paris to Tangier and then on to Marrakech, where he and Marianne would converge with other friends—including Christopher Gibbs, Michael Cooper, Robert Fraser, the painter Brion Gysin, and the illustrious photographer and costume designer Cecil Beaton. A contemporary of Noel Coward, Beaton was considered to be a man of such uncompromising good taste that he permitted only white flowers to be grown in his garden.

Meanwhile, Keith, Brian, and Anita Pallenberg were to drive from England to North Africa in Richards's chauffeur-driven powder-blue Bentley, which he called "Blue Lena" after Lena Horne. Halfway down Brian suffered a severe asthmatic attack and was rushed to a hospital in Toulon, France. Jones urged Keith and Anita to go on without him—a suggestion he would later rue. As chauffeur Tom Keylock steered a course for Morocco, Keith and Anita made unfettered love beneath a pile of furs in the backseat. "Amazing things can happened in the back of a car," confessed Richards, "and they did." Several days later Pallenberg retrieved the wan and bloodshot-eyed Jones, and the once-golden couple rejoined the party in Morocco.

The sun-splashed minerets and lush palms provided a perfect backdrop for the Stones' surreal caravan. Brion Gysin, who lived in Morocco, served as the group's self-appointed host, offering running commentary as Jagger and his party meandered unrecognized through the casbah. After an afternoon spent dickering with local merchants over caftans, fezzes, and hookahs, everyone retreated to the hotel, where the Stones occupied the entire tenth floor. At nine P.M. Cecil Beaton came upon "Mick Jagger and a sleepy-looking band of gypsies" in the lobby.

Beaton, according to an acquaintance, "fell in love with Mick instantly." Still, he was careful not to ignore Jagger's retinue. "It was a strange group," Beaton wrote in his diaries. "The three 'Stones': Brian Jones with his girlfriend Anita Pallenberg—dirty white face, dirty blackened eyes, dirty canary drops of hair, barbaric jewellery—Keith Richards in eighteenth-century suit, long black velvet coat, and the tightest pants; and, of course, Mick Jagger. . . .

"I didn't want to give the impression that I was only interested in Mick, but it happened that we sat next to one another as he drank a Vodka Collins and smoked with pointed finger held high. His skin is chicken-breast white and of a fine quality. He has an inborn elegance."

Jagger told Beaton of the Redlands bust, and that he was thinking of leaving England because, in his words, it had become "a police state." Later, while dining at a local restaurant, Beaton observed that Jagger was "very gentle and with perfect manners. He has much appreciation and his small, albino-fringed eyes notice everything."

When Jagger observed that the women of Marrakech were "more rustic, heavy, lumpy," Beaton concluded that his new friend had "an analytical slant and compares everything he is seeing here with earlier impressions in other countries."

Then, listening to a black singer, Jagger "sent his arms jerking about him," Beaton recalled. "I was fascinated with the thin concave lines of his body, legs, and arms. The mouth is almost too large; he is beautiful and ugly, feminine and masculine: a rare phenomenon."

Jagger, who with the others had been dropping acid all day, urged Beaton to experiment with LSD: "Have you ever taken LSD?" he asked Beaton. When the distinguished-looking Beaton, the epitome of an English gentleman, allowed that he hadn't, Jagger began to quiver like a tuning fork. "Oh, you should," he gushed. "It would mean so much to you: you'd never forget the colors. For a painter it is a great experience. One's brain works not on four cylinders but on four thousand. You see everything aglow. You see yourself beautiful and ugly, and other people as if for the first time. Oh, yes, you should take it in the country, surrounded by all those flowers. You'd have no bad effects. It's only people who hate themselves who suffer."

Beaton asked if the authorities weren't cracking down on

the drug. "Oh, no, they can't stamp it out," shrugged Jagger. "It's like the atom bomb. Once it's been discovered, it can never be forgotten, and it's too easy to make."

The illustrious Beaton was less interested in Jagger's opinions than he was in his body. The two men returned to the hotel at three A.M., and they listened to music for another two hours. Beaton was disappointed when Jagger nodded off "without taking off his clothes."

The next morning by the pool Beaton was stunned when Jagger walked toward him: "I could not believe it was the same person. . . . The very strong sun, reflected from the white ground, made his face look a white, podgy, shapeless mess; eyes very small, nose very pink and spreading, hair sandy dark. His figure, his hands, and arms were incredibly feminine."

Taking Jagger into the woods to be photographed, Beaton "gave his face the shadows it needed. The lips were of a fantastic roundness, the body almost hairless and yet, surprisingly, I made him look like a Tarzan by Piero di Cosimo. He is sexy, yet completely sexless. He could nearly be a eunuch. As a model he is a natural."

Beaton was actually so impressed with a certain part of Jagger's anatomy that during this holiday he asked Mick to take off his pants. Beaton then snapped a photo of Jagger's naked posterior and committed it to canvas. Sir Cecil, a friend of the queen whose credits included the costumes for *My Fair Lady*, obviously considered Jagger's derriere a modern work of art. He gave the painting to a friend living in Tangier, and in 1986 it was auctioned off for a reported $4,000.

Meanwhile the atmosphere grew tense as Brian slowly realized that Anita had slept with Keith. During one drug-fueled evening Mick twirled about for Robert Fraser in a bizarre "magic dance" while Brian eyed Pallenberg and Richards suspiciously.

That night Jones brought two tattoo-covered Berber prostitutes to the hotel and ordered Pallenberg to join in a ménage. She refused, and he pounded her mercilessly. The next day, while Brian listened to the magical pipes of the hashish-puffing musicians of JouJouka, Anita fled with Keith back to London. When he returned to his hotel, Jones found himself abandoned, utterly alone.

It was a final, shattering blow for Brian—the ultimate betrayal by a friend and a lover. "They took my music; they took my band. And now they've taken my love." Richards was less than sympathetic. "Hell," Keith shrugged. "Shit happens."

On March 18 the London *Daily Mirror* blared the news that—regardless of the $12,000 payoff—Mick Jagger and Keith Richards were to face charges stemming from the Redlands bust. The trial was scheduled to begin May 10. In the interim the band was scheduled to embark on a tour that would take them to Sweden, West Germany, Austria, Italy, France, Poland, Switzerland, Holland, and Greece.

As defendants in a highly publicized drug case Jagger and Richards's names automatically went on Interpol's "red list." That meant that customs officials at every airport, forewarned of their arrival, tore through luggage and subjected all the Stones to a rigorous and humiliating body search. It also meant that, before they arrived at their destination, a long line formed at the rear of the plane as the Stones and their entourage hastily flushed all manner of illegal substances down the toilet.

The Rolling Stones' first concert behind the Iron Curtain occurred in Warsaw, where, true to form, Communist party officials and their families packed the Palace of Culture while Polish soldiers held back thousands of teenage fans outside.

The stalemate continued until Jagger, eager to fire up the kids outside, had one of his underlings rush outside and toss copies of the Stones' latest single ("Ruby Tuesday"/"Let's Spend the Night Together") just outside police barricades. With that three thousand fans overran the barricades and stormed the iron gates leading to the Palace of Culture. Two armored cars rolled into position, and the crowd was bombarded with water cannons and tear gas.

In Zurich a crazed man vaulted onto the stage and attacked Jagger. Before police could pull the man off, he had hurled a dazed Mick to the floor and stomped on him.

Paradoxically, Jagger now seemed to feed on the violence he instilled in others. Marianne got a frightening glimpse of this when she hooked up with Mick in Milan. It was the first time she joined him right after a concert—and the last.

Following the Stones' show at Milan's Palazzo dello Sport, Jagger joined Faithfull at their hotel. Still in full costume and makeup, he was literally frothing at the mouth and growling like an animal. Jagger grabbed Faithfull and flung her against the wall. She would later describe Jagger as "absolutely terrifying—like somebody possessed. He was a berserk stranger . . . like a mad creature from some hostile planet." Jagger behaved like the incident never happened, and Faithfull believed he had no memory of it.

Through it all the atmosphere in the Stones' office in London remained unchanged. "The place was always full of sycophants," recalled Stephanie Bluestone, who with her boss, Laurence Myers, handled the Stones' financial accounts. "There were lots of people around who weren't that nice to know—dangerous people, people operating just this side of the law." The first day she met Jagger, Bluestone said, "he drove me around in this little black Mini he owned and told me who to stay away from. He was very sweet, very protective of me."

According to Bluestone, who worked inside the Stones organization for years, Allen Klein was "a dreadful, dreadful man. He was greasy and fat and vulgar. He carried a gun, and used to walk around swigging Scotch out of a bottle."

Andrew Oldham, meanwhile, was "like something out of the Gestapo," said Bluestone. Gobbling painkillers like jellybeans, Oldham now experienced violent mood-swings that left workers in the Stones' office reeling. Tantrums were a daily occurrence; staffers were fired with regularity. Bluestone also observed a schizophrenic quality to Oldham's particular management style. "One minute he'd be calm, the next he'd be shrieking and turning over desks. He seemed to have this need to frighten people." Toward that end Oldham traded in Reg the Butcher for a more upscale but equally sinister-looking bodyguard named Eddie.

In contrast to all this Bluestone recalled Mick as being "sort of sane compared to everyone else. He was very kind to Marianne, very considerate to the people in the office." Contrary to popular belief Bluestone also insists Jagger was "immaculate in his appearance. Always very together—especially when he was around businessmen."

Jagger had also developed a compulsion for cleanliness. "I couldn't say the same about the rest of the Stones," said Bluestone, "but Mick was amazingly clean, absolutely scrupulous about his personal hygiene." That extended to taking several showers a day. Said Bluestone: "Mick was always forgetting to turn the water off; several times his bath overflowed and flooded the flat one floor below."

As Jagger awaited trial, he saw no reason to curtail his social schedule in London—particularly in light of his new friendship with member of Parliament Tom Driberg. To be sure, Mick was well aware that he might soon need all the well-placed allies he could get.

Driberg was no stranger to controversy. Between his election to the House of Commons in 1942 and his elevation to the House of Lords thirty-two years later, the Labor party gadfly raised eyebrows—as much for his homosexual exploits as for his decidedly left-wing beliefs.

Although he was godfather to Mick's former girlfriend Cleo Sylvestre, Driberg did not actually meet Jagger until the spring of 1967. But two years earlier Driberg had sprung to Mick's defense when a Glasgow magistrate lectured a fan convicted of smashing a store window following a Stones concert. "I am surprised you go along and mix with the long-haired gentlemen called the Rolling Stones," said Magistrate James Langmuir. "What is the attraction for you? Complete morons like that wear their hair down to their shoulders, wear filthy clothes, and act like clowns. You buy a ticket to see animals like that?"

Driberg fired back by introducing a motion censuring the magistrate for "using his privileged position to make irrelevant, snobbish, and insulting personal comments of a pop group, the Rolling Stones, who are making a substantial contribution to the public entertainment and the export drive." As a result Driberg himself was denounced as a "certifiable lunatic" and a "bloody fool" by outraged constituents.

Jagger and Driberg finally met through their mutual friend Allen Ginsberg, the American beat poet. Ginsberg, who like Driberg was gay, had met Jagger at a party in New York's Greenwich Village and, he told friends, was instantly smitten with the androgynous young rocker.

Ginsberg's interest in Driberg was more cerebral. He was surprised that Driberg was an advocate of legalizing marijuana, and that he had been a student of the "Great Beast" Aleister Crowley, Britain's infamous father of twentieth century witchcraft.

When Ginsberg was visiting London in April of 1967, he dropped by Jagger's apartment one evening with Driberg in tow. The three men had spent nearly five hours sipping wine and discussing everything from art and religion to Satanism when Driberg noticed a rather large ceramic phallus on the mantle—a sculpture presumably made by Chicago's famous "Plaster Casters," who similarly immortalized the likes of Jimi Hendrix, Jim Morrison, and all the members (literally) of Led Zeppelin. The conversation came to a dead stop as Driberg, seated next to Jagger on the couch, leaned over and put his hand on Mick's thigh. Staring at the sculpture, and then at Jagger's bulging crotch, Driberg squealed "Oh, my, Mick. What a big basket you have!"

"I was slightly embarrassed, as Driberg was my guest," recalled Ginsberg. "I was also astounded at his boldness. I had eyes for Jagger myself, but I was very circumspect about Jagger's body. Yet here was Driberg coming on crude."

The direct approach may have worked. A number of

times the poet reportedly told Mick's friend Miles that Ginsberg, Jagger, and Driberg had shared a night together in bed.

What neither Jagger nor Ginsberg—nor, for that matter, the British public—knew was that Tom Driberg was a spy. Beginning in 1942, when he first entered the House of Commons, Driberg worked as a double agent for the KGB and for Britain's espionage agency, MI-5. According to a report issued in the mid-1980s, Driberg "reported on the personal and political activities of his friends and colleagues in Parliament to both agencies." After he was elevated to the peerage in 1974, Driberg's espionage activities continued. It was then that he acquired a new nickname among those in the intelligence community—a twist on the homoerotically charged William Golding novel *Lord of the Flies*. Driberg was referred to simply as "Lord of the Spies."

Whether or not the relationship between Driberg and Jagger was romantic remains open to question. The undisputed fact is that Driberg pursued Jagger on both a sexual and intellectual level, and that at the very least they became intimate friends and confidants. More disturbingly, Driberg began to see Mick as a messiah to the young, someone whose almost hypnotic powers of persuasion could be harnessed to reshape society. Over the years, as Driberg actively courted Jagger behind closed doors, the friendship between Mick and the man they would call "Lord of the Spies" would evolve into one of political mentor and protégé.

For now, as he prepared to face drug charges, it certainly did not hurt for Jagger to have an advocate in the House of Commons.

On the morning of May 10, 1967, Mick Jagger, Keith Richards, and their friend Robert Fraser pleaded not guilty before a local magistrate and were released on bail of £250 (around $500) awaiting trial in June.

Four hours later Brian Jones and Stones hanger-on Prince Stanislaus ("Stash") Klossowski de Rola, still reeling from the previous night's festivities, were jolted awake by someone pounding on the door of Jones's Chelsea apartment. Scotland Yard detectives burst inside, and within minutes their search yielded quantities of cocaine, hashish, and methedrine.

Reporters, obviously tipped off to the raid, waited outside the Chelsea police station as Brian and Stash were hauled inside and formally charged with drug possession.

By planning Brian's arrest to coincide with the formal arraignment of Jagger and Richards, British authorities were announcing to the world that they had declared war on the Rolling Stones. As the most visible members of the group (and frankly, the easiest to nail on drug charges), Jagger, Richards, and Jones were now to be held accountable not only for their own sins, but for the preening petulance of England's anti-Establishment youth. This was the Establishment's revenge.

Jagger and Richards hired one of the priciest criminal lawyers in England to defend them, Michael Havers. A future attorney general and lord chancellor, Havers told Jagger the case against him and Richards was shaky at best. The possession of a few airsickness pills—that is how Havers would now characterize the amphetamines—hardly constituted a crime against society. His only advice to Jagger was that he drop the phony cockney accent; like it or not, a jury was more likely to believe a gentleman.

On June 27, 1967, hundreds of fans, some wearing T-shirts emblazoned MICK IS INNOCENT and FREE THE STONES, gathered outside the West Sussex courthouse in Chichester. Inside, another eighty fortunate fans crowded the public gallery, breathlessly waiting for their idols to take the stand.

Jagger, wearing a pale green blazer, ruffled white shirt, and striped tie, stepped up into the dock of the Dickensian courtroom to a chorus of sighs from the mostly female gallery. The jury of one woman and eleven men struggled to ignore the giggling and rustling that would be the leitmotiv of the proceedings.

As sunlight filtered down through the high, cathedrallike windows, Queen's Counsel Malcolm Morris perfunctorily described the raid at Redlands. Under court rules Morris was forbidden to disclose the identity of the woman who was present, though every newspaper in the country—and quite a few around the world—identified Marianne as the famous "Naked Girl in the Fur Rug." She did little to quell speculation by showing up in the courtroom that day to cast loving glances at Mick.

(While Jagger was in jail, Richards and Faithfull actually posed for their photographer friend Michael Cooper on the front lawn of Redlands. The pictures show Keith and Marianne holding up front-page headlines blaring NUDE GIRL AT STONES PARTY.)

QC Morris's first witness was Detective Sergeant Stanley Cudmore. The sergeant testified that he had found four pills in Jagger's jacket and that Jagger had admitted they were his. Under laboratory analysis the pills had turned out to contain amphetamine sulfate and methyl amphetamine hydrochloride. In more common terms, speed.

Havers's only defense witness, Jagger's physician Raymond Dixon Firth, testified that he had not prescribed the pills for Mick—they had apparently been purchased when Jagger was traveling in Italy—but that he would have if his patient had asked him to.

With that, Judge Leslie Block turned to the jury and told them that Dr. Dixon Firth's remarks "cannot be regarded as a prescription by a duly authorized medical practitioner." Therefore, Judge Block concluded, "I direct you that there is no defense to this charge."

Havers was horrified. Six minutes later the jury returned a guilty verdict. Jagger went white. Judge Block, a former naval officer with little tolerance for the likes of Jagger, then denied Havers's request for bail. Sentence would be postponed, the dour judge added, until the completion of Richard's trial.

Along with Robert Fraser, who had changed his plea to guilty and thrown himself on the mercy of the court, Mick was handcuffed, bundled into a police van, and driven through mobs of sobbing fans to Lewes prison. There Jagger, tears streaming down his face, was processed, fingerprinted, and given a prison uniform. Marianne brought him cigarettes and newspapers, and seriously contemplated the distinct possibility of being apart from him for a very long time. Jagger and Fraser spent their first night of incarceration in a small room in the prison's hospital wing.

As soon as photographs of a handcuffed Jagger appeared in the London papers, Tom Driberg questioned the necessity of such rough treatment on the floor of the Commons. When pressed on the issue, prison officials would merely state that this was standard procedure, and they had not been officially asked to do otherwise.

The next morning Jagger and Fraser were manacled once again and led to the courthouse. They waited in a small holding cell while Richards, clad in a black suit and trying his best to be polite, listened as the prosecutor laid out the case against him.

For the first time Queens Counsel Morris alluded to the mysterious David Schneiderman, at first simply as "Mr. X." Schneiderman had been charged in absentia for possession of sixty-six grams of cannabis resin.

To paint a picture of depraved, drug-induced decadence, Morris then spoke of "the young lady on the settee. All she was wearing was a light-colored fur-skin rug, which from time to time she allowed to fall, disclosing her nude body. She was unperturbed and apparently enjoying the situation."

In his opening statements to the jury Michael Havers named Schneiderman, and implied strongly that a "well-known national newspaper" that was being threatened with a libel suit by Jagger had set him up.

As for "Miss X," Havers railed against the implication that she was "a drug-taking nymphomaniac. I am not going to allow this girl into the witness box," he gallantly stated. "I am not going to tear that blanket of anonymity aside and let the world laugh or scorn as they will."

To counter the suggestion that Faithfull was barely covered by a scrap of animal fur, Havers asked Sergeant Cudmore to describe the rug.

Havers: "Was it a large rug?"

Cudmore: "Quite large."

Havers: "Was it bigger than a fur coat?"

Cudmore: "Yes."

Havers: "But it's a bedcover, isn't it?" Six foot square. Here, take a look." [Havers spreads the rugs out over the defense table]. "It's enormous. You can see—it's about eight and a half feet by five."

After the day's testimony Richards remained on bail while Mick returned to jail in handcuffs. ("Jagger Cuffs" became a trendy jewelry item during this period, selling at boutiques throughout London.) He returned the next morning to wait in the holding cell once again while Richards took the stand.

Defense counsel Havers allowed Richards to detail the curious events leading up to the Redlands raid, and the suspected role of Schneiderman and the *News of the World*.

Under relentless and at times insulting cross-examination by the prosecutor Morris, Richards struck the respectful tone requested by his defense attorney—for a time.

Morris: "Is it your defense that Schneiderman had been planted in your weekend party as part of a wicked conspiracy by *News of the World*? Is that any part of your defense or not?"

Richards: "Yes, it is, sir."

Morris: "Is your defense that Schneiderman was planted by the *News of the World* in an attempt to get Mick Jagger convicted of smoking hashish? Is that the suggestion?"

Richards: "That is the suggestion."

Morris: "Are you quite clear of what you are saying?"

Richards: "Yes."

After hammering away on this point without riling Richards, Morris turned his attention to the girl in the fur rug.

Morris: "Would you agree, in the ordinary course of events, you would expect a young woman to be embarrassed if she had nothing on but a rug in the presence of eight men, two of whom were hangers-on and the third a Moroccan servant?"

Richards: "Not at all."

Prosecution: "You regard that, do you, as quite normal?"

Richards: "We are not old men. We are not worried about petty morals."

Havers cringed at that final line, for it betrayed the languid arrogance for which Richards and Jagger were truly on trial.

The jury deliberated for seventy minutes before delivering its verdict: Guilty.

Jagger and Fraser were then brought up from their holding cell and led to the dock to stand beside Richards. Amid protests shouted from the gallery, Keith was sentenced to one year in prison, and a five-hundred-pound fine.

Judge Block then sentenced Fraser to six months and two hundred pounds.

The room fell suddenly silent as Block turned to Jagger. "Michael Philip Jagger," the judge intoned with all the gravity of a lord high executioner, "you will go to prison for three months. You will pay one hundred pounds towards the costs of the prosecution."

Jagger, the wind knocked out of him, appeared on the verge of collapse. "I just went dead when I was sentenced," Mick later recalled. "It was just like a James Cagney film except everything went black."

Marianne was already on her way to the courthouse in Richards's blue Bentley when news of the sentencing came over the car radio. Weeping, Marianne made her way through the crowd of eight hundred fans milling outside the courthouse to the front gate. Helped inside by the police, she met with Mick in his holding cell. They sobbed in each other's arms for fifteen minutes.

At the news, mass hysteria gripped the mob outside the courthouse. There were plaintive cries of "Shame!" and "Let them go!" As the fans wailed and shook their fists in protest, Jagger was taken by van to serve out his sentence at Brixton prison. Richards and Fraser, meanwhile, were bound for the onomatopoetic Wormwood Scrubs.

Those who visited Mick at Brixton prison were shocked at the immediate effect it had on him. He was wearing a prison uniform and did share a cramped cell, but unlike other prisoners he had not been deloused, subjected to any degrading body-cavity searches, or even asked to cut his hair. Yet, perhaps with some justification, the wraithlike pop star feared that he might become the unwilling object of some felon's affection.

Pale and shaking, weeping inconsolably, Jagger teetered on the verge of a complete nervous breakdown. Faithfull began to wonder if he had the strength to survive the experience.

Outraged at the severity of the sentence, disc jockeys around the world played Stones records nonstop or called for moments of silence. Thousands of protestors marched on British consulates in the United States and throughout Europe, chanting for authorities to "Free the Stones." The Who hurriedly released its own version of "Under My Thumb" and "It's All Over Now," vowing to keep the Stones' music out there so long as Mick and Keith were unjustly behind bars.

Several hundred people milled menacingly outside the offices of *News of the World*, which denied any involvement in framing Jagger and Richards. "A monstrous charge was made against *News of the World* in the trial of Keith Richards," countered the paper in a July 2 editorial. "It was a charge made without a shred of evidence to support it."

Letters to the editor from some of England's leading citizens voiced outrage at the sentences. The case was kept alive in Parliament, where Tom Driberg once again protested that the Stones were being treated like convicted murderers. None of his colleagues, however, was aware that Driberg's zeal was at least partially motivated by his affection for the well-equipped Mick.

The next day Jagger and Richards were released on seven thousand pounds bail pending appeal. Yet the harsh legal treatment of the hapless Stones would continue to be a hotly debated issue in the press.

The *Observer* complained that the severe sentences had "produced two martyrs," while the *Sunday Express* felt the penalty was "monstrously out of proportion to the offence." The London *Evening News* ran editorials for and against the verdict. "Teenagers wept, I read, when Jagger and Richards were sentenced," wrote Charles Curran. "Well, I decline to imitate them. I prefer to applaud. . . . The law applies to everybody, including pop music millionaires."

Countered journalist John Heyes: "Every ten years or so the British public seems to need a scapegoat, a scandal. It is a safety valve for society, a blowing-off of steam. . . . Some would regard this as yet another case of British hypocrisy. Another classic case."

Perhaps the biggest and most unexpected blow on their behalf was struck by the congenitally stodgy London *Times*. William Rees-Mogg, the tweedy editor of the *Times,* borrowed an obscure quotation from Alexander Pope as the title for his editorial: WHO BREAKS A BUTTERFLY ON A WHEEL?

In his piece Rees-Mogg observed that Jagger was not accused of any major drug use or of drug trafficking, and that in nearly all such minor drug cases the penalty had been probation. Pointing out that the pills had been purchased in Italy, Rees-Mogg offered the following scenario: "If after his visit to the pope, the archbishop of Canterbury had bought proprietary airsickness pills in the Rome airport, and imported the unused tablets into Britain on his return, he would have risked committing precisely the same offence.

"There are many people who take a primitive view of the matter," the *Times* continued. "They consider that Mr. Jagger has 'got what was coming to him.' They resent the anarchic quality of the Rolling Stones' performances, dislike their songs, dislike their influence on teenagers and broadly suspect them of decadence. . . .

"As a social concern this may be reasonable enough, and

at an emotional level it is very understandable, but it has nothing to do with the case. One has to ask a different question: Has Mr. Jagger received the same treatment as he would have received if he had not been a famous figure, with all the criticism and resentment his celebrity has aroused?" Rees-Mogg went on to conclude that "Mr. Jagger has received a more severe sentence than would have been thought proper for any purely anonymous young man."

The case gained momentum as an American doctoral student at Oxford named Steve Abrams seized the moment to take an ad in the *Times* calling for liberalized marijuana laws. The ad, paid for by the Beatles, was also signed by the Beatles manager Brian Epstein, writers Graham Greene, Kenneth Tynan, and Jonathan Miller, artist David Hockney, and, of course, Mick's close friend Tom Driberg.

The ad called for, among other things, commuting the sentences of convicted pot smokers, legalizing marijuana use in private, and legalizing possession altogether.

One week after the ad ran, on July 31, Jagger stood before none other than England's lord chief justice, Lord Parker, and awaited word of his fate. (Richards, suffering from a case of chicken pox, was excused from the proceedings). Again, the court chambers were packed with squirming pubescent girls. Their gaze occasionally fell on Marianne, who, though wearing a skin-tight micro-miniskirt, somehow managed to look beatific. (At the time of the ruling Keith Richards's love, Anita Pallenberg, was in Rome costarring with Jane Fonda in Roger Vadim's science fiction romp *Barbarella*).

Flanked by two bewigged appellate judges, Lord Parker struck down Richards's conviction, noting that there was scant evidence to support the notion that the rug-wrapped "Miss X" had been smoking pot.

There was a fleeting moment of anxiety when Lord Parker upheld Jagger's conviction; the four amphetamines found in Mick's jacket were, after all, illegal drugs. However, a squeal of joy went up when the judge threw out Jagger's prison sentence and put him on one year's probation. If he got into trouble any time over the ensuing twelve months, Lord Parker warned, Jagger would receive stiff sentences for both crimes.

Jagger was not about to escape without a lecture. "You are, whether you like it or not," said Lord Parker, "the idol of a large number of the young in this country. Being in that position, you have very grave responsibilities. If you do come to be punished, it is only natural that those responsibilities should carry higher penalties."

Assuming that his sentence would be overturned, Jagger had agreed to appear on Granada Television's *World in Action* broadcast immediately after his court appearance. The whole affair would soon take on the dimensions of a three-ring media circus.

Leaving the High Court, Jagger climbed into the back of a waiting limousine, downed several Valium, and sped away to a press conference at Granada's headquarters. To symbolize his Phoenix-like rise from the ashes, Jagger had shed his green double-breasted courtroom suit for flashier plumage: purple satin plus pants, an off-white shirt, off-white shoes, and a tunic with embroidered red, yellow, and green trim.

Looking nervous despite the large dose of Valium, Jagger perched on a windowsill and fielded reporters' questions. "Do you think you do have a responsibility to the young in this country, as Lord Parker said?" asked one television reporter.

"I've been given that responsibility," replied Jagger, "pushed into the limelight. I don't try to impose my views on people. I don't propagate religious views like some pop stars do, I don't propagate drug views like some pop stars do. This was all pushed upon me by the prosecution." He claimed he had prepared himself for jail "mentally, physically, and businesswise." Apparently fully recovered from his nonstop crying jag at Brixton, Jagger claimed that he "really felt quite good. I got myself in the frame of mind to accept it."

The Stones' unflappable publicist, Les Perrin, called a

halt to the press conference after fifteen minutes. Jagger and Faithfull were then whisked away in a white Jaguar to a waiting helicopter.

Twenty minutes later their chopper touched down at its top-secret destination: Spain's Hall, the Georgian estate of Sir John Ruggles-Brise, lord lieutenant of Essex. In this bucolic setting *World in Action* cameras were set up to film a kind of generational summit between Jagger and several substantial pillars of Britain's Establishment.

Making up the panel were the stalwart likes of Lord Stow Hill, former home secretary and attorney general, the Jesuit priest Father Thomas Corbishley, and Dr. John Robinson, bishop of Woolwich and, fittingly, Jagger's champion William Rees-Mogg.

Before the inquisition was to begin, Marianne and Mick excused themselves to "freshen up" inside the manor house; a few minutes later a Granada staffer who had gone to fetch Jagger paused outside their bedroom. Clearly audible even through the heavy oak door were squeaking mattress springs and moans building to a crescendo—the unmistakable sounds of two people in the throes of sex. The staffer waited a few minutes before knocking, but it hardly mattered to the unselfconscious couple inside. In due time. . . .

Facing his interrogators Jagger was treated with the same respect usually accorded a royal personage or a head of state. In a turnabout worthy of Lewis Carroll the drug conviction that only hours before had hung over his head like a sword of Damacles now somehow transformed him into a respected spokesman for the young. Statesmen and churchmen and press lords now beseeched him for answers to society's deepest ills.

"Do you feel," asked Rees-Mogg, "that society has a great deal in it today that ought to be rebelled against?"

"I didn't think my knowledge was enough to start pontificating on the subject," replied Jagger. His speech was slower and more deliberate than it had been at the earlier conference, the result of yet another heavy dose of Valium.

"I didn't ever set myself up as a leader in society. It's society that's pushed one into that position."

As for whether taking drugs could be considered a crime against society, Jagger pointed out that "until recently attempted suicide was a crime. . . . Anyone who takes a very bad drug, such as heroin, commits a crime against himself. I cannot see how it is a crime against society. I can't see it's any more a crime against society than jumping out a window."

Sweet revenge for Jagger, so roundly vilified by the very same institutions whose gray-templed representatives now hung on his every word. Before millions of skeptical Britons he had shown himself to be articulate, thoughtful, and—when the situation called for it—remarkably civilized.

Brian's deteriorating condition cast a pall over Jagger's triumph, however. The effects of his drug arrest were devastating. He was relying more heavily than ever on tranquilizers that deepened his depression and aggravated his paranoia.

One way Jones coped with stress was by going on a shopping spree. Always the Beau Brummell of the group, Brian spent thousands of dollars on exotic furs, velvet Edwardian and Regency-style suits, brocade jackets, and broad-brimmed hats. Brian had a special fondness for expensive silk scarves that he tied around his knees, and for flashy costume jewelry.

After Anita left Brian for Keith, Jones often appeared at her doorstep unannounced and begged her to return. He traveled through dozens of women in the following months, at last settling on a Pallenberg look-alike, Suki Poitier. A stunning blond model, Poitier had survived the car crash that had killed Brian's friend, Guinness heir Tara Browne. (Sadly, Poitier herself would die in a separate car crash a decade later.)

Neither profligate spending nor his new lover could forestall the inevitable, however, and while awaiting his trial Jones suffered a complete nervous breakdown. Brian's psychiatrist, Dr. Leonard Henry, had him admitted to the Priory Nursing Home for treatment. For days on end staff psychiatrists heard the sorry tale of how Brian had founded the world's greatest rock and roll band only to have it stolen from him. Stolen from him by Mick Jagger.

While Jones poured out his torment to the psychiatrists at Priory hospital, Jagger, Faithfull, and her two-year-old son, Nicholas, moved into a stately Queen Anne–style town house on Cheyne Walk along the banks of the Thames. In the garage: a gleaming new cream-colored Bentley.

Guided by Christopher Gibbs, Marianne set out to transform the interior of their new home into a kind of Moroccan bazar. Mick had gained a deserved reputation for being frugal; he always looked for bargains when he shopped for his own clothes, and carefully scrutinized restaurant and hotel bills.

Yet the house on Cheyne Walk was to be Jagger's showplace, a reflection of his vaunted social status. Faithfull was not exactly given carte blanche, but close to it. She filled every room with costly antiques, Oriental carpets, and tapestries. Nor did she hesitate to plunk down £7,000 (about $16,000) for a 350-year-old uncut crystal chandelier to hang in the foyer. "My God," Jagger would say to guests as he pointed to the ceiling, "seven thousand quid for a fuckin' light! Ain't it," he'd add, his face breaking into that famous megawatt smile, *"Marvelous?"*

"My whole life isn't rock and roll. It's an absurd idea that it should be."

More than any politician or royal or rival rock star—including any of the Beatles—Mick Jagger was in the summer of 1967 the most respected and reviled, loved and feared, shunned and sought-after figure of his generation. Now that Britain's Establishment had, in a sense, taken him to its ample bosom, Jagger felt invulnerable.

Only days after he had gobbled enough Valium to get him through his appearance in appeals court, Jagger was calling for insurrection. "We have got them on the run now and we have to finish what we have started," Jagger told the press. "The time is right now, revolution is valid." Some of his public proclamations, issued without the slightest hint of self-consciousness, were unintentionally hilarious: "Anarchy is the only slight glimmer of hope. . . . There should be no such thing as private property."

The messianic nature of the pop star phenomenon was showcased that August in *Privilege*, a film dealing with a Jagger-like rock star who is so idolized by the public that he is latched on to by the church as a redeemer. In reviewing the film many critics drew parallels between its protagonist (played by Paul Jones) and Jagger. Although the movie was filmed months before Mick's trial, it contained a scene uncannily like the "summit" between Jagger and members of the Establishment. "As an attack on mass adulation, hypocrisy, and mod materialism," wrote one critic, reflecting the public's growing resentment of too-smug rock stars, "*Privilege* is unequaled."

Jagger's brush with the law did little to alter his habits or those of his highborn friends. He and Marianne spent some evenings at home with little Nicholas, smoking pot and listening to music. Most nights, however, were spent sharing conversation and drugs in the homes of the privileged class, or at hot London hangouts like the Ad Lib, the Bag of Nails, the Speakeasy, and the Scotch.

The epicenter of social life in Chelsea was Christopher Gibbs's oak-paneled living room overlooking the Thames on Cheyne Walk. Located just a few doors down from Jagger's elegantly narrow Queen Anne manor, Gibbs's house, once the residence of the American painter James McNeill Whistler, was virtually indistinguishable from the other imposing brick and stone structures that surrounded it.

Inside, as might have been expected of the man who had transformed Jagger's home into a Moroccan bazaar, Gibbs's house was a dreamlike vision straight out of the Arabian Nights. At every turn there were Moorish lanterns, leather camel saddles, and jewellike Persian carpets—all viewed through an acrid haze of burning incense. Guests draped in caftans or Victorian lace luxuriated on huge embroidered cushions strewn about the floor. "It was a wondrous room," said John Michel, a frequent guest at Gibbs's near-nightly soirees, "a temple of the Mysteries." Appropriately, the room was used for the famous party scene in Michelangelo Antonioni's classic sixties thriller *Blow-Up.*

Gibbs's living room was no more exotic than the people who inhabited it. According to Michel, Gibbs's parties attracted "the confused, the catatonic, and the ecstatic. Night after night gathered the select pipe-dreamers of sixties Chelsea: poets and mystics, artists and musicians, courtesans, hustlers, and hangers-on."

Gibbs threw one of his more memorable parties in July of 1967 to celebrate the return to London of Allen Ginsberg, who had been traveling in Italy. Princess Margaret, two viscounts, a marquess, and miscellaneous lesser aristocrats chatted with cabinet ministers, Oxford dons, and even the odd American as the Beatles' landmark paeon to psychedelia, *Sergeant Pepper*, played in the background.

Mick's friend and neighbor Paul Getty II dropped in with his stunningly beautiful wife, Talitha, who, as was her habit, wore a flimsy see-through dress and absolutely nothing underneath. (Talitha later died of a drug overdose.)

Yet all eyes were on the true stars of the evening. Mick wore a mauve tunic with ruffled cuffs, Marianne a thigh-gripping miniskirt, an equally tight lavendar blouse, and no bra. They seldom took their hands off one another.

"Mick broke down the social barriers," contended Michel. "More than the Beatles, who were never really accepted into the upper strata, Jagger was more or less accepted as one of them. And why not? He was a very glamorous figure, and all the aristocrats wanted to be near him. He always asked a lot of questions and said he was 'learning to be a gentleman,' but the patricians were learning as much from him as he was from them—probably much more."

John Dunbar offered a different perspective: "Mick wanted to be one of the 'aristos,' and he still does. But they would never really accept him as an equal. He was and remains a curiosity for them."

Around ten P.M. the night of the Ginsberg party, a butler brought around a large silver tray piled high with hash brownies. "Back then it was the 'in' thing to use the recipe from the *Alice B. Toklas Cookbook*," recalled Miles, a guest at the party. "Only this time someone obviously doubled the recipe. What they were eating was very toxic, very dangerous."

As a result, said Miles, "everybody got hashish poisoning. People began freaking out. All these ladies and lords, curators from the British Museum, various members of Parliament, were rushed away in their chaueffeur-driven cars to have their stomachs pumped."

Jagger and Faithfull dashed into the night air and, to overcome the effects of the hashish, began "running up and down Cheyne Walk at high speed. Mick came up to me," Miles remembered, "and said, 'I feel very high, but happy.' " The incident was never reported in the press. "If it had been," said Miles, "it would have been a huge scandal. There were members of the Royal Family, politicians, and other big names there, it would have rocked the government, definitely."

Buckingham Palace was not amused. Though Queen Elizabeth regarded the Beatles with a detached bemusement, Jagger was another matter. Her Majesty viewed the Rolling Stones as a bad influence on Britain's youth, and took personal offense at Jagger's remark in the press that she was England's "Chief Witch."

The queen, devouring every detail about Jagger's arrest at Redlands and the subsequent trial, was shocked by what she read. She was also concerned about Jagger's high-profile friendship with her sister, and summoned Princess Margaret to the palace to tell her so.

Just one week after the Gibbs affair Miles encountered Jagger at another soiree in Ginsberg's honor—this time thrown by the wealthy American hostess Panna Grady, a patron of William Burroughs and other veterans of the Beat Generation. Arriving at Grady's Regent Park address, Miles looked up to see "Jagger, a flowing white scarf around his neck, sitting cross-legged on a balcony while Allen Ginsberg taught him a mantra." They were then joined by Tom Driberg. *Ommmmm.*

Secure in their invincibility Mick, Marianne, and their pampered coterie flouted drug laws and decorum wherever and whenever they felt the urge. Invited by their friend Desmond Guinness to watch Lord Ormonde hand over historic Kilkenny Castle to the government of Ireland, Mick and Marianne showed up stoned on LSD. "We were all doped up, slithering about with all the pictures falling off the walls," recalled Gibbs, who accompanied them. "We were in a terrible state." On their return to London photographers swarmed over Mick and Marianne; they were turned down by several disapproving taxi drivers before finding one who was willing to drive them into town.

No matter. Marianne, far from being tarnished by the scandalous Redlands episode, was offered several acting parts. She had starred on the London stage in Chekhov's *Three Sisters*, but now she was offered a shot at a role in a major motion picture, playing a leather-jacketed "biker chick" opposite French heartthrob Alain Delon in the Jack Cardiff–directed *Girl on a Motorcycle*. Meanwhile the Stones' record label was busy capitalizing on all the publicity generated by the drug trials and their aftermath. London Records, Decca's U.S. subsidiary, released an album entitled *Flowers*, a patchwork quilt of old tunes and outtakes. *Flowers* would have a nine-month run on the American Hot 100, rising all the way to No. 3.

Mick and Keith had contributed background vocals to the Beatles' "All You Need Is Love" single. The Beatles returned the favor when the Stones recorded their answer to "All You Need Is Love," the blatantly derivitive "We Love You." Jagger had purportedly written the song in prison as a kind of love note to the fans who had supported him throughout his ordeal. By way of social commentary Jagger added shuffling feet and clanging cell doors.

To hype the single they made a four-minute movie on the trial of Oscar Wilde. Mick was dandied up even more than usual to portray Wilde, Keith was cast in the role of the marquess of Queensbury, and Marianne played Lord Alfred Douglas, Wilde's lover. It was an audacious step, and one that thoroughly infuriated the stuffy BBC. Despite pressure from some of Mick's high-placed acquaintances, the BBC refused to air the provocative anti-Establishment film.

That did not upset Jagger half as much as the disappointing sales of "We Love You." Jagger had expected it to soar to No. 1 on the strength of what he perceived to be his newfound popularity. Instead, it topped out at no. 8.

With *Sergeant Pepper* the Beatles had tapped into a creative wellspring that seemed to Jagger to be spiritual as well as musical. When they invited him to join them in seeking divine guidance from the Maharishi Mahesh Yogi, Jagger jumped at the chance.

A curious cross between Gandhi and Truman Capote, the Maharishi achieved global celebrity as the era's leading exponent of transcendental meditation. Speculation swirled about the peculiar little figure who giggled like a Munchkin; there were even widespread rumors that the Maharishi was a woman—to be specific, a "dyke from Yorkshire," according to Anita Pallenberg.

Still, the Maharishi counted many movie stars as rockers among his followers, and the Beatles were far and away his best-known disciples. Jagger had hoped to find some answers at the foot of the Indian mystic. But when he rushed off with the Beatles to meet the guru at a teachers' college in Wales, Mick was sorely disappointed—not so much in the bewhiskered guru as he was in John Lennon and Paul McCartney. Likening the Mahareshi's lecture to a circus sideshow, Jagger later said he had expected the more ethereal-minded George Harrison to "fall for all that peace, love, and pay-the-bill crap." However, he had expected Lennon and McCartney to be less gullible.

That weekend, as it turned out, the Beatles were to require all the spiritual guidance they could find. Between sessions with the Maharishi they learned that Brian Epstein, their longtime manager and mentor, had taken his own life with an overdose of sleeping pills.

Sergeant Pepper was widely considered to be the Beatles' greatest achievement to date. If the musical taste of his generation was moving in a psychedelic direction, Jagger did not want the Stones to be left behind.

Mick's solution: *Their Satanic Majesties Request*, a "concept" album along the lines of *Sergeant Pepper*. The title was taken from the language found on all British passports: "Her Britannic Majesty's Principal Secretary of State for Foreign and Commonwealth Affairs Requests and Requires in the Name of Her Majesty . . ." Decca hesitated to approve the original title *Their Satanic Majesties Request and Require*, fearing it struck a little too close to home.

As the title suggests, *Their Satanic Majesties Request* conjured up all manner of demons for the Stones. Brian Jones felt from the outset that the album represented an ill-conceived departure from the Stones' musical roots. Yet, now all but resigned to a secondary position in the band, he showed up dutifully at Olympic Studios in London to contribute his formidable skills on every instrument from the guitar to the Mellotron and sitar.

For Andrew Oldham *Their Satanic Majesties Request* represented nothing less than the closing chapter in his long relationship with the Stones. Ever since Allen Klein entered the picture, Oldham's grip on the Stones—and on reality—had been steadily slipping.

By the summer of 1967 Oldham had squandered much of his fortune and all of his creative energy on drugs. His system was so inured to chemicals that by now no pharmaceutical could lift his spirits. Ironically, he owed much of his anxiety during this period to the Redlands bust and the headline-making drug trials that followed. Fearing that the Stones were bent on self-destruction, Oldham felt utterly powerless to stop them. He reacted by withdrawing from the scene, leaving the old publicity war-horse Les Perrin to handle hostile members of the press.

A psychiatrist diagnosed Oldham as suffering from a textbook case of clinical depression. His recommendation: electroshock therapy. Each Friday afternoon Oldham would go to London's Bethan hospital. There electrodes would be attached to his temples, and a device placed in his mouth so that he could not shatter his teeth or bite off his tongue. Then a jolt of electricity would be sent coursing through his body, often rendering him unconscious.

After each series of shock treatments Oldham would be driven to a convent in London's Highgate district where he spent the rest of the weekend being cared for by nuns.

During the week Oldham functioned surprisingly well. But when he arrived at Olympic studios to do business as usual, it was painfully clear that Mick no longer had any use for him. Week after week during the recording of *Their Satanic Majesties Request*, band members kept Oldham waiting in the studio for hours. When they did show up, often in the middle of the night, they made a point of dismissing Oldham's ideas out of hand.

Photographer Gered Mankowitz, who was present for several of the *Satanic Majesties* recording sessions, recalled the night when Mick came into the studio with photographer Michael Cooper and told Oldham what the album's cover would look like. "When it came to the look, the image of the Stones, they had always deferred to Andrew's genius," said Mankowitz. "But not this time. By not consulting Andrew on this Mick was basically telling him he was finished. I remembered the look on Andrew's face so clearly. He knew what was going on, and that he was powerless to do anything about it."

Oldham persisted for several more weeks until the band agreed to include two blues numbers on the album, songs more in keeping with the Stones' musical past. When it came time to record these tracks, however, they played them as badly as they could. "Finally," Ian Stewart remembered, "Andrew just walked out."

It was *finis* for Oldham and the Stones. The band's business affairs were now solely in the hands of Allen Klein. "Andrew was a mass of energy, ideas, and madness," said his friend Mankowitz. "He was bonkers, in a way. A very difficult man to deal with. Yet working with Andrew could also be magic."

At the time Jagger claimed that the group had simply outgrown its need for Oldham. "If someone opens a door for you," observed Mankowitz, "and *everything* you want is on the other side of that door, then you can't dismiss him as a doorman."

In mid-September of 1967 the Stones converged on New York to shoot a cover for *Their Satanic Majesties Request* and to meet with Allen Klein about their divorce from Oldham. Arriving at Kennedy Airport, Mick and Keith were once again subjected to a degrading customs search and interminable questioning. This time they were allowed to remain in the U.S. for no more than two weeks—more than enough time to accomplish what they wanted this trip. There was an ominous-sounding caveat: Jagger and Richards would not be permitted to return to America until immigration officials had reviewed the outcome of the various drug charges that had been brought against them in the United Kingdom.

From Klein's offices the following day the Stones announced Oldham's departure to the press. Guided by Les Perrin, most members of the group struck a conciliatory tone. Most, but not all: Mick told newspaper reporters that he felt Oldham had become superfluous. "We were practically doing everything ourselves anyway," said Jagger. "Allen Klein is really just a financial scene. We'll really be managing ourselves."

Oldham claimed that it was he who left the Stones, not vice versa. "We just weren't on the same wavelength anymore," he said. "We'd gone as far as we could go together. It was time to move on." As much as he tried to conceal his pain, Oldham felt betrayed by Jagger. "It was excruciating for Andrew," said his wife, Sheila. "He was devastated by the whole thing, and I don't think he recovered."

When he went to collect his share of the group's proceeds, Oldham was shocked to find that the $1.25 million in royalties (the equivalent of nearly $10 million today) was not where he thought it would be. Oldham and Jagger had both assumed the money had been deposited in the Stones' British holding company, Nanker Phelge Music. Instead, Klein had the $1.25 million deposited in Nanker Phelge USA. As luck would have it, Nanker Phelge USA was run and owned by none other than Allen Klein.

In what would be the first in a long series of legal skirmishes, Oldham sued Klein, and eventually a settlement was reached. For the sum of $1 million Oldham officially stepped aside as comanager.

Klein controlled the purse strings for the time being, but

for all intents and purposes the Rolling Stones were managing themselves. Or, to be more accurate, they were being managed by Jagger.

Now that the Stones were forced to move out of Old-ham's offices, Jagger's first task as de facto manager was to find a new headquarters for the group. The Stones' unsavory reputation preceded them; several landlords refused to let Jagger even look at vacant office space.

Accordingly, Jagger rented space in a Maddox Street town house that had once been the home of a scandalous figure from another era: Lillie Langtry. (Even then, the landlord was told only that the space would house offices for an unnamed "music company"). Mick's antique-filled upstairs office had actually been one of the rooms where Langtry carried on her notorious affair with the very-married King Edward VII. Their downstairs neighbors were another sixties group of note, the Kinks.

By way of setting himself apart from his fellow Stones, Mick hired a "personal assistant": Jo Bergman, a cheerful, frizzy-haired San Franciscan who had once run the Beatles fan club for Brian Epstein and had become a close companion of Marianne's. Bergman, later to become a top executive in Warner Records' video division, was paid out of the Stones' collective kitty but answered to only one person: Mick Jagger.

Within days of moving into their new quarters on Maddox Street, the Stones were rocked by yet another judge's decision—this time concerning drug charges stemming from the raid on Brian Jones's apartment. After months of plea-bargaining Jones donned a conservative pinstripe banker's suit and drove to Inner London Sessions court in his gleaming silver Rolls-Royce sedan.

Before court chairman R. E. Seaton, Jones took full responsibility for any marijuana smoking that might have occurred at his apartment, immediately letting his codefendant, Prince "Stash" Klossowski de Rola, off the hook. In exchange for this and a guilty plea to cannabis possession, authorities dropped the more serious speed and cocaine possession charges.

Jones threw himself on the mercy of the court. Citing his client's precarious mental health, Brian's legal counsel, James Comyn, called Jones's psychiatrist to the stand. Dr. Leonard Henry testified that any prison time would "completely destroy his mental health, and he would go into psychotic depression, as he could not possibly stand the stigma of a prison sentence and he might well attempt to injure himself."

The judge was unmoved. Citing what he called a growing drug "canker," Seaton vowed to make an example of Jones. He sentenced Brian to six months at the dreaded Wormwood Scrubs prison. Shouts of "No, no" went up from fans in the gallery. Denied bail, Brian was handcuffed and led to a holding cell as dozens of teenage girls filed out of the courtroom in tears.

None of the Stones were on hand in court to lend moral support to Jones, contributing to his acute sense of abandonment—and his swelling paranoia. Brian even began to suspect that Jagger and Richards might be behind his arrest.

There was one Jagger present at Brian's trial, however: Mick's younger brother, Chris, who with several others blocked the prison van that was to ferry Jones and other prisoners to Wormwood Scrubs. They stood their ground, shouting protests at the police before being carted off to jail themselves for abusive behavior.

Outraged at the severity of the sentence, attorneys Comyn and Henry pleaded with a High Court judge to grant Brian bail while his case was being appealed. Their request was granted, provided that Jones agree to be examined by a court-appointed psychiatrist. After a single terror-filled night in the dank, almost medieval confines of Wormwood Scrubs, Brian was released. That night he picked up two teenage girls, purchased a fresh supply of LSD, and celebrated his release with a psychedelic threesome. When

Jones turned violent, both girls fled from his apartment, naked and bleeding.

By comparison, Mick, Marianne, and her two-year-old son, Nicholas, were leading a life of domestic bliss at 48 Cheyne Walk. Jagger had taken a paternal interest in the boy—in the coming two years he would teach Nicholas, among other important things, how to urinate standing up.

Although Mick's affection for the child was genuine, Nicholas spent weekends with his biological father and most of his time at Cheyne Walk in the care of nannies. After Faithfull broke up with Jagger in 1970, her addiction to drugs became so powerful that Nicholas was taken to live with his grandmother the baroness. Dunbar took custody of Nicholas when he was six, and raised his son from that point on.

Entering the Cheyne Walk house was like stepping into a pasha's harem, or an opium den. Blinds shut out the midday sun, and only a small table lamp illuminated the huge living room, with its walk-in fireplace and massive furniture. "Mick likes as little light as possible," remarked a visitor to the house. "The house has a feeling as heavy as incense, slightly opulent, very comfortable."

Padding about the house in women's bedroom slippers, Mick, added the guest, "walks like a housewife." Faithfull and Jagger seemed dwarfed by their Brobdingnagian surroundings: "There is a faint impression of both Mick and Marianne themselves being the children of the house rather than the owners. And, like children out on a spree, they have the money to spend on what they fancy."

One game they enjoyed—a game Mick would continue to play with the other women in his adult life—was dress-up. Just as Anita Pallenberg routinely exchanged clothes with both Brian and Keith, Marianne and Jagger enjoyed rummaging through each other's closets in search of just the right thing to wear. The slightly built Mick, who now wore heavy kohl makeup around his eyes, would wriggle into Marianne's dresses, blouses, skirts, and furs, top them off with a feather boa and lots of jewelry—and then slink about the house. If Marianne was lucky, he might entertain her with his Tina Turner impersonation.

Casual cross-dressing of this sort had always been popular among the British upper classes, and often gave no clue as to the participants' true sexual orientation. In the case of Mick and Marianne it indicated an open relationship in every sense of the word.

More than once Mick returned home unannounced to find Marianne in bed with another woman. Rather than exploding in a rage, his reaction was to strip off his clothes and join them.

"I did have girlfriends and I did have affairs with them," said Faithfull. "Mick knew about my girlfriends. His attitude was that he'd much prefer me to have a girlfriend than a boyfriend. Same as I preferred him to be in bed with a man rather than a woman."

Over their years together he would allegedly be found in bed with both. On one occasion Jagger was reportedly discovered in bed with Eric Clapton, then lead guitarist with the hugely successful "supergroup" Cream. "Eric and Mick were caught in bed together, it's true," claimed Marianne's ex-husband John Dunbar. "It was a very narcissistic scene, very ambivalent sexually. Bisexuality and androgyny are not only accepted, but they are encouraged."

Others close to both men were not aware of any such relationship between Clapton and Jagger; they could only confirm that the two men were close friends. They also remembered that, when it came to his appearance, Clapton was every bit as camp as Jagger in the mid-1960s. Chrissie Shrimpton recalled that Eric was the first man she ever saw who wore nail polish and back-combed his hair—"quite a personal statement at the time."

Dunbar's assertion did not surprise writer Victor Bockris, who covered the late-1960s rock scene in London. "There was a lot of extremely hedonistic, dope-induced behavior at the time. Clapton was very much a part of that," said Bockris, pointing to Clapton's longtime heroin addiction. "Nothing was sacred. The idea was to break every taboo.

This was a time period when there was no sense of finger-pointing if you were bisexual. It wasn't perceived as something to be ashamed of. Everyone was experimenting, including heterosexual rock stars."

Why Jagger and Clapton? "They were both being worshiped, and they were isolated by sycophants," observed Dunbar. "After a while rock stars of their magnitude begin to believe their own press. They become deluded, as fooled by it as the public is."

Dunbar offered another theory for such an affair: "I think it has a lot to do with Mick's attitude that all women are groupies. It's a more equal mating with other men because they're your peers. I'm only speculating, but I've heard that's what he believed."

Marianne added that homosexuality is a more accepted part of English life, and that "it's at the heart of narcissism. It's just the desire, a very strong desire, to have people be in love with you. Whether it's a man or a woman isn't really important."

During this time the convent-bred aristocrat played cultural Pygmalion to Jagger's willing Galatea. Marianne escorted him to the theater and the opera, providing him with a running commentary on each production. Once he saw Rudolf Nureyev perform onstage with Margot Fonteyn, Jagger was instantly smitten—with Nureyev. Mick rhapsodized repeatedly about Nureyev's power and grace onstage, and admitted that he often fantasized about being in the toe shoes of the great Russian dancer.

On one of their many cultural forays Jagger and Marianne ventured backstage to meet Nureyev. "It was fascinating to watch," said a witness to the meeting, "but something clicked between Nureyev and Jagger instantly. I felt a little sorry for Marianne, she seemed sort of left out in the cold." For her part Marianne was struck by what she felt was an uncanny resemblance between the two men. "My God," Faithfull told friends, "Mick and Nureyev even *look* alike. I mean, those lips!" When she told Jagger this, he kiddingly struck a balletic pose. "Do you really think so?" Increasingly, Jagger would become drawn to people who seemed to reflect his own image. (The personal relationship between Nureyev and Jagger intensified over the years, reaching its peak sometime during the ambisexual seventies in New York.)

That autumn of 1967 Mick decided that a Queen Anne mansion on Cheyne Walk would not suffice for a man of his stature. Keith had Redlands, Bill Wyman had Gedding Hall in Suffolk, and now Jagger, too, wanted a country house. "Jagger still desperately needed to be a true English gentleman," said his friend John Michel. "And for that you must have a country house."

A relative of Michel's just happened to have one for sale near the Berkshire town of Newbury in south central England. Mick and Marianne drove down in a caravan that included Gibbs, Keith and Anita, Robert Fraser (newly sprung from prison), and the American writer Terry (*Candy*) Southern. After a half-dozen pub stops along the way, they arrived at their destination four hours late, and well after sunset.

Even in the pitch darkness it was hard not to be impressed with Stargroves. An Elizabethan manor of kingly proportions, it had once been the headquarters of Oliver Cromwell. It was in need of some refurbishing, but its stables and outbuildings set on forty thickly wooded acres made it all but irresistible. Besides, it dwarfed both Richards's Redlands *and* Wyman's Gedding Hall. Mick had to have it.

Jagger was willing to pay the full asking price, but the owner had his doubts. A pillar of the local community, he was reluctant to sell the cherished family home to a rock singer—particularly one as notorious as Jagger.

Jagger took the owner by the arm and, leading him through the house, described what changes he intended to make to restore Stargroves to its sixteenth-century grandeur. Most of the renovations Jagger and Faithfull had in mind were precisely what the owner himself had wished to do—if he'd had the money. Mick bought the house for the then-substantial sum of $55,000.

Mick quickly lost interest in the property, however, and wound up spending little time there. His friends, on the other hand, made themselves right at home. In 1967 and 1968 Stargroves would serve as the starting-off point for a series of "New Age" hippie caravans led by John Michel. Shunning modern transportation, the golden children of Britain's aristocracy journeyed through the English heartland riding in horsecarts and aboard barges, searching for UFOs, ley lines (straight lines running through the countryside that supposedly intersected at UFO landing spots), and other totems of the Age of Aquarius.

The Chelsea set had become so enthralled with the idea of UFOs that a house on Tottenham Court Road was turned into the UFO Club, where, said Michel, "contact with alien minds was stimulated by flashing lights and the weird sounds of Pink Floyd. Those who wanted the real thing took their acid tabs to ancient hilltops in Wiltshire and Somerset, the renowned centers of UFO experiences."

Michel and his friends came to view their expeditions "not as holidays, but as essays in Grail questing." Sir Mark Palmer, owner of the English Boy modeling agency, brought along some of his titled young friends, including Julian Ormsby-Gore and Viscount Gormanston. Lord Harlech and his daughter Jane Ormsby-Gore were also among the New Age grail-questers.

Pushing their carts out of ruts and ditches, their silk scarves trailing in the mud, these New Age pioneers more closely resembled a ragtag band of gypsies than the cream of British nobility. When they arrived at Stargroves, the local town council was in an uproar; it took the intervention of Stargroves' esteemed former owner, now a buddy of Jagger's, to calm down the villagers.

On one of the pilgrimages that included Jagger and Faithfull, they hit the jackpot. Camping at a spot called Glastonbury Tor, Michel claimed the group saw "almost nightly displays of UFO lights, and once the luminous, cigar-shaped 'mother ship' with smaller lights going in and out of it."

Not all their expeditions were so fruitful. Heading off toward Hereford in search of ley lines, Mick, Marianne, Keith, Anita Pallenberg, Kenneth Anger, and assorted aristocrats and malcontents got sidetracked in Gloucestershire. Jagger, a lifelong cricket fanatic, recalled that a famous cricketer named Tom Graveney owned a nearby pub. They dropped in to pay their respects, and wound up spending the afternoon. "Graveney was not even sighted," said Michel, "much less any UFOs!"

On these trips Mick sometimes struck a comically effete pose. While the others were slogging through muck, Jagger put one hand on his hip and daintily refused to soil his velvet frock. "Mick had a witty, self-deprecating humor," recalled Michel. "He is a natural comedian, really. The quintessence of camp."

Jagger's interest in UFOs stemmed from a natural curiosity and, as Cecil Beaton had observed earlier, an analytical mind. "Mick is the Great Observer," said Michel. "He is interested in everything that goes on around him. He asks questions constantly. He takes nothing for granted. He's thinking all the time, and he wants to know what everyone else is thinking."

Michel felt there was also something of an ulterior motive behind Jagger's interest in unexplained phenomena. "Above all else Mick is a showman. He is interested in presentation, in glamor," said Michel. "I got the feeling that everything he learns he somehow incorporates in his work." It would not be long before Michel's theory was proven correct.

Whatever his motives, Jagger did plunge headfirst into the worlds of mysticism and the occult. Marching in lock-step with their peers, Mick and Marianne had already embraced astrology; they charted their every move according to the *I Ching*.

* * *

Miles, Mick's friend and owner of the Indica bookshop, noticed a distinct change in Jagger's reading habits. Always a voracious reader, Mick had long had a fondness for Ginsberg, Burroughs, Kerouac, Ferlinghetti, and the other Beat writers and poets. But by late 1967 his interests had veered in another, more sinister direction.

Jagger began calling Miles with some bizarre requests. "Mick had an account with us," recalled Miles, "and he started ordering *lots* of occult stuff during this time." There were requisite titles like *The Book of the Damned* and *The Golden Bough*, but Jagger also purchased *Manuscripts of Witchcraft, Fairy Faith in Celtic, Masks of God, Mysterium Coniunctionis*, and *The Master and Margarita* (a Russian novel that served as the inspiration for the Stones' later hit "Sympathy for the Devil").

Ever the chameleon, Jagger had been searching for a way to outrage and offend his fans' parents, and nothing fit the bill better than Satanism. The black arts offered it all: heresy, violence, spectacle, and—best of all—sex.

What better role model for rock's quintessential antihero than the Antichrist? Jagger was encouraged in this by Kenneth Anger, a former Hollywood child actor turned master of the occult, and arguably the most disquieting member of Gibbs's inner circle. Anger was a disciple of the notorious Edwardian black magician Aleister Crowley and, like Crowley, claimed to be a magus, a kind of satanic wizard of the highest degree.

Whether or not he actually possessed satanic powers, Anger did his best to keep Jagger and his friends off-balance. He would often appear without warning and then vanish just as suddenly. When Robert Fraser unveiled several all-white sculptures by his clients John Lennon and Yoko Ono, all the guests were told to wear white. Anger materialized in their midst—clad in black, of course—was spotted by Lennon, Yoko, Fraser, and half the guests, only to disappear. He later claimed to have been out of the country the entire time.

On another occasion Fraser, who stammered slightly,

opened an envelope to find a razor and a note from Anger: *The final solution to your stuttering problem.*

Foremost among Anger's admirers was Anita Pallenberg. A willing student, she hung on his every spell and incantation. Over the next several years she would herself become a polished practitioner of the black arts. "Some people do have the power," she said of Anger. "If you practice it a lot, you can do it."

Anger was also an underground filmmaker of some note. Not surprisingly, Anger's cult classics such as *Fireworks* and *Scorpio Rising* were heavily laced with gay sex and occultism.

For years Anger had been working on a cinematic tribute to the devil entitled *Lucifer Rising*. In the title role Anger cast Bobby Beausoleil, a Hollywood-handsome guitarist with the rock group Love. Beausoleil may have gotten a little carried away with his portrayal: After a heated argument with Anger on the set, he grabbed several cans of film that had already been shot and burned them. Several days later he committed a brutal murder after which he scrawled satanic references on the wall in his victim's blood. (When Charles Manson was tried for the sensational murders of Sharon Tate and five others, it was revealed that Beausoleil had been a close Manson Family friend).

With Beausoleil out of the picture Anger turned to Jagger for the role of Lucifer. In truth Anger was intrigued by the mesmeric sway Jagger held over his audiences. The magus saw Mick as nothing less than a modern day Lucifer, a demonic pied piper capable of luring millions over to the Dark Side.

Mick was flattered. He volunteered to write music for *Lucifer Rising* and even took charge of the sound recording, but when Anger kept pressuring him to act in the movie, Jagger reluctantly bowed out.

Anger was displeased, and that in and of itself was enough to cause Mick some concern. Once, Anita and Keith had taken a number of Anger's books and talismans and loaded them in their car. When they became involved in an auto accident, they placed a frantic call to Mick. "Then we did this ritual fire burning of all Anger's stuff that was in the car," said Pallenberg. "But that was just panic, and to be safe."

Two years later Anger would salvage the music Mick had written for *Lucifer Rising*, as well as Bobby Beausoleil's performance. He used them in a weird film called *Invocation of My Demon Brother*, which also juxtaposed Stones concert footage with stomach-turning newsreel footage of the carnage in Vietnam.

Anita, meanwhile, was fully immersed in practicing the black arts. Speeding along in her limousine on the road between Marrakech and Fez, Pallenberg came upon an accident victim bleeding to death at the side of the road. She ordered her driver to stop, got out, and dipped her silk scarf in the man's blood.

It was a widely held belief that a dying person's blood was imbued with mystical qualities. Anita used this scarf to cast spells on her enemies and, when she briefly came to believe that Mick might be Satan's emissary on earth, over Jagger as well.

As the release of *Their Satanic Majesties Request* approached, Jagger dreamt of a critical and commercial success as colossal as *Sergeant Pepper*. At this point the Beatles and Stones were closer than ever, clandestinely contributing to one another's projects, sharing at times what seemed to Mick a common musical vision.

With Brian Epstein and Andrew Oldham now out of the picture, the world's two reigning supergroups stood at a crossroads. Mick proposed that the Beatles and the Stones pool their resources to open a studio and management office. Lennon and McCartney were initially thrilled with the idea, but after they had picked out a site for the studio, the ambitious plan fizzled.

From this point on, however, they agreed to time the release of their records so that they would not always be competing head-to-head as they had in the past. "It was an incredibly shrewd strategy," said one of their former executives. "That way the Beatles and the Stones never deprived each other of a Number One hit."

After toying with the idea of renaming the new album *The Rolling Stones' Cosmic Christmas* to take advantage of the holiday-season release date, *Their Satanic Majesties Request* hit record stores on December 12, 1967. It would be difficult to imagine an album produced under more trying circumstances. Oldham's departure, the psychically draining drug trials, and Jagger's obsession with besting *Sergeant Pepper* all served to prolong the making of the album over ten months and drive the budget well past the then-outrageous $100,000 mark. It was, as Mick observed, a miracle that it was ever completed at all.

It had been nearly a year since their last hit-filled album, *Between the Buttons*, and the publicity generated by the Stones' legal tribulations only served to whet the record-buying public's appetite further. The huge advance orders for *Their Satanic Majesties* had raised Jagger's hopes, but they were soon dashed. The album was an unmitigated catastrophe, universally panned for being precisely what it was—a feeble imitation of the Beatles' brilliant *Sergeant Pepper*.

One did not even have to remove the record from its sleeve to realize what the Stones were up to. Jagger had employed Michael Cooper, the same photographer who had created the stunningly psychedelic *Sergeant Pepper* album cover (which, incidentally, included a reference to the Stones) to conjure up another whimsically surreal image for the *Satanic Majesties* jacket.

To do so Cooper imported a special 3-D camera from Japan at a cost of $40,000. The result: a headache-inducing three-dimensional portrait of the Stones encircled by a kaleidoscopic blur of fruit and flowers. In the center foreground Jagger stares intently from beneath his wizard's cap emblazoned with a crescent moon. The others, clad in all manner of medieval and Elizabethan finery, try to look equally serious against a backdrop featuring mountain peaks, heavenly spheres, and an onion-domed mosque. By way of reciprocity, pictures of the Beatles were hidden among the flowers on the cover. A maze was planned for the inside cover, with a nude photograph of Jagger at its center. As much as he admired the photograph, Decca Chairman Sir Edward Lewis yanked it from the layout at the last minute.

The Stones came to regard *Their Satanic Majesties* as far and away their worst album, though it did produce one memorable hit: "She's a Rainbow," a pretty Elizabethan-sounding tune reminiscent of "Lady Jane" and "Ruby Tuesday." With its thinly disguised references to LSD and sex ("She comes in colors"), "She's a Rainbow" was, said one critic, "a suitable flower-power type song." The rest of the album, unfortunately, fell flat.

December 12 was indeed a day of decision for the Stones, and not just because it was the release date of their new album. As a million copies of *Their Satanic Majesties* went on sale in the U.S., Jagger sat among the spectators in the Court of Appeals waiting to hear Brian's fate.

As before, the testimony of experts as to Jones's mental state would weigh heavily in the court's findings. The court-appointed expert in forensic psychiatry, Dr. Walter Neustatter, had examined Brian four times before rendering his opinion.

Dr. Neustatter concurred with Jones's own doctors that he suffered from free-floating anxiety and paranoia. He then offered a Freudian explanation for Brian's self-destructive behavior. "He is very involved with Oedipal fixations," Neustatter testified. "He experiences strong resentment toward his dominant and controlling mother who rejected him and blatantly favored his sister. Mr. Jones is, at present, in an extremely precarious state. . . . His grasp on reality is fragile." Without further intense psychotherapy, Neustatter concluded, Brian's prognosis was "very poor. Indeed, it is very likely that his imprisonment could precipitate a complete break with reality, a psychotic breakdown, and significantly increase the suicidal risk for this man."

Lord Chief Justice Parker threw out Jones's nine-month

prison sentence. In lieu of hard time Jones received three years probation and a one-thousand-pound fine. "Remember, this is a degree of mercy which the court has shown," warned Lord Parker. "It is not a let-off. You cannot go boasting, saying you have been let off. You are still under the control of the court. If you fail to cooperate with the probation officer or you commit another offense, you will be brought back and punished."

As he left the court, Brian glanced over at the only other Stone in the room and smiled. Brian was, said his psychiatrist, "pathetically grateful" that Jagger had finally come to lend him moral support.

The next day Fleet Street had a field day with the psychiatrists' testimony, printing large chunks of it under the blaring headline THE MIND OF BRIAN JONES. Publicly humiliated, Brian went on another spree. His pharmaceutical favorites: Quaaludes alternating with amphetamines, usually washed down with Scotch. Barely thirty-six hours after he had narrowly escaped a prison term, Jones was back in the hospital.

Furious, Jagger reacted by calling a press conference to discuss the new album. "There's a tour coming up," he told reporters. "There are obvious difficulties. One of them is with Brian, who obviously can't leave the country."

This would be a recurrent theme, as Les Perrin's office issued press release after release stating that the Stones would soon hit the road again—with or without Brian. According to "Spanish Tony" Sanchez, a longtime Stones insider and sometime drug-supplier, Mick saw Jones "as a threat. It could be only because he knew what no one outside the Stones' immediate circle knew—that Brian really was what Jagger pretended to be."

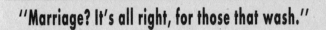

"Marriage? It's all right, for those that wash."

It was arguably the single most tumultuous twelve-month period since the end of the Second World War. The year 1968 was chockablock with milestone events: the assassinations of Martin Luther King and Bobby Kennedy, President Lyndon Johnson's decision not to run for reelection, bloody clashes between police and demonstrators outside the Democratic Convention in Chicago, race riots in Washington, Detroit, and Los Angeles—all set against the bloody backdrop of Vietnam.

The peace and love generation, once content with placing daisies in rifle barrels, had now taken to the streets. From Berkeley to Paris to London antiwar protestors were shouting slogans, throwing rocks, smashing windows, storming police barricades.

In liberal salons everywhere the only guests more sought after than Maoists were scowling, gun-toting members of the Black Panther party. It was the year of Radical Chic.

Jagger, who had been calling for revolution ever since his televised "summit" with members of Britain's power elite, seized the moment. When antiwar protestors stormed the U.S. embassy on Grosvenor Square that spring, Jagger rode to the affair in his Bentley, then jumped out and mingled among the rioters. Between signing autographs and allowing himself to be shot by press photographers, Jagger joined arms with demonstrators and actually led the protest before climbing back into his limousine. (A young Rhodes scholar would organize another round of demonstrations at the embassy that fall. His name: Bill Clinton).

When he got back to Cheyne Walk, Jagger sat down and began scribbling the incendiary lyrics to "Street Fighting Man." When the single was released in the U.S. the following August, urban tensions were running so high that many radio stations simply refused to air it.

It was about this time that Tom Driberg began his political seduction of Jagger. Ever since their first meeting, when Driberg had complimented Jagger on his physical endowments, the two men had forged a close personal bond. Mick felt a deep gratitude to Driberg for having stood up in Parliament and, at some considerable political risk, criticized the courts for their treatment of Jagger and Richards after the Redlands bust.

Nearly every week the aging homosexual politician and the flamboyant rock star shared a table for two at the curiously named Gay Hussar, a Hungarian restaurant popular with politicians and journalists. Often, Driberg and Jagger would spend long afternoons or evenings together at Cheyne Walk.

Inevitably, dinner conversation at Cheyne Walk turned to politics. In sharp contrast to the other Stones the former London School of Economics student desperately wanted to be taken seriously outside the sphere of music. He was not unaware of his influence among the young, and how that influence might be harnessed for some greater purpose.

Mick and Marianne grilled Driberg relentlessly about the inner workings of Westminster. They could not understand why the government seemed to be so unresponsive to the people's needs. They wanted to know what, if anything, Driberg or any member of Parliament, for that matter, could do to end racism and the war in Vietnam.

Jagger, a self-described anarchist, parroted the slogans and leftist rhetoric of the era. Yet he seemed earnest in his desire to hone his ideas. He had once confessed his desire to "learn to be a gentleman." Now Mick yearned to be a sophisticated political thinker as well.

Finally, Driberg blurted out the obvious question at one of their get-togethers: "Mick, why don't you go into politics?"

Jagger raised his eyebrows, leaned back in his chair, and tried to look surprised. It wasn't as if the idea hadn't already occurred to him. "If a man with anarchistic feelings did go into politics," he asked, "where would he fit?"

Driberg, ex-chairman of Britain's Labor party, didn't hesitate to answer. "The Labor party, of course. Labor is the only hope."

The old party war-horse was practically vibrating with excitement at the idea of Jagger standing for a seat in Parliament. He could bring thousands, perhaps millions, of young voters along with him, breathing new life into the party's left wing and forcing the more centrist Labor prime minister Harold Wilson to take notice.

Driberg, the future Lord Bradwell, was so caught up in the moment, he actually told Jagger he felt revolution was right around the corner. "I know that's the view of some of the Trotskyites, that it is all breaking up and loosening up," Driberg said. "And the Labor party is where a young man should be when it happens."

Did Driberg agree with the Trotskyites, Jagger wanted to know. Did he feel the social unrest would lead to revolution in England—"not necessarily fighting in the streets, mind you, but revolutionary change?"

Driberg would later say that he was "carried along" by Jagger's zeal, not to mention his sexual charisma. "One begins to share that revolutionary hope when one is in the company of someone like Mick." Downing another glass of claret, Driberg told Jagger exactly what he wanted to hear. "The Trotskyites may be right," said Tom. "Revolution may be starting at this moment."

Once Driberg had departed, Mick turned to Marianne. "I'm going into politics," he said. It was the first of a dozen or more such proclamations he would issue over the coming months.

Jagger's coquettish posturing frustrated Driberg, but the

seasoned pol persisted in his efforts to lure Mick into the Labor party and convince him to stand for a seat in Parliament. Over fishbowl-sized glasses of red wine Jagger now insisted that there was no way to bring about significant change by working within the system. Caught up in the from-the-hip rhetoric that made intelligent political discussions all but impossible, Mick now advocated tearing the system to the ground and starting over.

Jagger's passionate call for insurrection should have come as no surprise to Driberg—by now "Street Fighting Man" had become the anthem of barricade-crashers everywhere. Yet, for the first time, Driberg was nonplused. He had matched wits on the floor of Commons with every political figure since Winston Churchill, but he proved no match for Mick. Jagger pointed out that the Labor government of Harold Wilson supported American policy in Vietnam and sided with Nigeria in the Biafran War—policies which Driberg abhorred. Before long the rock star had the Labor stalwart doubting his own party.

At this moment Driberg hit on a stunning idea: the formation of a new political party, with Mick Jagger as its leader. Driberg contacted a number of political allies, and found them receptive to the idea. All that remained was a nod of approval from Mick.

One can only speculate as to Driberg's true motives. As a double agent, did he wish to tip Britain's delicate political balance in the direction of anarchy? Or did he wish to flush the revolutionaries out into the open, where they could be more closely monitored by Britain's security agencies? Certainly, future "Lord of the Spies" Driberg would have benefited from either scenario, or both.

Unfortunately for Driberg, Jagger managed to elude capture. During one of his attempts to corner Mick at Cheyne Walk, Driberg encountered a sobbing Marianne. Mick was busy rehearsing and had left her alone. Claiming she was broke, Faithfull implored Driberg to go to the corner pub and buy her a few bottles of red wine.

(Driberg remained close with both Jagger and Faithfull,

even after the couple's 1970 breakup. Years later he invited
Marianne and Mick's brother, Chris, to a dinner party for
W. H. Auden at the Gay Hussar. Seated next to Marianne,
Auden leaned over and asked, "When you're smuggling
drugs, do you pack them up your arse?")

As for Driberg's infatuation with Jagger, it only endeared
him to the older man. According to Stones intimate Spanish Tony Sanchez, "Many of Mick's closest friends are men
who he knows long to go to bed with him. The feminine
side of his complex personality seems to delight in their
flattery and admiration."

Politics and revolution aside, Jagger had more pressing
issues on his mind—namely, scoring another No. 1 hit.
They had a number of Top Ten hits, but it had been two
years since the Stones actually topped the single charts
with "Paint It Black." In the wake of the wan *Satanic Majesties* album, the band was already being consigned to the
scrap heap by critics eager to move on to the next hot
group. "We *had* to have a Number One hit," recalled Wyman.

It was Wyman himself who stumbled onto their next
chart-topper while "mucking around" with a few chords on
the studio piano. Jones and Watts began building on the
riff, and when Jagger and Richards walked in a half hour
later, they were "floored" by the sound. Within an hour
Jagger had written the lyrics for "Jumpin' Jack Flash."

Musically, the song marked a much-needed return to
their rock roots. The strangely skewed lyrics, akin to a de-
mented nursery rhyme, cast Mick as one part Nimble Jack
and four parts spawn of Satan. With their new producer,
Jimmy Miller, at the controls, the Stones laid down a track
so perfect that even Brian Jones began phoning people
with the news that the Stones were back in the rock and
roll business.

Not one to leave anything to chance, Jagger hired ITV's
Michael Lindsay-Hogg to produce a promotional film
clip—forerunner of a modern video—to hype the song on
television. Jones, his hair dyed brown for the occasion,

wore green-rimmed sunglasses and orange lipstick. Meanwhile, Mick, wearing a tattoo on his forehead and gold war paint, glared into the camera like a modern-day Rasputin. The record shot straight to No. 1 on both sides of the Atlantic. For Jagger it was truly a "gas gas gas."

Despite his enthusiasm over "Jumpin' Jack Flash" Brian soon resumed his role as a major thorn in Jagger's side. To mollify him Mick agreed to let Brian contribute a song to the upcoming *Beggars Banquet* album (the oxymoronic title with medieval overtones, suggested by Christopher Gibbs, struck a suitably cynical note).

When guitarists Eric Clapton and Dave Mason were brought in to contribute to the album, Jones became unraveled. Convinced they were ganging up on him, Brian confronted Jagger. In the studio control booth Jones accused Jagger and Richards of ignoring the tunes he had written so they could hog the song royalties. Jagger replied that he had become a "whiny pain in the ass" who was no longer good enough to be a Stone. "Christ, Mick," he replied, "it's my fucking band!"

Strangely enough, Jagger had resisted Allen Klein's entreaties to dump Jones. Mick was not known for his loyalty, but even he could not bring himself to betray the original Stone. For the most part Jagger merely ignored him. At one session Jones walked up to Mick and asked him what to play.

"You're a member of the band, Brian, play whatever you want," Jagger replied. Jones began playing, and Mick abruptly cut him off. "No, Brian, not that—that's no good."

So what should he play, Jones asked. And again, Mick told him to play whatever he wished. Jones began one more time, and Mick stopped him yet again. "No," said Jagger, shaking his head in exasperation, "that's no good, either, Brian."

Jones put down the guitar and moved over to the conga drums. As if he were dealing with a small child, Jagger thumped out a rhythm and instructed Brian to follow it.

Brian, biting his lip until he drew blood, tried and tried, but to no avail. Jagger could not be pleased.

"Brian ended up drunk in the corner," a musician told the rock magazine *Creem*, "stamping his foot out of beat, and blowing harmonica with a bloodied mouth. Jagger stared at him icily, threw his coat over his shoulder, and exited the studio."

It may not have been deliberate, but some began to view Mick's treatment of Brian as a subtle form of psychological torture. In this Keith was a coconspirator. At times the other Stones would not let Brian in on recording dates until after they were finished in the studio. Then they would call him in to lay down his tracks on sitar or guitar or dulcimer alone. Often he would be banished to another cubicle, where he sobbed softly as his fellow band members laughed and joked in the main studio.

There were other complications in Brian's life. That spring his lover-of-the-moment, Linda Keith, decided that he was seeing other women. She took an overdose of sleeping pills, stripped off all her clothes, phoned all her friends with news that she was killing herself, then bolted the door so police would be forced to break it down. They did, and she eventually recovered—but not before the newspapers had a field day with the lurid story. Brian was summarily evicted from his apartment.

On May 21 Les Perrin called Mick with the news: Brian had been busted again. This time the police had arrived in the early morning, and when Jones refused to open the door, they crawled in through the window. They found a small chunk of hashish hidden inside a ball of yarn that had been stuffed in the back of a bureau drawer. Jones claimed he had never seen the ball of yarn; it was, he told Perrin, a frame-up.

Brian was released on two thousand pounds bail and ordered to appear for his trial in September. He celebrated the following night by going to the Revolution Club in Mayfair, gobbling down several Quaaludes, and crashing unconscious to the floor.

Over the next few weeks Brian was even more psychotic than usual. He called up people at any hour of the day or night and ranted on about the way he was being persecuted by the police, and ignored by Jagger.

The latest bust spelled an end to the Stones' plans for a tour to promote *Beggars Banquet*—unless the band decided to tour without Brian. There were also rumors that Bill Wyman was about to be replaced by Eric Clapton once Cream ceased to exist after Christmas. Since Clapton played lead guitar—a job handled very nicely by Keith Richards—that particular rumor made little sense.

Even though the gossip about Clapton had centered on the erroneous assumption that Wyman was leaving, Jones was convinced Mick and Keith intended to sack *him* in favor of Clapton. Such a move would, he reasoned, enable them to tour. As spokesman for the Stones, Mick sought to quell the gossip with a terse but unmistakably clear statement: "The five Rolling Stones remain the five Rolling Stones. There is to be no alteration."

There was no doubt in Mick's mind that Brian had been set up, and as the group's most visible member, he worried that he would be next. If these were the opening salvos in a full-scale war against the Stones, then it was important they maintain a united front.

That summer, as Brian nervously awaited his trial, Mick and Keith invited him for a weekend of solidarity-building camaraderie at Redlands. There they were invited to shoot around the grounds on Richards's futuristic Hovercraft or, armed with shotguns, join Keith's deerhound Syph (short for Syphilis) in hunting the giant water rats that populated Redlands' moat.

Instead of bonding, Mick and Brian argued violently. Jones knew that he faced a stiff prison sentence, and accused Jagger of having a plan in effect to replace him. Suddenly he made a headlong dash for the moat, screaming, "I'm going to kill myself." He jumped in and disappeared below the surface. Reluctantly Jagger, a rope tied around his waist, went in after him. The water turned out to be about four feet deep where Jones was crouching, but Mick did not appreciate the joke. He had ruined his expensive velvet pants. "You stupid, stupid bastard," Jagger screamed. "I hope you do go to jail, and for a long bloody time too."

While Keith and Anita stayed in London, it was agreed that Brian should remain out of harm's way. He was to spend the rest of the summer at Redlands with his girlfriend, Suki Poitier.

One afternoon Mick and Marianne made an emergency run to Redlands, prompted by Faithfull's ominous reading of the *I Ching*. All the signs had pointed to impending doom for Brian. He was a double Pisces, the water sign; Marianne saw him being swallowed up in a watery grave. The moat at Redlands, perhaps?

Mick managed to cut the usual travel time by thirty minutes; a demon behind the wheel even under normal circumstances, this time he churned up the countryside like a man possessed. When Jagger's Bentley pulled up in front of the thatch-roofed mansion, they found Brian and Suki sitting in front of the fire. He was off drugs, but drinking heavily.

Jones insisted they stay for a dinner, but when Brian's house servent brought out a platter heaped with roast beef, Jagger declined. With Marianne in tow, Mick left to dine at a local pub. When they returned two hours later to resume the evening, Brian was drunk—and furious that Mick had spurned his offer of dinner.

Without warning Jones lunged at Jagger with a carving knife. Jagger pirouetted out of reach, then grabbed a knife of his own. The two dueled for several minutes, Brian on the offensive, Jagger jumping over furniture, twirling just out of reach. While Marianne and Suki screamed in terror, the fencing match spilled out onto the terrace and then the lawn.

Suddenly Brian threw down his knife, ran to the edge of the moat, and jumped in. Again he shouted that he wanted to end his life, that he did not want to exist in the same world with Mick Jagger. Mick pulled him from the water not once but three times, before finally picking Brian up and carrying him back into the house.

Jagger and Richards made a point of being present in the courtroom when Brian's case finally did come up later that year. When the jury rendered its guilty verdict, there were the customary cries of outrage from the gallery. Jagger glared at the jury, but before he could really get worked up the judge pronounced sentence: "Mr. Jones, I am going to treat you as I would any other young man before this court. I am going to fine you according to your means, fifty pounds and one hundred guineas [$400] court costs."

Jagger, Richards, and Jones posed for pictures outside the courthouse in a rare display of unity. It would, alas, be short lived.

By the time Mick was halfway through his twenties, Eva Jagger could brag to her neighbors in Dartford that he was truly a gentleman of wealth and taste. Certainly, he could claim all the trappings—the Bentley, the London town house, the country estate.

Yet, painfully aware of his suburban roots, Jagger feared that it could all evaporate in an instant. "Mick is and always was terribly frugal," said a former lover. "Mick loved to buy his women expensive gifts, but he would spend hours combing the racks of a clothing store for a bargain. Another, somewhat less charitable friend claimed Jagger "was always flat-out cheap. Tipping? Forget it. If he left five percent, the waiter was lucky." More often than not Jagger would claim not to be carrying cash and ask whoever was with him to foot the bill.

By all accounts Jagger's penury would grow worse as his fortune swelled. But even in 1968 Jagger and Richards bristled at being routinely overcharged by nightclubs merely because they were nouveau-riche rockers. The obvious solution: a club of their own.

Vesuvio, coowned and operated by Keith's drug-supplier friend Spanish Tony Sanchez, opened with a bacchanalian twenty-fifth birthday party for Mick on July 26, 1967. Scheherazade would have felt right at home. Draped with

Islamic tapestries, the black-lit interior was divided into sections, each heaped with cushions and featuring its own hookah.

The fact that Vesuvio was located scarcely a block from the Tottenham Court Road police station did not deter Sanchez from serving the kinds of delicacies for which he was famous. There were the requisite hash brownies, as well as rolled joints lined up at every place setting like party favors. The punch was laced with methedrine.

All of the Stones were there, of course, as were John Lennon and Yoko Ono, the Gettys, and half of London society. Songs from the not-yet-released *Beggars Banquet* album pulsated over the sound system all evening—until Paul McCartney slipped the Beatles' new single on the turntable. Jagger, according to Sanchez, did not try to conceal his resentment when the room began swaying to "Hey, Jude."

Once the room had emptied out, Robert Fraser presented Jagger with his birthday present. That night, according to Sanchez, Mick and Marianne lay back on their Moroccan cushions and, passing around the pipe at their table, drew deep breaths of pure Thai opium.

Jagger received another, even more memorable birthday gift that year: the news that Marianne was expecting his baby.

The pregnancy had been an accident; Faithfull, her memory clouded by an almost steady diet of drugs and alcohol, simply forgot to take her birth control pill. Although Jagger had already proved himself to be a relatively caring father figure for Nicholas, she worried that a baby of his own might make Mick feel trapped.

Faithful needn't have worried. Jagger was ecstatic at the prospect of becoming a dad. From the very beginning he was convinced the baby would be a girl. He and Marianne even picked out a name: Carena.

When the press learned of Marianne's condition in September, it became clear that not everyone shared in Jagger's unwedded parental bliss. Once again Jagger was a lightning rod for controversy.

Did Mick and Marianne intend to marry? "Can't see it happening. Just don't believe in it," Jagger shrugged. Behind the scenes, however, Jagger was pressuring Faithfull to go ahead with her divorce from John Dunbar so they could be married. Yet Faithfull, clinging to what remained of her identity, feared that it would be altogether obliterated if she took this final step and became Mrs. Mick Jagger.

Faithfull agreed to go ahead with the divorce, but she made it clear to Mick that she did not want to rush into marriage. He agreed, in retrospect just a little too quickly, perhaps.

Ever since she had left her sensitive artist husband to live with the planet's leading hedonist, Marianne had been pilloried in the press. When she announced that she was leaving her husband to have Mick's baby, but had no intention of making the baby legitimate, Marianne became one of the most scorned women in Britain. Even the powerful archbishop of Canterbury went so far as to denounce her from the pulpit of Westminster Abbey, calling upon the faithful to pray for her soul.

As Britain's fallen angel Marianne bore the brunt of criticism. Whether it was out of sympathy for her pain or a desire to once again pontificate on social issues, Jagger jumped at the chance to cross swords with their detractors.

The opportunity came when David Frost invited Jagger to debate Mary Whitehouse, the nation's self-anointed guardian of public decency, on Frost's highly rated television program. Jagger had squared off with Whitehouse once before, and if nothing else respected her tenacity.

Before the sparring with his ideological opponent began, Jagger was asked by Frost what he felt about marriage in general.

"It's very important that you shouldn't get married if you think that you could get divorced," replied Jagger, taking a more conservative position than his audience might have expected. "If you want to get married and you consecrate your union to God, you can't break it, not even with God. You just have to carry on." Evoking one of the most painfully idiotic adjectives of the era, Jagger went on to describe the institution of matrimony as "groovy."

So, asked Frost, "Why did you decide against it?"

"Ah, well, the lady that I am with is already married, so it's a bit difficult. I could be a bigamist, I suppose." Frost agreed that would be "a bad idea."

"Wouldn't be such a good idea, would it?" Jagger mused. "But I don't really want to get married, particularly. . . . I don't feel that I really need it. But if I were with a woman that really did need it, well, that's another matter. But I'm not with that kind of woman."

Then the fireworks began. Whitehouse blasted Jagger's lack of moral fiber, and branded both him and Marianne un-Christian. "The fact of the matter," she said smugly, "is that if you're a Christian or a person with faith, and you make that vow, when difficulties come, you have this basic thing you've accepted. You find your way through the difficulties."

Whitehouse had barely finished speaking when Jagger fired back. "Your church accepts divorce," he pointed out. "It may even accept abortion—am I right or wrong? I don't see how you can talk about this bond which is inseparable when the Christian church itself accepts divorce."

For once Whitehouse was rendered speechless. "Either you're married and you don't get divorced," Jagger continued, "or you don't bother and you can't come along with some compromise Christian opinion on marriage." Jagger felt better for having bested his rival in a debate viewed by millions. Marianne, closeted alone at Cheyne Walk with a supply of cheap wine and cannabis, wondered if he really understood her pain.

Jagger had always been in awe of Faithfull's acting talent—she now had two small films to her credit, as well as parts in several West End productions—and paid attention when she urged him to make the transition to celluloid.

That spring the Stones had allowed the noted French

film director Jean-Luc Godard to film them recording "Sympathy for the Devil" at Olympic Studios. The song was inspired by the Mikhail Bulgakov novel *The Master and Margarita,* in which Lucifer drops in on Moscow to assay his handiwork following the Bolshevik Revolution. Jagger's painstakingly crafted lyrics, generously sprinkled with historical references, conjure up a dark tale of evil let loose in the world. "Sympathy for the Devil," which went a step beyond "Jumpin' Jack Flash" to establish Jagger as a kind of swivel-hipped Beelzebub, would come to be regarded as something of a rock masterpiece.

In the film, Godard's first in English, shots of the Stones' recording sessions at Olympic Studios are interspersed with scenes of young black men shooting white women in a junkyard, girls painting slogans on walls, and political diatribes delivered by such diverse figures as LeRoi Jones and Adolf Hitler.

Needless to say, practically the only footage worth salvaging dealt with the Stones' recording sessions. Here, Jagger unintentionally revealed the rift between Brian Jones and the rest of the group. Clearly treated as an outsider, Jones was often shown sitting alone in a corner. If he played at all, it was usually only a small acoustic guitar part. And when he screwed up enough courage to make a suggestion, Jagger, unquestionably the man in control, ignored him.

To cash in on the Stones' appeal the original title of the movie, *One Plus One,* was changed to *Sympathy for the Devil.* A wise move. Trounced by the critics on its release over a year later, this maddeningly disjoined effort would nonetheless turn a healthy profit at the box office.

Over the previous two years Jagger had rejected scores of movie scripts, including several from big-name directors and top studios. "Mick was always wary of taking risks," said John Dunbar. "He'd go way out on a limb when it came to making records. But movies—it was something he knew nothing about, and he didn't want to look foolish. The whole idea scared him. That's where Marianne came in. She kept popping up his ego, and gave him the confidence to at least give acting a try."

Chronically suspicious of strangers, regardless of their qualifications, Jagger was invariably swayed in his professional decisions by friends and friends of friends. So, after turning down offers from established filmmakers, Jagger agreed to star in *Performance*—a first-time effort from his old buddy Donald Cammell, the expatriate American painter living in Paris.

The story of a hit man on the run and his bizarre encounter with a washed-up rock star who makes him doubt his own heterosexuality was written with Jagger in mind. Once Mick had agreed to do the movie, Warner Bros. snapped it up on the assumption *Performance* would be a charming musical romp along the lines of the Beatles' smash hits *A Hard Day's Night* and *Help.*

Since Cammell had no experience at filmmaking whatsoever, he asked Nicolas Roeg, the brilliant cinematographer whose credits included *Lawrence of Arabia,* to work alongside him as codirector. Donald's brother David, a maker of television commercials and another pal of Mick's, signed on as the film's coproducer with the Stones' then-agent Sandy Lieberson. At Jagger's suggestion Christopher Gibbs was brought in to conjure up a set design similar to the tomblike environment he had created for Mick and Marianne on Cheyne Walk.

To lend the film's portrayal of the underworld authenticity, Donald Cammell enlisted the unofficial aid of his childhood chum David Litvinoff. A shadowy figure, Litvinoff counted among his closest associates the infamous Kray brothers, kingpins of organized crime in Britain. The brothers were so notorious that in the 1980s they became the subject of a major feature film, *The Krays.*

Donald Cammell wanted Marlon Brando for the part of the hoodlum, but when Brando turned the part down he hired James Fox, a patrician-looking English actor who had already begun to make his mark in films like *King Rat* and

The Servant. Fox was reluctant to take the part at first, and was advised against it by his agent-father Robin Fox.

To prepare himself for the role Fox took a small flat over a pub in the East End, chopped off his fashionably long blond hair, and began frequenting mob hangouts. His education was speeded along by Litvinoff, who introduced Fox to the Krays and even hired one of his underlings, boxing promoter Johnny Shannon, to show him the underworld ropes.

Fox became so absorbed in the role of the sadistic cockney gangster that Lieberson's secretary was terrified when Fox, in his character of Chas, paid an unannounced visit to the producer's office. Even Johnny Shannon, who wound up playing Chas's mob boss in the film, became concerned about Fox's obsessive identification with his character. At one point Fox was even said to have accompanied some of his new associates on a heist.

Jagger, meantime, was having his doubts about assaying the role of Turner—a task made all the more difficult by the fact that there was no script per se. "We never had a script," said Roeg, "only an outline. It was very organic, growing out of the relationships between the characters as we went along. You couldn't do that today. The stakes are so high, no studio could afford to take the chance."

Both Roeg and Cammell pushed Jagger to take the reclusive, bisexual Turner as far as he could. "The whole androgynous look stemmed more from Donald and I," recalled Roeg. "We'd say, 'Gee, Mick, wouldn't it be great if you wore this body stocking?' or 'God, Mick, this makeup would be great for the character.' Mick would resist at first, but eventually he'd come around." Jagger would spend most of the film wearing an assortment of body stockings, frilly blouses, and billowing caftans, his face smeared with blue eye shadow and fire-engine-red lipstick.

As for his actual performance in *Performance*, Jagger was instructed not to act at all, but to simply "be you." Marianne urged him to reject his directors' advice. Instead, she suggested that the character of Turner be a combination of

Brian and Keith. "You've got to imagine you're poor freaked-out, deluded, androgynous, druggie Brian," she told Mick, "but you also need a bit of Keith's tough, self-destructive, beautiful lawlessness." Jagger took her advice, and the result was a mincing, preening cross between Jones and Richards that, in truth, did not stray all that far from the real Jagger; one character even refers to Turner as "Old Rubber Lips."

Faithfull herself had originally been cast as one of the two women who inhabit Turner's surreal netherworld of drugs, sex, and cynicism. But she bowed out when doctors warned her of complications in her pregnancy. Jagger packed Marianne off to Ireland, where for $250 a week he rented a friend's mansion outside Galway.

With Marianne temporarily out of the picture, the role went to Anita Pallenberg. Keith's lover was also pregnant, but she was not about to have a little thing like impending motherhood stand in her way. She had an abortion, and was on the set the following day.

To heighten the tensions between the androgynous retired rock star and the malevolent gangster who hides out in his basement, Roeg had wanted both men to actually move into the mansion on Lowndes Square where much of *Performance* was shot.

That, as it turned out, proved unnecessary. Jagger and Fox had known one another before shooting began and, said Donald Cammell, "had a sort of romance . . . but they were both such closet queens." Lieberson would only say the two men had "an intense personal relationship. Everyone on the set knew each other. They were all, er, intimate friends."

There was no doubt that *Performance* was, above all else, out to shock. Even before Jagger makes his appearance, Chas is shown pouring acid on a rival's Rolls-Royce one minute, then making love to a woman in the backseat of another Rolls the next.

Nudity, profanity, and drugs abound in the film. Turner's curious coterie seems to be constantly smoking dope and nibbling on psychedelic mushrooms; in one of the many graphic scenes Pallenberg stands before a mirror injecting smack into her derriere. She clearly knows what she is doing.

In their first scene together Chas hides behind a screen while interviewing his prospective tenant. When Turner finally makes his appearance, he is wearing a black body stocking, a necklace, and a hip-hugging belt with an oversized silver buckle. Chas looks him over and then delivers a portentious line: "You'll look funny when you're fifty."

During the course of the film, however, it is Chas's world that is turned upside down—and Fox's along with it. In one scene Anita, playing Jagger's nymphomaniacal secretary, seduces Fox and then begins chiding him about his sexuality. To demonstrate that no one is entirely male or female, she holds a mirror up to his body, so that her breast is reflected on his chest. The image is at once arresting and disquieting. Under the influence of Turner and his minions Chas eventually dons a wig and makeup to explore his feminine self.

Life imitated art as Jagger, trying to keep his character alive, taunted his costar between takes. Jagger had rehearsed diligently, but Fox was a perfectionist who demanded retake after retake. When Mick was satisfied—often after a single take—he simply refused to do any more. Fox would follow Mick, pleading with him to do a scene just one more time. "Fuck off, Jimmy," Jagger would reply, his voice dripping with contempt. He then, as a rule, would slam his dressing room door in Fox's face.

"Mick was constantly trying to do James Fox in," Cammell told British writer Carey Schofield, "because that's the only way Mick can operate. Mick was very unkind to Jimmy, but he'd always been unkind to him. . . . In that sense he's a little destructive, Mick."

The making of *Performance* proved to be a traumatic experience for Fox. Once filming was completed, he gave up his acting career and spread the Gospel as a born-again Christian.

Indeed, whatever action took place on the screen paled to the soap opera that swirled around the making of *Performance*—a real-life drama that for the first time seriously threatened the partnership of Jagger and Richards.

When they first read the script synopsis, the two men laughed at the prospect of Mick and Anita acting out a spirited ménage à trois with a boyish teenager named Michele Breton. Once filming was under way, however, Richards was consumed with jealousy. "Keith refused to come onto the set," recalled Lieberson. "He just sat outside the house on Lansdowne Square in his car, fuming." Robert Fraser, who shared Richards's passion for drugs, served as Keith's spy on the set. Early in the film's shooting schedule Fraser would watch from the sidelines, then report to Richards as he waited in his blue Bentley. Eventually, Cammell barred Fraser—and everyone else, for that matter—from the set.

No one seemed to enjoy all the fuss more than Pallenberg, who admitted that she was stoned through the entire film. Anita took sadistic pleasure in tormenting Richards with the admission that she had slept with him and with Jones just to get to Jagger. To make matters worse, Richards was supposed to write the music for a song to be used in the film, "Memo to Turner." So long as he suspected Anita and Mick of carrying on an affair under the guise of acting, he refused to finish the song.

Richards, as it turned out, had every reason to be jealous. The film's controversial orgy scene begins with Anita getting Mick's attention by sticking her tongue in his nostril. Then, by way of lending the film that extra dash of realism, Jagger made energetic love to both Pallenberg and Breton. After some judicious editing all the moviegoer would see were bodies writhing beneath sheets and an occasional glimpse of thigh and nipple. The uncut version later surfaced at a pornographic movie festival in Amsterdam. It won first prize.

What neither Jagger nor Richards knew was that Pallenberg was in the throes of another torrid affair at the time.

While Mick and Keith postured for one another, Anita was also sleeping with Donald Cammell.

Lieberson described the atmosphere as "high drama. Mick, Keith, and Anita are all extremely volatile personalities, and they made sure there were lots of eruptions, arguments, tantrums. Mick in particular is very high strung, very mercurial. I got the impression everything had to be very *large* or he just didn't feel alive."

Amid all the confusion Warner Bros. got wind of what was transpiring on the set and actually shut the film down while they decided whether or not to pull the plug on the project. "Shooting was held up for about a week," said Lieberson, "until we managed to convince them that we had everything under control."

After constant rewrites and a grueling schedule that pushed everyone to the brink of exhaustion, an unexpected crisis reared its head at the lab where the film was being processed. One of the female technicians was so distraught over the graphic sex scene between Jagger and the two women that she complained to her boss. He, in turn, phoned Roeg in the middle of the night, threatening to destroy the film.

"I told him to wait until I got there," recalled Roeg. "When I arrived, the lab's managing director was in a panic. He told me that the material was probably pornography and that he could go to jail for printing it. I tried to talk him out of destroying the film, but he was adamant. I had to stand there and watch as he cut it up." Fortunately Cammell grabbed the negative, and the film was processed at a lab with more liberal standards.

One final hurdle remained: getting Jagger and Richards to mend their relationship long enough to record the movie's theme song, "Memo from Turner." Keith, still bristling over Mick's fling with Anita, dragged his feet. Finally Cammell and Roeg cornered Jagger and begged him to take matters into his own hands. They were stunned when Mick broke down sobbing. "The rift with Keith," said Roeg, "had really taken an emotional toll on Mick."

A compatriot of the Stones was more blunt: "Keith and Mick were having what amounted to a lover's quarrel over Anita. She knew she could never be as important to either one as they were to each other, so Anita got even by driving a wedge between them. A lot of us thought she was evil."

Jagger agreed to take matters into his own hands. He invited Steve Winwood and Jim Capaldi of the group Traffic to join him at Olympic Studios, and within days delivered the completed track to *Performance*'s musical director, Jack Nitzsche.

Shortly before Thanksgiving Warner Bros., still under the impression that *Performance* was another musical romp à la *A Hard Day's Night*, held a private screening for studio executives and their families. Just a few minutes into the film several perceptive parents rushed their teenagers out of the screening room. One of the women in attendance got up during one of the many graphic sex scenes and, after managing only a few steps, threw up on a studio vice-president's shoe.

"The first thing they wanted to know," said Lieberson, "was if Michele Breton, who was quite flat chested, was a boy or a girl." Overall, Warner executives were "displeased with the tone and the morality of the movie," recalled Lieberson. "The violence and straight sex didn't bother them half as much as the drugs and bisexuality." Pallenberg was not surprised at Warner's reaction. "They thought," she said, "we were a bunch of dirty hippies."

Despite dozens of angry phone calls from Roeg, Cammell, Lieberson, and Jagger himself, the studio shelved *Performance* indefinitely. They refused to even consider releasing the film until it was dramatically recut.

The dispute dragged on as each side threatened to sue the other. "*Performance* nearly destroyed us," said Roeg. "It was a very painful time." Eventually Fred Weinbtraub, one of the producers of the film *Woodstock*, came to Warner Bros. and interceded on *Performance*'s behalf. After nearly two years of haggling the movie was at long last released in

1970—with a dreaded X rating. Despite all the angst surrounding the movie Roeg was pleased with the results—even though the film received decidedly mixed reviews. "I'm glad I did it," said Roeg. "It was quite a seminal piece of cinema, and besides, it was my *life*. A lot of my blood went in *Performance*, but I guess nobody had more at stake than Mick."

At her mansion on the Irish coast Marianne was blissfully oblivious to the potboiler that unfolded during the filming of *Performance*. She had been warned by the doctors to stay away from drugs, so Faithfull dutifully restricted himself to wine, grass, and lots of cocaine.

An avid horseback rider since childhood ("There are only three things that I do well: ride, cook, and fuck," she once said), Faithfull saddled up every morning for a gallop across the Irish countryside. Marianne claimed never to have felt stronger or healthier.

Marianne was in the middle of her seventh month when, without warning, her water broke and she miscarried on November 22, 1968. The stillborn infant was a boy. (By some tragic twist of fate Yoko Ono miscarried John Lennon's baby only hours later. Ono, who was still married to the American movie director Anthony Cox, was also seven months pregnant.)

Faithfull was devastated. Not only had she suffered the loss of a child, but she was told in no uncertain terms that she was to blame: Faithfull's years of drug abuse, said the doctors, caused her to miscarry.

Mick rushed to Marianne's side, comforting her and reassuring her that they would try again to have a child. For a moment it seemed that this shared tragedy might bring them closer together.

Once they returned to London, however, it was clear that their relationship had been altered forever. Mick quickly distanced himself from Marianne, submerging himself in preparations for the December release of *Beggars Banquet* and an upcoming television special, the Rolling Stones' *Rock and Roll Circus*.

Marianne was resentful of how quickly Jagger seemed to snap back. He showered her with flowers and gifts, but as she wandered from room to room in the Cheyne Walk house, Marianne felt alone and abandoned. When he did find a few fleeting moments with her, the tenderness that had been there during her pregnancy was gone. He had hardened toward her.

Although he tried assiduously to conceal it, the miscarriage had a crushing impact on Mick. Faithfull still had Nicholas, but all Jagger's dreams of fatherhood had been dashed by Marianne's carelessness. Jagger was, as he repeatedly told Faithfull, determined to try again. Only not, as it turned out, with her.

"When I go on the road I just go crazy. I become a total monster."

As 1968 drew to a close, it seemed to Jagger that life was fast becoming nothing but a mind-spinning succession of crises. This time he was locked in a very public battle with Decca Chairman Sir Edward Lewis over the jacket art for the new album.

The original cover for *Beggars Banquet*, as conceived by Jagger and Richards, was simply a black-and-white photograph of a graffiti-covered men's-room wall. A number of pithy remarks were squeezed in among the song titles and credits, including GOD ROLLS HIS OWN!! and PETER IS A FAGGOT.

Lewis, who publicly denounced the lavatory-wall design as "childish" and privately feared that it might leave Decca vulnerable to an obscenity charge, stood his ground. The release date was delayed four months, until the Stones finally caved in.

Beggars Banquet was released the first week in December with a cover that was the absolute antithesis of the filthy lavatory wall: the group's name and the album title in elegant script, with a simple RSVP in the lower left-hand corner—all against a plain white background.

By way of revenge the Stones launched the album with an irreverent "banquet" at London's Queensgate Hotel. Lord Harlech, England's ambassador to the U.S., was a spirited combatant in the food fight that quickly ensued. Brian Jones grabbed Jagger's gray top hat, put it on, then—looking like a man possessed—crammed a custard pie in his nemesis' face with inordinate force.

Coming on the heels of the embarrassing *Their Satanic Majesties Request*, it was vitally important to Jagger that *Beggars Banquet* be an unqualified hit. There was a hitch: Because of the unforeseen delay in releasing *Beggars Banquet*, the Stones album hit record stores at precisely the same moment as the Beatles' new LP, *The Beatles*. This marked the very first time the two groups had issued albums simultaneously.

In this contest the Stones emerged victorious. Richards was lauded for his composing talent and musicianship, but most of the praise went to front man Jagger. *The New York Times* was especially effusive about Jagger's rendition of "Stray Cat Blues," the story of a fifteen-year-old groupie climbing the stairs to a rock star's apartment ("Bet your ma don't know you can fight like that, I bet she never saw you scratch my back"). "Jagger himself is demonic," wrote the *Times*'s critic Nik Cohn. "He comes in on a tiny snicker, fat lips flapping, and builds all the way to flat-out hysteria, flinging out abuse at random. In every way it's a sick performance, pure sadism, and it's also wildly exciting."

Widely hailed as their best album to date, *Beggars Banquet* was not only embraced by diehard blues and rock fans who had deserted the Stones after *Their Satanic Majesties*, but also by left-wing activists who viewed its "Street Fighting Man" as a call to arms. "The Stones were the first band to say, 'Up against the wall, motherfucker,'" wrote John Landau in *Rolling Stone*, "and they said it with class."

While *Beggars Banquet* climbed the charts, the Stones began work on a BBC television special that was intended as a gift to fans who had not seen them perform live for nearly two years. Jagger also intended to best the Beatles once again; their much-ballyhooed *Magical Mystical Tour* TV special never got off the ground, and Mick was confident his Stones would succeed where their middle-of-the-road pop counterparts had failed so miserably.

Filmed over a three-day period before an audience of

eight hundred invited guests at London's Wembley studios, the *Rolling Stones Rock and Roll Circus* featured all the standard circus fare—jugglers, animal acts, clowns, and acrobats—as well as Brian in wizard's robes, Charlie Watts in a military uniform and top hat with silver satyr horns, Bill Wyman in ruffled finery, and Keith wearing a drum major's brass buttons and epaulets. Since Jagger was calling the shots, he literally cracked the whip as a crimson-jacketed ringmaster.

While fire-eaters belched flame and trapeze artists swung overhead, a roster of megastars appeared in a variety of wild getups: John and Yoko were there, he in a harlequin's outfit, she wearing a peaked witch's cap and cape; Eric Clapton smiled from beneath a giant Artful Dodger's cap; John Entwistle was a beruffled court jester; and Roger Daltry and Pete Townshend dressed as medieval peasants.

There were performances by Lennon, Clapton, and the Who—even a song from Marianne, who seemed more beautiful than ever less than a month after her tragic miscarriage. But the highlight of the *Rock and Roll Circus* was the Stones' rendition of "Sympathy for the Devil." By the time the Stones came on, it was five A.M. on the last day of shooting.

The late hour seemed to have no effect on Mick. Ripping off his shirt to show a large fake "tattoo" of Lucifer emblazoned across his narrow chest, Jagger writhed and slithered his way through the number six times—until he was at last satisfied with the take.

"Everybody agreed that it was a terrific show, an incredible one-of-a-kind event," said Sandy Lieberson, who was hired by Jagger to produce the show. Everybody except Jagger. When he screened the program, Mick was struck by how old and tired he looked—in stark contrast to the Who's perpetually youthful Roger Daltry. Despite the enormous cost Jagger nixed the project. *The Rolling Stones Rock and Roll Circus* has never been seen on the BBC, or anywhere.

If nothing else, the ill-fated TV project seemed to bring

Jagger and Richards back together—even though, behind Keith's back, Mick still pursued Anita. According to Pallenberg, Jagger repeatedly implored her to dump Richards and replace Marianne in his life; as an inducement he offered to find another film project for them to star in together. "Mick wanted for us to be a couple," Pallenberg told Victor Bockris, "but I just didn't want it. Mick just wanted to walk around and show me off like he did with all his women. Keith needed a more human kind of attention and care and love."

As soon as the Rock and Roll Circus was wrapped up, Mick suggested that he and Marianne run away to Majorca on holiday. Faithfull had grown tired of the Spanish resort. Reminding Jagger that he was now a "man of wealth and taste" who could easily afford to go anywhere in the world, she suggested they join Keith and Anita on a cruise to South America. Keith had insisted on a relaxing boat trip because Pallenberg was again pregnant, and he did not want the same fate that befell Marianne to befall her.

With Nicholas in tow the curious foursome sailed from Lisbon for Rio de Janeiro on December 18. Jagger and Richards spent much of their time together at the ship's bar, where an outgoing middle-aged woman asked them every night who they were. As she guzzled one pink gin after another, she became increasingly insistent. "Come on, now, who are you?" she'd ask. "Won't you give us a glimmer?" From then on, Jagger and Richards called themselves the Glimmer Twins.

Pallenberg, still immersed in witchcraft and Satanism, had originally conceived of a month-long trek across South America as a way to commune with native shamans while "looking for flying saucers." Richards told a British journalist that they were "hoping to see this magician who practices both black and white magic. He has a very long and difficult name which we can't pronounce. We call him 'Banana' for short."

They stayed at a posh suite in Rio, then at a coffee plantation outside São Paulo, and finally in a hut on the beach at Recife on Brazil's northeastern coast. Tanned and sporting a small beard, Jagger had never looked or felt more relaxed.

One afternoon Mick and Marianne were strolling on the beach with Nicholas when they heard drums and chanting. Drawing closer to the primitive sounds, they came upon a group of blacks practicing the secret rites of a form of Roman Catholicism that incorporates elements of voodoo.

Spotting the white strangers in their midst, their first reaction was to pelt them with rocks. Before Mick and Marianne could scoop Nicholas up and start running, their "priest" ordered them to stop. He then walked up to Jagger and, carefully studying Mick's face, began to smile. The religion-obsessed Brazilians thought that Jagger, with his long brown hair, beard, and lanky physique, bore an uncanny resemblance to Jesus Christ.

Covered from head to toe against the tropical sun—"She wore big hats and boots and veils and long sleeves; not one inch of her skin was showing," said Pallenberg—Faithfull nevertheless succumbed to the heat and returned to London.

Pallenberg, though pregnant, pressed on with the men to Peru. Jagger had been reading about the Inca civilization, and spent most of his time "just walking around looking at the Indians. You can get an idea of what people are like just by walking about. I could have found out more. You could take a tent and spend days, driving out somewhere, but I haven't got the time."

Jagger was impressed that the Inca civilization grew "despite the fact they didn't have the wheel, and there were messengers who had to carry little bits of colored wool because there was no writing." The main impression he took away from the experience was the observation that Peruvians "got stoned on a funny kind of beer." The Aztecs, he decided, were probably more interesting.

Jagger's South American sojourn is perhaps most memorable for the songs it produced. With Pallenberg as their sounding board Jagger and Richards wrote "Honky Tonk

Women" and "You Can't Always Get What You Want" on this trip. (Faithfull had also contributed to the Stones' repertoire. Drawing on her own harrowing experience, she wrote "Sister Morphine" about drug addiction ending in overdose.)

On his return to London, Jagger discovered to his chagrin that Marianne had already plunged back into work, acting opposite Nicol Williamson in Tony Richardson's Roundhouse Theatre production of *Hamlet*. "Mick was jealous of Marianne's acting," said a friend of the couple's. "It was something she could do well and that he was very frightened of doing." Added John Dunbar: "He didn't like to be upstaged—not by any woman, much less *his* woman."

Not long after, Tony Richardson approached Mick to play the title role in *Ned Kelly*, the noted director's ambitious film biography of the legendary nineteenth-century Australian Robin Hood. This was an instance of casting against type, to be sure, since Jagger seemed to possess none of Kelly's rugged outlaw qualities. Yet Richardson, a homosexual who was later said to have a crush on Jagger, apparently saw the possibilities. To secure the deal Richardson offered Faithfull the part of Kelly's feisty girlfriend. Jagger was also to write the score. Shooting was to begin that July in Australia.

On May 28 Les Perrin's office announced that Jagger was slated to star in *Ned Kelly*. That evening Mick answered the front door and had barely opened it a crack when the police shoved their way in, pushed Jagger into the dining room, and searched the house. The police quickly uncovered a small box containing about a quarter ounce of pot.

Mick, who showed up in court wearing a purple suit and a violet shirt, claimed that the marijuana had been planted there by the police, and that the arresting officer had solicited a thousand-pound bribe to forget the matter. Both allegations were denied by the police.

Once again Jagger took the fall for Faithfull. She was acquitted, but Jagger was eventually convicted of possession and fined £200 (about $500).

This latest bust, conducted by the same officer who had last arrested Brian Jones, convinced Mick beyond a shadow of a doubt the Stones were being singled out for harassment. Brian could hardly be blamed, he thought, for coming apart at the seams under such pressure. (The arresting officer, Detective Sergeant Robin Constable, sued Jagger for claiming that he had solicited a bribe. The suit was later dropped).

His newfound empathy for Jones notwithstanding, Jagger had a tour to think of. Given his arrest record there was no way Brian would be allowed into the U.S. A strategy was devised to dump Brian and still leave his dignity intact.

With the aid of Allen Klein, Jagger devised a scheme where Brian would be asked to step aside temporarily so the rest of the Stones could tour. In truth, he would be asked to leave forever, for which he would continue to be paid royalties for previous Stones records and a lifetime annual stipend of £100,000. Having worked out the details, all that remained for Jagger was to fire the founding member and first leader of the Rolling Stones.

Unaware of all the intrigue, Brian had found something approaching peace at Cotchford Farm, an eleven-acre estate in Sussex that had once been the home of *Winnie-the-Pooh* creator A. A. Milne. Cotchford Farm was, in fact, something of a shrine to Milne. In one corner of the garden was a life-size statue of Christopher Robin; in another, a sundial decorated with images of Pooh, Eeyore, and Piglet. Legend had it that Milne buried all his manuscripts on this spot.

Though steeped in rustic charm, Cotchford Farm was not without creature comforts. There were three reception rooms, six bedrooms, three bathrooms, a staff apartment, garages, and a heated Grecian swimming pool.

There were signs that Brian was trying to pull himself back together. He claimed to have given up everything but alcohol, and was so fearful of being busted again that he searched the belongings of all his houseguests to make certain they didn't bring illegal drugs onto his property.

Jagger was unimpressed. "Mick was very forceful about this," Ian Stewart later recalled. "He said that it was imperative that we get rid of Brian and replace him with someone who could perform."

To prepare Brian for the inevitable, Jagger dispatched their old friend and mentor Alexis Korner to Cotchford Farm. There Brian played the perfect host, pouring glass after glass of wine for his guest as he rambled on about future projects—recording an album of Moroccan JouJouka music, for example, or starting a blues band along the lines of Creedence Clearwater Revival. Jones had actually grown obsessed with the John Fogerty–fronted group, playing "Proud Mary" on his stereo system continuously.

Jagger, meantime, was already breaking in Jones's replacement, a twenty-year-old John Mayall–trained guitarist named Mick Taylor. Summoned to the Olympic Studios late on the night of June 1, Taylor made his debut contributing to a little ditty called "Honky Tonk Women."

One week later Jagger and Richards drove to Cotchford Farm, bringing Charlie Watts along to act as referee if tempers flared. As it happened, everyone behaved in a surprisingly civilized manner, given the bitter feelings that had been harbored for so long.

Jagger pointed out that the situation had become untenable, and Brian acted as if he were relieved to be leaving. "I no longer see eye-to-eye with the others over the discs we are cutting," Jones explained in his official press release. "The Stones' music is not to my taste anymore. The only solution," he concluded, "was to go our separate ways, but we shall still remain friends. I love those fellows." Once they were gone, Jones locked himself in his room and cried all night.

"We'd known for a few months that Brian wasn't keen," Jagger told reporters the next day. "He wasn't enjoying himself and it got to the stage where we had to sit down and talk about it. So we did and decided the best thing was for him to leave."

Jagger would never again see Jones alive. On the drive

home Mick had to confront the fact that, next to him, Brian remained the group's most popular member. The best way to soften Brian's departure and introduce Mick Taylor to the world, Jagger figured, was to provide the masses with an unforgettable spectacle.

Jagger, never one to think small, had already concocted a scheme to reshoot the ill-fated *Rock and Roll Circus*, only this time at the Coliseum in Rome. When that fell through, he and Marianne showed up in London's Hyde Park at an unprecedented free concert by Blind Faith, the new group formed by Steve Winwood and Eric Clapton. The concert drew more than 150,000. Swept along by the rapturous mood of the crowd (aided by copious quantities of grass, LSD, and cheap wine), Jagger decided that the Stones would throw a free Hyde Park concert of their own. The date was set for July 5. When he got wind of the planned concert, Brian wondered aloud if he would be the only one the Stones would charge to see it.

With the long-postponed business of axing Brian Jones at last out of the way, Jagger began "auditioning" young beauties to appear in publicity photos for their "Honky Tonk Women" single. One, the black daughter of a Phila-delphia psychiatrist, had made quite a splash singing in the West End production of *Hair* and posing nude for *Vogue*. When Marsha Hunt's breasts popped out of her blouse dur-ing a live broadcast of British television's *Top of the Pops*, Jagger was convinced he had to have her as the Stones' prototypical "Honky Tonk Woman."

Hunt felt otherwise. "I was established then," she re-called. "It wasn't like I needed the exposure." Besides, she added, "the last thing black women needed was for me to denigrate us by dressing up like a whore among a band of white renegades."

Jagger showed up at her apartment at midnight to try and change her mind. His first gesture upon meeting—pull-ing his hand out of his pocket, pointing it at her like a gun, and saying "Bang"—disarmed her completely. Jagger opened up to Hunt about Marianne's growing drug dependence, her miscarriage, and their deteriorating relationship. He also confided in Hunt that, in order to save the band, he had been forced to sack Brian Jones. What most impressed her was that he confessed unashamedly that he was lonely. They talked, drank tea, and then made love until seven the next morning.

Their affair continued, with Mick sneaking away from Marianne to see his new mistress several times each week. Part of Hunt's appeal was that she was stone-cold sober at a time when Faithfull, under the destructive influence of her friend Pallenberg, was "popping" heroin four times a day (actually, Faithfull was too squeamish to stick herself with a needle; she had friends do it for her). Hunt's trademark sky-high Afro made it easy for Jagger to come up with a nickname for her. He called her "Miss Fuzzy."

Professionally Mick was increasingly absorbed with the Stones' business affairs. "He obviously loved the money end of things," said Stephanie Bluestone. "He would walk into the boardroom, and all these very proper-looking men in dark suits jump to their feet. Everyone was very impressed with the very specific, intelligent questions he'd ask about foreign sales and taxes and so on. It probably wouldn't have come as such a shock to them if they'd known he attended the London School of Economics."

Preparing for life sans Brian, Jagger took stock of the Stones' finances and was shocked by what he found. By Mick's estimate, in the two and a half years since Allen Klein took over as business manager, the group had grossed at least $17 million. Yet, as they ended the decade as the world's top musical attraction next to the Beatles, the Rolling Stones were for all intents and purposes stone broke.

Mick, as well as the others, owned up to having squandered fortunes on houses, cars, country estates, drugs, and the high life in general. But by any reckoning the $1 million or $2 million they may have collectively spent between 1966 and 1969 should still have left them with a healthy seven-figure after-tax balance.

It did not help that Klein was preoccupied with four new

high-profile clients with fiscal woes of their own. When they'd hired Klein in 1966, they recommended him whole-heartedly to the Beatles. By the time Lennon, Harrison, and Ringo Starr had themselves hired Klein to sort out the well-publicized mess over Apple Records (McCartney cast the sole opposing vote), Jagger was trying to warn them off.

While Klein jousted with such British entertainment heavyweights as Sir Lew Grade and EMI over the future of Apple, Jagger quietly turned to an unlikely source for help. At one of his famous get-togethers Christopher Gibbs introduced Jagger to Prince Rupert Loewenstein, a pear-shaped patrician who could trace his Bavarian ancestors back to Friedrich I.

Prince Rupert asked Gibbs to repeat the young fellow's name; he had never heard of Mick Jagger, or the Rolling Stones, for that matter. Once he was briefed on the global fame of the man and the group, Loewenstein, then a partner with Jonathan Guinness in the long-established firm of Leopold Joseph, was all too happy to become Mick's personal financial advisor; he assumed there would be a few extra million to invest. To his dismay Prince Rupert discovered that Jagger was, on paper at least, virtually destitute—his debts far exceeded his assets.

Mick informed Loewenstein that the group was in similar straits, and hinted that the "German Dumpling," as the *Tatler* dubbed the prince, might ultimately be called in to sort out the financial tangle created by Allen Klein. For now, however, Loewenstein was to concentrate solely on protecting Mick's interests. "In Mick Jagger's mind only one thing came first," recalled Keith Altham. "Mick Jagger."

At Cotchford Farm, Brian was on a manic high. "It was almost as if someone had taken a weight off his shoulders," said Ian Stewart. Exuberant over his newfound freedom, he had already set out to form a band of his own. Jones had also talked to John Lennon, Jimi Hendrix, and Jeff Beck; all expressed serious interest in working with him.

On the evening of July 2, 1969, Jones and his new Swedish girlfriend, Anna Wohlin (another Pallenberg look-alike), watched *Rowan and Martin's Laugh-In* on television. Brian had hired a work crew to do some renovations, and, as they sometimes did on warm summer nights, these laborers took the liberty of inviting their girlfriends over to party by the pool. Around ten P.M. Jones and Wohlin joined them.

The brawny workmen clearly resented the coddled, effete rock star in their midst, and when he took to the diving board to impress their girlfriends, the festivities turned nasty.

There had been a lot of pollen in the air that day, and the asthmatic Jones had been using his "puffer" (inhaler) every half hour or so to clear his bronchial tubes. He had also, in typical fashion, washed down several tranquilizers with a half-bottle of whiskey. None of this, however, prevented him from paddling about the pool and flirting with the ladies.

Fed up, the workmen began to get rough with Jones, shoving him underwater, then letting him up for only a few seconds before pushing his head under again. Brian was flailing his arms, gasping for air, his inhaler just a few feet from his grasp at the pool's edge.

It was at this time, around eleven P.M., that Nicholas Fitzgerald and Richard Cadbury came upon the scene. Fitzgerald, a longtime friend of Brian's, drove up to Crotchford Farm and heard a commotion as soon as they got out of their car. Peering through the bushes, they saw three men and a woman standing at poolside, watching as a fourth man kept shoving a blond head under water.

"Out of the bushes right next to us stepped a burly man wearing glasses," Fitzgerald recalled. "He made a fist, which he put in my face menacingly. 'Get the hell out of here, Fitzgerald, or you'll be next.' "

Terrified, Fitzgerald and Cadbury fled. So, apparently, did the workmen—leaving only Jones's live-in foreman, Frank Thorogood, and his girlfriend, Janet Lawson, a nurse.

Anna Wholin, who had gone in to change, emerged from the house to see the couple staring down at the pool. Brian, wearing multicolored trunks, was spread-eagle on the bottom.

According to Anna the others "were just *standing there*" while she dived in and fished Brian out of the water. Thorogood and Wohlin lifted Jones out of the water, and Lawson tried artificial respiration and heart massage. Wohlin said she "gave him the kiss of life, suddenly felt his hand grip mine . . . and then he just stopped moving."

When police arrived, no one mentioned the party, or the presence of anyone at the house other than Wohlin, Thorogood, and Lawson. Coroner Angus Sommerville would rule that Jones had died as a result of "drowning by immersion in fresh water associated with severe liver disfunction caused by fatty degeneration and ingestion of alcohol and drugs." At the time of autopsy there were traces of amphetamines, the tranquilizer Mandrax, and of course alcohol in his bloodstream. Waxing poetic, the coroner's inquest labeled Brian's demise "death by misadventure."

Shortly afterward Anna Wohlin left the country, and Fitzgerald's friend and fellow witness Richard Cadbury moved without leaving a forwarding address. Within hours of Jones's death the house was stripped of millions of dollars' worth of antiques, artwork, and other possessions.

"Some very weird things happened that night," Richards later said. He claimed never to have seen Brian suffer from an asthma attack, and doubted that he could have drowned because he, alone among the Stones, was an exceptionally strong swimmer. "We had these chauffeurs working for us and we tried to find out. . . . Some of them had a weird hold over Brian. There were a lot of chicks there, they were having a party. . . . None of us were trying to hush it up. We wanted to know what was going on. But goddammit, to find out is impossible. It's the same feeling with who killed Kennedy. You can't get to the bottom of it."

Mick was with Keith and Charlie Watts at Olympic Studios mixing tracks for "Let It Bleed" when he picked up the phone at two A.M. on the morning of July 3. The wife of Brian's assistant Tom Keylock told Mick that Brian had drowned.

Keith Altham walked into the studios moments after they had heard the news. "I hadn't heard the news yet," recalled Altham, "but when I walked into the room everyone looked stunned and ashen-faced. The place was utterly silent. Jagger sat at the control board, looking stricken. He was not crying, but he was as close to it as I've ever seen."

Altham asked Jagger what had happened.

"Brian," he replied.

"Dead?"

"Yeah."

Altham asked if Jagger and the others were going to call it quits for the night. "No!" Jagger snapped, turning his attention back to the control panel. "It goes on."

Headlines around the world blared the news of Brian Jones's death. Asked for a reaction, the Who's Pete Townshend shook his head and replied, "Oh, it's a normal day for Brian. He died every day, you know." It was the most heartfelt and intelligent comment made about Brian's death and his life, but one for which Townshend was harshly criticized by Les Perrin.

That first morning following Jones's death Mick joined the other Stones at the Maddox Street offices. Mick Taylor, who had never met Jones, could only look on in respectful silence. Watts's face was tear stained.

Jagger paced nervously about the office, weighing what impact Brian's death would have on the fortunes of the Stones. Certainly all the publicity could only help their double-A single "Honky Tonk Women" and "You Can't Always Get What You Want," which, coincidentally, was being released that very day.

To promote the single the Stones were scheduled to appear on the TV program *Top of the Pops* the afternoon of July 3. It was an important show, and Jagger saw no reason to cancel. For personal reasons Jagger also wanted to press ahead with the Hyde Park concert. If Mick showed up on the Australian set of *Ned Kelly* any later than July 9, the producers of the film would sue. For Jagger to make it Down Under in time, the concert would have to be held as scheduled.

How could they hold a mass celebration just two days after Brian's death without seeming heartless? Watts came up with the simple solution, suggesting they go ahead with the concert, only now as a memorial to Jones. Jagger co-opted the idea, and announced it to the press: "We will do the concert—for Brian," Mick said. "We have thought about it an awful lot, and feel he wanted it to go on."

That night, less than twenty hours after Brian Jones's lifeless body had been pulled out of his swimming pool, Mick and Marianne arrived at a party thrown by Prince Rupert Loewenstein in a tent on the grounds of his Kensington estate. All the guests were told to wear white for the occasion, so Jagger was clad in a white "party dress" by the avant-garde designer Michael Fish; the dress had actually been ordered by Sammy Davis, Jr., but was loaned to Mick.

Marianne, seemingly more distraught than anyone else over Jones's death, had hacked off great swatches of her beautiful blond hair. She was the only guest at the "White Ball" dressed in black, out of respect for Brian.

It turned out to be a raucous affair, with three rock bands filling the night air. The guest list included Peter Sellers, the fashion mogul Hardy Amies, Lord and Lady Tavistock, and Lord Harlech. But nothing created more of a stir than the couple of the evening—Mick Jagger and Princess Margaret—comparing hem lengths, then shaking it up on the dance floor.

Before retiring that night Faithful heard Jagger sniffling in the bathroom. When he came out, his eyes were puffy and swollen; Mick could not raise his voice above a whisper. Finally, she thought, the enormity of Brian's death had hit Mick. Before she could put a comforting hand on his shoulder, Marianne realized that Mick was merely fighting off the effects of hay fever—his first allergic attack in ten years. One of the symptoms was a sudden onset of laryngitis, and for a few terrifying hours Jagger wondered if he'd be in any condition to sing the next day. When he awoke, however, his voice had returned.

As tens of thousands of people in various states of undress spilled into Hyde Park on the hot morning of Saturday, July 5, six TV camera crews were setting up to provide live coverage of what promised to be the year's premier rock event. Meanwhile Jagger, still biding his time at 48 Cheyne Walk, offered some random observations on the nature of free concerts.

"A concert," he explained, "is an excuse as much as anything to come together, embrace each other, and have a common feeling." Then, offering a crash course in rock economics, Jagger explained why playing before anything but an enormous crowd just isn't worth it. "You don't make any money when you play a house that holds two thousand people. An average of ten shillings—that's two thousand pounds. One thousand pounds goes to the promoters. Another seven hundred pounds goes to pay the supporting groups. You're left with three hundred pounds. It cost you a hundred fifty pounds to get there. What's left is divided by five. I mean, really. . . ."

Jagger also offered a few thoughts about Brian. "Oh, Brian will be at the concert. . . . He'll be there," Mick said. "I don't believe in Western bereavement. I can't wear a long black veil. . . . But it's still very upsetting. We want to make it so that the audience will be filled with as much love as possible."

At two-thirty P.M. Mick, Marianne, and Nicholas piled into a limousine and were whisked to the Stones' concert headquarters at the Londonderry House Hotel. During the ride Mick looked out at the crowds jamming the side streets and swallowed hard. "I'm really quite nervous," he confessed to a smiling Marianne. Floating on a pharmaceutical cloud, Faithfull looked on serenely.

By now the throng had swelled to 250,000—a great blur of beads, feathers, flowers, and tie-dyed T-shirts stretching to the horizon. The crowd was particularly mellow, politely listening to bands like the Third Ear, King Crimson, the Screw, Family, Alexis Korner's new group New Church, and the Battered Ornaments as they waited for the main attraction.

Stones announcer Sam Cutler sounded like a school principal as he told the crowd when to stand up and stretch their legs, where to get help if they started feeling faint, and why they should climb down out of the trees (watching TV coverage from his Londonderry House suite, Keith Richards worried aloud that some of the fans perched on high branches ran the risk of serious injury). Cutler also read out the names of lost children, and suggested that they should meet up with their parents at the boat shed.

Nazi-helmeted, beswastikaed Hell's Angels, pale British cousins of the fearsome California motorcycle gang, were brought in to patrol the area around the stage. Given the mellow attitude of this crowd, their presence was hardly necessary. More mayhem could have been found at a grade-school assembly.

Marsha Hunt arrived, clad head-to-toe in fringed white buckskin, and was escorted to a perch atop a thirty-foot-high scaffold that rose on the left-hand side of the stage. Mick wanted to be able to see Marsha while he performed, and in this obvious spot she was impossible to miss. Faithfull was not likely to overlook Hunt's presence either. The two exchanged knowing glances as Marianne, dressed in a long white dress, took her place on the stage with the Stones' wives and official girlfriends.

Giant color portraits of Brian were quickly nailed up, and a roar of anticipation began to build. Suddenly, Jagger stood before them in his Fish-designed billowing white party dress over tight white pants, a gold-studded leather collar tight around his throat. No woman in sight was as heavily made up as Mick, in dark blue eyeshadow, rouge, and his favorite shade of Joan Crawford red lipstick. A large wood crucifix dangled from his neck.

Jagger blew kisses to the crowd, and then asked them to

be quiet. "I'd really dig it," he said, "if you would just cool it. I want to say a few words about Brian . . . and about his going when we didn't expect him to."

With that Mick opened a small book and began to read from Shelley's *Adonais*:

"Peace, peace! He is not dead, he doth not sleep—
He hath awakened from the dream of life—
'Tis we, who lost in stormy visions, keep
With phantoms an unprofitable strife,
And in mad trance, strike with our spirit's knife
Invulnerable nothings. *We* decay
Like corpses in a charnel; fear and grief
Convulse us and consume us day by day,
And cold hopes swarm like worms within our living clay."

People were weeping openly as Jagger jumped ahead to another stanza, and resumed his slightly stilted delivery:

"The One remains, the many change and pass;
Heaven's light forever shines, Earth's shadows fly;
Life, like a dome of many-colored glass
Stains the white radiance of eternity,
Until Death tramples it to fragments. —Die,
If thou wouldst be with that which thou dost seek!
Follow where all is fled! —Rome's azure sky,
Flowers, ruins, statues, music, words, are weak
The glory they transfuse with fitting truth to speak."

With that, helpers opened several cardboard boxes at the edge of the stage, releasing a quarter of a million white butterflies. This fluttering cloud lingered for a time over the stage, then dispersed to wreak considerable damage on the park's meticulously cultivated trees and shrubs.

Then the cowbell clanged, and Jagger ripped into "Honky Tonk Women." Whipping himself into a frothing frenzy, Jagger unbuttoned his dress and peeled it off like Gypsy Rose Lee to reveal a tank top underneath. At one point he unhooked the studded antique leather belt that had been slung low around his hips and began thrashing the stage floor with it. When the leather-worshiping Hell's Angels reached up to grab it from him, Jagger whispered, "No. It's the only one I have."

Muscles straining, veins snaking over his arms, the mascara-smeared Head Stone pranced, pouted, and pumped for the audience for the next hour. With a television audience of millions—not to mention a small army of police—looking on, Jagger fell to his knees and wrapped his lascivious lips around the head of his hand mike. Decades before Madonna caused a stir by fellating an Evian bottle, Jagger seemed to be doing the same thing—to himself.

Jagger's bravura performance notwithstanding, the band's playing was uneven, almost amateurish. The Hyde Park Concert would come to be regarded as their worst effort ever.

The event also fell short as a memorial to the fallen Jones. "We all thought he'd cancel the concert," recalled Stones fan club organizer Valerie Watson Dunn, who was there. "But he carried on anyway. I was surprised that Mick didn't seem too affected by Brian's death. He seemed sort of heartless, as if nothing happened. I thought differently of him after that, and I think a lot of Stones fans did. . . ."

Mick told Marianne he had some unfinished business and spent the night with Marsha Hunt at her flat. They parted at sunrise so he and Marianne could catch their flight to Australia and be on the set of *Ned Kelly* the next day. "I laughingly shrugged off Mick's last kiss," remembered Hunt, who bade Jagger farewell in a driving rain. "I hate good-byes, especially when the lump in my throat threatens to get the better of me."

The Australian trip also provided Mick with an excuse to miss Brian's funeral; the services were scheduled for the same day Jagger was to appear on the *Ned Kelly* set.

Exhausted by the flight to Sydney, Mick went to bed as soon as they checked into their hotel. Marianne, still haunted by the image of Brian lying facedown at the bottom of a swimming pool, found it harder to fall asleep.

So, as she had done a hundred times before, she sat at

the vanity table and took her sodium amytal sleeping pills, washing each down with a swallow of hot chocolate. The difference this time was that she would not stop.

Confusing herself with the Shakespearean character she had recently played, Ophelia, Faithfull began to hallucinate. She took the entire bottle of pills—150 in all—and then climbed into bed alongside Jagger.

An hour or so later Mick awakened and noticed the empty bottle of pills on the table. He grabbed Marianne and shook her, but when she didn't respond he quickly called an ambulance.

After her stomach was pumped at the hospital, Jagger kept a vigil at Faithfull's bedside. Since she was also suffering from heroin withdrawal, doctors warned Mick that she might never regain consciousness.

During this time Marianne imagined herself floating through space with Brian—until the voices of her mother and son summoned her back to the living. After six days in a life-threatening coma she came to. Had Mick not called an ambulance immediately, Faithfull would not have survived. She was grateful to Jagger for having saved her life. Marianne also knew that, to keep from trying to take her life again, she would have to find some way to leave him.

Reading about Marianne's overdose in the papers, Marsha Hunt worried about what impact it would have on Jagger. "I was frantic, because I didn't think that Mick had the stamina to deal with another crisis," she said. "There is only so much a person can take."

Marianne was promptly replaced in *Ned Kelly* by her understudy, and spent the next two months at Mount St. Michael Hospital outside Sydney recuperating. At Brian's funeral the rector read from the parable of the Prodigal Son, and also asked the congregation to pray for Marianne's soul. Charlie Watts and Bill Wyman were the only members of the Stones's huge organization to attend.

On the set Mick, who was required to speak Ned Kelly's lines with an Irish accent, butted heads with the film's director, Tony Richardson, over what he felt was a mediocre

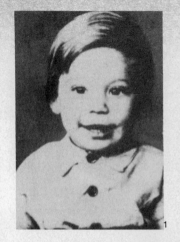

1 His contrived cockney accent aside, Michael Philip Jagger (shown here at age two) grew up solidly middle-class in the London suburb of Dartford. When he was ten, the family moved from **2** this duplex into a larger home **3** in an exclusive neighborhood called The Close.

4 Captain of the Dartford School basketball team, Jagger (standing at right) bit off the tip of his tongue during a game, changing his speech forever.

5 The original Rolling Stones. From left: Ian Stewart, Keith Richards, Charlie Watts, Brian Jones (standing), Bill Wyman, and Jagger. Stewart, looking far too normal, would soon be bumped into the background.

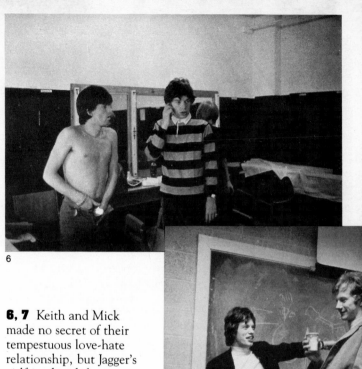

6, 7 Keith and Mick made no secret of their tempestuous love-hate relationship, but Jagger's girlfriend said she was surprised when she found him in a compromising position with manager Andrew Oldham.

6

7

8

8 Shills had been planted at early concerts to start audiences screaming, but by their 1965 U.S. tour, Jagger and the Stones were the world's top hard rock band—and causing full-scale riots wherever they played.

9 Primping in the dressing room. The son of an Avon lady, Jagger has been an expert on cosmetics, hair care, and fashion since adolescence.

9

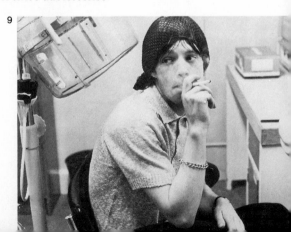

10 The rock star and his first major purchase: a jet-black Aston-Martin.

11 Jagger and fiancée Chrissie Shrimpton returning from a holiday in the Bahamas in 1965. When their stormy four-year affair ended the following year, she attempted suicide over Mick.

10

11

12 Cloak and Jagger. Mick posed as a sort of pop Byron for photographer-designer Cecil Beaton, who gushed in his diaries about Mick's physical attributes.

13 Jagger and his new love Marianne Faithfull in 1967, before her descent into heroin addiction.

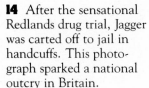

14 After the sensational Redlands drug trial, Jagger was carted off to jail in handcuffs. This photograph sparked a national outcry in Britain.

15 Jagger shares a bath with Anita Pallenberg and Michelle Breton in his first feature film, *Performance*. Keith Richards fumed while Mick and Pallenberg carried on a steamy affair offscreen as well.

16

16 Brian (lower left) and Mick after a custard pie fight at the press launch for *Beggar's Banquet*. In all the excitement, Jagger apparently failed to notice that the seams of his pants were coming undone.

17 At his own drug trial in the fall of 1968, Jones gets a kiss from girlfriend Suki Poitier and moral support from Keith and Mick. This rare display of unity would be short-lived.

17

18 The Rolling Stones' *Rock and Roll Circus*. The cast of the TV special also included John Lennon, Yoko Ono, Roger Daltry, Pete Townshend, and Eric Clapton.

19 After Jagger engineered Brian Jones's departure from the group, Mick Taylor (second from left) was introduced to the press on June 13, 1969, as the newest Stone.

20 Seven months after she miscarried their baby, Faithfull and Jagger were back in court on drug charges in the summer of 1969.

21 Jagger, wearing his "party dress," at the July 5, 1969, Hyde Park concert in memory of Brian Jones. More than 250,000 people attended the concert, held just two days after Jones's mysterious death.

22 One of the unlikely getups worn by Jagger in the embarrassing shoot-em-up *Ned Kelly*. While on location in Australia, Faithfull became the second woman in Mick's life to attempt suicide.

23 The Day the Music Died. The carnage at Altamont, chillingly detailed in the documentary *Gimme Shelter*, would haunt Jagger for years.

22

23

24 Jagger goes boating with Richards, Pallenberg, and their toddler son, Marlon. Her obsession with satanism profoundly influenced both men, and their music.

25 Mick and Bianca's media circus wedding on May 12, 1971, in St. Tropez.

26 As usual, Keith enjoyed himself at the reception.

25

26

27 Marsha Hunt and daughter, Karis, Jagger's eldest child. Mick would not admit paternity for years—and only then after Hunt, by that time living on welfare, filed two lawsuits.

28 For the Rolling Stones' record-smashing 1972–73 tour, Jagger wore glitter, spangled jump suits, lots of jewelry, and even more makeup.

29 Jagger, wearing nail polish, shares a tender moment with Lou Reed and Bowie at London's Cafe Royal in 1973.

30 A forty-foot-long phallus was unquestionably the most memorable prop of the 1973 tour.

31 Wielding her trademark walking stick, style-setting Bianca ruled over the night world at New York's legendary Studio 54 in the 1970s.

32 One look says it all. Bianca called the misogynistic Stones "the Nazi State," and became so enraged over Mick's affairs that, according to Jagger, she once pulled a gun on him.

33 Jagger and Princess Margaret had already been close friends for a decade when they got together backstage after a 1975 concert. They also maintain neighboring hideaways (along with David Bowie) on the tiny island of Mustique.

34 Talking shop with the urbane chief of Atlantic Records, Ahmet Ertegun.

34

35, 36 Jerry Hall and Jagger. The Texas-reared model described her methods for keeping Mick happy to their friend Andy Warhol in graphic detail.

35

36

37

38

37 Paul and Linda Mc-Cartney pay a backstage courtesy call. Jagger remained friendly with all the Beatles, though he was closest to John Lennon.

38 Partying with Catherine Guinness, one of several Guinness women with whom Jagger has been romantically linked over the years.

39

39 The Jaggers: a bearded Michael Philip, younger brother Chris, proud parents Eva and Joe. He described his mother as "very working class" and his father as "bourgeois."

40, 41 During the headline-making 1981 tour, Jagger proved he could still whip millions of fans into a frenzy.

42 The enigmatic Mick.

41

42

43 Jagger partying at Regine's with eighteen-year-old debutante Cornelia Guest. Jerry retaliated by running off with racehorse mogul Robert Sangster.

44 Much to Jerry's delight, Jagger offers one of his favorite gestures to an L.A. photographer.

45

45 Mick gets a hug from Pete Townshend of The Who. In a fortieth-birthday tribute to his friend, Townshend admitted that he had always been physically attracted to Jagger.

46 Mick takes Jade, twelve, to New York's Lenox Hill Hospital to see Jerry and her new half-sister, Elizabeth Scarlett.

47

47 The proud grand-parents—Joe, Eva, and Marjorie Hall—join Mick and Jerry at Elizabeth Scarlett's christening.
48 At the historic 1985 Live Aid concert, Jagger and his onstage role model, Tina Turner, stole the show with their steamy renditon of "Honky Tonk Women."

48

49

50

49 Jagger and thirteen-year-old Jade, backstage at Live Aid.

50 Costar Rae Dawn Chong was nude in the hour-long video to promote *She's the Boss*, but Jagger wore a dress.

51 A scene from the video for his *Lucky in Love* solo single. He sometimes packs a gun off camera as well.

52 Cecil Beaton's portrait of Jagger's posterior was auctioned off at Sotheby's in 1986.

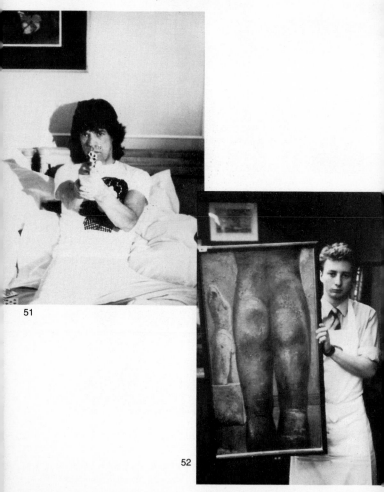

51

52

53 A Jagger family portrait at Heathrow: Karis holds two-year-old Elizabeth Scarlett while Jerry has her arm around Jade. A nanny pushes James, seven months.
54 After the success of 1985's *Dancing in the Streets*, Mick Jagger and David Bowie considered donning drag to remake *Some Like It Hot.*

53

54

55 A family picnic at Mustique.

56 At the 1988 Rock and Roll Hall of Fame dinner in New York, Jagger presented the Beatles with their award, then jammed with George Harrison and Bruce Springsteen.

57 Jagger cutting loose during the Steel Wheels tour—the biggest in rock history.

58 Hall took Elizabeth Scarlett and James to join their father in the U.S. as he rehearsed for the Stones' 1989 Steel Wheels tour.

57

58

59 While they sit for a group portrait, Charlie Watts catches the most narcissistic Stone in the act.

60 The Glimmer Twins could not have been more delighted when the Rolling Stones were inducted into the Rock and Roll Hall of Fame in 1989.

61 Jade and boyfriend, Piers Jackson, father of Mick's first grandchild.

62 Jagger played a bounty hunter with a heart in the futuristic *Freejack*.

63 Jagger's alleged affair with Carla Bruni pushed Mick and Jerry to the brink in 1992.

64 The Lion in Winter.

script. Mick also was fed up fumbling through retake after retake with Marianne's replacement, who hadn't had a chance to learn her lines.

It was also a physically demanding role, requiring Jagger to make at least a few convincing moves before the stunt double stepped in to finish off the fight scenes. Jagger, as luck would have it, suffered the only serious injury during the making of the film, nearly losing his right hand when a handgun accidentally fired off a blank at close range. The wound required sixteen stitches.

As he had with Cleo Sylvestre years before, Mick showered Marsha Hunt with love letters and telephone calls. The letters were often addressed to "Miss Fuzzy," and Hunt was impressed with their sensitivity and unrestrained romanticism. "He wrote laughing, sad, pensive, deep, observant, touching letters to me," she recalled.

On July 20, 1969—the day American astronauts landed on the moon—Jagger was moved to share the awe-inspiring moment not with Faithfull, but with Hunt. He sat down and penned a letter to her, dated simply "Sunday the moon." During one of his almost daily phone calls to Marsha, Mick told her he was in the middle of writing a song about her. He wanted to call it "Brown Sugar." (He did not let her in on the *entire* working title: "Brown Sugar aka Black Pussy").

After Jagger's hand was nearly blown off on the set of *Ned Kelly*, he scrawled one or two of the letters with his left hand. Mick shared the details of the accident with Hunt, but spared Marianne the added upset. When she inquired about his bandaged hand during one of his daily visits to her hospital room, Jagger told her it was merely part of his *Ned Kelly* attire.

It was not all bad news that summer: Anita and Keith had purchased a mansion just a few doors down from them at 3 Cheyne Walk. A few days after moving in Pallenberg gave birth to a healthy baby boy. They named him after Keith's favorite Hollywood rebel. Marlon Richards slept soundly in his nursery, unaware that every night his parents shot up heroin in the next room.

As soon as filming was over in September, Jagger and Marianne took off for a holiday away from prying reporters and intrusive fans in Indonesia. While they tried to pick up the broken pieces of their relationship in seclusion, the Stones released *Through the Past Darkly*, a collection of their hits in memory of Brian. The epigraph:

> When this you see, remember me
> And bear me in your mind
> Let all the world say what they may
> Speak of me as you find.

Once they were back on Cheyne Walk, Mick and Marianne picked up where they had left off. She tried to run the household on the measly twenty-five pounds a week Jagger budgeted for that purpose. He concentrated on a secret plan to wrest control of the Stones' finances from the dreaded Allen Klein.

By this time Klein's machinations were legendary. In an article titled "The Toughest Wheeler-Dealer in the Pop Jungle," the venerated *Sunday Times* of London described Klein's operation as a "startling blend of bluff, sheer determination, and financial agility, together with an instinct for publicity and the ability to lie like a trooper."

The group's contract with Klein ran until July 31, 1970, as did their contract with Decca. But Klein was still distracted by the Beatles debacle, and if there was ever a chance of wriggling free, Mick would have to put some plan into effect now.

Jagger told Prince Rupert Loewenstein that, in addition to handling Mick's personal finances, he would be hired as the Stones' business manager as soon as Mick could devise a plan to dump Klein. In the meantime, at a private meeting in Loewenstein's Kensington home, Prince Rupert told Mick the only solution to their long-range plans was for the

Stones to leave England—permanently—to avoid that country's crippling tax bite.

Fleeing England was far less daunting than the process of separating from Klein. Now was not a propitious time for such a delicate maneuver. The formal changing of the guard would have to wait until after the upcoming tour of America—their first in three years. As a tentative first step toward freedom, however, Jagger cagily convinced Klein to let his nephew and deputy, Ronnie Schneider, handle the tour instead of Klein himself. Jagger's first order of business: hiring B. B. King and the Ike and Tina Turner Revue as opening acts.

Predictably, news of the upcoming tour triggered a scramble among producers on the other side of the Atlantic. Fillmore founder Bill Graham, the best-known rock promoter in the country, was first in line to book the entire tour. But Schneider kept Graham waiting while he walked his dog ("It was something he was really good at," sniped Graham, "and something he actually knew how to do"), then turned him down because, in Schneider's estimation, Graham hadn't done anything "really big." The William Morris Agency got the job, but Graham did get the chance to put on one of the tour's biggest shows, at the Oakland Coliseum.

The Stones arrived in Los Angeles on October 13 and set up their headquarters in the Du Pont mansion above Sunset Strip. Mick and Keith, meanwhile, stayed with friend Stephen Sills in a palatial Laurel Canyon estate built by the composer Carmen Dragon and previously occupied by Monkee Peter Tork.

During these three weeks prior to the actual launch of the tour, Mick availed himself of the ready supply of willing females—sweet young teens as well as seasoned twenty-something troupers with names like Suzie Suck and Suzie Creamcheese.

Yet for Mick, nothing was quite as satisfying as sleeping with the lovers of friends—particularly the lovers of other rock stars. Jagger's fling with Pallenberg had whetted his appetite for cockoldry, and it was not long before he zeroed in on his next conquest.

Pamela Des Barres was destined for a peculiar sort of celebrity as one of the premier groupies of the late 1960s and '70s. Yet when she first peered in Mick Jagger's hotel room window during the 1966 U.S. tour, she was just Pam Miller of Reseda, California.

Mick thought nothing of her at the time, but by 1969 she was a member of an all-girl band, the GTOs. More significantly, she was now the girlfriend of Led Zeppelin's Jimmy Page. Jagger had to have her.

In the weeks before the tour began, Jagger's campaign to lure Jimmy Page's woman into his bed was unremitting. Mick charmed, cajoled, stroked, kissed, fondled, and begged the girl he called "Miss Pamela" to sleep with him, but to no avail.

Jagger wondered if he would have as hard a time winning over American audiences. Indeed, the Mick Jagger they would behold in 1969 bore scant resemblance to the snarling rocker who had belted out "Under My Thumb" and "Paint It Black" back in the summer of 1966. This time, at their "break-in" concert at Colorado State College, the lights went up on the spitting image of *Performance*'s androgynous Turner—a leaping, twirling, eye-rolling sprite wearing a skinny black top, wide studded belt, tight flared pants, a crimson scarf, and red, white, and blue Uncle Sam top hat. "The audience just *sat* there," marveled Jagger. "They were, I think, too stoned to move."

Once they stepped off the plane in Oakland, the Stones faced the first crisis of the tour. In the torrid political climate of 1969 a number of radical groups had asked for the Stones' endorsement. Except for the Oakland-based Black Panthers, who did not ask but *demanded* that the street-fighting Mick publicly back them. His refusal brought death threats. Ike and Tina Turner took these warnings seriously; they surrounded themselves with armed bodyguards, and carried their own handguns for good measure.

That night in Oakland it looked as if Jagger might need

extra security—to protect himself not from the Panthers but from the fans. When Tina Turner tore up the stage, Mick was so reluctant to risk comparison that he kept the crowd waiting forty-five minutes before the Stones went on. The audience response to Jagger's opening number "Jumpin' Jack Flash," was neither immediate nor tumultuous. "So happy to be here," sneered Jagger, "and all that bullshit. . . ."

Halfway through "Satisfaction" Graham and tour manager Sam Cutler got into a shoving match right onstage. It was two A.M. by the time the Stones started the second show—fully two hours behind schedule. "It was 'fuck you' for the sake of 'fuck you,' " Graham later recalled. "I had to spend the whole night dealing with that."

By Jagger's own admission the band's playing was "ragged,"and he was finding it hard to breach the wall that had been erected over the past three years between Jagger the Myth and his audiences. "We had to look at him to make sure he was really there," wrote Greil Marcus in *Rolling Stone*. "The giant TV screen up above the stage held images that in an odd way were more real than the show itself—somehow it made more sense to see a *picture* of Mick Jagger than to see Mick Jagger himself."

While Jagger was still trying to seduce Jimmy Page's "Miss Pamela," he unexpectedly found himself on the receiving end of infidelity. The tour had reached Dallas when newspapers picked up the story that Marianne Faithfull had run off with wealthy Roman painter Mario Schifano, Anita Pallenberg's long-ago boyfriend. Mick was stunned and angry—not only at Faithfull's betrayal, but at her timing. In the middle of a tour that depended on the public perception of his sexual supremacy, Jagger was being shown up by an Italian pretty boy.

Sobbing, Jagger phoned Rome immediately and pleaded with Faithfull to return. Then, at last, he nailed Miss Pamela in a booth at the Whiskey-a-Go-Go on Sunset Strip. "He gave new meaning to giving head," she recalled. "Those lips!!! Please!! We made love for hours. . . . All I really care about is that he LIKES me, genuinely. . . ." Afterward she helped him pack his seven suitcases, pulling out one of his outfits and holding it up to her. "Oh, it's *you*, Miss Pamela," Jagger gushed, and gave it to her.

By the time they reached New York on Thanksgiving day, the Stones had hit their stride—and the audiences responded accordingly. The crowds at Madison Square Garden rushed the stage, a forest of hands reaching up to grab Jagger's trailing red scarf. Jagger's friend Andy Warhol and a thoroughly inebriated Janis Joplin watched from VIP seats while Jimi Hendrix, who had tried to steal Faithfull away from Jagger, crouched behind some amplifiers to watch the show.

Leonard Bernstein did the same thing, transfixed by the pumping, thrashing dynamo that drove the Stones' engine. "Lenny was excited by the Stones' music," said a friend, "and most of all by Mick Jagger's sexual charisma. He had a crush on Mick." Between shows the bisexual conductor-composer embraced Jagger, lingering long enough to make his interest known. Mick was flattered, but declined Bernstein's advances.

Jagger's unisex posing kicked up quite a lot of speculation in the press, and even among those who knew him. The Stones' stage manager, the ingeniously named Chip Monck, confessed to having somewhat confused feelings toward his boss. "Before I saw Mick," he recalled, "I had this old lady. Every now and then when I look at Mick from the side he looks like her. I don't know if this puts me in the latent homosexual category, but it makes me feel very warm toward him."

"Mick definitely has a kind of bisexual charm," said Kenneth Anger. "I'm sure that's part of the appeal for the chicks. It reacts in their unconscious, it brings out the beast." Abbie Hoffman, who unsuccessfully tried to get Jagger to pay for part of the Chicago Eight's legal defense, thought Mick was nothing less than the Woodstock Generation's Myra Breckinridge.

Jagger might well have been the self-assured Myra as he

held court during a press conference in that masterpiece of Art Deco architecture, the Rainbow Room. Jagger had kept everyone waiting while his minions dashed around looking for pills to get him through the ordeal. "Can anybody get any Librium for Mick?" pleaded one. "It's very, very urgent!" At the last minute Jo Bergman managed to borrow a Valium from a reporter, and the show went on. "Mother's little helpers," quipped one wag, "get mothers' sons through busy days, too, it seems."

The room buzzed when a female reporter asked if Jagger was any more "satisfied" with this tour than previous ones.

"Do you mean financially? Sexually? Philosophically?" he asked.

"Financially and philosophically satisfied," she replied, careful to omit one category.

Jagger thought a moment before answering. "Financially, dissatisfied," he said, aware that Allen Klein was standing behind him. "Sexually, satisfied—you know? Philosophically, still trying."

"Are you sadder but wiser?" someone asked.

"Just a little wiser," said Mick.

Jagger had every reason to be satisfied financially. The Stones had shattered attendance records across the nation, and their estimated take of $2 million would be the largest in history.

The huge gross was due in part to the sky-high ticket prices commanded by the Stones—a fact that did not go unnoticed in the press. After veteran San Francisco rock critic Ralph J. Gleason accused the Stones of "despising their audience," there was no shaking the perception that Jagger and Co. had merely come to America to shake down the fans.

Jagger had been hinting for weeks that the Stones would pay back their American fans with a free concert. Now, in the Rainbow Room, he confirmed it. When did he decide to do a free concert? a reporter asked. "It was when we first fucking got to Los Angeles, the first stop," Jagger answered testily. "We decided right then to do it after the tour was over. We wanted to do Los Angeles, because the weather's better. But there's no place to do it there, and we were assured we could do it much more easily in San Francisco. . . ."

"If I go into a village grocer's they all act real scared. What do they expect? That I'll rape their daughters or stick a needle in my arm?"

Place: The San Francisco editing room of Albert and David Maysles. The Maysles Brothers are about to screen a rough cut of their Altamont film *Gimme Shelter* for Mick Jagger and Charlie Watts. Before they do, they listen to Hell's Angels leader Sonny Barger ranting on about the Stones on a local radio talk show. "This Mick Jagger put it all on the Angels," protested Barger. "He used us for dupes, man. As far as I'm concerned, we've been the biggest suckers for that idiot I've ever seen. They [the Stones] told me that if I sat on the edge of the stage and I didn't let anyone get by me, I could drink beer until the show was over. When they started messin' over our bikes, they started it. . . ."

Mick, visibly shaken by the anger in Barger's voice, shook his head and turned his attention to the film. The fatal stabbing of Meredith Hunter had been captured by the Maysles in gruesome color, and as it was rerun for Jagger in slow motion, he carefully studied the footage. "Wow," said Jagger, enthralled. "It's so horrible." Moments later he was off to join Miss Pamela.

Gimme Shelter would not be released for another year— around the time Hell's Angel Alan Passaro went on trial for Meredith Hunter's murder. Since he was clearly visible on the Maysles Brothers' film, Passaro could not deny that he had stabbed Hunter. But several Angels whose identities could not be determined were also shown plunging knives and fists into the young black man. There was no way of proving that Passaro had struck the fatal blows. Moreover, Passaro's lawyers argued that Hunter had pulled a gun on their client, and that he was merely acting in self-defense. The jury, to the astonishment of millions viewing the film over and over again on the local news, voted to acquit.

Despite their legal vindication the Hell's Angels would hold Jagger personally responsible for their troubles. Years later, much to Mick's horror, it would be revealed just how deep seated their resentment was.

The fallout from Altamont lingered for decades. Landowners in the area sued the Stones for damage to their property. The family of Meredith Hunter sued the Stones, and the Stones, in turn, sued Sears Point Raceway for $10 million. If Sears Point hadn't canceled at the last minute, they reasoned, there never would have been an Altamont.

Beyond the legal entanglements Altamont would leave the Stones and Mick with a bitter and lasting legacy. "Altamont, it could only happen to the Stones, man," said Richards, shaking his head. "Let's face it. It wouldn't happen to the Bee Gees and it wouldn't happen to Crosby, Stills, and Nash." Composer-singer Don McLean immortalized Jagger in his landmark song "American Pie": "No angel born in Hell/could break that Satan's spell."

Indeed, Altamont was widely (if somewhat disingenuously) regarded as the Dark Side of Woodstock—a singularly bloody event that marked an end to the so-called peace and love era. It also solidified Jagger's global reputation as a kind of pop Antichrist. As Jagger packaged and repackaged himself over the coming decades, this taint of malevolence would always remain.

The 1970s dawned on a Mick Jagger filled with apprehension over the changes in his personal and professional lives. With Marianne gone, the only woman in the house at 48 Cheyne Walk was Bruna Girardi, Jagger's Italian housekeeper. Marsha Hunt moved in for a short time, but was unnerved by his friends down the block. Keith and Anita, hopelessly hooked on heroin, frightened her. "Mick doted on Keith," she recalled, "but I decided to keep my distance."

On a day-to-day basis Mick was hardly devoid of female companionship. A dizzying succession of women—many Americans, for whom he had a special fondness—hopped in and out of Jagger's bed. Christopher Gibbs said that often when he dined with Jagger, women who had slept with him would come up to the table and "he'd have absolutely no idea who they were."

Yet as the holidays drew closer, he became increasingly emotional about Marianne and the way in which she had deserted him. Faithfull returned to England with Mario Schifano and Nicholas to spend Christmas with her mother, the baroness. On Christmas Eve, Jagger drove down from Redlands, where he was staying with Keith, and confronted them. "I suppose that his motivations were not so much to get me back," she later said, "but to overcome his public humiliation. He had to do it to preserve his personal machismo."

If anything, she felt Mario was a superior lover, but Marianne had to concede that she felt more comfortable around Mick. She took her customary handful of sleeping pills and decided to let them battle it out. When she awoke the next morning, Mick was in bed beside her. Mario was asleep on a couch in the living room, and departed for Rome early the next day. "Wop in your bed, girl?" he said. "A bleedin' Eye-tie?" Mick had won.

They returned to Cheyne Walk the day after Christmas. Hours later he sneaked out and met Marsha in the kitchen of her friend's apartment. She gave him her Christmas present—a puppy. He told her he loved her.

Once again on Cheyne Walk, nothing had changed, and Marianne sank deeper and deeper into depression. Mick was roaming once again, and Marianne was expected to remain true to her surname. But it was more than that. Faithfull came to believe that Jagger wanted her to stay at home like a traditional English housewife because she was more valuable to him that way. "I was giving him fantastic food for material and that was much better than me being a little actress in my own right."

As she alternated between heroin and cocaine, Faithfull began to come unhinged. Screaming matches and suicide threats were commonplace now, but still Jagger would not let go. "It's like having a butterfly or an insect on a pin," she explained. "It's beautiful and fascinating. I was, and I am, so complex and get so disturbed and he couldn't let me go. He had me on a pin and he was watching me flail and writhe, but it was something that fascinated him as an artist."

It was over dinner at Mr. Chow's in January that Jagger suggested to Marsha Hunt that they have a baby. Watching Keith with little Marlon over the Christmas season had made him realize that he still wanted to be a father. Hunt, who had always shunned the birth control pill because of its side effects, obligingly removed her IUD.

Seven weeks later, as they cut through Hyde Park on the way to a meeting with Atlantic Records mogul Ahmet Ertegun, Hunt told Jagger that his wish had been granted: she was due to give birth in November. Hunt told him that if he had changed his mind, she was willing to have an abortion. But Jagger was jubilant. It was agreed that, for the time being, they would keep Mick's name out of the papers. Then Mick returned to the truly important business of the day, listening to Ahmet Ertegun lay down the reasons why the Stones should leave Decca for Atlantic.

By midspring it was clear that Marianne's heroin addiction had taken a horrifying toll. She was unkempt, there were great circles under her bloodshot eyes—and she didn't care. More than once she fell down in the streets; more than once she passed out in restaurants and at chic dinner parties, pitching headfirst into her plate. Once Jagger returned to Cheyne Walk to find her sprawled on the bathroom floor, unconscious.

Marianne knew that, when he said he was working at the studio, Mick was at Hunt's flat in St. John's Wood. She also knew that Stargroves, the Berkshire estate that had once been Oliver Cromwell's headquarters, now was Mick's favorite trysting place for one-night stands.

Jagger hired Maldwin Thomas, his former hairdresser and one of Sir Mark Palmer's traveling band of UFO buffs, to look after Stargroves. Thomas was startled awake several times a week by Jagger pounding away on the door, shouting to be let in with yet another young woman. Ironically, Thomas himself married Jenny Fabian, one of the era's best-known groupies.

This became somewhat more problematic when Eva and Joe Jagger decided to move into Stargroves for long stretches, lording it over the locals and ordering the help about. Eva's brusque manner eventually drove Thomas away.

In the press Jagger hardly lavished praise on his parents. "I owe my parents nothing," he declared publicly. "They are my parents, that is that. I liked them and I still do, but there are no dues to be paid by me to them. I was never part of home life. I knew I'd break away and I did."

By way of replacing Thomas, Mick invited his brother, Chris, still struggling to emerge from his sibling's looming shadow, to move in with his American girlfriend. With Chris ensconced, Stargroves was once again in operation as Mick Jagger's Elizabethan answer to Motel 6.

It was in May that Mick bumped into Miss Pamela, fresh from Los Angeles and living with a friend of his, a co-owner of the fashionable London boutique Granny's. The fact that Miss Pamela was again involved with someone he knew made Jimmy Page's former girlfriend all the more desirable.

Jagger spirited her off one afternoon to the old Edith Grove flat he had shared with Brian, Keith, and the dreaded Jimmy Phelge. They stripped off their clothes and "checked out each other's buns and had a great laugh." One afternoon Jagger and Miss Pamela made love in his friend's double bed while he was off at work. "My nerves flew out the window as he threw me on the mattress and turned me into a cheating trollop. It was fantastic," she later said. "Just as our moans started harmonizing, we heard a key in the door. . . . One-two-three, Mick came and went." The unexpected visitor turned out to be the cleaning lady.

During one of her nightly scream fests with Mick, Faithfull once again declared that she was leaving. This time Mick pulled her back inside and quietly asked her to listen to a song he had just recorded. Faithfull sat there coolly and listened to the lyrics of "Wild Horses":

Graceless Lady you know who I am
You know I can't let you slide through my hand.
Wild horses couldn't drag me away. . . .

She leapt to her feet and, weeping, threw her arms around him. "I can't leave you. Ohhh, such a beautiful song. You wrote that for me? I love you!"

Faithfull stayed, but within days Jagger had slipped back into his old ways, and she felt more resentful than ever. "I had no way of expressing my anguish," Marianne recalled, "and Mick was using mine to make him even better than he was, and it made me mad. The only way I could see out of it was for me or him to die. And then I thought, *Even if I die or he dies I still won't get away from him!*"

With "Nicholas under one arm and a Persian rug under the other," Faithfull left the house on Cheyne Walk, moved in with her mother, and began an affair with another man—Lord Rossmore, an Eton-educated Irish peer sixteen years her senior.

Undaunted, Jagger launched yet another campaign to win her back. In desperation Marianne, still hopelessly hooked on heroin, deliberately gained fifty pounds to turn Jagger off sexually. "Mick is very conceited about his body, and about the women he is seen with. He basically has contempt for women; they only exist as reflections of *him*." Jagger was stunned when he saw the new, dowdy Marianne. "And that," she said, "was the end of that. He never came back."

Faithfull continued using heroin, cocaine, and a wide range of other drugs long after her final split with Jagger. Marianne also claimed she suffered an unanticipated side-effect from her time with Jagger: "I can't have an orgasm anymore," she said years later ". . . and that's come from flooding myself with too much feeling. But I think it'll come back. . . ."

Jagger's assessment of their five-year affair is equally charitable. "Marianne, you know, she nearly killed *me*, forget it! I wasn't going to get out of there alive, Marianne Faithfull and Anita Pallenberg! I mean, *help!*"

That July, Jagger wept. Not over a broken love affair or impending fatherhood, but over *Ned Kelly*. Since Warner Bros. was still refusing to release *Performance*, this marked the first time Jagger had actually seen himself on the big screen. The experience was shattering. He knew the film would be a catastrophe, but he had also imagined that his director, Tony Richardson, would somehow be able to salvage the damage in the editing room. If anything, he looked and sounded even more ridiculous than he remembered.

In this, audiences and reviewers were in complete agreement. The film premiered in London on June 23, and Mick wisely chose not to attend. "When he reaches for his gun," said the *Daily Mail*, "we expect peas to issue from it. He's just about as lethal as last week's lettuce."

Before its release Down Under the film was shown to residents of Glenrowan, the Australian cattle town where Ned Kelly's gang had been wiped out in a gunfight and Kelly himself taken alive and hanged. The townspeople of Glenrowan were markedly less charitable than the London critics in their assessment of Mick's performance. Noting that the real Ned Kelly was over six feet tall and some two hundred pounds, one local pointed out that Jagger "has shoulders like a Coke bottle. He looks too sissy, and too bloody scrawny, to be Ned Kelly."

Colin Bennett of the Melbourne *Age* blasted Jagger as being "too fey in his strange Irish drawl, too vulnerable and vague to make a leader, let along magnetize or menace anybody." UPI agreed Jagger was incapable of playing "the iron man of legend."

Jagger's comments left no doubt as to his opinion of his film debut: "*Ned Kelly!* That was a load of shit. I only made it because I had nothing else to do. You never know until you do it whether a film will turn out to be a load of shit, and if it does, all you can say is, 'Well, that was a load of shit.' "

The day after the London premiere of *Ned Kelly*, Jagger hired a leggy blonde from Los Angeles, Janice Kenner, to be his housekeeper and personal assistant. Before giving her the job he asked Kenner, "Where do you like to wake up, the country or the city?" She chose the country. Jagger got behind the wheel of his Bentley and drove his new housekeeper to Stargroves at breakneck speed.

After a marathon lovemaking session with Kenner, Jagger left her behind at Stargroves and drove into London to spend the afternoon strolling through Chelsea with Pamela Miller. They wound up at Cheyne Walk, where they put on some Dylan, smoked grass, and, according to Miss Pamela, "fell into such a beautiful mood, we fucked on a pile of pillows . . . bodies so gentle; him saying how I make him feel so relaxed. . . ."

Once Miss Pamela left 48 Cheyne Walk, Jagger rang up another nineteen-year-old American girl he was seeing, New Yorker Patti D'Arbanville, and invited her over for an intimate "picnic" in his backyard.

D'Arbanville, an actress-model who had already posed for Richard Avedon, Patrick Lichfield, and Bert Stern, had just finished her first feature film when she met Jagger. Within days she moved into a flat just a few doors away. "Mick is so exciting," she gushed at the time, "but at the same time so peaceful to be with. We don't have to go anywhere exotic to enjoy life." (Not long after, Pamela Miller—later Des Barres—and D'Arbanville would begin long-term affairs with the actor Don Johnson).

With all this Jagger still found the time to carry on simultaneous affairs with Suki Poitier (again, the temptation of sleeping with Brian Jones's ex-lover proved irresistible), Caroline Coon (she had hoped Jagger would match George Harrision's fifteen-thousand-dollar donation to a drug program called Release; Jagger declined), and another stunning Californian, Catherine James. This rundown does not include innumerable one-night stands with women whose names Jagger could not recall—if he ever knew them in the first place.

Janice Kenner did not exactly welcome Catherine James into the Stargroves fold. Although she only occasionally slept with Jagger and was willing to tolerate his dalliances with other women, Kenner more or less considered herself the chatelaine of Stargroves. James's addition to the resident cast of characters might have been expected to provoke a heated response from Kenner and—much to Jagger's obvious delight—it did. For the next few months the two women battled constantly over Jagger.

Amazingly, even with all these distractions Jagger managed to keep a firm grip on the tiller of the Stones organization. The group officially severed ties with Allen Klein on July 30. The next day they announced the termination of their arrangement with Decca, leaving them free to pick a new label from the two dozen record companies clamoring for their business.

Jagger instructed the group's lawyers to file a $29 million action against Klein in Manhattan, accusing him of manipulating the Stones' finances "for his own personal profit and advantage." The way things were organized by Klein, the Stones essentially worked for him: proceeds from the group's lucrative record deals were paid directly to Klein, who in turn doled out modest sums to the Stones on request. Jagger & Company remained virtual paupers while Klein continued to rake in millions.

The lawsuit was only the first salvo in a protracted legal war. Klein did, in fact, control the master tapes and copyrights dating from the creation of the Stones up until 1970. He still does, along with all the publishing rights to the

Stones' songs written over that period. And there is no way of proving that songs recorded by the Stones in after years were not written prior to 1970, giving Klein an indefinite claim on the group's future "product."

Jagger heeded Prince Rupert's advice to cut the group's loss and settle out of court for $2 million—half of which would go to the songwriting team of Jagger and Richards and the rest to be divided equally among the four remaining Stones and Brian Jones's estate. (Bill Wyman demanded and got an extra $50,000 each for himself and Watts; Mick Taylor, still a salaried employee, received nothing in the settlement.)

This left the Stones completely free to sign with the record company of Jagger's choice. In negotiating the new deal Mick once again played the pivotal role. At face-to-face meetings with button-down corporate executives in teak-paneled boardrooms, Richards, Wyman, and Watts struck a languid, sphinxlike pose; Jagger was as canny, knowledgeable, and precise as any bean-counter in the room.

Jagger was not proud of his reputation for being a world-class wheeler-dealer; like other performers with a rebel image, he did not want to alienate his young, antiestablishment audience. "I read these things always: 'Mick's the calculating one; Keith's passionate,'" Jagger complained. "But, I mean, I'm really passionate about getting things right. And if I'm not passionate about the details, some slovenly person that's employed in this organization will just let everything go."

Jagger had little choice but to assume total control of the Stones' business affairs. "The descent of Marianne and Keith and Anita into heroin addiction really upset and changed Mick," observed Victor Bockris. "Jagger *had* to take control. Just as the Stones reach this important crossroads, Mick's closest friends *evaporate*. If Mick didn't make the hard decision, who would?"

In choosing a new label Jagger looked for the company that offered the most hard cash—and a touch of class. Ahmet Ertegun possessed both in abundance. The son of Tur-

key's ambassador to the United States, the urbane, bald,
goateed Ertegun was passionately fond of all things American—particularly jazz and rhythm-and-blues. In 1948 he
founded Atlantic Records and began recording such early
jazz and R & B greats as Joe Turner, Ray Charles, and Wilson Pickett. In the 1960s and '70s his stable of stars would
swell to include the diverse likes of Crosby, Stills, Nash,
and Young, Aretha Franklin, Bette Midler, and Led Zeppelin.

Yet it was Ertegun's polished style that won Jagger over.
Already one of the industry's most colorful characters, Ertegun was as much at home ordering Dom Perignon at Paris's Tour d'Argent in flawless French as he was talking riffs
with Eric Clapton at the Garden or hobnobbing with Miles
Davis at the Blue Note in Greenwich Village. With his
comely wife, Mica, who cofounded the interior design firm
of Mica and Chessy with Chesebrough-Pond's heiress
Chessy Rayner, Ertegun had already infiltrated Park Avenue society by the time he began courting Jagger.

It was a lengthy courtship. Two years earlier Ertegun had
sold Atlantic to Warner Records, giving him access to the
company's lavishly appointed corporate jet, the Wickey
Bird (*Wicky* being an acronym for Warner Communica-
tions, Inc.). For ten months Ertegun would wine, dine, and
fly Jagger anywhere and everywhere before finally being
given the nod.

Almost as important as Ertegun's panache was Atlantic's
R & B catalogue. "I think Jagger would have liked to be on
Excello," said Ertegun, referring to a tiny blues label. "We
were the closest he could get to Excello and still get five
million dollars."

Before the Stones could officially jump to Atlantic, Sir
Edward Lewis informed them that they were obliged by
their old contract to provide Decca with one more single.
At this stage the Stones were not kindly disposed toward
Decca; they had bristled at the record company's repeated
attempts at censoring their songs and their album covers.
The final straw was the revelation that a significant por-

tion of the $160 million they had grossed for the company went into developing Decca's radar manufacturing subsidiary. "We found out," said an indignant Richards, "that all the bread we made for Decca was going into making little black boxes that go into American Air Force bombers to bomb fucking North Vietnam. . . . That was it. Goddamn, you find out you've helped to kill God knows how many thousands of people without even knowing it."

By way of a parting gesture the Stones took a mobile unit to Stargroves and recorded a charming little Jagger-Richards ditty entitled "Cocksucker Blues." The song, a graphic celebration of gay sexual practices, was one of Jagger's favorites, and he belted out the X-rated lyrics with special conviction. From the moment he heard the opening lines—"Where do I get my cock sucked? Where do I get my ass fucked?"—Sir Edward Lewis knew there was no way Decca could release it.

To rub salt in the wound Jagger reportedly marched in to Sir Edward with a solution. Dripping with sarcasm, he recommended that "Cocksucker Blues" be included on an adults-only "party album" along with such other charming songs as "How Much Pussy Can You Eat?" Lewis politely declined.

Right after they dropped their bombshells on Allen Klein and Decca, the Stones hit the road again. Before he left, Jagger bade passionate farewells to Miss Pamela, Patti D'Arbanville, and Marsha Hunt, now five months pregnant. At Stargroves it was a case of coitus interruptus when another of Jagger's women happened upon Mick and Catherine in bed; when he suggested a threesome, Catherine flew into a rage.

The next morning the London *Daily Mail* carried a lengthy interview with Jagger. Initially worried that he might be a "grubby corrupter of youth, a sort of evil Peter Pan," writer Barry Norman concluded that Jagger was actually "rather shy and very affable. God fearing and patriotic and—would you believe—curiously innocent."

While he popped grapes into his mouth, Jagger told Norman he was not a candidate for marriage. "I don't envisage a time when I shall ever get married and settle down," he said. As for children: "I might have kids and I might get married but I'll never settle down. I'm not the type. For me life has always got to be on the move and exciting. I love kids, I really do . . . but it's not something I'm thinking about." Jagger neglected to mention that Marsha Hunt was expecting their first child in three months.

The six-week, fourteen-city European tour confirmed that the Stones had lost none of their power to inspire mayhem. As the Stones' fifty-man caravan hauling forty tons of equipment swept across the continent like a plundering army, virtually the same scene was replayed again and again. From Helsinki to Milan to West Berlin: riot police clashed with rioting fans, cars were overturned and burned, storefronts were smashed, and ambulance sirens filled the night.

There were also more than a few fits of petulance behind the scenes. When a waiter at his hotel in Copenhagen told Jagger the table he was sitting at was reserved, he threatened to tip the table over. In Hamburg, Mick told the German newsmagazine *Der Spiegel* that he never voted in British elections because he regarded the choice "like between polio and cancer." He went on to deny that he was a Marxist-Leninist, but conceded that he admired Mao and Lenin. In a turnabout Jagger—apparently forgetting Black Panther threats against the Stones back in Oakland—now said he would support the Panthers if he was asked.

Throughout the tour Jagger phoned Marsha Hunt and boasted about his conquests on the road; "He kept me laughing," recalled Hunt, "about whose girlfriend he'd had." They talked about her pregnancy rarely. Jagger not only decided that the baby would be a boy, but that he would be sent to England's most prestigious boy's school, Eton. As a black woman Hunt was also understandably insulted by the name Jagger had unilaterally picked out for their child: Midnight Dream.

The Stones were accorded their standard twenty-one-tear-gas-canister salute when they arrived in Paris on September 23, triggering the worst riots since students had manned the barricades in May of 1968. After their sold-out show at the Olympia Theater, there was a postconcert party at the elegant George V Hotel. The party would change Jagger's life.

For months Donald Cammell, an accomplished womanizer in his own right, had been pestered by one young female acquaintance who wanted desperately to meet his famous friend. He finally relented, escorting her to the Olympia concert and to the party afterward. As soon as Jagger entered the room, Cammell cornered him.

"Mick, this is Bianca," he said, noticing for the first time the striking resemblance between them. "You two are going to have a great romance," Cammell declared. "You were made for each other."

Blanca (she changed her first name as a teenager) Perez Morena de Macias was Nicaraguan by birth but reeked of Paris chic. She was one of the most exotically beautiful women Jagger had ever met: dark, sleek, dangerous-looking, she exuded a faint air of disdain to match his own. She spoke several languages in a sultry purr, and obviously possessed a keen intelligence.

Most important, Jagger found in Bianca something he could find nowhere else—an uncanny reflection of himself. "There wasn't ever any doubt that Mick would fall for Bianca," said one of Jagger's on-again, off-again lovers. "Mick looked into Bianca's face and saw—Mick. It was as close as he could get to making love to himself." Said a male friend of Mick's: "Both are moody, sullen, and secretive. They were fantastic together right from the start."

Bianca was not conscious of the similarity at first. "I wasn't attracted to Mick for physical reasons," Bianca later insisted. "I found him shy, vulnerable, human—the opposite of everything I had ever imagined. It sounds silly, but it was like a bolt of lightning."

After the party Mick and Bianca wound up at Cammell's

apartment, where they talked for hours over caviar and several bottles of Louis Roederer Cristal. When Cammell invited them to join him and his Ethiopian girlfriend, Myriam, in bed, the two new lovebirds demurred. They did, however, spend the night together in one of Cammell's guest bedrooms. The next morning Mick called Marsha Hunt to tell her he had met someone new and was taking her to Italy.

Always cloaked in mystery, Bianca continually revised her resume. There was the matter of her age. When she met Mick in 1970, Bianca insisted she was twenty-one. But that would have meant she was only fourteen when she arrived in Paris seven years earlier. In truth, Bianca was twenty-five when they met.

As for her family background, Bianca first claimed she was the daughter of a diplomat, then the daughter of a coffee baron, then the daughter of a well-to-do commodities broker. In truth, her uncle was Nicaragua's ambassador to Cuba. When she was eleven, her parents divorced ("A shock in a country as feudal as mine") and her mother was forced to scrape by running a lunch counter in Managua.

Spoiled by her doting mother ("I never washed a dish, boiled an egg, or cleaned"), Bianca went through the "terrible sexual repression" of convent schools before heading off at seventeen for Paris, where a second cousin was cultural affairs attaché at the Nicaraguan embassy. Vowing to someday become her country's first woman ambassador, she won a scholarship to the prestigious Insitut d'Etudes Politiques.

For two years, said Bianca, "I studied hard and remained a virgin until eighteen and a half." Then, hard pressed for money, she dropped out and returned to Managua. Bianca was offered a clerical job with the Nicaraguan Foreign Office staff, but decided it was beneath her and returned to the high life in Paris.

During this period she lived in a dollar-a-day room and took a variety of jobs—including a brief stint as a hostess greeting businessmen at the main stand of the Paris Meat

Fair. When she was just twenty, she landed a job on the Nicaraguan ambassador's staff, and was soon a fixture on the embassy party circuit.

Yet it was certainly not enough to finance her haut monde life-style. "I don't know how she did it," marveled a male friend of the period. "She bought all her clothes at Yves St. Laurent."

Bianca was staying at a friend's flat in Mayfair when she wangled an invitation to meet Michael Caine. The actor quickly became her "almost first lover," and in 1965 she took up residence in Caine's suite at London's Dorchester Hotel.

Bianca and Caine, in the words of a mutual friend, "fought like cats and dogs all the time—in restaurants, on the street, at parties. It was very fiery, very passionate, and very entertaining for the rest of us. But it must have really been hell for them."

"Caine was unkind, superficial, and kept me like I was his geisha," Bianca recalled. Caine put Bianca in a category by herself: "She is totally different from any of the girls I have known before—like a panther cub who is potentially dangerous but who still needs help."

No one was surprised when the affair ended a year later—although the relationship had a lasting impact on Caine. "You notice after me," quipped Bianca, "there were no more blondes in his life." Caine's second wife, Shakira, would in fact be a Bianca look-alike.

After her breakup with Caine, Bianca moved back to Paris, and after six months began an affair with record mogul Eddie Barclay. Bianca admitted that falling in love with Barclay, who was much older than she was and married at the time, was part of her search for a father figure.

"Until Mick," she allowed, "the search was for a father figure—for the protection and affection a father can provide. And the day I think I grew up a little bit—the day I didn't need a father figure anymore—was when I fell in love with Mick." Jagger, she added, was more like an "older brother."

Reflecting on her initial infatuation with Jagger, Bianca later claimed she was swept up in "the romance of the moment. For me fantasy is so much more important than reality," she said. "My dream—I am so romantic that for me the greatest thing will always be a book by Saint-Exupéry called *The Little Prince*. I shouldn't say it—because he is so arrogant—but when I met Mick he became for me the Little Prince and the rest was part of reality, but with him it was all fantasy."

So, some argued, was the sterling background she invented for herself. The gaps in Bianca's history—not to mention the unanswered questions concerning her fast-lane life-style—gave rise to the persistent and unproven rumor that Bianca was, in fact, a "Madame Claude Girl"—one of the elegant, multilingual young women who blended in so seamlessly with the well-born beauties who frequented Rue Princesse, Maxim's, and Régine's from the late 1950s through the late 1970s.

Madame Claude was so discreet, and her standards so high, that her list of clients included monarchs (the shah of Iran had one of her girls flown in to Tehran every Friday), presidents, prime ministers, dictators, ambassadors, generals, captains of industry, Hollywood actors, and rock stars.

"It reached the point," remarked one Wall Street banker who was a Madame Claude customer in the 1960s, "where if you walked into a room in London or Rome, as much as Paris, because the girls were transportable, and saw a girl who was better dressed, better looking, and more distinguished than the others, you presumed it was a girl from Claude. It was, without doubt, the finest sex operation ever run in the history of mankind."

Many Madame Claude girls went on to become the wives of some of the world's wealthiest and most powerful men. They graced society pages wearing Scaasi gowns and posed in their penthouse drawing rooms for *Town & County* and *Architectural Digest*.

However false the gossip, Mick inadvertently helped to

perpetuate it by joking about Bianca's reputed past. Years later, when a musician friend named Ronnie Lane broke up with his girlfriend, Jagger made a suggestion. "Come on, Ronnie, I know a great whorehouse in Paris, I'll take you there."

"I don't want some old scrubber," Lane replied.

"Watch what you're saying," Jagger cracked, "that's where I got my wife from."

Donald Cammell called his friend Bianca "an old-style courtesan, the sort who was always basically saying to herself, 'Well, who's going to be paying the rent five years from now?'"

There were other indications that the glacially beautiful, enigmatic South American with the Tallulah Bankhead voice might have been exaggerating her pedigree. One acquaintance from the old days claimed her father was not a diplomat or wealthy commodities broker, but a shopkeeper. After gossiping with Bianca for nearly an hour in a twangy patois that was recognizable only to them, a Brazilian housekeeper claimed the downscale dialect they were speaking was the kind employed "only by tarts."

"Bianca really is a complete mystery to us all," said a woman who described herself as a close friend of Bianca's. "A lot of people know her very well, but none of us really has the slightest idea where she came from or who she is. I wonder if even Mick knows."

Understandably the press pounced on the "mystery woman" who seemed to have replaced Marianne Faithfull in Jagger's life. When one overzealous paparazzo rushed up to snap Bianca's picture, Jagger chased him down and struck him in the face—a maneuver that resulted in Mick's being fined $1,400 for assault. In Vienna, Mick let his bodyguards run interference while he and Bianca eluded the press by scrambling over a wall.

When Jagger and Bianca arrived back in London they were besieged by reporters wanting his reaction to news that Marianne Faithfull's divorce from John Dunbar had finally been granted—and hoping to learn something of the coffee-colored exotic who had obviously replaced Faithfull in his life. Bianca merely stated, "I have no name," and answered all questions by saying—in perfect English—"I don't speak English."

Jagger was equally coy. "Sorry," he told reporters, "I can't tell you who she is. That's our business." As for their relationship, Jagger merely smiled and said enigmatically, "We're friends."

While the Stones were storming Europe, Warner was still vacillating about what to do with *Performance*. At a preview in Santa Monica members of the audience screamed in protest, hurled popcorn at the screen, and marched out. Some studio executives actually recommended burning the negative while others proposed giving the film to an independent producer to avoid damaging Warner's sterling reputation.

When Jagger returned to London with Bianca in October, *Performance* went into worldwide release. While critics differed sharply in their assessment of the film, most were fascinated by Jagger's performance. Stephen Farber, writing for *Cinema* magazine, praised the film for being "fierce and abrasive—the most provocative, searing, uncompromising, imaginative vision of the future that any youth film has yet provided." Roger Greenspun of *The New York Times* was fascinated by the film's "sadism, mashochism, decorative decadence, and languid omnisexuality."

Attention focused on *Performance*'s baroque sex and freewheeling portrayal of the drug culture, but there were also those who were offended by the film's graphic violence, particularly in the wake of Altamont. Donald Cammell told the Sunday *Telegraph* that Jagger was not at all squeamish or hesitant about the film's gorier scenes. "Mick will probably be annoyed at this," said Cammell. "But his dilemma is that he knows what he's into. He *knows* about the violence. This movie was finished before Altamont, and Altamont actualized it."

Coinciding with the world premiere of *Performance* was the release of the 1969 tour album *Get Yer Ya-Ya's Out!*

(taken from a voodoo chant), recorded live the previous winter at Madison Square Garden. "The music of the Rolling Stones," said *The Washington Post*, "epitomized everything our mothers told us to avoid: sex, drugs, and violence. And it's for this reason their music is so powerful, so intense, and so exciting." *Rolling Stone*'s Lester Bangs called it "the best rock concert ever put on record. The Stones, alone among their generation of groups, are not about to fall by the wayside. And as long as they continue to thrive this way, the era of true rock-and-roll music will remain alive and kicking with them."

With Jagger and Bianca ensconsed in their own suite at Stargroves, Cromwell's former headquarters had suddenly become the epicenter of the Stones operation. Unwilling to be away from his new love for more than a few moments, Jagger insisted that the Stones work on their next album at Stargroves. They were willing to accomodate Mick, but whenever Bianca visited the makeshift studio, work ground to a halt while he went off with her to make love.

Jagger's new love wasted no time dispatching the competition. Devastated over the breakup of another relationship, Pamela Miller called Mick at Stargroves. Bianca answered the phone, and told Miss Pamela in a husky growl "never, ever, under any circumstances, to call Mick, ever again. Get the picture?" That scene was repeated over and over again as Bianca circumvented attempts by old lovers to contact Mick.

Bianca faced a tough adversary in Anita Pallenberg, who took an instant dislike to Mick's new mistress. With Marianne Faithfull out of the picture Pallenberg wielded more influence than ever before within the Stones' inner circle. By virtue of her common law marriage to Richards and her past liaisons with Brian Jones and with Mick, Pallenberg reigned over the Stones' court like a dowager empress. The other Stones women—Watts's wife, Shirley, Mick Taylor's fiancée, Rose, and Bill Wyman's Swedish girlfriend, Astrid Lundström—wisely steered clear of her.

Pallenberg made no secret of the fact that she regarded

rock wives as a docile species. "I remember when John Lennon used to bring Cynthia along," she recalled of pre-Yoko days. "She would go straight upstairs and lock herself in the loo. And this was the last we would see of her all night." Bianca also liked to barricade herself in the bathroom. "She was totally self-obsessed," complained Anita. "She'd come to my house and disappear into the bathroom for four hours and do makeup and then have these airs and barely talk to anybody. She was always incredibly aloof."

What disturbed Pallenberg was the effect Bianca had on Mick. "Mick was changed—he was responsible for her," said Anita. "And then nobody liked her in the group, so I'm sure it was really hard for her to try and fit in. . . ."

Not that Anita made it any easier for Bianca. Pallenberg had actually begun her campaign against the Nicaraguan interloper while the Stones were still on tour. One of her favorite ploys was to borrow a designer dress or fur-lined jacket from the obliging Bianca, then leave it, grimy and torn, in a heap on her hotel room floor.

Once they were back on home turf, Pallenberg approached Keith's friend cum connection Spanish Tony Sanchez and asked him to dig up whatever "dirt" he could on Bianca. She offered Sanchez a small fortune to provide proof that Bianca had undergone a sex-change operation.

When Sanchez laughed off the suggestion that Bianca was anything but a woman, Anita resorted to black magic. Pallenberg and Richards had rejected Kenneth Anger's suggestion that they be married in a satanic wedding ceremony, but she still draped garlands of garlic around the house on Cheyne Walk to ward off vampires and conjured spells of her own. In a locked case in her bedroom Pallenberg also kept human hair, scraps of bone, skin, and various animal parts for the occasional curse or incantation.

Pallenberg, who now took to wearing a garlic necklace to bed, worked overtime on Bianca. Among other things, she wrote a voodoo curse on a scrap of paper, slipped it in her shoe, and at a party nonchalantly walked around

Bianca three times—a ritual designed to rid the Stones of the interloper once and for all.

Keith also loathed Bianca but, in the interest of maintaining harmony within the group, publicly proclaimed that he felt Bianca was a "groovy chick." Jagger, meanwhile, told Bianca to do whatever was necessary to get along with Pallenberg. "Anita is one of the Stones now," he said. "You'll have to sort it out between yourselves. Put up with her as best you can."

On November 3, 1970, Marsha Hunt gave birth to a baby girl in the maternity ward at St. Mary's Hospital, Paddington. As she held her daughter for the first time, Hunt could not help noticing that the baby's lips were "a perfect replica" of Jagger's. Passing on Jagger's original suggestion that the infant be named Midnight Dream, Hunt unilaterally named her Karis. From her hospital bed Hunt called Stargroves and shared the news with Mick.

After he hung up the phone, Jagger matter-of-factly told Bianca that Hunt had just given birth to his child. Bianca, who up until this time was unaware of Hunt's pregnancy, reacted to the news with stunned disbelief. So long as he was bound to another woman by a child, Bianca knew she was placed at a distinct disadvantage. It was an imbalance of power that Bianca was determined to rectify.

Jagger sent a limousine to take mother and child from the hospital to her modest apartment in St. John's Wood. When she arrived, Jagger's housekeeper, Bruna, was there to greet her, along with a dozen red roses from the proud father.

Mick himself arrived later that day, but when he did it was clear to Marsha that he was "in a hurry to be somewhere else." He returned ten days later, again dropping by on his way to another appointment. This time she flew into a rage over his obvious lack of interest in their child.

"I never loved you," he screamed back, "and you're mad to think I ever did." Hunt burst into tears, but Jagger was unmoved. "She's my child," he said. "I could take her away from you any time I felt like it."

"Try it," Hunt replied coolly, "and I'll blow your brains out." Jagger stormed out, slamming the door behind him.

Two weeks later Mick and Bianca flew off to the Bahamas to celebrate Thanksgiving at Ahmet Ertegun's seaside estate in Nassau. On a stopover in Miami, Jagger decided to deal with the disapproving stares of two matrons sitting in the lobby of his hotel. "These women look like hookers to me," bellowed Jagger, pointing to the blue-haired ladies. "Say," he continued, motioning to a member of his ever-present entourage, "you want a couple of hookers?"

Even as the two dowagers in the hotel lobby turned up their noses at the scruffy pop star in their midst, Jagger was being given England's sartorial seal of approval. *Tailor and Cutter*, the menswear bible which had previously praised Prince Philip and then–Prime Minister Edward Heath for their sense of style, praised Jagger's wardrobe. "He is," the trade magazine declared, "one of our more elegant popocrats."

A somewhat more influential publication, *Newsweek*, put Jagger on the cover of its Christmas-week issue. The story, titled "Mick Jagger and the Future of Rock," proclaimed that "of all the charismatic figures produced by rock—Paul McCartney, Bob Dylan, John Lennon, Jimi Hendrix, Janis Joplin, Eric Clapton—Mick Jagger is undoubtedly the most startling in his sustained flamboyance, his demonic power to affect even people who instinctively recoil from him, his uncompromising refusal to ingratiate."

That winter Mick and Bianca spent more and more time in the company of their Cheyne Walk neighbors Paul and Talitha Getty. According to Tony Sanchez this foursome snorted so much cocaine that Sanchez would often have to "calm them down" by giving them heroin. It is doubtful that Paul's father, J. Paul Getty, at the time considered to be the richest man in the world, approved of his son's lifestyle—or his friends.

Coinciding with the start of a nine-city "Farewell to Britain" tour, Les Perrin formally announced on March 4, 1971, that the Stones would be relocating to France. Fleet

Street reacted as if a major corporation were departing, and of course they were right.

At a press conference Jagger was careful not to make it look as if the group was fleeing to avoid Britain's ninety-seven percent tax bite.

"If you know me," Jagger told reporters, "you know I shall most probably be back in Britain more often than I have been in the past. We felt a change of scene, temperature, and climate would be good for us." A tax maneuver? "There's nothing," said Jagger, "to be gained or lost by it." In truth, by bailing out in fiscal 1971–72, the Stones were avoiding taxes on their income going back to 1969. If things went as planned, the relocation would save them millions the first year alone.

As the Stones crisscrossed Britain, Mick underwent a transformation; by the time they reached Glasgow, he already looked like a Parisian in his tight ribbed sweater, suede maxicoat, flared bell-bottoms, and blue cap. When Bianca wasn't whispering into his ear in French, she played gin with the boys—trouncing one tour member to the tune of $10,000.

All of pop London turned out for the Stones' final performance at the Roundhouse. In the dressing room Bianca, looking like Mata Hari in a human-hair boa and with a green peacock feather in her cloche cap, waved an ivory-colored cigarette holder as she held court.

It was at this inopportune moment that a bumptious groupie aptly nicknamed Joyce the Voice pushed her way past security and marched up to Bianca. "Excuse me," said the Voice, "but didn't I see you with Osibisa in their dressing room last week?"

"What is Osibisa?" Bianca asked, incredulous.

"Oh, wow," boomed Joyce. "There's someone with your exact vibration around. I mean, like a twin sister. You know? Someone who is walking around with your face."

Bianca responded to the suggestion that she had been a groupie for another band with glacial indifference. She had merely to glance in the direction of a bodyguard, and Joyce the Voice was gone.

The following day the group was scheduled to bid a final farewell to London with a television performance at their old stomping ground, the Marquee Club. History was about to repeat itself. Their old nemesis Harold Pendleton, the jazz purist who had tried to stand in the way of the Stones eight years earlier, was still the club's manager. Although Mick strictly forbade him from doing it, Pendleton hung a huge neon "Marquee Club" sign behind the stage. When Pendleton refused to take the offending sign down, Richards, arriving two hours late and intoxicated, picked up his red Gibson guitar and swung it at Pendleton's head, missing him by a fraction of an inch.

It was Mick's turn to throw a tantrum two weeks later, at a lavish farewell party at Maidenhead's Skindles Hotel. When the hotel asked Jagger and his noisy guests to depart at four A.M., Mick was outraged. John Lennon and Eric Clapton both tried to quiet him down, but Jagger, shouting obscenities, picked up a chair and flung it through a plate glass window.

At the end of March the Stones finally made good their promise and went into tax exile in France. Watts was the first to arrive, settling with his family into a secluded farmhouse in Provence. Wyman rented a house in Grasse, while Richards leased a gleaming white palace, Nellcôte, overlooking the harbor town of Villefranche. Mick and Bianca, meanwhile, were living at the Byblos Hotel in Saint-Tropez. Before long they would move into a lavish, white-walled villa of their own in Biot.

Less than forty-eight hours after their arrival in France, the Stones finally formalized their arrangement with Kinney Services, the holding company for Ertegun's Atlantic Records. Under the terms of the four-year, $5 million deal, the Stones agreed to record six albums that would be distributed by Atlantic on the new Rolling Stones record label.

Recalling those early days when he wrote away to Chess

Records for his Chuck Berry albums, Jagger brought in Marshall Chess, son of Chess Records founder Leonard Chess, to head Rolling Stones Records. Keenly aware of the Beatles' painful experience with its Apple label, Jagger downplayed the importance of Rolling Stones Records. "We're not gonna try and make some big corporate image and build a skyscraper in the corner of Saville Row," he said. "We just want to keep it a very small thing; a small operation which we could handle."

Chess and Trevor Churchill, London-based manager of Rolling Stones Records in Europe, had actually lobbied against the Atlantic contract. "We wanted them to make an independent deal so that they would eventually get an even bigger slice of the pie," said Churchill. "But all that up-front cash Ertegun was waving at them was just too tempting."

As much as in the bedroom and onstage, Jagger was a veritable whirlwind of activity in the boardroom. "Mick held meetings constantly," recalled Churchill. "We would sit, but he had all this nervous energy that made it impossible to remain still. He would be pacing up and down, fidgeting, asking questions."

Even with Prince Rupert and an army of accountants hovering about, it was clear that one man ran the day-to-day operations of the Stones empire. "Mick was very much in control," said Churchill. "He was incredibly well versed on the business side. He used to come up with extraordinary things to keep you on your toes. You never knew when he'd ring you up and ask, 'What are the sales this week in Sweden?' He also handled all the liaison work with the bankers."

Only one person could veto a Jagger decision. "Before he put anything into effect, Mick ran it by Keith," said their longtime business associate Sandy Lieberson. "If Keith said no, then Mick was fucked."

A constant source of frustration for anyone involved with Rolling Stones Records over the years was Jagger's unwillingness to sign other acts. Although Atlantic had anted

up a substantial sum for this purpose, the Stones preferred
to pocket it for themselves.

"Mick is very cautious," observed Churchill. "Contrary
to his public image he is not a risk-taker. Everything is
tightly budgeted and strictly controlled. Jagger is afraid of
failure, and of rejection. That's why he never really got his
movie career off the ground. Too much of a gamble."

As a result Jagger passed on signing Queen, Roxy Music,
the Average White Band, Genesis, and a number of other
major acts over the years. "The Stones wanted acts to sort
of stumble toward them," said Churchill, "but when they
did, Jagger just brushed them off. The Stones were just not
willing to share the money, or the spotlight."

Even after their tax exile Jagger managed to hold frequent business meetings at 48 Cheyne Walk. The lady of
the house did not approve. "Bianca was a cool cucumber,"
remembered Churchill. "She was polite, but it was obvious
she resented having us at Cheyne Walk. This was her
house, after all." For the most part Bianca treated Jagger's
business cronies like "the hired help. As far as she was concerned, we were riffraff."

One week after signing the deal with Atlantic, the
Stones released their first record on their new label. Jagger
was particularly proud of *Sticky Fingers*, and rightly so.
Among the classic cuts it contained was "Brown Sugar."
He wanted to make as big a splash as possible with *Sticky
Fingers*, so he hired his friend Andy Warhol to design the
jacket for the album.

After they first met in 1964, Warhol had exerted a quiet
but lasting influence over Jagger. "Mick borrowed some
from Marlon Brando and some from Marilyn Monroe, but
a lot from Andy," said Warhol biographer Victor Bockris.
"Jagger is extremely clever, and he is always waiting to pick
up on the next trend. This all grew out of Mick's desire to
be wild, to be on the cutting edge. In his field Andy was a
genuine pioneer. He took chances. He was the Mick Jagger
of the art world."

It was not a one-way street, by any means. Jagger offered

Warhol what the celebrity-obsessed father of pop art craved most—proximity to a bona fide superstar. Befriending Jagger was also a shrewd business move. "Andy lent Mick a kind of artsy respectability," said Warhol confidant Christopher Makos. "But Mick brought Andy something more important commerically—exposure to the wider rock audience."

The *Sticky Fingers* cover symbolized the fusion of rock, fashion, and art: a bulging, Levi's-clad crotch with an actual fly that could be unzipped to show the label's Warhol-designed logo—Jagger's rubber lips ("child-bearing lips," comic Joan Rivers would later call them) and his taunting, Satan-red tongue stuck out at the world.

The back of the jacket, appropriately, was a denim-clad derriere. Since the assumption would be that Jagger occupied the pants on the cover (he did not), Warhol screened several male models before picking one that lived up to Jagger's reputation in the frontal department. To guarantee the necessary shock value Warhol borrowed one of Jagger's own tricks and had the model stuff a rolled-up sock down the front of his pants. This famous "zipper cover," said Bockris, added "gay prurience to the steamy aura around rock's favorite bad boys."

The erotic lapping-tongue logo, which would become as recognizable as the corporate symbols for Coke and McDonald's, removed any doubt that Mick was the driving force behind—and in front of—the Stones. Once again Jagger's attention to detail came into play when record outlets in Spain refused to stock *Sticky Fingers* because of its suggestive cover. Francisco Franco was still very much in power, and the government threatened to jail anyone selling what it deemed obscene material.

To get around that problem Jagger called in graphic artist John Pasche to redesign the cover for Spain to depict fingers sticking out of an open can. Jagger was not so accommodating when Spanish authorities then demanded that the many obvious drug references be cut. Jagger excised the offending lines, but as a protest decided merely to leave silences where the lyrics would have been.

It is no wonder that the Franco regime took umbrage at some of the material in *Sticky Fingers*. The record contained language that was unsettling even by Stones standards. Since so much of the album is awash in drug argot— particularly the depressing "Sister Morphine"—it was logical that so many critics would guess that "Brown Sugar" was about cinnamon-colored Mexican cocaine. Instead, the Marsha Hunt–inspired song graphically described sex on a southern plantation between white masters and black slave girls ("Hear the boss whip the women and taste them just around midnight").

At the same time, Decca retaliated over the "Cocksucker Blues" insult by releasing *Stone Age*, an anthology of old Stones recordings. Jagger fired back by denouncing the Decca album as inferior and taking out ads urging their fans not to buy it.

If he seemed to be at odds with the rest of the universe, Mick had at least found happiness close to home—though he was not yet ready to let the world in on the secret. "We're definitely not getting married," Jagger lied to reporters who cornered them shopping in Saint-Tropez. Not only had she already accepted his wedding proposal, but in order to be married at the tiny Roman Catholic Church of Ste. Anne overlooking the Côte d'Azur, Anglican Jagger was already taking private catechism lessons from the church's pastor, Father Lucien Baud. The priest had no idea who Jagger was until reporters, tipped off to the location of the wedding, began badgering him for interviews.

Three weeks later Eva Jagger sobbed with joy when her elder son called to invite her to his wedding. He neglected to mention that Bianca was also four months pregnant, and that even under those circumstances he had had to talk her into getting married.

Staffer Shirley Arnold was not so thrilled with the news; Mick phoned her on May 11 to say he and Bianca would be wed on May 13, and that Arnold was to make all the necessary arrangements.

Originally only a few close friends were supposed to be in attendance—Mick's parents and brother Chris, the actress Nathalie Delon, film director Roger Vadim, Keith, Prince Rupert. But the guest list quickly swelled to seventy-five. Arnold's first task was to round them all up virtually overnight and put them on a chartered jet out of London's Gatwick Airport.

Jagger had said repeatedly that he wanted to avoid a circus atmosphere, but of course that is precisely the atmosphere he seemed determined to create. Working feverishly, Arnold managed to corral nearly all the guests, and the following day Paul and Linda McCartney, Ringo Starr, Queen Elizabeth's cousin Lord Litchfield, Keith Moon, Eric Clapton, and Eva and Joe Jagger were among the celebrity pack headed for the wedding of the year. Even though McCartney and Starr were traveling with their children, most of the rockers on board had no compunction about smoking dope on board. One passenger was given special treatment even by VIP standards. While the others had ridden a bus to Gatwick, Spanish Tony Sanchez claimed Jagger arranged for a special limousine to transport him in style to the airport with the evening's supply of top-quality cocaine.

Getting off the plane in Nice, Mick's parents were besieged by reporters. Flustered, Eva let on that the ceremony was set for the following day. "I'm just not used to it," she said of all the cloak-and-dagger secrecy surrounding the wedding plans.

"We can never understand all this fuss about him," Joe Jagger said of his son. "The stage image is not the real Mick at all. He is basically a very serious boy." Mom conceded that she was happy "that Mick is going to settle down at last."

In their suite at Saint-Tropez's Byblos Hotel only hours before the wedding, Mick and Bianca were locked in mortal combat over the terms of their prenuptial agreement.

Under French law they were required to sign a document stating whether their property would be held jointly or remain separate.

Jagger, mindful of the fact that his tax exile would net him an additional million dollars in 1971 alone, pressured her to sign. Understandably she was not eager to relinquish any future claims and begged him to cancel the wedding plans. "Are you," Mick shouted, "trying to make a fool of me in front of all these people?" Bianca relented, and the signing was witnessed by Alan Dunn, Jagger's longtime driver.

The wedding was to be a two-part affair: a brief civil ceremony conducted by Mayor Marius Estézan at Saint-Tropez's town hall, followed by the religious ceremony at the storybook Ste. Anne Chapel. When he received word that more than one hundred photographers had crowded into town hall, Mick sent a message to the mayor that the happy couple would not arrive until the premises were cleared.

The town hall was a public place, replied Mayor Estézen, and any citizen had a right to be there. Now Jagger threatened to call the whole thing off. "If there is going to be all the crowd," he said, "I'm not going to get married. I am not a fish in a goldfish bowl and I am not the king of France!"

On hearing this the mayor ripped off his tricolor sash and issued an ultimatum of his own: Either Mick and Bianca showed up within ten minutes, or the show was off. Fully fifty minutes behind schedule the bride and groom arrived at the packed hall and, to the accompaniment of popping flashbulbs and shouted questions, tried to make their way to the mayor's chambers.

Once they managed to get inside, the crush proved too much and Jagger, grasping Bianca's hand, turned to leave. "I'm not going on," said Mick, "I'm not doing it like this." Les Perrin spun the couple around and gently shoved them in the mayor's direction.

With a scruffy-looking Roger Vadim and Nathalie Delon

as witnesses, Mick and Bianca went through the motions and signed the register. She signed "Blanca Rosa Perez-Mora" and gave her age as twenty-six—she had blithely told Mick when they met eight months earlier that she was not yet twenty-one.

The groom, clad in a cream-colored three-piece summer suit with a floral-print shirt and no tie, looked like any Parisian dandy. The bride, choking back tears, wore a wide-brimmed picture hat trimmed with rosebuds and a white St. Laurent suit with a neckline that revealed more than just a hint of décolletage—a visual package that artfully distracted attention from her already protruding abdomen.

Keith Richards, holding a diaper-clad Marlon, looked on from the sidelines. Dressed in black leggings and a combat jacket, Richards had at first been barred from the proceedings by police. "I've had four fights just to get here," he shouted, smashing an ashtray on the marriage table.

Simultaneously the chief of the local gendarmes refused to move the photographers to a single spot in the room. "The floor is weak," he explained, "and if they go stand there we shall all go through."

Wyman, Watts, and Taylor were noticeably absent from the ceremony. "We were shocked to find that apart from Keith, none of the Stones or our ladies were invited to the wedding," said Wyman, "and only to the celebrity-packed Saint-Tropez reception by a casual phone call from Mick the day before."

A handful of local leftists who had read news reports that the wedding would cost more than $50,000 kicked at the tires of Jagger's rented Bentley, but they managed to make it up the hill to Ste. Anne's Chapel. There Mick and his bride climbed the steps up to the front door, only to discover that they were locked out of their own wedding.

As the crowd of onlookers and photographers descended on them, Jagger pounded on the door furiously. Finally someone heard his cries, and the door swung open just in time for the newlyweds to scramble inside, a half-step ahead of the mob. Fuming, Jagger marched up to the alter rail.

While an organist played the theme from the hit film *Love Story* (Bianca's request), the bride was escorted down the aisle by Lord Litchfield—hardly a close friend of Bianca's, but mute testimony to the Jagger's vaunted social status nonetheless.

Father Baud was clearly unnerved by the bride's nipple-baring attire, but he cleared his throat and pushed on. During the ceremony he paused for a moment to talk directly to Jagger. "You have told me you believe that youth seeks happiness and a certain ideal and faith," said the priest. "I think you are seeking it, too, and I hope it arrives today with your marriage. But when you are a personality like Mick Jagger," he added with a sigh, "it is too much to hope for privacy for your marriage."

For the reception at Saint-Tropez's somewhat shabby Café des Arts, Bianca changed into a sequined turban and a see-through blouse. Her wedding present from Mick—a $10,000 diamond bracelet—glittered on her left wrist.

A local band started the festivities and bombed miserably, leaving a pounding reggae group called the Rudies to bring the affair to life. Prophetically, they struck up "It's All Over Now" as the bride and groom took to the dance floor; the tune would be replayed throughout the evening.

Terry Reid kept the momentum going, but the high point of the all-night affair came when a sloshed Jagger jumped onstage to join Doris Troy and comely Ikette P. P. Arnold for a twenty-five-minute-long soul medley. Bianca, unaware that her new husband had had a torrid affair with Arnold, gazed through the thick haze of marijuana smoke as they bumped and ground their way through several steamy numbers before the two hundred–plus invited guests and assorted gate-crashers.

Keith Richards spoiled Jagger's plans for an impromptu performance by the Stones. He had already passed out, mouth open wide, on the floor.

Eva and Joe Jagger spent hours trying to corner their son

and his new wife just so they could give them their wedding present—a linen tablecloth. Around midnight the senior Jaggers returned—neatly wrapped package in hand—to the sanctuary of their hotel room. Meanwhile Bianca, irritated with the way Mick was ignoring her, retired to the Byblos alone.

The party rocked on until the early morning hours without her. "Girls kissed and cuddled each other," recalled one of the guests. "Men in hot pants and with short hairy legs did the same. Couples lay about the floor on cushions. And if a girl wasn't showing at least one nipple, she was out of fashion." The groom, oblivious to his wife's absence, drank it all in.

Next afternoon the newlyweds boarded the 120-ton yacht *Romeang* with its six-man crew for a ten-day honeymoon cruise around the Mediterranean islands of Sardinia and Corsica. Cost: $20,000—all paid out of one of Jagger's Swiss bank accounts. As the Jaggers boarded the yacht, they were asked by reporters if any of their famous friends would be accompanying them. Replied Mick: "You must be joking."

Back home in Dartford, Eva Jagger told a local reporter that she and her husband were "glad that Mike is married—just like any parents would be." She was less than effusive in her assessment of Bianca, whom she had met at the wedding for the first time. "I just want my son to be happy," she said, "and as long as he's happy, I'm happy. You wouldn't try to stop your son marrying a girl just because you didn't like her, would you?"

That summer Mick and Bianca spent the odd weekend at their rented Saint-Tropez villa, but for the most part they lived at Paris's exclusive L'Hôtel, best known as the place where Oscar Wilde died uttering history's most memorable last words: "Either this wallpaper goes, or I do."

They considered staying in the very room where Wilde breathed his last. Bianca, however, deemed it too small.

Jagger himself had planned for the Stones to invade the U.S. in early January, and that meant renewed pressure to deliver a blockbuster album that would coincide with the tour. Since the others all lived full-time in the south of France, it was agreed that they would record the album at Nellcôte.

As soon as they moved in, Richards and Pallenberg transformed the stately manor into a squalid drug den over-run with fellow junkies, drug dealers from Marseilles, and an assortment of flunkies, derelicts, and weirdos. Local gossip raged about the bestial orgies and bizarre satanic rituals going on at Nellcôte, and Richards did nothing to discourage it.

By way of thumbing his nose at French officials, Richards named his yacht after one of his favorite prescription drugs: Mandrax. In a fight with the Villefranche harbormaster Keith went so far as to grab an authentic-looking toy pistol out of son Marlon's hand and threaten the harbormaster with it. Richards narrowly escaped death when the harbormaster returned with a very real gun of his own and aimed it squarely at him.

The one thing Nellcôte did have was space. There was room enough for the Stones' recording facilities, and for the usual supporting cast of technicians and gofers.

Jagger hated the condition at Nellcôte. It was so unbearable in the basement studio during those sweltering summer months that Mick sweated buckets as he tried to record "Tumbling Dice" and the overtly sexual "Rocks Off" for their new double album. Jagger recalled that Richards's "disgusting" basement "looked like a prison. The humidity was incredible. I couldn't stand it. As soon as I opened my mouth to sing, my voice was gone." When the temperature reached 120 degrees, Jagger disrobed completely and sang several numbers in the nude.

There were vexing technical problems as well. The power intermittently flickered and surged, wreaking havoc on the Stones' sound system and forcing retake after retake.

Tempers also became frayed when Anita, four months pregnant at the time, loudly complained that Keith had not made love to her in months and flirted outrageously with practically every man who came in the door—from musicians like fellow heroin addict Eric Clapton to pushers to hapless local tradesmen. Keith, suddenly besotted with fatherhood, would disappear in the middle of a session to put Marlon to bed. Then he would shoot up and not return to the studio until the early morning hours.

Most of the band's anger, however, was directed at Jagger. Bianca refused to accompany Mick to Nellcôte, and with good reason. Anita and Keith still hated her. Nor did the bizarre, heroin-centered environment they had created seem appropriate for a woman entering her final months of pregnancy.

Back at L'Hôtel word reached Bianca that Pallenberg and her husband had picked up where they'd left off on the set of *Performance*, and were once again sleeping together. To placate his bride Jagger rushed back to Paris several times a week, leaving his fellow Stones to record without him.

Late that September Mick invited Marsha Hunt to bring Karis along to visit him in Saint-Tropez. Hunt, reluctant to ask Jagger for money but hoping that he might offer to help support his daughter, was broke when the call came from Mick.

Jagger's longtime chauffeur and assistant Alan Dunn met Hunt and Karis at the Nice airport and drove them to Mick's house in Grasse—not Mick *Jagger*'s house, but Mick Taylor's. Bianca did not exactly welcome the idea of Jagger's former girlfriend and her child sleeping under her roof, so it was arranged that they would stay with Taylor and his fiancée, Rose.

Dunn picked up Hunt and the baby the next afternoon and drove them to the Jagger's sun-washed villa. During dinner Jagger and the very pregnant Bianca cuddled and murmured to one another in French, completely ignoring Marsha and Karis.

As she left, Hunt screwed up her courage to ask Jagger for a five-hundred-dollar loan. He reluctantly wrote out the check, but never looked Hunt directly in the eye. "I guess," she later sighed, "he couldn't."

"A lot of my friends have died in car crashes, in plane crashes, and from drug overdoses. I've learned from that. I've always made sure I avoided driving while on a drug overdose during a plane flight."

12

As mid-October approached, Bianca demanded that Mick be on hand for the imminent arrival of their first child. When he called from Nellcôte to tell Bianca he was going to stay a few extra days to complete work on the double album, she flew into a Latin rage and slammed down the receiver. Jagger caught the first available plane back to Paris, but when he arrived at L'Hôtel, she was gone.

Jagger tried for several days to reach his eight-months-pregnant wife, but to no avail. When she finally materialized, he asked for no explanations concerning her absence; she offered none.

On October 21, 1971, Bianca gave birth to a six-pound baby girl at Belvedere Nursing Home in Paris. She would be nearly two days old by the time her parents finally decided on a name: Jade, because, as her father explained, "she is very precious and quite, quite perfect."

Two weeks later they all flew back to England to show the new arrival off to the proud grandparents. Jagger also asked Marsha Hunt to drop by at 48 Cheyne Walk, where he took snapshots of her holding Karis and the newborn Jade.

After that, Hunt would not hear from Mick for another month, and then only after she approached him for a small loan to help pay for some of Karis's clothing and food. By now she was beginning to accept the fact that the father of her child would never offer financial assistance without considerable prodding.

Jagger doted on Jade as much as he ignored Karis. "I'm a terrific dad," he bragged. "Jade is a fantastic kid, a lovely baby, very sweet and good-tempered. . . . I've always been a good father, and the kid makes it easy to be that way."

Jade's nanny, Janie Villiers, remembered that Mick "enjoyed fatherhood. It made an incongruous scene: Mick Jagger in a silk shirt, white satin trousers, and green eye shadow he wore in the evenings, bringing all his flamboyance and charisma to the nursery."

Bianca, conversely, was not exactly the maternal type. According to Villiers, Bianca "saw less of Jade than Mick did and when she carried her, she'd give her an awkward kind of fireman's lift. Once, she actually dropped Jade down the stairs."

"I'm under tremendous strain here," Bianca told Villiers. "Nobody knows what a strain it is to keep a house, to look after Jade, and be dressed properly all the time." Forced to take care of Mick Taylor's daughter, Chloe, at no extra pay, Villiers allowed Jade and Chloe to use half a dozen of the Stones' gold records as bathtub toys. "They were getting bent and dirty," she shrugged, "and no one seemed to care."

That December, Jagger flew with Bianca, Jade, and their entourage for a working vacation in Los Angeles. Prince Rupert Loewenstein and Ahmet Ertegun had convinced Mick that a 1972 U.S. tour was an economic necessity for the Stones. But memories of Altamont lingered, and, if anything, American audiences strung out on dope, coke, and speed seemed more prone to violence than ever. On this fact-finding trip Jagger hoped to map out a tour of smaller venues—concert halls seating a few thousand—where riots were less likely to erupt.

To many it seemed as if the Stones had only themselves to blame. The songs on their new double album, retitled *Exile on Main Street*, were as tauntingly profane and violent as ever. Jagger himself set the tone even before his Pan Am

747 took off for L.A. After jumping ahead of other passengers in line and taking their seats in first class, Jagger and his party were told they were occupying the wrong seats.

According to stewardess Pauline Laugh, Jagger grabbed her by the arm, spun her around, and let fly with several blistering epithets. "You talk like that to me," he reportedly said, "and I'll kick you up your ass." Jagger denied that he grabbed her. "But I'd like to have given her a good slap in the face," he said, "because she deserved it."

In March of 1972 the Rolling Stones formally settled their $29 million lawsuit against Allen Klein. It was made abundantly clear that, while Klein still controlled their pre-1970 material, his ABKCO Industries no longer represented the Stones.

By this time Jagger was aware that, if he was ever going to get the group's financial house in order, this would have to be the biggest-grossing Stones tour ever. That meant jettisoning the concept of modest venues and booking only the major arenas in the largest cities.

Jagger hired an efficient young Cambridge student named Peter Rudge to secretly book the biggest coliseums around the U.S., then stand back when the promoters stampeded for the rights to promote each city's appearance. The first day they received an offer of $1 million to book the Stones into the Indianapolis Speedway. Jagger wanted this tour to be big, but not that big and—shades of Altamont—definitely not at a speedway.

Meanwhile, after nearly a year in tax exile, Jagger was beginning to feel homesick. Bianca was an avowed Francophile, but Jagger was no fan of the French. "Everybody treats you like a tourist," he complained. "They all try to fleece you." When Jagger was asked if his wife shared his love of England, his answer betrayed their growing indifference to one another. "I haven't," he said with a shrug, "asked her."

Jagger kept an eye on British politics, and when a bill was introduced to limit the number of people at rock festivals he replied in the press. "It's a load of Tory rubbish,"

Jagger told the *Daily Mail*. Slamming the apathy of the English, Mick also took aim at Conservative Prime Minister Edward Heath. "Unfortunately," Jagger observed, "from this distance it looks as though he has made a mess of everything. He's out of touch with the people. He should be put down a mine for a week—I'd go with him. Direct action, it's the only thing." Harkening back to his lunches at the Gay Hussar with Tom Driberg, Jagger was now telling friends that he ought to go back and run for office. "But," he would sigh, "I haven't got the right wife."

That spring Jagger traveled to New York to meet with Ahmet Ertegun and discuss plans for the upcoming tour. There he ran into James Taylor, whose *Sweet Baby James* album had set the musical world on its ear the year before. Taylor had already spent time in a mental hospital suffering from suicidal psychosis by the time he fled to London, where he was discovered by Jagger's old friend Peter Asher. Since the success of "Fire and Rain," Taylor, like so many people around Jagger, had been fighting a losing battle with heroin addiction.

Taylor had had a long and highly publicized affair with folk singer Joni Mitchell, but he had a new love now and he wanted Mick to meet her. With hits like "That's the Way I've Always Heard It Should Be" (inspired by a run-in with a casting-couch producer in Nashville) and "Anticipation," Carly Simon was a major star in her own right.

Mick was intrigued with Simon's background. Her father had founded the publishing house of Simon & Schuster and during Carly's childhood it was not unusual for Albert Einstein or Richard Rodgers to show up at the dinner table. She went into analysis at the age of nine to overcome her stutter, but when that failed her mother discovered a way for Carly to communicate: Carly sang whatever it was she wanted to say, and her voice emerged clearly and beautifully.

Simon was involved with Warren Beatty when she met Taylor at a Carnegie Hall concert in late 1971. Now they seemed to Jagger to be very much in love—reason enough

for Mick to pursue her. Then there were her looks. Rangy,
wild-maned, and lush-lipped, Carly had those physical
qualities he found most irresistible: She looked like Mick
Jagger—or an All-American version of Bianca.

"Carly was awfully innocent compared to Jagger," said a
family friend. "He was one of the most worldly men she'd
ever met, and one of the most exciting. He'd fly all over
the world at the drop of a hat, he seemed to know everybody, to have *slept* with everybody. He was very knowledgeable on a wide range of topics, and to top it all off he
was this pop god."

When word of Jagger's affair with Simon reached Europe, Bianca threw a full-fledged tantrum. She went into
Mick's closet and ripped all his shirts to shreds—with her
teeth. "There's a certain American female singer," she became fond of saying, "I'd like to tear to pieces."

On his return home to the south of France, Jagger found
himself once again locked out of the house. Once he'd finally talked his way in, he wished he hadn't. Bianca, in a
jealous frenzy, was brandishing a revolver. After a few tense
moments she settled for throwing Mick out of the house.

Bianca often carried a derringer with her when she traveled. One night Mick thought he heard a robber fumbling
at the window of their hotel room and grabbed the gun,
aiming it at the intruder. The burglar turned out to be
Mick's loony friend Keith Moon of the Who. Moon had
climbed up the exterior of the hotel and into the Jagger's
sixteenth-floor window. "Dear boy," said Moon, "I thought
I'd just pop up and tuck you and the lady in."

Bianca later confided to Andy Warhol that of all Mick's
lovers the one who concerned her most was Carly Simon
because, said Andy, "Carly Simon is intelligent and has the
look Mick likes—she looks like Mick and Bianca."

Late in 1972 Simon would wed James Taylor and spend
much of their nine-year marriage helping him get off heroin. All three—Jagger, Simon, and Taylor—remained close
friends. When Simon recorded her hit single "You're So

Vain," it launched a flurry of speculation about the identity of the song's subject. To anyone familiar with the details of their affair, the answer was obvious from the lyrics ("your scarf it was apricot . . . one eye in the mirror as you watched yourself gavotte . . . the wife of a close friend, the wife of a close friend. . . ." To add fuel to the controversy Jagger sang anonymously (but very recognizably) in the background, and Carly hinted the song was about Beatty, not Mick.

That May of 1972 the Stones rehearsed for a week in the Swiss reort of Montreaux so they could be close to the clinic where doctors were trying to wean Anita Pallenberg off heroin before she gave birth to her second child by Keith. (Their daughter, Dandelion, would be born on April 17 with a harelip, but otherwise apparently undamaged by her parents' relentless drug abuse.)

Before launching his grueling eight-week assault on the U.S., Jagger took off with Bianca in search of a little anonymity in Southeast Asia. While Bianca shopped and lolled on the beach, Mick ostensibly explored ancient Siamese ruins. He also managed to sample the sexual smorgasbord served up at Bangkok's famous houses of ill repute. (When he bumped into Marianne Faithfull five months later and managed to talk her into bed, Jagger told her about Bangkok and claimed he hadn't "had a good fuck since.")

Bianca wanted to tag along with her husband on the U.S. tour, but he ordered her to stay at home with Jade. Jagger was standing in the hallway of 48 Cheyne Walk, surrounded by twenty suitcases and waiting for the limo to take him to the airport, when Bianca struck back.

"If I can't go," she screamed, "then my silk scarf's not going either. You can just unpack every suitcase until you find it."

According to Jade's nanny, Janie Villiers, Jagger actually burst into tears at this juncture. "I was going to wear it for my act," Mick whined. "You can't expect me to find it now!" But he did, plowing through every suitcase until he finally pulled it out of the last one.

Even before they landed on North American shores that June, *Exile on Main Street,* heralded by many critics as the Stones' most accomplished effort, had already sold one million copies—a staggering number for a double issue. The tour was no less ambitious in scope: fifty concerts in thirty cities, nearly one million fans standing in line up to forty-eight hours to plunk down upwards of $4 million for tickets. Price was no object; scalpers were selling six-dollar tickets for fifteen times that amount, most often a combination of cash and drugs. Demand was so overwhelming that it could not have been met even if the Stones had had the fortitude to perform twice a day every day for a full year. They were at the summit of the miltibillion-dollar record industry, but how long could the Stones stay on top? "The end," replied an Atlantic executive, "is infinity."

Jagger had his own, highly personal reasons for enduring the rigors of the road once again. At the end of the tour he would turn twenty-nine—well into middle age by pop-star standards of the time. The Beatles were already seen as quaint relics of another, distant era, and all-important teenage consumers were now flocking to buy the latest offerings of relative newcomers David Cassidy, the Jackson Five, and the Carpenters.

Elton John and David Bowie were cashing in on the gender-bending "Glitter Rock" trend for which Jagger had laid the groundwork. It was essential that Mick reclaim the young audience. Toward that end he decreed that VIPs and the press be banished from the first twenty rows in favor of screaming fans. "He feeds off their energy," said a tour member, "sort of like a vampire." Agreed Mick: "I can feel 'em down there. I need each and every one of 'em."

Jagger did not disappoint. Leaping onstage in a white jumpsuit slashed to the pubis, he was all purple eye shadow, gold sparkles, and bulging genitalia ("Makes me look like I have a permanent hard-on. If that's what they want, that's what I'm givin' them.") The apricot satin scarf clung to his hips, as narrow as any sixteen-year-old's.

Midway through the tour Jagger would appear, snarling into a microphone and drenched with sweat, on the cover of *Life* magazine. Although the story was headlined "The Stones Blast Through the Land," *Life* writer Thomas Thompson zeroed in on the charismatic Mick. "Above all there is Jagger," he wrote. "He is possessed, as few performers are—Callas, El Cordobés, Nureyev come to mind— with a stunning, electric-shock stage capacity. Watch him prowl the space, pantherlike at first, suddenly a marionette abandoned by the string-puller, now cheerleader at an orgy."

Taking swigs of Jack Daniel's and, in the fleeting moments he was not center stage, a snort or two of coke, Jagger worked himself up to "Midnight Rambler," with its troubling lyrics about bloody sexual prowls and the Boston Strangler. Again he whipped off his studded belt and, as he brought it down with a crack on the floor, was suddenly bathed in blood-red light.

At the end of each show he dipped into a silver bowl and scattered rose petals over the audience like a benediction. As the tour began to get to the roadies, someone concealed a chicken leg among the rose petals as a practical joke. Not seeing it, Jagger tossed it into the crowd and it bounced off a fan's head. Later, Jagger dissolved in hysterics when he reached in among the roses and pulled out a bloody liver. The next time he had a roadie check the bowl first—in time to prevent his tossing a bloody pig's leg, hoof and all, into the crowd.

Carried on a tsunami of record sales and sustained air play—as well as copious quantities of pot, amyl nitrite, and cocaine—STP (Peter Rudge's shorthand for "Stones Touring Party") once again swept across the continent like a Mongol horde—with similar results offstage and on. Before their sold-out concert at Vancouver's Pacific Coliseum, two thousand angry fans who had been unable to buy tickets clashed with a phalanx of red-coated Mounties, injuring over thirty.

A search of all fans entering the Seattle Coliseum yielded several guns and knives, and in San Diego fans set fire to police barricades, touching off a battle with police that resulted in sixty arrests and fifteen injuries. Police lobbed tear gas grenades into an unruly Stones mob in Tucson, and the ensuing mayhem resulted in a dozen injuries and over three hundred arrests.

It was about this time that Jagger received an urgent call from Marsha Hunt. The mother of Jagger's eldest child, still unkown to the press, was herself touring Germany when nineteen-month-hold Karis knocked over a glass of hot tea at a café and severely scalded herself. Karis was refused medical attention by the Germans because her mother appeared to have no money, so Hunt hopped the first flight back to London.

During the ten days Karis spent in the hospital, Jagger phoned twice to offer assistance. Hunt asked him to send along half the $200 hospital bill. Jagger promised he would have his office wire the money. He never did, and Hunt was forced to skip without paying. Later, he told her he did not send the $100 because, as Hunt later wrote, she would "probably have bought shoes with the money." That cavalier remark would send Hunt straight to a lawyer.

Across the Atlantic, Jagger wisely abandoned plans to celebrate July Fourth in Washington resplendent in full Revolutionary War regalia, but the results were the same: chaos, and another sixty-five fans thrown in jail. In Montreal, while three thousand holders of counterfeit tickets rioted outside the Forum, Quebec separatists set off a bomb planted underneath an equipment truck, injuring no one but destroying several amplifiers. In Rhode Island, Jagger and Richards were arrested for slugging a press photographer.

The city most prone to violence—where some sort of retaliation for Altamont, perhaps from disgruntled Hell's Angels, might take place—gave Jagger his warmest reception. Eager not to witness a repeat of the bloody events of 1969, promoter Bill Graham sequestered the Stones on a floor of San Francisco's fortresslike Miyako Hotel and ordered a private security force to secure a four-block radius around the Winterland auditorium.

"The biggest difference between 1969 and 1972 was Mick Jagger's ability to control an audience," Graham later said. "He was a marked man. All it would have taken was one maniac. Yet Jagger performed with a kind of open looseness without ever giving up control. He knew just how far he could go."

There was only one tense moment—the sudden, heart-stopping crack of what sounded like a gunshot in the middle of "Under My Thumb." Security guards scrambled to investigate, but Jagger, the color drained from his face, kept singing. It was only a firecracker.

Richards had described Altamont as "just another gig—a gig where I had to split quick." It now seemed that Altamont had indeed faded from the collective memory of San Franciscans. As the Stones boarded the Lapping Tongue, their private DC-7 with Jagger's trademark oral features emblazoned on its fuselage, a miniskirted woman ran up to Jagger and handed him an envelope. It contained a summons from Altamont landowners claiming their property had been damaged. Jagger's response was to slap the process server across the face and literally throw her off the plane.

Had she not looked so much like one of the Stones' battalion of long-legged, braless groupies, the writ-server would never have gotten so close to Jagger. Two burly bodyguards accompanied him at all times, and even then Jagger packed a .38 pistol in his jacket pocket. "You could see that look of dread come over him practically every time somebody he didn't know came up to him in a restaurant or on the street," said a Stones staffer. Jagger was now saying that he expected to die violently, and that he worried about being shot every time he stepped out onstage.

Assassination wasn't Jagger's only concern on the 1972

tour. After spending almost as much time in the air as a commercial pilot, Mick inexplicably became a white-knuckle flier. Takeoffs and landings had suddenly become events fraught with terror, and even the slightest turbulence could trigger a panic attack.

Angst aside, life on the road for the Rolling Stones was as insane as ever—much of it captured by filmmaker Robert Frank for a never-released tour documentary. Among the many revealing vignettes: Keith shooting up heroin; Mick and Keith, obviously stoned, babbling nonsensical answers and unselfconsciously rolling joints during an interview; Jagger belting out "Cocksucker Blues"; a man whose face we cannot see masturbating inside his satin pants; Bianca's breasts popping out of her dress during a fitting in Mick's hotel room; Jagger walking around the swimming pool of the Stones' rented L.A. headquarters, his hands down the front of his swim trunks playing with himself; tour members and naked groupies alternately rolling about on hotel beds and shooting themselves/each other up; Bianca photographing her husband smoking pot in the back of their limousine as it barrels down a country road in the Deep South, and Jagger just before a performance snorting cocaine through a rolled-up hundred-dollar bill—then, just before he reaches the stage, running back for more. For obvious reasons Jagger would not allow the film, titled *Cocksucker Blues*, to see the light of day.

Still, Jagger drew the line at heroin. He did not believe in going onstage stoned, though by stoned he obviously meant out of control and unable to perform. "I think it's completely wrong," he insisted, "to get totally fucked up and go out and play."

Whatever his rationale, Jagger frequently dipped into the Stones' pharmaceutical cookie jar. *Rolling Stone*'s Robert Greenfield personally witnessed thousands of dollars' worth of drugs being snorted, smoked, injected, and swallowed. "Five bottles of Demerol and a bottle of 500 Quaaludes and now they're all gone; a quart-sized jar of coke just for an energizer; four Quaaludes to get to sleep, but if you start to speed on them drop a Placidyl—they use them for bad acid trips; $500 of coke laid out in a four-foot line on a mirror and they did it all up; one guy keeps his stash in a rubber—calls it *real* prophylactic medicine, ha-ha."

In a typically surreal scene groupies and hangers-on are shoving poppers—amyl nitrite—under each other's noses, snorting lines of cocaine, and having sex in dark corners. At the center of it all is a naked Jagger, sitting up in bed with a woman writhing in the sheets next to him. He is holding a mirror up to his face, staring into it like the Wicked Queen in *Snow White*. No one thinks this is odd, and in this grotesque world it isn't.

The debauchery reached its nadir some thirty-five thousand feet above sea level aboard the Lapping Tongue. With Jagger playing tom-toms and cheering them on, several roadies stripped three young groupies and began chasing them around the cabin. One roadie picked up a girl, spun her upside down, and plunged his face between her thighs. The tour doctor appeared to be most rapacious of all, having sex with one of the groupies in every conceivable position while Jagger and the others looked on.

This accommodating young groupie was supposedly doing research for her high school newspaper. Truman Capote, who was assigned to cover the tour for *Rolling Stone*, claimed to have witnessed the event. "Well," he told the girl, "you came to get a story for your high school newspaper and you're sure getting one." (In truth, the girl was nineteen and attended a secretarial school. But she, like Capote, was taking notes for an article that was never written).

Capote had been allowed considerable access, and hovered backstage with his best friend, Princess Lee Radziwill, sister of Jacqueline Kennedy Onassis. "It was a case of dueling bitches from the start," said a friend of Capote's. "Mick disliked Tru for being 'on' all the time." Jagger described Capote as "tryin' to make everyone laugh. Everyone laughs at a cocktail party, but no one laughed with him because he wasn't funny."

Capote dismissed Jagger as "a scared little boy, very much off his turf." Predicting the Stones would never tour the U.S. again and would probably disband after three years, Capote went on to slam Mick: "Jagger can't sing, his voice is not in the least charming, he can't dance . . . he has no talent save for a kind of fly-eyed wonder. He will never be a star. That unisex thing is a no-sex thing. Believe me, he's about as sexy as a pissing toad."

Keith Richards may have contributed to the obvious animosity. Trying to roust Capote for one of the Stones' pre-dawn orgies, Richards banged on his hotel room door shouting, "C'mon, you old queen . . . you bitch. Fuckin' WAKE UP!" When Capote told him to leave, Keith moved on to Radziwill's room: "Princess Radish! C'mon, you old tart, there's a party going on downstairs." Not surprisingly, Radziwill remained in her room.

Capote did concede that Jagger was probably a superb businessman. He also figured that, while he was whipping the crowd with his belt during "Midnight Rambler," Mick actually imagined that he was flogging Prince Rupert Loewenstein toward bigger and bigger profits. Ultimately, Capote would grow tired of working on the *Rolling Stone* magazine piece and abandon it altogether.

Bianca joined Mick only twice during the tour, and that suited him perfectly. "Ah, I find it very difficult to travel with anyone on tour," he explained. "Bianca's easier than some people, but I just have to be on my own." And free to partake, as he always had, of the road's many and varied pleasures. For their series of concerts in Chicago the Stones were guests at the Playboy mansion. While Hef puffed away on his pipe with the Playboy logo on the stem, Jagger drifted upstairs each night with the voluptuous playmate(s) of his choice.

Even then there were moments where fear overtook his libido. "Did ya see men leapin' onstage the other night?" he asked Keith. "Great big men they were too. With clenched fists. . . ." Another night a burly fan loudly begged Jagger to whip him during "Midnight Rambler"—"pleading for it and grabbin' at the belt. His eyes . . ." Then another man in the audience held up a burning cigarette to get Jagger's attention and then snuffed it out in his palm and held it up "all black with ash and fucked up. Weird, eh?"

Not all of Jagger's many sexual encounters on the road were with nameless groupies. At a party in Los Angeles he spotted a familiar face across the room. "Miss Pamela, the girl of my dreams," he shouted to Pam Miller. Her current lover, an as-yet unknown blond actor named Don Johnson, was cheating on Miss Pamela with Tippi Hedren's sixteen-year-old daughter, Melanie Griffith. A very drunk Miss Pamela responded to Jagger's clarion call. "I ran through the trendy mass, half out of my skull," she recalled, "knocking him down into a flock of pillows, where I plunged my hand down his pants and into the crack of his sweet famous ass." Jagger's competitive instincts were aroused once again when Pamela informed him that her new beau, Don Johnson, was the best-endowed lover she'd ever had.

On July 24, Mick and Bianca, traveling under the aliases "Mr. and Mrs. Shelley," checked into Richard Nixon's favorite suite at New York's Sherry Netherland Hotel. The two shows at Madison Square Garden on Wednesday, July 26, would mark the tour's climax—and Jagger's twenty-ninth birthday.

As the star of his own ABC talk show, Dick Cavett had himself recently landed on the covers of both *Time* and *Life* magazines. Now he was standing in the wings at Madison Square Garden in a fringed buckskin coat, cheering Capote on with "Go, Truman, go" as café society's "Tiny Terror" danced onstage next to the Stones.

To boost ratings Cavett came to give his audience an exclusive backstage look at the "World's Greatest Rock and Roll Band." During a brief interview with Bill Wyman, Cavett asked him if he chain-smoked. Waving a joint in front of the TV cameras, Wyman said he didn't. Cavett coyly replied, "But you *are* smoking a cigarette." Wyman merely shook his head and inhaled deeply. One-on-one with Jagger in a small dressing room, Cavett found the man "charming and frustrating. A very elusive character. He was getting ready to go on and he was obviously keyed up." Cavett and Jagger would become quite close in the mid-1970s, when Mick and Bianca rented the house next door to his summer home on Long Island.

Once Cavett had finished their interview, Jagger took his customary snort of coke and, surrounded by bodyguards, made his way down a series of passageways and bounded up a ramp to the stage.

Chip Monck had planned an enormous surprise for Mick on his birthday. But Garden management barred him from hiring an elephant to gallumph onto the stage. Nor was Monck permitted to dump five hundred live chickens on the heads of the audience. The Stones had to settle for hurling custard pies at each other while the throng of twenty thousand sang "Happy Birthday to You."

From there Jagger was whisked to another, celebrity-packed party hosted by Ahmet Ertegun at the St. Regis Hotel on Fifth Avenue. It was a Felliniesque finale to the tour. The guest list was, to say the least, eclectic: Tennessee Williams, Huntington Hartford, Woody Allen, Oscar and Françoise de la Renta, Gianni Bulgari, Winston and C.Z. Guest, Lord Hesketh, Diana Vreeland, Lady "Slim" Keith, Andrea Portago, Cy Newhouse, George Plimpton, and of course Capote and Princess Lee. Bob Dylan, in a white fedora, chatted with Dick Cavett and then asked to have his picture taken with Zsa Zsa Gabor. Andy Warhol snapped Polaroids while Pat Ast and transvestite Candy Darling kibbitzed with Tennessee. Bianca, still telling friends she wanted to "tear her apart," was steered away from Carly Simon, who nonetheless found a spare moment to nuzzle Mick when Mrs. Jagger wasn't looking.

With the lapping-tongue logo unfurled on the drapes behind him, Count Basie and his orchestra played as Warhol Factory girl Gerry Miller popped out of a cake wearing only minuscule pasties and gyrated through an adults-only routine. Then four septuagenarian tap dancers emerged and did a soft-shoe. "It's exploitive," said evangelist-turned-actor Marjoe. "I felt like we should have thrown pennies."

Jagger, dressed in a white satin suit, spent most of the evening drinking champagne and discussing grosses and percentages with Ertegun. Around them some of the world's most famous names openly passed around joints and snorted cocaine. As two A.M. approached, Mick joined in a jam with Stevie Wonder and Muddy Waters, then he and Bianca opened their birthday gifts—among them a photograph of a nude woman, a silver cross, and a cocaine snuff box—and left.

Rex Reed unaccountably compared the party, which did not end until six A.M., to "a Doris Day movie." Dylan proclaimed it "encompassing—the beginning of cosmic consciousness."

Syndicated columnist Harriet Van Horne viewed the celebration differently. Pointing to the open drug use and the nude woman popping out of a cake, Van Horne likened the whole spectacle to a Roman orgy "where 'a sweet lass naked' often rose from pies in a flutter of thrushes. As reclining guests gorged themselves on such delicacies as dormice baked alive in honey, platters of nightengales' tongues, and combs torn from living roosters, the dancing girls performed sexual acrobatics and slave-clowns told obscene stories." Sniffed Van Horne: "I thought of all the ancients who would have been perfectly at home at such a Bacchanale as Jagger's birthday party. Nero, Caligula, the Marquis de Sade. I also thought of *Clockwork Orange* and the Manson Family."

Mick Jagger's birthday party made the front pages of *The New York Times*, the *Daily News*, and the *New York Post*. The fact that there was a total eclipse of the moon that night did not.

"Everyone knows everyone is
basically bisexual."

13

A silvery confection of turrets and domes, the Ansonia Hotel reigned like a dowager empress over Manhattan's Upper West Side. The basement of the Ansonia, however, more closely resembled a steamy cross between Hades and an Esther Williams movie.

These were the famous Continental Baths, the subterranean gay mecca where Bette Midler, Barry Manilow, Melissa Manchester, and other performers got their start playing to howlingly appreciative homosexual audiences.

The principal activity at "the Baths" had nothing to do with music—or baths, for that matter. There was indeed an Olympic-size swimming pool, and there were steambaths. But the real action took place inside dozens of cubicles where all manner of ménages, orgies, and S & M extravanganzas took place.

When Jagger stepped down into this tile-walled Gomorrah, the reception he received was hospitable—unsettlingly so. One man wearing nothing but a towel walked up to Jagger, dropped his towel, and stood there waiting for Jagger to do something. Mick turned away only to have another man walk up to him, rip off his towel, and stand there with the same look of anticipation on his face. A half dozen other hopefuls similarly bared themselves to Jagger as he beat a hasty retreat.

Not that Mick was in any way intimidated by gays or the lives they led. Onstage and off he embodied the bisexual chic that had taken firm hold in 1972. That summer Jagger spent several days in the company of another glamorous symbol of the new sexual philosophy, Rudolf Nureyev.

A full decade after his spectacular defection from the Soviet Union, Nureyev was at the peak of his powers, dazzling audiences around the world with his gravity-defying leaps and his sheer animal presence. Away from the concert stage the flamboyantly exotic figure with the pouting lips and high Tartar cheekbones strutted through life much like Jagger—driving himself past the point of exhaustion onstage, then partying fiercely until dawn.

Nureyev seduced women as well as men, including his famous partner Margot Fonteyn, designers Halston and Giorgio Sant'Angelo, Leonard Bernstein, and Anthony Perkins. "Rudolf had a sex life," observed his friend, movie director James Toback, "that was probably as wide ranging as anyone's in this century."

When he was still living with Marianne Faithfull, Jagger dreamt of becoming another Nureyev. After they became friends in the late 1960s, the two spent hours together partying and debating the relative demands of their professions. "Me and Nureyev have flaming rows about whether it takes more talent and discipline to be a ballet dancer or a pop singer," Jagger said. "He used to put me down a lot, but I think I've converted him. I told him I would have wanted to dance myself, but I never had the opportunity."

An incident at the home of television personality Geraldo Rivera that summer of 1972 provides some insight into the relationship between Nureyev and Jagger. Rivera threw an impromptu party at his apartment on Manhattan's Lower East Side, and Nureyev and Jagger were among the guests. While the two men smoked marijuana and danced in his living room, Rivera went into the kitchen to mix some drinks.

"Suddenly," recalled Rivera, "someone snuggled up behind me. I felt an arm around my waist, and I made a kind of half pivot to see who it was. It was Nureyev, and he was moving in time to the music, pressing himself against me from behind. He was being playfully suggestive, overtly sexual, and before I had a chance to even think how to respond, Jagger approached me from the front and started doing the same thing. They were kidding, and giddy, but there was also something seriously competitive going on between them."

As Jagger continued to run his hands over Rivera's chest, Nureyev ran his fingers through Rivera's hair. "He's a virgin, you know," Rudolf told Mick.

"Oh, well," laughed Jagger, "we can break him in."

Rivera remembered that he "squirmed out from between this odd sandwich and laughed the whole thing off." But he was convinced that, playfulness aside, they were making a serious attempt to seduce him.

Rivera declined. But, he conceded, "if I were ever going to have a homosexual experience, it would have been that night, with Rudolf Nureyev and Mick Jagger."

(Throughout the next two decades Jagger and Nureyev would maintain their intense personal friendship. In 1984 Nureyev was diagnosed HIV positive, and nine years later he died of AIDS at the age of fifty-four).

Mick was not the only Jagger who found Rivera charming. Bianca later appeared on Geraldo's ABC series *Good Night America*, and blurted out that "Mick doesn't think much of women." The remark enraged Jagger, igniting another of the knockdown drag-out arguments for which the Jaggers had now become famous on two continents.

After the landmark 1972 tour Jagger and Bianca returned to London that September and announced that they were fed up with life on the Côte d'Azur—though they would in fact continue to avoid paying taxes by shuttling from one residence to the next.

All the Stones decided to stage a homecoming. None too soon for Richards and Pallenberg. After a year's surveillance of all the Stones, French authorities decided to issue an arrest warrant only for Keith and Anita; it seemed that a cook at Nellcôte complained to the local gendarmes that Pallenberg had introduced his teenage daughter to heroin.

With the exception of cricket, sex, and making money, few endeavors appealed to Mick more than toying with the press. He had always been able to speak volumes without revealing anything of substance, and had developed a strategy about what to dish out to each publication: for *Vanity Fair*, insouciant wit; for *The New York Times* and the London *Sunday Times*, cautious introspection. For *Rolling Stone*, music-industry savvy, with a dollop of sex.

This time he decided to make headlines by declaring his intention to retire in four years. "When I'm thirty-three I'll quit," he said. "That's the time when a man has to do something else. I can't say what it will definitely be. . . . But it won't be in show business. I don't want to be a rock 'n' roll singer all my life."

Why not? "I couldn't bear to end up as an Elvis Presley and sing in Las Vegas with all those housewives and old ladies coming in with their handbags," shuddered Jagger. "It's really sick. Elvis probably digs it. That's his good fortune if that's the way he wants it. Not me."

Settled back on Cheyne Walk, Mick and Bianca resumed their marital free-for-all. It seemed to most of their friends that Jagger simply did not love Bianca; there were no displays of affection, and it was rare for them to appear in public together at all. When they did spend time together, it invariably ended badly. "Mick and Bianca fought *constantly*," said a former personal secretary. "You couldn't be around them for two minutes without both of them erupting like Vesuvius."

At a going-away party for Shirley Arnold, who had been with the Stones organization for nine years, Mick and Bianca each showed up with a present—she with perfume, he with a topaz necklace. To everyone's embarrassment they almost came to blows over who had been given the assignment of bringing Arnold's gift.

Chrissie Shrimpton and Marianne Faithfull had both put

their careers on the back burner to tend to Mick's fragile
ego during their years with him. Although she had no career, Bianca made it clear from the outset that she had no
intention of becoming just another rock and roll wife. "I
am a person in my own right," she proclaimed. "Mick's
achievements and his accomplishments are his. Nothing to
do with me. I must achieve my own. He's a musician, and
I am not. The people who surround the Stones bathe in
the reflected light. I refuse to."

After Jade's birth Bianca claimed to have experienced a
"change" in herself. "I feel life is just beginning. I need to
concentrate on something. Mick's just starting to notice."

How could he not? They had just added a house in Ocho
Rios, Jamaica, to their string of homes, but Bianca seemed
to prefer hotel rooms. Sashaying about London, New York,
and Paris, Bianca capitalized on her newfound visibility.
Dipping into a wardrobe that included everything from velvet capes, boas, and cloches to see-through sheaths, lace
mantillas, and a collection of silver, gold, and ivory-tipped
walking sticks, Bianca was undeniably a fashion original.
That year she would join her husband on the Best Dressed
List.

Publicity aside, Bianca still complained loudly that her
husband was not paying enough attention to her. While
Mick was in Jamaica working on the Stones' new album,
Goat's Head Soup, she did something about it. In an act of
desperation reminiscent of Marianne Faithfull's scalping,
Bianca chopped off most of her hair. When he saw what
she'd done to her beautiful mahogany-colored hair, he did
the same to his. Even more than before Mick and Bianca
looked like mirror images of each other.

With Keith and Anita now wanted on a new set of drug-
possession charges in France, all the Stones returned home
to London for the holidays. Bianca and Mick made an effort to get along, for Jade's sake, when a disaster half a
world away effectively ended their Christmas.

On December 23, 1972, a news bulletin flashed across
the Jaggers' television screen: a devastating earthquake had

struck Managua, killing more than six thousand people. Bianca burst into tears, convinced that her family had died in the disaster.

Nicaragua had been cut off from the outside world. No matter what strings he pulled, Jagger was unable to find out where Bianca's relatives were, or even if they were still alive. There were no direct commercial flights to the stricken country, so Jagger chartered a private jet and filled it with medical supplies for the journey.

As the Jaggers drove from the airport into Managua, Bianca was stunned by the devastation. Searching the rubble where her mother's tiny diner had been, Bianca could not find a trace of either of her parents. On New Year's Eve they tracked down both Bianca's mother and father in a nearby village; miraculously, they had managed to escape injury.

On January 4 Mick and Bianca returned to their house in Jamaica only to learn that they had also been reported by several news agencies as "missing in Nicaragua" for forty-eight hours. While Mick stayed behind to resume work on the album, Bianca returned to Nicaragua and rented a small house there for herself and her mother. She soon found herself in a situation not unlike Marsha Hunt's, repeatedly phoning Mick and imploring him to send money for her food and lodging.

Mick was more forthcoming, however, when Bianca told him that the thing her stricken country needed most was hard cash. Jagger moved swiftly, and on January 18, 1973, a Rolling Stones benefit concert held in the Los Angeles Forum raised a staggering $787,500 for the relief effort.

Meanwhile, the Stones were dealt a few setbacks of their own. Japanese officials, unmoved by Jagger's fund-raising efforts on behalf of Nicaragua, ruled that because of his 1966 drug conviction he would not be allowed into their country. That meant cutting Japan from the group's long-planned Far Eastern tour. Australia then threatened to bar Keith Richards because of his heroin addiction, but backed down at the last minute. This would set the pattern over the next two decades, as the Stones' arrest records made all-important visas increasingly difficult to obtain.

Japan was not the only country where the Stones—and Jagger in particular—were in imminent danger of being branded persona non grata. All rock groups were now candidates for surveillance—John Lennon, for example, ranked high on the FBI's list of so-called "subversives" even before he and Yoko gave their highly publicized antiwar press conference in bed.

Not surprisingly, the Stones were singled out by several government agencies for special attention. Both the U.S. Customs Service and the Immigration and Naturalization Service had put them on their special "watch list" of undesirables after the series of drug arrests in the mid-1960s. The State Department and the CIA also began dossiers on Jagger after he joined in the 1968 march on the U.S. embassy in London. Finally, in 1972 Jagger was officially added to Richard Nixon's Enemies List after the President spotted a photograph of Mick cavorting onstage in an Uncle Sam hat.

Yet no agency took more interest in the Stones than the FBI. Beginning in 1969 undercover agents donned disguises and mingled with the crowds at most of their U.S. concerts. At Altamont a dozen FBI operatives, some posing as bikers and drug dealers, infiltrated the crowd. By the early 1970s the Bureau had informers working inside the Stones' operation.

J. Edgar Hoover himself took a special interest in Jagger. In addition to his history of drug arrests Jagger had publicly described himself as a Maoist and an anarchist. Jagger had also proclaimed his support for the Black Panthers, a group that Hoover was intent on destroying. Radical chic aside, anyone who aligned themselves with the Panthers automatically wound up under some form of FBI surveillance. (In 1967 Hoover issued a secret memo ordering his agents to "expose, disrupt, misdirect, discredit, or otherwise neutralize" all black nationalist groups and particularly the Panthers.)

Hoover's interest in Jagger extended beyond Mick's political pronouncements. The venerated Hoover, a bachelor prude who concealed his own homosexual orientation from the public, was horrified by the lyrics to Jagger's songs. He was also offended by the Stones' use of profanity in general. Transcripts of wiretaps on the phones in Jagger's hotel rooms were censored; the more egregious obscenities were replaced with a series of asterisks so as not to offend Hoover's delicate sensibilities.

Hoover considered Jagger a negative, even dangerous, role model for American youth. But his singular interest in Mick went beyond that. Jagger's androgynous persona angered and upset Hoover. The director's own tough-guy image had been cultivated to offset persistent rumors that he was gay. Toward that end Hoover professed a hatred of "queers" and often instructed his agents to dig up evidence of homosexual activity with which to blackmail his political opponents.

By turns a strutting cock-of-the-walk and a beglittered, sloe-eyed faun, Jagger seemed to Hoover to be, well, un-American. According to one former FBI agent "Hoover hated Jagger probably more than any other pop culture figure of his generation." Jagger's pansexuality and his unequaled charisma both repelled and fascinated Hoover.

The quake in Nicaragua offered Jagger and the Stones a golden opportunity to wipe the slate clean. In May of 1973 Mick and Bianca were scheduled to appear in Washington to personally present a check for $787,500 to the Pan American Development Fund. Work at the Senate office building came to a virtual standstill when word flashed through the corridors that Jagger would soon be arriving— "and not only Mick Jagger," gushed the normally dignified *Washington Post*, "but the newest superstar of the family: Bianca Jagger, his wife and twin in sullen-lipped looks, darling of the social and fashion worlds."

A galaxy of Latin American ambassadors and several United States senators were on time for the ceremony, but the guest of honor, as usual, was not. "All we have to do now," sighed a weary Senator Jacob Javits, "is wait for Hamlet."

When they did materialize, Mick and Bianca lived up to their sartorial image—he in an open white shirt and a blue-and-white striped blazer with a yellow rose in the lapel. For this occasion he had borrowed his wife's trademark accessory: an ebony-and-ivory walking stick. Bianca, meantime, wore an Ossie Clark coat with Joan Crawford shoulder pads, green sequined shoes, and a green straw hat.

Mick and Bianca were presented with a golden key in appreciation of their fund-raising efforts, and, after politely sitting through a series of speeches, made their way through the crowd to their waiting limousine. From there they decided to drop in for lunch at Washington's trendiest restaurant, Sans Souci, and were promptly turned away. Why? "No reservation," sniffed the maître d', "and no tie."

According to Bianca, Mick had hired attorney William Carter, a former Secret Service agent during the Kennedy and Johnson administrations, to help him obtain a permanent U.S. visa. At a Washington dinner that May, Carter reportedly told Mick that as a result of his charitable donation for earthquake relief, a permanent visa was his "for the asking."

By that time, recalled Bianca, Mick wasn't interested. "Mick said to me that since he was trying to avoid paying United States income taxes, he did not and would not apply for a permanent visa, since if he had one this would give the impression he was recording in the United States and this was something he did not want known.

"He told me many times," continued Bianca, "that he wanted to give the impression that he was not recording in the U.S. when he actually was." More than the FBI, the CIA, or the INS, Jagger feared the IRS.

American tax authorities made no claim on Jagger's income for the time being. Not so Marsha Hunt. Tired of having to pursue Mick for the occasional meager handout, she arranged a bizarre cloak-and-dagger meeting with him on the steps of the Albert Memorial in London's Hyde

Park. Together they hammered out the details of a £20,000 (about $50,000) trust fund to be put in Karis's name. By the end of the day Jagger had knocked the figure down to £17,000 ($42,000).

It was all academic; after months of waiting for Jagger to sign the trust documents, Hunt filed suit on July 16, 1973. In the whirlwind of publicity that followed, Jagger denied paternity and, in an effort to stall legal proceedings, insisted on a blood test—thus implying that Marsha was promiscuous. Hunt, meantime, was portrayed as a home-wrecking gold-digger. Mick, stung by what he viewed as Hunt's betrayal, sarcastically suggested that Hunt had gone public merely to hype her own flagging career.

While Hunt literally skipped over rooftops holding Karis to avoid reporters staked out in front of her London house, Jagger's lawyers made a settlement offer: £9 a week to pay for a nanny and a £10,000 (roughly $25,000) trust fund once Karis left school. In exchange Hunt would be required to sign a document stating Jagger was not the father. She accepted the deal.

Even when it came to Jade, Jagger acknowledged that he was not exactly a model father. "I don't see the baby," he confessed. "I'm always fuckin' *on the road*. It's my own choice, but I'm fucking negligent, I just am. But when I was a kid, my father was away a lot. It's important to be there in the formative years, but I'm not there. And short of carrying the kid about in the next room, which I also don't particularly dig, you just see your kid when you can, same as anyone else. It's *the American way*."

That July the world press, as expected, did not let Mick's thirtieth birthday pass unnoticed. "Age shouldn't bother you," Jagger protested. "People are really too concerned about it. It's really something very strange how people are all hung up about age. . . . I suppose you wonder do you look as beautiful as you did when you were nineteen or twenty," Jagger mused. "I didn't look very nice when I was nineteen anyway. . . . I don't promote the image of being an eternal twenty-year-old, that's a very dangerous thing to do."

The Jimmy Miller–produced *Goat's Head Soup* was released on August 31, but only after a furious battle with Ahmet Ertegun over one of the final cuts on the album. "Starfucker" was just a little too raunchy even by Stones standards. Ertegun worried that with lines like "bet you keep your pussy clean" and "giving head to Steve McQueen," at the very least the Stones left Atlantic open to a lawsuit from McQueen.

Since Jagger had apparently witnessed the incident described in the song, he merely sent a tape of the song to McQueen and asked him to promise in writing that he wouldn't sue. McQueen obliged. Jagger ultimately relented on the title, however, agreeing to change it to "Star Star"—not enough of a change to keep it from being banned by the BBC and most American radio stations.

To launch the new album Mick invited Princess Margaret, the Ormsby-Gores, Lord Litchfield, and the heavies of the British music industry to a party at Winston Churchill's birthplace, magnificent Blenheim Palace. An unkempt Anita Pallenberg stopped the show when she stormed into the palace, called Bianca a "fucking bitch," and dragged Keith out in search of another fix. Two weeks later Richards was at a Swiss clinic having his entire blood supply replaced—the only way he could get off heroin in time for the Stones' upcoming British and European tour.

Turning the gender-blender on high this time, Jagger was depicted on the cover of *Goat's Head Soup*, lips parted, staring through layers of gauze. He looked very much like a proper Victorian Lady in a turn-of-the-century motoring veil.

For all the controversy surrounding "Star Star" and the bizarre jacket photo, the critics praised *Goat's Head Soup* as one of the Stones' best efforts ever. "They have regained their musical confidence," intoned the *Times* of London, "that arrogance and rawness that brought them out of the Richmond clubs in 1963." *The New York Times* reserved its most glowing phrases for Jagger. "Too little respect," wrote *The New York Times*'s Loraine Alterman, "is given to his brilliant vocals."

Only one cut from the album was a hit, however; all other songs were eclipsed by a single, plaintive-to-the-point-of-whiny ballad that fluttered up to the No. 1 spot on the singles charts and perched there for thirteen weeks—"Angie."

To promote "Angie" Jagger again recruited Michael Lindsay-Hogg to make one of the group's famous pre-MTV videos. For this the Stones sat on the lip of a stage while Jagger sang in a blizzard of rose petals. For "Angie" 's U.S. television debut on *Don Kirschner's Rock Concert*, Jagger wore what *The New York Times* described as "full female makeup."

Meanwhile rumors flew that the inspiration for "Angie" was David Bowie's wife. Not quite. David, not Angie, was the inspiration for the song.

Bisexual chic owed much of its appeal to the outrageous exponents of a new musical subgenre called Glitter Rock. Elton John strutted and romped around concert stages all over the world in feather boas, foot-high platform shoes, and sequined capes, flashing his trademark—$50,000 worth of eyeglasses, ranging from a simple rhinestone pair to solid gold and flashing neon numbers with rims the size of tennis rackets. Although his sexual preference hardly needed to be stated, in 1977 after the first of his two suicide attempts, John announced that he was fervently bisexual and had sex three times a week—"more female than male."

No one personified this epoch's excesses more than David Bowie. Brought up in a working-class row house in South London, David Jones (his real name) often visited the orphanage where his father worked to play with the orphans. A high school dropout at sixteen, he tried to make it as an artist and worked as an ad designer to support himself until the well-known mime Lindsay Kemp took him under his wing.

As a teenager David Jones saw himself onstage as a rock performer who combined the universal appeal of the Beatles with the shock value of Mick Jagger. When it came time for him to choose a stage name he used both as his model. Mick often pointed out that in Old English, a "jagger" was a knife. So, Jones reasoned, his pseudonym would have to relate to knives, and begin with a *B* in deference to the Beatles. The Bowie knife had been named after the nineteenth-century frontiersman Jim Bowie, and for David it carried an added bonus: it was quintessentially American.

In 1969 the bisexual Bowie met an aspiring American actress named Mary-Angela Barnett through a mutual boyfriend. As Bowie would later put it, "We were both laying the same bloke." Angie had been expelled from Connecticut College for women for having a lesbian affair, and was pleasantly surprised when Bowie, rather than being shocked, was sympathetic.

The night before their wedding in 1970 David and Angela engaged in a ménage à trois with a friend of theirs named Clare; she served as a witness at the ceremony the following day. Throughout their marriage both Bowies continued to carry on relationships with members of both sexes.

Early on, Angie pushed David not just to copy Mick's unisex look, but to perfect it. When Bowie was reluctant to put on one of Michael Fish's dresses, Angie pointed out that Jagger had looked wonderful in the same dress the year before. Soon Bowie's Day-Glo orange hairdo, plastic disco boots, and painted fingernails had established his stage character, Ziggy Stardust, as the androgynous king of space rock.

Jagger eyed Bowie with envy. Although only four years younger than Mick, Bowie was being touted as pop music's hottest new star since the Beatles. And he did not have to share the glory, not to mention the proceeds, with anyone. Prompted in part by Bowie's meteoric rise, Jagger began talking openly about plans for a solo album.

At a Bowie concert in the spring of 1973, Jagger ventured backstage and was greeted warmly by the star in full Ziggy attire. It was apparent to bystanders that both men were taking the opportunity to size each other up.

Several months later Jagger invited Bowie and his companion, Scott, to the Stones concert in Newcastle, England. Jagger paid for their hotel suite along with roses and champagne. The note read *Love, Mick.*

In the middle of "Jumpin' Jack Flash" Jagger noticed a sudden surge in the audience. Looking over his shoulder, he caught sight of Bowie hovering stage left, his trademark orange mane in clear view. Stagehands acted quickly to move Bowie out of sight, and all eyes were once again on Jagger.

That night Mick and Bianca went to Bowie's hotel room, but before knocking they could hear voices inside. Bowie was saying that he had hated the show—from Mick's costume to his dated dance steps. At that moment the Jaggers walked in on Bowie and Scott, together in bed. They threw back the covers to reveal they were still dressed. All four went straight to a gambling casino.

Both as a star and as a man Bowie fascinated Mick. While Mick had pioneered high camp, he had been careful to dance around the subject of his own sexuality. Bowie, on the other hand, openly declared that his stage persona was not merely an act—that not only was he bisexual but so was his wife, and they often enjoyed sharing partners. Having focused his sexual energies on the pursuit of women, Jagger was now intrigued by Bowie's unfettered ambivalence—not to mention the positive effects it might have on a pop icon's career.

For his part Bowie was flattered at the attention being given him by an established giant of the music industry. If Jagger was a willing student, Bowie was an enthusiastic teacher.

The two soon became inseparable, hanging out together every night at the London disco Tramps, sitting ringside at the Ali-Norton title bout, attending a Diana Ross concert. At Bowie's "retirement" party at the Cafe Royal in London, Jagger was squeezed between the guest of honor and Lou Reed. The crimson-nailed Reed had scored a hit with the Bowie-produced "Walk on the Wild Side." Bowie, who always called Jagger "Michael," never Mick, also took his new companion Jagger to gay films. "David," said British television producer Kevin Kahn, "is a born proselytizer." Soon this oddest of couples would be photographed in a hotel room, Bowie cradling Jagger's head in his lap.

At first Angela tried to discourage the friendship. She felt that Jagger's glory days had passed, and that by associating with him David ran the risk of alienating his hip young audience. "There was this feeling," said a Bowie associate, "that Mick was washed up and that David was the wave of the future. And David *was* huge at the time. But he also knew that, when it came to longevity in the business, there was a lot he could learn from Mick."

That fall of 1973 the Bowies moved into a house on Oakley Street, not far from 48 Cheyne Walk. Ava Cherry, a black backup singer with blond, close-cropped hair, moved in with Angie and David. The three slept in the same bed, and occasionally David would cruise London nightspots in search of a young man to join them.

One morning Angie returned from a night on the town and went straight to the kitchen to make some tea. The Bowies' maid, who had arrived for work an hour earlier, coyly told the lady of the house that someone was in her bed.

When she pushed open the door to her bedroom, Angie Bowie saw her husband and Mick Jagger naked in bed together. Both men were startled awake. David looked up at his wife and said, "Oh, hello. How are you?"

"I'm fine," she replied. "Do you want some coffee?" Jagger said nothing. Without skipping a beat Angie went downstairs to the kitchen and returned with orange juice and coffee. She then obligingly served Bowie and Jagger breakfast in bed.

Although she did not catch them in the act, Angela later said she "felt absolutely dead certain that they'd been screwing. It was so obvious, in fact, that I never even considered the possibility that they *hadn't* been screwing.

"Even though I cared, there really wasn't much I was going to do about it. So I made breakfast." While they ate, Angie left the house to run some errands, and when she returned Jagger was gone. "I wish it had been me with Mick. I've always thought Mick must be a wild man in bed. He is a very sexy guy." The one time he did try to seduce Angie she "could not stop giggling. I looked at him and all I could see was this billy goat. I just couldn't get that image out of my head."

Ava Cherry apparently became a participant in Jagger's nocturnal games. "Mick and David were really sexually obsessed with each other," she reportedly told a friend. "Even though I was in bed with them many times I ended up just watching them have sex. They became very close and practically lived together for several months."

Leee (sic) Black Childers, former executive vice-president of Main Man, the management firm that handled Bowie, said the relationship between Bowie and Jagger was scarcely a well-kept secret. "We all knew about Angie catching Mick and David in bed together," said Childers. "Everyone knew what was going on between them." Maybe, Angela once quipped, the two men "were composing 'Angie'" when she discovered them in bed together.

Rumors also flew that Angie and Bianca were having an affair, adding a whole new dimension to wife-swapping. It was also suggested that, if such an affair was indeed going on, it might have been in retaliation for their spouses' mutual infidelity.

"Angie" had already reached No. 1 when singer Chuckie Starr met Mick at a party in Beverly Hills. "It was the glitter era and everybody wanted to be part of the bisexual revolution," said Starr. "Mick was no different. He was wearing rhinestones, blue eye-shadow, and platform shoes. When I asked him why, he said, 'Because I have a lot of respect for David Bowie.'"

Mrs. Jagger was less cordial. "Bianca was a bitch," said

Starr, who was also sported full glitter regalia. "She took one look at me and was appalled. Nothing happened between Mick and me, and as drunk as we all were it could have. But Bianca told me to get lost."

Andy Warhol, or at least the strange universe he had fashioned, attracted and inspired both Bowie and Jagger. In lurid films like *Trash, Bike Boy, Nude Restaurant, Chelsea Girls,* and *Bad,* the white-thatched perennial boy wonder unflinchingly depicted drug use, sadomasochism, douching, masturbation, and every sexual permutation imaginable. The Velvet Underground, a group founded by Warhol in 1967, became the springboard for seventies New Wave stars Lou Reed, John Cale, and Nico.

In February of 1973 Jagger actually agreed to write a musical that Warhol would then produce on Broadway. The show, which never got off the ground, was intended to be a star vehicle for Bianca. Warhol protégé Paul Morrissey also wanted to direct the couple in his film version of André Gide's *The Caves of the Vatican.* Mick and Bianca were to play brother and sister.

Although Bianca would turn out to be the most important Jagger in Andy's life, he was, by all accounts, attracted to Mick. "Mick liked to dance, and he would get drunk and dance with Andy at Max's Kansas City," recalled Chuckie Starr. "Andy claimed that he had slept with Mick. He told me that several times, and I believed him."

Chris Makos remembered that Jagger often appeared to be interested in members of his own sex: "Mick was always pointing out cute men. He would say to me, 'Wow, look at that good-looking guy over there.' But I really think he was more heterosexual than bi."

Liz Derringer, ex-wife of rocker Rick Derringer and a close friend of Jagger's since the mid-1970s, conceded that Jagger has a strong feminine side. "Mick is a girl's guy," she said. "He is chatty, bitchy, gossipy. He engineers that whole henhouse atmosphere. You know, 'Girls, let's dish!' "

But, she added, "Mick is not some freak. When you're with him you never think, *What is* this? He is a *man*."

Another longtime friend of both Jagger and Bowie, influential Los Angeles music industry insider Rodney Bingenheimer, said "Mick and David were lovers, of course. They didn't exactly make a secret of it." But he added that Jagger "was always more interested in women." Years earlier, when *Beggars Banquet* was on the charts, Bingenheimer and Jagger went to a party for Marc Bolan of the group T. Rex in L.A. On the way back to Jagger's bungalow in Bel-Air, they stopped at the House of Pies on Hollywood Boulevard at one A.M. "to pick up girls. All these teenyboppers would come up to Mick and say, 'You look like Mick Jagger!' and he'd say, 'Yes, everybody says that.' Then he'd take a couple home with him."

According to Bingenheimer, Jagger never stopped crusing the streets in search of female company. "His marriage to Bianca didn't change things at all," said Bingenheimer. "He'd still drive around picking up girls. The younger the better."

Few people are as well qualified as Bebe Buell to offer insights into Jagger and Bowie. The strikingly beautiful former Ford model and *Playboy* centerfold carried on lengthy affairs with both men. In fact, at various times Buell was romantically involved not only with Jagger and Bowie, but with Todd Rundgren, Rod Stewart, Jimmy Page, Elvis Costello, punk rocker Stiv Bators of the Dead Boys, and Aerosmith's Steve Tyler.

Buell was just eighteen and seriously involved with Rundgren when she first met Bowie in 1973 at Max's Kansas City in New York. The fact that she was already a rock star's girlfriend made Buell all the more irresistible to Bowie—a competitive streak he clearly shared with Jagger. Bowie quickly seduced Buell, but she drew the line at leaping into bed with Bowie's tour members and their girlfriends.

Buell also met Jagger in 1973, at an Eric Clapton concert. "Mick tried to kidnap me that first night," she said.

"He didn't care if I had a boyfriend. That made it more interesting." At the party afterward, Jagger persisted. "He made a tremendous fuss over me," said Buell. "He was flirting outrageously. He kept coming over and telling me to ditch Todd. It was quite overwhelming to say the least."

Still, Buell resisted Jagger's advances. *He's kind of cute,* she thought, *but not cute enough* to leave Rundgren. As the evening wore on, she recalled, "people were drinking a lot of champagne, smoking pot. Eric and Mick were in the corner whispering, being terribly discreet. Things were becoming extremely euphoric."

It was then that Bebe went to the kitchen to get a drink. "Mick followed me," she said, "and Todd hit the roof. 'We're going home *now,*'" he said. On the cab ride home Rundgren warned Buell to "watch out for guys like Warren Beatty and Mick Jagger. It was a simple fatherly lecture, and it had its desired effect, for a while."

In the ensuing months Buell's and Jagger's paths "were continually crossing—we kept bumping into each other, and he kept up the pressure." Ultimately Jagger talked her into joining him for dinner. "Mick took me out for my first sushi," she said. "He ordered expensive bottles of wine. You've got to remember, here is a man who can go slumming downtown with the gutter pigs and have high tea with Baron So-and-so. Mick is very versatile, very multifaceted. He dominates every social situation. I was impressed."

They did not go to bed after the first date, however. "Mick wanted to sleep with me," Bebe surmised, "but he didn't want to *scare* me." When they did sleep together for the first time, it was at Jagger's suite at the Plaza Hotel— across the street from Bowie's suite at the Sherry Netherland.

When Jagger shed his clothes, Buell was somewhat taken aback. "I was very, very shocked by his smallness, his fragility. Such tiny little bones. But," she added, "Mick was not fragile or demure as a lover. Being with him was not like sleeping with a bag of bones. He was very aggressive as a lover, very strong and confident. But sex was not the dominant thing in our relationship."

Perhaps. But, during that decade before the advent of AIDS, casual sex was far from rare. "Fidelity was not exactly the call," admitted Buell. "Nobody was monogamous. There was a lot of incestuous behavior, in that if someone you slept with introduced you to someone, then you slept with him. In the end, everybody was sleeping with everybody." Buell didn't mind. "My only two taboos were drugs and orgies."

Not that both Jagger and Bowie didn't try to corral Buell into group-sex situations. "I used to get some pretty strange phone calls from Mick and David at three in the morning, inviting me to join them in bed with four gorgeous black women," she said. "You could hear giggling and moaning over the phone. Sometimes they wanted me to join them with four gorgeous black *men*. Mick had affairs with several black men that I know of. Nobody famous—just great-looking guys from Long Island."

Once, however, Jagger came to Bebe's rescue when they paid a call on Bowie at his Sherry Netherland suite. A woman named Dana Gillespie was there with David, and after their guests arrived she produced a set of vibrating "benwa balls"—a sexual device used to enhance a woman's pleasure.

"They wanted Mick and I to join in with them and this thing, but it scared me," recalled Bebe. It was then that Jagger jumped up and stood between Bebe and the advancing benwa balls. "Okay, luv," Jagger said to Buell, "It's time for us to leave."

"Mick saved me from an orgy"—Buell laughed—"but if they hadn't waved that thing around I think he would have been all for it." From then on, said Buell, "I was known as the orgy-aborter."

As with all of his mistresses of long standing, Jagger took a keen interest in Buell's appearance. "Mick demanded a certain chic of his women," she recalled. "Before we went out, if he didn't like what I was wearing he would send me back to put on another outfit." Jagger seemed particularly interested in what shoes his women wore—"Mick always kidded me about my platforms," recalled the five-foot-ten-inch Buell—and would sometimes show up for a date with a shoebox under his arm. "If you had a dress and you couldn't find the right shoes to go with it," said Buell, "you called Mick."

In fact, Jagger lavished expensive gifts on all his women. "Mick bought me dresses, flowers, expensive perfumes," said Buell. "He would fly me to meet him on his private plane. He would think nothing of spending five hundred dollars for wine at dinner." But, she added, "he is also, to put it charitably, frugal. He'd spend hours looking for bargains." (Jagger has always been a notoriously lousy tipper. Keith Altham recalled taking a $2.50 cab ride with Jagger in Manhattan: "Mick gave the driver three dollars and asked for a quarter change.")

Jagger was generous, however, when it came to sharing beauty secrets. He often visited Buell's apartment just to give her facials. "Mick's a genius with skin," said Buell. "He always knew what creams to use, and he often shared his beauty products with me. He'd say 'Let me look at that, Bebe,'" and then produce a jar and start massaging the contents into my skin. He told me how to steam my face, what herbs to use. No woman on earth knows more about cosmetics than Mick."

Throughout their on-again, off-again affair, Buell knew she was only one of many Jagger kept dangling on a string. The exotic model Apollonia Vonravenstein (Jagger called Apollonia "Apples,"), socialite Barbara Allen, and Sabrina Guinness were just a few of the women Jagger carried on affairs with while seeing Buell.

"I wasn't very territorial," shrugged Buell. "I loved Mick dearly, but I wasn't *in* love with him. Our affair was a sneaky thing, but *everybody* cheated."

Only one woman was capable of emotionally wounding Jagger, Buell claimed, and that was Bianca. Jagger referred to his wife disparagingly, either as "my old lady" or simply as "B." But, insisted Liz Derringer, "Mick was madly, passionately in love with Bianca. We all thought he loved her and she didn't love him." Concurred Buell: "He loved her so much more than he admitted. Mick was a very traditional Englishman when it came to his marriage. He wanted her to stay home and take care of the kids while he did what he pleased."

Gone were the days when Bianca banished Pamela Des Barres with a husky command or threatened to tear Carly Simon to shreds. Realizing that she had lost that battle before it had begun, Bianca treated some of her husband's lovers with courtesy, even warmth.

"Bianca was very sweet to me," allowed Buell, who was a full head taller than the five-foot-four-inch Mrs. Jagger. "She would clutch my hand and ask me to sit next to her at parties." Bianca always referred to Bebe as "Mick's little friend"—which, said Bebe, "was quite amusing since I was two inches taller than Mick and six inches taller than Bianca."

Once at P J Clarke's in New York ("Mick always said they had the best hamburgers"), Buell was sitting with both Jaggers and guitarist Ron Wood. "I used to clip my nails very short, which was against the trend, and paint them bright red." Bianca pointed them out and said how chic they looked. That was typical of her—she always complimented me on my hair, my clothes. She tried to make you feel like a million bucks."

Buell determined that this was Bianca's way of sending her husband a message. "She was saying to him, 'You can have your little girlfriends, Mick. It doesn't matter to me.'"

Bianca had by no means relinquished control entirely, however. One of her favorite ploys, according to Buell, was to "lose" an expensive piece of jewelry and then rope Mick into helping her look for it—a search that invariably lasted for hours. "She'd say, 'God, I've lost my $40,000 bracelet! I must have left it at the restaurant!' Then she'd pull Mick back into the limo," recalled Buell, "and he was out of circulation for the rest of the evening. Mick called this 'one of her little stunts.'"

Over the course of their marriage Bianca led safaris in search of misplaced or stolen rings, earrings, and pins—

none worth less than $10,000. Amazingly, the missing items always seemed to turn up—only to vanish again.

Mick tolerated Bianca's "little stunts." He was deeply upset, however, that Bianca carried on her affairs with a degree of indiscretion that equaled his own. Around this time, she was linked to actors Elliott Gould, Helmut Berger, and Ryan O'Neal—to name but a few.

"She can dance with anyone she likes," replied Jagger, "and so can I. If she dances with people, I don't mind. I think women should do what they want. After all, men go around doing what they want."

In truth, Jagger was livid over Bianca's on-again off-again affair with the star of *Love Story*. While he was in England filming Stanley Kubrick's *Barry Lyndon*, O'Neal started a romance with Bianca that would stretch over several years. During this time the inexhaustible O'Neal, who once served fifty-one days in jail for punching a movie critic, would also number Joan Collins, Barbra Streisand, Ursula Andress, and Anouk Aimée among his conquests before settling on Farrah Fawcett.

Technically, the marriage of Mick and Bianca Jagger would survive the decade. But in court documents Jagger would later contend that "in every true sense of a marriage" they separated in 1973. To be sure, as they ricocheted from one tax haven to another, Mick and Bianca already seemed intent on spending as little time together as possible. "It was rare," said Buell, "that you ever saw them in the same room."

Not so Bowie and Jagger. Normally, when he was in New York during this period Mick stayed at the Pierre Hotel or, less frequently, the Plaza. Bowie preferred the Sherry Netherland. But when both men were in the city at the same time, they both stayed at the Pierre. "Mick would come out of one entrance," said photographer Vinne Zuffante, "and Bowie another. They were careful never to be seen coming out of the hotel together."

In a perverse twist, in the winter of 1973 Bowie had simultaneous flings with Marianne Faithfull and model

Amanda Lear. A protégée of Salvador Dalí, Lear was rumored to have had a sex-change operation.

As the haunting strains of "Angie" flowed over the airwaves and out of stereo speakers around the world, Jagger kept the public guessing. "Sexually, Mick pushes himself to the limits—sampling all colors, all classes," said Bebe Buell. "He has absolutely zero prejudice. He loves blondes. He loves blacks. He loves Indians, Latins, and Asians. There is no stopping him."

As for his orientation: "You can't say he's homosexual, or even bisexual," said Buell. "He's beyond that. Mick Jagger is the world's greatest practitioner of cosmic sex."

Jagger's art had always fed off personal experience. Just as he had dabbled in Satanism, drugs, rebellion, and high society, the chimerical Jagger was now exploring his own sexuality.

"How do those lyrics to 'Cocksucker Blues' go?" Sandy Lieberson asked rhetorically. " 'Where do I get my cock sucked, where do I get my ass fucked'? Well, *that's* Mick."

Even this preposterous posturing was carefully mapped out, insisted Lieberson. "Mick has always been so together, so calculating, so conscious of what he's doing," he said. "He's always been able to flirt with taboos and come out whole. It's not learned. It's something inherent, something in his character. He does it all, but he *never* loses control."

Asked by a magazine to name the person with the most sex appeal, Jagger picked Noël Coward. Mick was the only male celebrity to pick another male, but the choice was logical. The sublimely sophisticated Coward possessed all the qualities to which Jagger aspired. Although he was gay and conceded that the feeling was mutual, Sir Noël was somewhat embarrassed by Jagger's very public vote of confidence. Coward's own choice for most sexually appealing was, curiously enough, another bellwether for the androgynous age: Twiggy.

"I think when you start to feel married you should get divorced."

Jagger had played the press like a concert virtuoso for over a decade, so it was to be expected that some of this talent would rub off on his wife. The new year 1974 was less than a week old when she admitted to *Viva* magazine that her marriage was in trouble. "Perhaps Mick isn't attracted to me anymore," she said softly. "When I first met him I knew who he was. But I don't know now."

Bianca went on to basically accuse Jagger of being a liar and a cheat, but in the gentlest of ways. "All I need is to find a human being who is truthful," she said. "It's so sad when I discover that someone I cared for isn't truthful. If I have deep feelings for someone, and they do something to me, I get very hurt. That I can get over. But if someone I care for lies to me . . . I can't forgive lies. Lies are offensive to the intelligence."

Bianca was convinced that Carly Simon, now married to James Taylor for over a year, was still pursuing Mick. "It's something I still can't cope with," Bianca told *Viva*. "It's not so much intelligence as perception that is the great obstacle between Mick and I, because I am rather sensitive and perceptive. I hear everything. I see everything. I feel everything. Too much, and men hate that."

As for the future: "Maybe tomorrow I'll be out on the streets," sighed Bianca. "I have my identity. It is not so linked with Mick's. I could find something to do. I would find something exciting."

What concerned her most, revealed Bianca, was the effect all this was having on her daughter. "I am frightened sometimes when I look at Jade," she said. "My parents were divorced, and I remember how painful it was to be a child divided between two loves." Since Jade was cared for by a nanny and spent little time in the company of either parent, it was doubtful that she'd even notice.

Bianca's decision to go public was a brilliant ploy, to which Mick responded immediately. Admitting that he'd gotten married because it seemed like "a good idea" at the time, Jagger stated flatly, "I've never been madly, deeply in love in my life. I'm not a very emotional person."

In an obvious swipe at his wife Jagger claimed he couldn't "stand people who live out their loves in public." That did not prevent him, however, from outlining the only conditions under which he would remain married. "I am not in the least bit domesticated," he conceded. "To put it bluntly, I try not to hang around with my family more than I have to. If I am going to be Mick Jagger, then Bianca and Jade and I have to meet in a sort of compromise."

Jagger seemed at times to be less interested in keeping his marriage from being derailed than he was getting his movie career back on track. "I see films that I know I could have done—anything from *The Sting* to *Deep Throat*," he complained.

There were plenty of offers, but they evaporated almost as quickly as they were tendered. Bowie and Jagger talked about doing a film together, but the right script eluded them. After Jagger attended a private screening of Ken Russell's *Mahler* on March 7, 1974, the director approached Mick to portray the "deeply spiritual and sensuous" side of Franz Liszt in Russell's film biography of the great composer and pianist (Roger Daltry ultimately played the part). At about the same time Hollywood agent Sue Mengers brought Mick an offer to play the lead in *Joe Bunch and All That Glitters*. In that film Jagger was to play a con man.

Bianca was at least partly responsible for Mick's newfound desire to take another stab at movie stardom. She tore into Mick for wasting his life in the music business, and he responded by writing a song: "It's Only Rock 'n' Roll" ("I know it's only rock 'n' roll/But I like it").

"It's Only Rock 'n' Roll," which featured background vocals by Bowie, was the title track for the next album. Unable to stay in either Britain or the U.S. for longer than three months without suffering a tax liability, the Stones opted to record the new LP in Munich. Their longtime producer, Jimmy Miller, had moved on to other projects, so it was left to Jagger and Richards to find a replacement. They decided on their own alter egos, the Glimmer Twins.

Precisely one year after declaring his intention to retire at thirty-three, the fickle Mr. Jagger now said he "will never retire. I could go on forever, ya know. . . ." Perhaps, but the years of excess were taking their toll. His face was now lined and drawn, and everyone agreed that he looked a decade older than his thirty-one years.

The body, however, was as lean and limber as ever—the result of the sit-ups, push-ups, and weight-lifting that the obsessively fitness-conscious Jagger had always made part of his daily routine. In anticipation of the Stones' 1975 World Tour—their biggest ever—Jagger had also incorporated karate routines into his already punishing workout.

Jagger almost tried out some of his moves during one of his infrequent attempts to completely sever relations with Allen Klein. During a meeting at London's Savoy Hotel, Jagger chatted with his lawyers and remained cool—until Klein walked into the room. "You owe me $800,000!" screamed Jagger, who then proceeded to chase Klein through the hotel corridors.

This year it was interior designer David Mlinaric's turn to throw Mick's birthday party. Jagger wore a "buttercup-yellow" suit and white shoes, Bianca an off-the-shoulder white gown and matching turban. By two-thirty A.M. Bianca and Britt Ekland were involved in what one guest described as an "*intime* little dance" while Jagger gathered up his birthday presents and left, alone.

A month later Jagger was at New York's Plaza Hotel celebrating the opening of David Bowie's spectacular Diamond Dogs show at Madison Square Garden. Angie was there, as was Mick's old friend Nureyev, making for a few awkward moments.

At one point during the festivities Bette Midler, Bowie, and Jagger all stepped into a bedroom closet and shut the door behind them. The other partygoers were merely left to stare at the door and eavesdrop as nonchalantly as possible. After much giggling, moaning, and thrashing about, the three emerged an hour later. No one had the nerve to applaud.

It's Only Rock 'n' Roll arrived in record stores that fall. Yet again, a Lindsay-Hogg video was used to hype the single. The clip shows Jagger and his buddies, all clad in sailor suits, camping it up inside a tent. Jagger becomes increasingly manic as the tent fills up with bubbles. The silly vignette didn't hurt sales; the album spent eleven weeks at No. 1.

On December 12, 1974—one day before the Stones were to begin work on their *Black and Blue* album—Mick Taylor announced that he was leaving the Stones "to pursue new interests." It was no secret that he had felt hamstrung creatively. But Taylor's resignation was more in the interests of survival.

When he signed on with the group, the virginal Taylor was a nonsmoking, vegetarian teetotaler. Five years later he was consuming so much cocaine that he burned a hole in his septum that had to be surgically replaced with plastic. He had also begun to use heroin, and feared that he—like so many others—would only sink deeper into this quagmire if he remained in the company of Richards, Pallenberg, and the other druggies who swarmed around the Stones.

Over the years Jagger and Taylor had grown surprisingly close. One day Tony Sanchez and Marianne Faithfull walked into the house on Cheyne Walk and found the two Micks "dozing in bed together, like little boys."

Jagger was in Nicaragua with Bianca when he heard the

news. "No doubt," he sniffed, "we can find a brilliant six-foot-three blond guitarist who can do his own makeup."

Facetious remarks aside, Jagger launched a Scarlett O'Hara–like search for the next Stone. After running through a list that included Peter Frampton, Jimmy Page, Chris Spedding, Jeff Beck, Steve Marriott, and Rory Gallagher, they were about to tell Wayne Perkins he had the job when Mick learned that Rod Stewart's group Faces was about to disband. That left lead guitarist Ron Wood out of a job. Jagger, long a fan of Wood's, was eager to give him one.

"Woody" was not the most accomplished musician of the lot. But with his maniacal playing, scrawny physique, and dead-crow countenance, Wood blew away the competition.

In April of 1975 it was formally announced that Wood would be joining the Stones for the tour. Nine days later the Wick, Wood's mansion in the London suburb of Richmond, was raided by narcotics agents while Wood and Richards were in Munich recording *Black and Blue*. When the police burst into the Wick, they surprised Wood's then-wife, Chrissie, in bed with another girl. Nevertheless, the raid itself was tantamount to a rite of passage. Ron Wood was officially a Stone.

The 1975 World Tour was shaping up to be the most ambitious the Stones had ever attempted: twenty-nine Western Hemisphere cities in the first three months, then a sweep through the Middle East and Asia.

On New York's Fifth Avenue the tour got off to an official start when the Stones mounted a flatbed truck for a spur-of-the-moment jam. As Mick wailed "Honky Tonk Women," traffic on the avenue ground to standstill.

Before actually hitting the road, the Stones holed up at Andy Warhol's Long Island summer home rehearsing. Bianca, meanwhile, was making a splash of her own at the Cannes Film Festival, schmoozing, posturing, and talking up her own screen aspirations to the international film community.

Dashing from screenings to parties and back again in a dazzling series of see-through dresses, satin capes, and glittering turbans, Bianca secured her reputation as her generation's style-setter. This was only incidental to convincing producers, directors, and studio executives that she had the makings of a movie queen.

"I want to act now," she told them, "because I want to do something of quality, not just be a star. But the press turned me into something I was not. They wouldn't accept the fact that Mick had married a foreigner. So from that moment on I was a bitch." She certainly knew how to play the part. At the closing award ceremonies she angrily protested that her VIP seat assignment was not VIP enough and asked that actor Michael Caine relinquish his seat in the front row. Caine declined.

Bianca also set tongues wagging when she showed up at nearly every function on the arm of Helmut Berger, now breathlessly described by the European press as "the world's most beautiful man."

For this tour Jagger opted for flash over substance. At the start of each show the stage—a giant metal "flower" with bulletproof petals—would open to reveal the band inside. Looking down on the set one could see the points of a pentagram; His Satanic Majesty was clearly not quite ready to abdicate. This tour also marked the first time in years that Jagger sang "Sympathy for the Devil."

Days before he was to embark on the tour, Jagger got up to leave a restaurant and, mistaking a plate glass window for a revolving door, put his right hand through it. The gash ran seven inches up his arm.

"I wanted to photograph the stitches," said Annie Leibovitz, who had been assigned to cover the tour. "He hemmed and hawed." But when she started shooting the gory scene in black and white, he insisted on color.

"I went on tour to get to the heart of something," she

later said, "to see what it was really like. I was very reluctant to throw myself into something that deep for some time afterwards. People always talk about the soul of the sitter, but the photographer has a soul too. And I almost lost it."

Although Mick had said that he felt it was time to forsake high camp for the "butch lumber" look, he was more heavily tarted up than ever. When he could not find his underpants just before the start of the band's Toronto concert, he begged noted rock journalist Lisa Robinson to lend him hers. She reluctantly agreed, and Jagger went onstage wearing Robinson's white lace bikini panties—backwards.

The most memorable moment came midway through the show, when, at the push of a button, a forty-foot-long inflatable phallus unfurled from the back of the stage. To the delight of the throng Jagger climbed aboard the phallus as if it were an amusement-park ride and alternately stroked and pummeled it as he sang his X-rated ode to groupies "Star Star."

Still out to shock, Jagger also vamped outrageously onstage with singer-keyboardist Billy Preston. The two grabbed each other by the hips, ground their pelvises together suggestively, and kissed. (Preston, who had also played with the Beatles and enjoyed his own successful solo career, contributed to several Stones albums and remained a close friend of Jagger's.)

Jagger's coquettish posturings aside, there were moments when Mick dealt harshly with his fellow rockers. One night T. Rex's outlandish Marc Bolan stumbled up to Jagger in an alcoholic stupor and lunged for his testicles. "Get him out of here!" Mick commanded. "I didn't realize they were sacrosanct!" protested the hapless Bolan as he was pitched headlong into an alley by a half-dozen burly bodyguards. From then on Bolan had the same opening line whenever he encountered Jagger: "How's the old golden bollocks, then?"

The record-shattering crowds were huge and enthusiastic, but something was missing—the chaos and tumult that normally landed the Stones on the front pages on an almost daily basis during a tour.

It was not as if the Stones had cleaned up their act, offstage or on. For a quick pick-me-up during a show Jagger, Richards, and Wood could turn to the amplifiers hidden behind curtains on either side of the stage. On one amp there was a line of heroin for Richards and Wood, on the other a line of cocaine for Jagger and anyone who cared for a snort. (Jagger reportedly told a tour organizer that he had once asked a friend to smuggle hashish into the country for him. The friend panicked, swallowed the drugs before he could be searched, and was seriously ill for several days.)

In her book *You'll Never Eat Lunch in This Town Again*, Julia Phillips recalls her backstage encounter with Jagger on the 1975 tour: "We are shown into a particular room. On a high chair there is a small person with a lot of hair. It is impossible to tell if it is a boy or a girl. It turns its head and it is Mick Jagger in full makeup. Very depressing. He jumps off his chair to greet us. He has a huge head and a little body. . . . Bianca floats around in the background. She is wearing a sailor suit and cap. Her eyes are dead. There is a smelly Israeli named Freddie who seems to be very important to everybody. He carries two medium-sized bottles filled with rock cocaine."

Keith then appeared, whispered something to Mick, and the two disappeared. "Pregame blowjobs," Phillips whispered to Goldie Hawn.

After the show Phillips went to the Stones' suite at the Plaza, where Mick was checked in under the name Michael Phillips. There she found Mick and Keith on the floor between the beds, strumming on their guitars. "They form a freaky little unit, right there on the floor," she wrote, "but there is something peaceful about the scene." A block away, at the Pierre Hotel, Bianca was happily ensconced in her own suite. The Pierre register showed that she was a "Mrs. Benz" from London.

Kevin is the alias of a New York fashion designer who was a Rolling Stones groupie in the mid-1970s. He recalled that Jagger was a regular at New York's gay clubs. At Galaxy 21 on West Twenty-third Street, gay porn films were shown in the Pillow Room. "Mick was always surrounded by a bunch of gays," said Kevin. "He liked to dance, and when he danced everybody went nuts. Mick danced like a raging queen with his butt sticking out, just like onstage."

Jagger also went to Les Mouches, the 82 Club, and the Gilded Grape, an establishment with a large transvestite clientele. "Once at the Gilded Grape," claimed Kevin, "David, Angie, Mick, and Freddie Mercury were all whooping it up with a bunch of transvestites." Mercury, the lead singer of Queen, later died of AIDS.

Jagger, Warhol, and Bowie also reportedly had ringside seats at several gay orgies. "Andy's friend Victor Hugo would whip out his dick and wave it around anywhere, a complete weirdo," said Kevin, "and Andy would take pictures with his Polaroid." Jagger, however, was apparently never an active participant in these seamier games. "Mick witnessed a lot, but he hung back a little," added Kevin. "He preferred one-on-one, I think."

Kevin based that assessment on firsthand experience. He had been a friend of Ron Wood, but, Kevin confessed, "my ultimate goal was to sleep with Mick Jagger, and I did." It was late one night in 1975, and Kevin was waiting, as he did almost every night, in the Plaza Hotel lobby.

"Mick was stoned, doing a lot of cocaine," said Kevin. Returning home to the Plaza late one night, he spotted Kevin and invited him upstairs for a drink. "I was an innocent-looking, skinny, beautiful boy. He was obviously attracted to my type."

Kevin followed Jagger to his hotel room. "I was thrilled," recalled the ex-groupie. "When he went to get the drink, I grabbed a scarf of his thinking it was the greatest thing in the world—'Ooooh, Mick Jagger's scarf'—and I stuffed it down my pants."

Jagger returned with the drink and, remembered Kevin, began quizzing the young man about his clothes. "I was very fashion conscious then. I was wearing seventy percent women's clothes, but they looked masculine on me for some reason. He started picking my brain. 'You look *ravishing*,' Mick would say. 'Where did you get those shoes, where did you get that shirt?' Mick was super-obsessed with appearance, with style. He was like a sponge."

It was not long, said Kevin, before Jagger turned amorous. "We started kissing, then that led to bed. Mick definitely took the active role sexually. I was the passive one. Basically, he overpowered me in bed."

When they woke up together in bed the next morning, remembered Kevin, "Mick was very nice and almost gentlemanly toward me." Jagger asked Kevin if he was hungry, then ordered up an elaborate breakfast from room service. "We lay there nude in bed," said Kevin, "eating from silver trays while people knocked on the door all morning long."

Apart from the sex, Kevin got the impression that Jagger was "trying to be sort of a big brother. But when I left," he conceded, "I felt degraded and used."

A few weeks later Kevin was working at a nightclub as a waiter, wearing red satin hot pants and nothing else. When Jagger sat down, Kevin approached him. "I went up to Mick and said hi, but he just stared blankly at me." From then on the two men ran into each other periodically but, said Kevin, "Mick always pretended not to notice me."

That was a sentiment echoed by Bianca, now in full revolt against what she called "the Nazi state" ruled by the Stones and their roadies. She did not accompany Mick on the road or even go through the motions of hooking up with him for a day as she had done in the past. Which suited Mick perfectly. Unless a woman had a job to do on the tour, he huffed, the only other valid reason for one to be there was "to screw."

They did, however, spend time together with Jade at the beachfront estate they rented from Andy Warhol in Montauk, Long Island, for $5,000 a month. For the next few summers they would flee Manhattan every weekend for the relative tranquility of this oceanside retreat.

Even at this windswept outpost the intrusions on their

privacy were constant. A sign was posted reading DO NOT
PROCEED DOWN THIS ROAD, but it did little to prevent fans
from swarming over the dunes to catch a glimpse of their
idol. Once, several girls with shaved heads sneaked onto
the property. They were upstaged by the young woman
who appeared nude at the Jagger's front door; she had dyed
her pubic hair green to amuse Mick.

There was another groupie who showed off her unusual
talent for Mick. "It was one of the most unusual things I've
ever seen," deadpanned Jagger's Montauk neighbor Dick
Cavett. "This girl smoked a cigarette, only not with her
mouth. . . ."

Unlike the Hamptons, where dozens of restaurants and
clubs catered to Manhattan's summering glitterati and the
Social Register set, Montauk was essentially a sleepy fishing
village devoid of nightlife. Mick and Bianca compensated
for this by flying in friends and transforming the million-
dollar clapboard "cottage" into a throbbing seaside disco.

John Lennon and Yoko Ono, John Phillips (of the Mamas and the Papas), Eric Clapton, David Bowie, Jack Nicholson, and Warren Beatty were just a few of their houseguests that first summer. The goings-on around the Warhol
compound scandalized some residents. Dense clouds of
marijuana smoke wafted up from the house's wraparound
porch and rolled down the beach. "Sure, they offered the
odd substance at social occasions," said Cavett. "Sometimes it smelled like a brushfire in Sonora over there."

There were also plenty of other diversions. "There was
an awful lot of screwing in the dunes," recalled one resident. "It wasn't at all unusual to be walking along and suddenly have several people shoot past you stark naked and
splash around in the surf."

Not all of the Jagger's guests at Montauk were show business folk. In addition to hosting the odd British aristocrat,
Mick also socialized with American royalty. Dick Cavett
was horseback riding on the beach when an attractive,
dark-haired woman walked down from the Jaggers' and mo-
tioned for him to stop. As she came into view, he realized

that the woman was Jacqueline Onassis. "Jackie is an accomplished equestrienne," said Cavett, "so she walked around my horse, checking it out. We chatted a bit, and then she returned to Mick's. I think he intrigued her, and of course Mick was sort of in awe of Jackie, like everybody else." An expert horseman himself, Jagger would later be spotted cantering along the beach with Jackie O at his side.

By now Jagger, who had purchased a house for his parents on the coast of Kent, invited Eva and Joe to visit them in Montauk. Dick Cavett recalled walking along the beach and spotting Mick walking along ahead of him. "It was like a scene from an Alfred Hitchcock film," recalled Cavett. "I kept calling his name, but he wouldn't respond. Finally he turned around and started walking toward me. It wasn't until he was just a few feet from me that I realized it wasn't Mick but Chris Jagger. The resemblance was remarkable." By this time Mick's younger brother, having tried and failed to get his own singing career off the ground, was scraping by waiting on tables, restoring guitars, and selling Christmas trees.

Many of the visitors to the Montauk house determined that the most likable member of the Jagger clan was Jade. A strikingly pretty girl with chestnut ringlets, Jade had her father's pale complexion and her mother's air of aloofness. "My favorite is Jade," said Warhol. "I love Mick and Bianca, but Jade's more my speed. I taught her how to color and she taught me how to play Monopoly. She was four and I was forty-four. Mick got jealous. He said I was a bad influence because I gave her champagne."

Cavett, an amateur magician, taught Jade card tricks. He remembered her as a "bright, adorable kid." Once Cavett took her for a ride over the dune roads when his Jeep suddenly went dead and refused to start up again.

Before he could stop himself, Cavett blurted out, "Shit! Oops . . . sorry, Jade."

"You needn't apologize," Jagger's six-year-old daughter told Cavett. "I've heard that and much, much worse."

Jade was on hand for a tiff between her parents that

nearly landed them and their houseful of weekend guests in jail. The argument revolved around what Mick perceived as Bianca's obsessive craving for attention. John Lennon was among those relaxing with the Jaggers out in Montauk the day Bianca hurt her knee while playing with Jade. She limped around the house, shouting that she had a broken kneecap and demanding that she be taken to the hospital.

John Lennon and a half-dozen other guests sat around smoking pot, pointedly ignoring Bianca. Mick took a look at the injury and told her it was nothing more than a bruise, but she continued screaming in pain. "You'll do anything," said Jagger, shaking his head, "to get attention."

Bianca threatened to phone the police if Mick didn't call a doctor. Twenty minutes later an ambulance, fire engine, and a police squad car arrived. While the police pounded on the door, Mick raced after his wife to keep her from letting them in. Meanwhile, Lennon and the others scrambled around the living room gathering up the pot and stashing it out of sight.

Finally the police burst in, their guns drawn in response to all the screaming. Bianca again demanded to be taken to the emergency room, and this time she was. The doctors on duty reassured her that her injury was not serious; Bianca insisted that the leg be bandaged anyway, and spent the next several weeks hobbling around on a cane.

The pressures on Jade were extraordinary, even by Hollywood standards. Her volatile parents fought constantly. Because of the family's nomadic life-style—Mom seldom stayed in one place longer than a few months, Dad never more than several weeks—Jade was shuttled from house to hotel and school to school. And then there was the weighty psychological baggage that came with being the daughter of an international cultural icon and his global-trotting, trend-setting, impossibly glamorous wife.

Their love of Jade was the glue that held their marriage together in the early years, but by the mid-1970s Bianca and Mick were bickering constantly over the child. Mick was willing to let his loveless marriage drag on rather than have Jade be emotionally scarred by divorce. Although he was not a constant presence in her life, Mick doted on Jade when he was with her. "To understand Mick," said Liz Derringer, "you have to understand that he is very old-fashioned. He expects the mother to stay home with the kids like his mother did."

Bianca did not quite see it that way. Often Eva and Joe Jagger would take care of their granddaughter at their seaside home in Kent. But most of the time Jade was left in the care of nannies in London or New York while her mother dashed from one opening to the next. Her displays of maternal interest often seemed designed for public consumption. "Bianca would doll Jade up in some fabulous party dress and then bring her along to a restaurant to show her off," recalled a friend. "Bianca would play mommy to the hilt, telling her to sit up straight, correcting her table manners, the whole bit. It was all very forced."

Jade quickly became a handful. One year Mick brought Jade to a children's Easter party held in the Central Park West penthouse of a British-born socialist (Bianca refused to come because she said it would be attended by "a bunch of English whores"). Jade found most of the eggs hidden around the elegant apartment, and when she did she smashed them on the parquet floor.

Not long after, Warhol visited them in New York. "Andy Warhol, you never come to see us anymore," said the six-year-old Jade, who then asked him what he wanted to drink. When Warhol and his friend asked for two vodkas on the rocks, the little girl turned to the Spanish-speaking maid and said "Dos vodkas con hielo."

Warhol then asked his little friend to sing "Satisfaction," but she said she had never heard of it. Instead, she made up a song of her own about a friend at the New York kindergarten she attended: "I invited another child at school to come for dinner/But they wouldn't come/They think we're crazy/But they're crazy."

Prohibited from eating sweets of any kind, Jade hit up Bianca's grown-up friends for candy and junk food whenever her mother's back was turned. The little girl's chief supplier was Warhol, who would surreptitiously slip Jade M & M's or jelly beans once the coast was clear—not unlike, he later observed, a pusher giving a junkie his fix.

For a time, while her mother was more or less in residence at Cheyne Walk in London, Jade went to Garden House School on Sloane Square. There she would disrupt class, then make up sweetly in an obvious play for attention. To several of the teachers the little girl simply seemed starved for affection. Left for long periods of time in the care of nannies and house servants, at times Jade fell through the cracks; the child would often wait at the school for hours after class while teachers tried to locate someone to pick her up.

That December of 1975 Jagger made at least a half-hearted effort to repair his marriage, taking Bianca to Rio de Janeiro for the holidays. According to Mick, Bianca spent the entire week in a "state of settled depression and antagonism" toward him.

In fact, Bianca seemed happiest in the company of her new best friends, Halston and Warhol. When she wasn't with them, she spent her time talking about movie offers that never quite seemed to gel, or being photographed on the town with another handsome bachelor.

Around that time Jagger's own relationship with Warhol took a decidedly commercial turn. Warhol was commissioned to do a portfolio of Mick Jagger silkscreen portraits to be signed by both Mick and Andy. Warhol chose the colors carefully—imperial purple and gold for His Satanic Majesty.

Jagger dropped by at Warhol's Factory studio and spent two full nights signing the 2,500 prints that comprised the portfolio. Mick asked if Andy could put on some music to sign by, but all the artist had available was RCA's *The Original Big Band Hits*, Volume II, featuring Benny Goodman, Glenn Miller, Artie Shaw, and Jimmy Dorsey.

Fortified during the signing session with Chinese food, coffee, and champagne, Jagger dealt with the monotony by teasing the godfather of pop. "Mick did this really funny imitation of Andy," remembered Warhol confidant Pat Hackett. "He sat there and affected this pose and did, well, nothing. Andy laughed, but I think it unnerved him a bit."

One fan of both Jagger and Warhol was the empress of Iran. A Warhol silkscreen portrait of Mick hung in the shah's palace in Tehran. "I like," explained Farah Diba, "to keep modern."

Warhol played a role in one of Bianca's more incongruous dalliances—her brief fling with Jack Ford, the twenty-three-year-old son of incumbent Republican President Gerald R. Ford. Bianca introduced young Jack to Warhol one night at New York's El Morocco, and later took him to the gay disco Le Jardin.

Bianca had been contributing pieces to Warhol's splashy *Interview* magazine, and managed to convince Jack to sit for an interview in the White House. In it Ford admitted to Bianca that he hated life in the White House, and that the atmosphere there was "stifling." Much to First Lady Betty Ford's consternation a photograph of Bianca and the President's son lounging in the Lincoln Bedroom began popping up in the press, seeming to confirm already rampant rumors that Mick Jagger's wife and the President's son were in the throes of a steamy affair.

Jagger was embarrassed by the scandalous headlines linking Bianca to a man at least seven years her junior, but he opted to dismiss the episode offhandedly. Mick mockingly branded his wife "the easiest lay on the White House lawn."

Jagger's unraveling marriage and the pressures of planning a new European tour took their toll. In February of 1976 Jagger was admitted at two A.M. to New York's Lenox Hill Hospital, reportedly suffering from a drug overdose. He had checked in under one of his standby aliases, "Mr. Benz."

After nine hours in the emergency room Jagger was transferred upstairs. Late the next day the news leaked out.

"Apparently when the newspapers heard of it," said a hospital spokesman, he just got up and walked out."

Whatever they did during daylight hours—in Mick's case often little else but sleep—the Jaggers and their vampiric crowd came alive after midnight in the surreal environs of a place called Studio 54.

Truman Capote, who went several nights a week, called it "the nightclub of the future. It's very democratic. Boys with boys, girls with girls, girls with boys, black and whites, capitalists and Marxists, Chinese, and everything else—all in one big mix!" Truman fretted that people like Toulouse-Lautrec, Oscar Wilde, and Cole Porter weren't around to see the place. Journalists reached for superlatives to describe the atmosphere—"the ultimate in decadence," "a temple of hedonism," "a throbbing, swirling orgy of light and sound." *The New York Times* simply proclaimed it "the new Oz."

Studio 54 might more accurately have been described as the Grand Hotel for the 1970s—a place where the lives of the famous, the notorious, and the anonymous intersected to weave a surreal tapestry of the times.

People magazine was scarcely out of its infancy when Steve Rubell and Ian Schrager opened Studio 54 in the old Henry Miller Theater on West Fifty-fourth Street. The magazine and the club had a symbiotic relationship: Studio 54 supplied the grist for *People*'s celebrity mill, and *People* in turn served to glorify and glamorize the club's denizens for a national audience.

Studio 54 did at times seem like the center of the celebrity universe—despite the fact that the club celebrated drugs with impunity. Several times each night a cocaine-snorting neon man-in-the-moon would swing down from the ceiling; its eye would then flash red to the approving roar of the crowd. Watching this, someone commented to fashion doyenne Diana Vreeland, "It's like ancient Rome." Vreeland replied with a shrug: "Darling, isn't that what we're aiming for?"

Over this particular hive Bianca reigned as "Queen Bee"—a sobriquet bestowed on her by writer Bob Colacello. He also invented nicknames for the rest of Bianca's pack: Halston was "His Highness," Capote "the Count," and Warhol "the Pope."

Murmurs swept through the crowd whenever Mick slipped in through the back door and made his way to the VIPs-only basement. But Mrs. Jagger held court at Studio 54 on a near-nightly basis, surveying her pulsating domain from an iron catwalk that swayed over the dance floor.

Bianca was careful to stake out her territory not long after the club's opening. At a party thrown in her honor the birthday girl rode around the dance floor astride a white stallion led by a large black man covered only in gold glitter.

The excesses were wretched indeed—a pattern set by Bianca's own equestrian extravaganza. Jackie Onassis, Arnold Schwarzenegger, Elton John, Calvin Klein, Elizabeth Taylor, Candice Bergen, and Mikhail Baryshnikov were duly impressed when an elephant was trotted in as a prop for a bash honoring wildlife photographer Peter Beard. Robert De Niro watched G-string-clad women and men swing on trapezes overhead during a party celebrating the premiere of his film *Raging Bull*.

For Roy Cohn's fifty-second birthday party (Cohn was the club's lawyer and protector), the walls were lined with fifty-two television sets—all flickering with images from the Army-McCarthy hearings in which a much younger Cohn had been a featured player. Henry Kissinger, Barbara Walters, William Safire, and Donald and Ivana Trump were among the guests. Even the famous physician who served as a veritable walking pharmacy for a host of celebrities was feted here. Atop a syringe-shaped birthday cake his nickname was spelled out in red letters: DR. FEELGOOD.

The bathrooms at Studio 54 were used mainly for drugs. High in the tiered balcony that overlooked the dance floor, scions of the Kennedy, Rockefeller, and Vanderbilt families were among those snorting cocaine and amyl nitrite, oblivious to couples—gay and straight—that at any given time could be found having sex in the shadows.

The sanctum sanctorum of Studio 54 was actually the basement, a very private, carefully guarded catacomb where free drugs were dispensed like candy and the famous indulged in a wide range of sexual games.

In its celebration of wealth, fame, power, and unbridled hedonism, Studio 54 was symbolic of the Decadent Decade—the rudderless, self-obsessed, out-of-control seventies. It would also leave a deadly legacy. AIDS would come to decimate the ranks of Studio 54 alumni, claiming Halston, Rubell, Cohn, and hundreds of others who partied or worked there.

During the last half of the 1970s, however, there was really no place else to be. Before leaving for Studio 54 Bianca often dropped in at Halston's black glass-sheathed town house on East Sixty-third Street off Park Avenue. The designer, then at the peak of his career, would dress his Latin American friend in satins and feathers before they hopped into a limousine for the ride across town.

The evening's revels were not considered to have officially begun until Bianca's arrival. There was a method to this madness; the next day newspapers across the country invariably carried photographs of celebrities laughing, drinking, smoking, and schmoozing on the famous couches that lined the club's enormous dance floor.

One night, during a party for Elizabeth Taylor, Jagger and his entourage entered through one entrance, Bianca and her coterie of friends through another. Snaking their way through wall-to-wall bodies, the two warring factions passed one another without ever connecting.

"There was definite competition between Bianca and Mick," said a mutual friend. "She was definitely the queen at Studio 54, and Mick resented being upstaged. If Bianca was not going to stay at home and cook and raise Jade, then at least Mick wanted her to have a job. He thought Bianca was a dilettante. Mick did not consider what she did work."

While Bianca partied in Manhattan that spring and summer of 1976, Jagger spearheaded a twenty-two-city blitz of Europe. As usual, all the tour dates were sold out within a matter of hours, disappointing millions of Stones aficionados from Frankfurt to Florence.

If anything, the use of heavy drugs escalated on the European leg of the tour. "Jagger, Wood, and Richards were all going off and doing vast amounts of drugs," said writer Nick Kent, who accompanied the Stones. "By that time the heroin abuse was so bad . . . it was really just incredible, it was heroin city."

At Les Abattoirs in Paris, Jagger was backstage getting ready to go on when a jealous boyfriend rushed at him with a loaded gun. The man was overpowered by Mick's beefy bodyguards and Jagger, visibly shaken but unhurt, went ahead with the show.

To repay the loyalty of British fans who had not been able to buy tickets, the Stones gave their first free concert since Altamont, playing before a crowd of over 250,000 on the grounds of Knebworth House in Hertfordshire on August 21, 1976.

Todd Rundgren's band Utopia was on the bill with the Stones at Knebworth, and he brought along the girlfriend he unknowingly shared with Jagger, Bebe Buell. When Buell misplaced her backstage pass, her friends Paul and Linda McCartney escorted her past the guards and up onto the stage. As always she obeyed the Stones' standing rule that women onstage must maintain a distance of at least fifty feet from the group. Bianca watched silently from the sidelines.

"Mick winked at me and came over," recalled Buell. "Then he pinned his pass on my blouse. He was extremely adorable." Once again, Jagger could not resist teasing Buell's boyfriend. While Rundgren was performing onstage, Jagger camped it up outrageously, shouting, "Oh, Todd! What a cute *ass* you have!"

"Todd was frustrated and angry," said Buell. "Then Mick started playing his favorite game: 'I'm going to steal you from the rock star you're already with.' " Jagger derived obvious pleasure from taunting Rundgren. "You better hold on to your girlfriend, Todd," he said. "I'm a *bigger* star than you. I'll nab her." Forewarned, Rundgren never took his eyes off Bebe.

Jagger was not Rundgren's only competition, to be sure. By this time Buell was already having an affair with Aerosmith's lead singer, Steve Tyler. Often deemed the poor man's Mick Jagger, the thick-lipped, bantamlike prince of heavy metal strutted about the stage with such fury that the pedometer strapped to his razor-thin leg clocked four miles for each performance.

With the possible exception of their heavy-metal rivals Led Zeppelin, Tyler and his cohorts were widely regarded as the wildest group on the rock scene. "Aerosmith," said Bebe, "made the Stones look like *Romper Room*."

Again, Jagger tried to lure Buell away from her new rocker-star boyfriend. Noting that Tyler was generally perceived as a Jagger clone, Mick asked Bebe, "Why go with him when you can have the real thing?"

Buell became pregnant by Tyler in October, but Jagger thought the baby was either his or Rundgren's. When Buell gave birth to a girl, Liv, on July 1, 1977, Jagger phoned up to say, "I'm coming over to see *my* child." He and Ron Wood were the first to visit mother and child. Jagger looked at Buell holding the baby and said, "All right, put her away now. I can see you're a mother."

Although Tyler acknowledged that he was Liv's father, both he and Bebe agreed that it would be best for her to be raised as Rundgren's child. "Steve was completely incapacitated by drugs," Bebe remembered. "We knew we both had to put our egos aside and do what was best for the child."

Most people in the rock community were unaware of Buell's affair with Tyler. "People thought she was Mick's baby," said Bebe. Jagger did little to discourage such speculation. When introducing Buell, Mick described her as "the mother of one of my illegitimate children."

In true soap-opera fashion Liv was raised as Rundgren's

daughter until, at the age of eight, she approached her mother with some pointed questions. Bebe told her daughter that Tyler was her real father. "You can't escape fate," shrugged Buell. "I told her who her real dad was, and now Liv and Todd are good friends."

Buell did not make this information public, however, for several more years. "I think part of Mick was a little jealous," she said. "He didn't know Liv was Steve's child, and I think that bothered him. There were a lot of shocked people when it turned out that neither Todd or Mick was the father, but Steve Tyler." (In 1992 Liv Tyler would become one of the modeling industry's top teenage cover girls.)

After Knebworth, Keith Altham was heading back to London when he spotted a hitchhiker dressed from head to toe in white, standing "in the middle of nowhere. We got closer and we realized it was Bianca. Her limo had broken down and she wanted to know if we could give her a ride back to town. She sat in the back, smoking a joint like one of the boys and being exceedingly charming."

That autumn both Jaggers were weighing film offers. Bianca's first film effort, *Trick or Treat,* collapsed after Bianca refused to do nude lesbian scenes that she claimed were not in the original script. The film had to be aborted halfway through shooting, at a reported cost to the producers of nearly $1 million.

From that catastrophe she went straight to *Flesh Color,* a French-English production costarring Dennis Hopper, in which she played the cheating wife of a Mafia don. *Flesh Color* fizzled when the producers were unable to find an American distributor.

If her movie career seemed hopelessly stalled, Bianca shone brighter than ever as a star of the fashion world. Praised by *The New Yorker* as one of the last women with a true sense of style, Bianca became the youngest member of the Best Dressed Hall of Fame. Yet she chafed under her clotheshorse reputation. "I used to be a dandy, a little showman," she allowed, "but not anymore." Bianca's chum

Halston agreed that, with her Tallulah voice and innate presence, Jagger's wife could "bring glamor back to Hollywood."

Jagger's film prospects were equally tenuous. He agreed to work on a Franco Zeffirelli film score and to appear with his old confidant Nureyev in Roman Polanski's *Othello* (both projects were eventually scrapped). Mick turned down an offer from his longtime friend Jack Nicholson to play an Indian in a western called *Moontrap*, then spurned an offer to star opposite Barbra Streisand in a remake of *A Star Is Born*. Kris Kristofferson got the part instead. After seeing the film Jagger was relieved that he had turned down the role of a "totally has-been rock star, even for the $1 million they offered me."

Jagger flew to Los Angeles to be duly courted by producers and to commune with members of Hollywood's tight-knit group of British expatriates. At a party thrown by Peter Lawford in 1976, Jagger, John Lennon, and Keith Moon, all joined their host for a friendly game of pool in Lawford's library.

"It was really a coke den," explained Lawford's widow, Patricia. "It was remarkable to stand there watching these great stars shooting pool while high on cocaine." At one point Lawford, who had been brother-in-law to John F. and Robert Kennedy, invited Mick to sit in JFK's rocking chair. "Mick just sat there cross-legged in Kennedy's rocking chair, loving every minute of it."

One day Jagger had been to visit Lawford at his apartment in the exclusive Sierra Towers and left behind what appeared to Patricia Lawford to be a small metal toolbox. According to Pat Lawford, inside the box were enough Quaaludes and Valium to stock a small pharmacy—not to mention a variety of other substances. Before long the Lawfords received a frantic phone call from Jagger's bodyguard looking for the missing box. Relieved, he arrived within minutes to pick it up.

In keeping with the holiday spirit Mick and Bianca stayed civil to each other long enough to host a small party at their newly purchased East Seventy-third Street New York town house on Christmas Day, 1976. Cocaine was kept in a covered dish on the coffee table. Jagger was apparently just about to place a coke spoon under the nose of a male guest when John Lennon and Yoko Ono entered the room. Jagger jumped up, ran to the door, and thrust the spoon heaped with coke under Lennon's nose.

It was evident to everyone who knew the Jaggers that theirs was a marriage in name only. Yet the awkward public charade continued. Branding reports of marital discord "absolute rubbish," Mick declared that he and Bianca were "still living together and in love with each other. . . . We have no intention of splitting up. So many people have been nasty and tried to divorce or divide us. I'm very thick skinned but it affects me a bit and Bianca gets very upset about it."

"Why do people keep talking about divorce?" demanded on outraged Bianca. "Touch wood, our marriage will go on and on. Talk about us breaking up is absolute invention."

As for all those extramarital liaisons? "I hate dining alone, so when we're apart I go out to dinner with other men," explained Bianca. "But they're friends." Hearing that she was supposed to be having a steamy affair with Mick's pal Warren Beatty, Bianca confronted Beatty in front of the hotel where he lived, the Beverly Wilshire. "I hear you had an affair with me," she yelled as a small crowd gathered. "You must have been pretty bad, because I don't remember."

Flustered, Beatty dashed over to Bianca and laughed. "Well, did I?"

"Believe me," Bianca shot back, "if you had, you'd have remembered it."

Not all of Mick's righteous indignation was aimed at gossip-mongers and the press. When he heard that Chrissie Shrimpton might sell their old love letters to the *News of the World*, Jagger filed a lawsuit claiming publication constituted a breach of confidence and copyright. The British courts agreed with Jagger, banning the sale of Mick's adolescent scribblings.

A full decade after their split the financially strapped Shrimpton once again found herself under Mick's thumb. Through it all Jagger protested that his reputation as an unrepentant misogynist was undeserved. "In actual fact I love women," he insisted. "I'm absorbed by them and if you ask any of my women friends, not just the ones I've had affairs with, they'll tell you that I'm very nice. I have a lot of sympathy for women."

"Mick screws many, but has few affairs."
—Bianca Jagger

As Mick careened toward his mid-thirties, a lifetime of drug-taking, womanizing, and frenzied overwork had begun to take its toll. A fine latticework of wrinkles was becoming visible at the corners of the eyes, and deep verticle grooves were starting to form at the corners of the famous mouth. Jagger considered plastic surgery, but opted for glitter instead.

To enhance his sparking smile Mick had an emerald inserted in the middle of his upper right incisor. When people mistook it for a piece of spinach, he switched to a ruby. After trying out the ruby for several weeks, he was tired of people pointing out the "spot of blood" on his tooth.

Ultimately Jagger decided on a diamond. "I tried each of the others out for a while," Jagger said. "They came from Cartier, who were very nice about it."

Ron Wood was dubious. "Trouble is," said Wood, "you never know whose mouth they've been in!"

Jagger had no difficulty explaining why he had gone through the painful process of having the diamond drilled into one of his few remaining good teeth: "To look pretty."

Jagger's dazzling grin was not lost on Linda Ronstadt. The first to fuse the country-western sound with driving California rock in the late 1960s, Ronstadt was by now regarded as the undisputed queen of torch rock. She was on her way to a half-dozen platinum albums and had already scored with such singles as "You're No Good," "It's So

Easy," "When Will I Be Loved?," "Blue Bayou," and "Tracks of My Tears."

Ronstadt's romantic life was almost as checkered as Mick's. She had never been married but had been involved with comedians Albert Brooks and Steve Martin, several ex-managers and as many rockers, singers J. D. Souther and Jackson Browne. She was also linked with then-President Jimmy Carter's son Chip. Her housekeeping relationship with California's offbeat young governor (and perennial presidential hopeful) Jerry Brown made her the state's closest contender to a First Lady.

Ronstadt denied she was the vamp the press made her out to be. "I wish I had as much in bed," she quipped, "as I get in the newspapers."

When Jagger went backstage after watching Ronstadt's show at L.A.'s Universal Amphitheater, it was to chide her for her choice of material. "You do too many ballads," he told her. "You should do more rock and roll songs."

Ronstadt replied that Jagger should do less rock and more ballads. "So we started to tease each other," she replied, "and then I thought, *Well, nobody's right. . . .*" Ronstadt told Jagger that she loved the Stones' hit "Tumbling Dice," but that she couldn't sing it because she didn't know the words. Mick scrawled down the lyrics for her on the spot, and the following year Ronstadt's version of "Tumbling Dice" made it onto the singles charts.

Ronstadt got more than a hit single out of her relationship with Jagger. The two began spending time together at Ronstadt's Malibu beach house, and it was not long before Bianca got wind of Mick's latest paramour. She flew to Los Angeles and accused Mick flat-out of having an affair with Ronstadt. After the requisite blowup Jagger hurriedly returned to New York. Left behind in California, Bianca took her revenge by renting a place near the Malibu home of her off-again, on-again lover Ryan O'Neal.

Looking ahead to another world tour the following year, the Stones planned a quiet stay in Toronto. There they planned to record parts of their *Love You Live* double album at a nightclub called the El Mocambo. It would be the first time all five Stones had been together in months.

For Richards the previous year had been filled with turmoil. While his spiritual brother, Mick, was living the high life, Keith sank deeper and deeper into heroin addiction. In March of 1976 Pallenberg had given birth to Richards's second son, Tara, named after the ill-fated Guinness heir Tara Browne. Three months later little Tara mysteriously choked to death in his crib.

Richards drowned his grief in Jack Daniel's and heroin. Openly resentful of Jagger's obvious social pretensions, Keith—the original punk rocker—continued to brawl, crack up expensive cars, scrap with the volatile Anita, and get arrested for minor drug offenses.

When he arrived in Toronto on February 20, 1977, Jagger was stunned that Richards was nowhere to be found. For the next five days the other Stones prepared Richards with phone calls and telegrams before he grudgingly boarded a plane for Canada.

In Toronto customs officers searched Pallenberg's luggage and found hashish and a spoon encrusted with heroin. Then, on February 28, Mounted Police raided Richards's Toronto hotel suite and uncovered so much heroin and cocaine that Richards was charged not only with possession but possession with intent to traffic. Under Canadian law the trafficking charge carried a maximum penalty of life in prison.

Front-page headlines blared the news of Richards's and the Stones' impending demise. Released on bail, Richards blithely joined the group at the El Mocambo and gave two of his best performances.

Incredibly, it was at this moment that the headstrong, twenty-nine-year-old wife of Canadian Prime Minister Pierre Trudeau decided to pal around with the raunchy Stones, sparking yet another international scandal and rocking her husband's already shaky government.

Fully twenty-nine years younger than her husband and a self-described "flower child," Margaret Trudeau picked this auspicious moment to break away from her domineering husband and the pressures of being First Lady.

Eluding her government bodyguards, Mrs. Trudeau checked into a room next to Keith Richards's at the Harbour Castle Hilton. Now a constant member of the Stones' entourage, she was escorted to the El Mocambo each night by Jagger. Mrs. Trudeau then spent hours wandering the Harbour Castle corridors in a white bathrobe, hanging out with the band in Mick's hotel suite. When Mick and Ron Wood returned to New York in March, Mrs. Trudeau canceled all her duties and joined them.

The furor over Maggie's apparent lack of discretion was such that it threatened to topple the beleaguered Pierre Trudeau from power. After defending his wife's odd behavior on the floor of Parliament, the prime minister bluntly told a radio interviewer that his wife's precise whereabouts were "none of your damn business." While Maggie was in Manhattan, Pierre spent their sixth anniversary at home in Ottawa with the Trudeaus' three children.

After her initial fling with Mick, Maggie found Wood more to her liking. This did not sit well with Jagger. "I wouldn't go near her with a barge pole," he later claimed, rather ungallantly. "She was a very determined young lady—er, older woman. I think she was just a very sick girl in search of something. She found it—but not with me."

Acting the injured party, Jagger took the opportunity to slam Americans for scandal-mongering. "You Americans think we are a bunch of male chauvinist pigs," he protested. "We can't talk to a woman without being romantically attached to her. And you American women have a worse attitude than the men. You think we can't say hello without wanting to be in bed with you."

Publicly Bianca joined her husband in ridiculing reports of Mick's Trudeau affair. "We laughed about it," she said. "We thought it was very funny." She said nothing about the two other women who were now keeping him occupied: the beautiful heiress Sabrina Guinness, and twenty-five-year-old British actress Carinthia West, daughter of former NATO general Sir Michael West.

"They are all nobodies trying to become somebodies," Bianca said of the women who paraded through her husband's life. "It's very strange. The mystique of women thinking they've made it if they've slept with Mick. It shows such a lack of respect for themselves. He finds it repugnant. Nothing could be less of a turn-on."

She conceded that Mick denied having affairs at all: "Mick is not famous for being the most honest person." But Bianca insisted that Jagger found out about her extramarital exploits because she told him herself. In addition to old standbys like Ryan O'Neal, these now reportedly included Princess Margaret's sometime boyfriend Roddy Llewellyn, socialites Mark Shand and Tony Portago, and actor Maximilian Schell. "I don't," she shrugged, "believe in telling lies."

Most of those who buzzed around the Queen Bee posed no threat to Jagger. "Homosexuals make the best friends," Bianca insisted, "because they care about you as a woman and are not jealous. They love you but don't try to screw up your head."

Of all Mick's lovers, Bianca still maintained the only one that ever really made her jealous was Carly Simon. She even forgave Jagger for his fling with Ronstadt—a woman Bianca later confessed to being personally fond of.

Deemed least threatening—at first—was a six-foot-tall Texas model with tumbling blond tresses, an equine face, and a disarming drawl. Raised the youngest (with her twin Terry) of five girls, Jerry Fay Hall grew up in the Dallas suburb of Mesquite. Her father, a truck driver, died when she was twenty. But it was his wife, Marjorie, who taught her daughters the importance of a work ethic and sexy lingerie.

Jerry would later submit that she became fixated on sex at an early age, and cheerfully described her first orgasm at twelve: "It was a bitterly cold day and I was leaning on my horse. I put my coat up against the horse and began rubbing on it. Then it happened. It was a surprise . . . but it was great."

A gangling, awkward teenager, Jerry was dubbed "Tall Hall" by her unsympathetic classmates. Hall described herself as an "icky" adolescent who had no boyfriends in high school. After she and a girlfriend picked up a copy of *Everything You Always Wanted to Know About Sex (But Were Afraid to Ask)*, Hall made the conscious decision to lose her virginity at fifteen. "We wanted to get it all over with," she later remembered, "so we asked the champion bull rider if he would do it to us.

"We did it in the hayloft, in the rain. It was quick and not so romantic, but I think it's always that way the first time." The event was made all the more memorable by the fact that the bull rider never bothered to remove his boots. Hall was working at the local Dairy Queen the following year when she was injured in a car wreck. The insurance settlement was enough to pay for a nose job and a one-way ticket to Paris.

Jerry was staying at a youth hostel on the Riviera when she was spotted by fashion agent Claude Haddad sunbathing in the nude on a Saint-Tropez beach. She quickly moved in with noted fashion illustrator Antonio Lopez, and was soon immersed in what she called the "sleazy" nightlife of Paris.

Hall's sidekick during this time was the Amazonian black singer-actress Grace Jones, who was even taller than Jerry. The two American women worked up a risqué cabaret act to perform at parties, and soon Jerry attracted the attention of none other than the shah of Iran. The ill-fated ruler was so fond of the outlandish Hall that he had her flown to Iran to be with him.

In 1975 British rocker Bryan Ferry noticed Jerry on the cover of Italian *Vogue* and hired her to pose as a mermaid for the cover of his forthcoming album. She did, they promptly moved in together and within months he gave her an engagement ring that she proudly flashed in front of her envious friends.

"She's got one of those faces," noted British *Vogue* photographer Willie Christie, "that if you look at it in a bad light without makeup, she's ugly as sin. It's a horsey face. But in a good light she looks better than anyone."

Envious of Jerry's bluff, down-home manner and her seemingly effortless success, other models began circulating nasty rumors about the big-boned Miss Hall. "They were saying she was a man in drag," recalled one fashion writer, "or at the very least a transsexual. Jerry was definitely not like the other girls. She was an outsider. She didn't have that ice queen attitude so many models have. They felt threatened by her."

By 1977 Jerry had been on forty magazine covers; the girl who was teased in high school for wearing her sister's falsies could now brag she was the first "nipple cover" in *Cosmopolitan*'s history.

Hall was now commanding modeling fees in excess of $1,000 a day—a substantial figure at the time, and more than enough to buy herself a two-hundred-acre spread in Lone Oak, Texas. She reveled in being independently, well-to-do. "If you have your own money," she said, "no one can buy you."

Jerry's financial independence was one of the things about the leggy Texan that most appealed to Mick. That, and the fact that she was about to wed another rock star.

Ferry was touring Japan in early 1977 when Jerry was seated at a Manhattan dinner party between Warren Beatty and Mick Jagger. The two men vied for her ear until Jagger angrily said, "She's with me."

Holding up her ring, Hall protested that she was engaged, but that was hardly enough to dissuade either man from pursuing her. Finally, Jagger grabbed Beatty and pulled him to a pay phone, where Mick set his insatiable pal up with another willing young model.

Mick then dragged Hall to Studio 54 and, at four A.M., offered to give her a lift home in his limousine. Instead, he took her to his house and maneuvered her into the bedroom for some "tea." Recalled Hall: "The next morning I was thinking, '*Oh, no, what have I done?*' I was pulling on my clothes, running out of the house, trying to grab a cab . . . it took me five seconds to get out of there."

The next day Hall came rushing to her friend Liz Derringer with the news. "She came back from that party all excited," recalled Derringer. "She was saying 'Mick this' and 'Mick that.' Finally I had to stop her and say 'Mick who?' Jerry just knew she met another maniac, but she also knew he was the man of her dreams."

Hall had no illusions about what had drawn them together in the first place. "It was sex," she said when asked by a friend. "What do you think?"

Jagger began flooding Hall with flowers and dinner invitations, and when Ferry called to check on his fiancée she told him she had "lost" their engagement ring. Once he learned from friends that Hall had dumped him for Jagger, he threatened to fly to New York and beat Mick to a pulp. Instead, Ferry got his revenge by dealing Hall a crippling blow: When she asked him to send along the closetful of clothes she kept at Ferry's house in London, he refused.

Hall and Jagger maintained a low profile until late June of 1977, when they both showed up at New York's 21 Club for a glittering birthday bash designer Diane Von Furstenberg was throwing for her then-husband, Egon. Andy Warhol recorded in his diary that Jagger "started going after" another man at the party.

Mick's indiscreet behavior at "21" may have had something to do with his pharmaceutical intake that evening. "Mick was so out of it," recalled Warhol. "His head was so far back and he was singing to himself. The top part of his body was like jelly and the bottom half was tapping 3,000 taps a minute. He was putting his sunglasses on and off. . . ."

Hall may have been the front-runner in the race for Jagger's extracurricular affections. But Mick was constantly adding to the field. Between sessions with Hall, Jagger now wept about his failing marriage to socialite Barbara Allen while the two carried on a torrid affair of their own.

Jagger continued to indulge his appetite for teenagers, becoming involved with Nenna Eberstadt, the pretty sixteen-year-old granddaughter of Ogden Nash. A student at Manhattan's exclusive Brearley girls' school, Nenna wore a knit school uniform not unlike his own daughter Jade's. Nenna's mother, Isabel, was a friend of Jane Holzer's and had met Jagger at Baby Jane's famous party a decade earlier.

Freddy Eberstadt fumed at the news that the lascivious Mick Jagger was pursuing his daughter. Eberstadt reportedly went to Jagger's house at four A.M. looking for Nenna (he didn't find her there). When Eberstadt blew up at Mick for phoning his daughter—"How dare you. . . . You, an older man of forty!"—Jagger pointed out that he was only thirty-four.

Jagger caused another international brouhaha when he claimed he wouldn't mind if Jade had an affair when she was thirteen. "Just as long as she didn't turn into a tramp and was having it with anyone on the street," he told British journalist David Wigg. "It wouldn't upset me at all if she had sex at an early age. When I was thirteen all I wanted to do was have sex. I just desperately wanted to— didn't you?" He then promised to "give Jade a little talk about not getting pregnant when she is ten."

Hall's talks with *her* mother a decade earlier had clearly prepared her for the daunting task ahead. "There are three secrets that my mother told me," she confided. "Be a maid in the living room, a cook in the kitchen—and a whore in the bedroom. So long as I have a maid and a cook, I'll do the rest myself."

Jerry proved herself an aggressive competitor. Whenever another woman made a play for Mick, Hall fought back— poking her with her elbows, stomping her toes, kicking her in the shins until she bled. "In Texas," she explained, "we tell other girls where to get off."

Hall's most valuable secret for keeping Jagger or any man, for that matter: "Even if you have only two seconds, drop everything and give him a blowjob. That way he won't really want sex with anyone else."

Hall's supporters and detractors were about evenly divided. Some found her to be a crude, money-obsessed social climber. "Jerry is real Texas with lots of trash and glitz," said a fellow model. One of Jagger's British friends allows that she had "entertainment value, but certainly no grace."

Desmond Guinness was instantly won over by Hall's lack of pretense. "She's very good with strangers," he said. "If a party's drooping she will magically lift everyone's spirits just by walking into the room. She turns every time into party time and is very generous." Concurred Keith Altham: "Jerry is sweet, kind, and extremely patient. She puts up with a tremendous amount. It's impossible not to fall for that genuine southern charm." Even Bianca's buddy Warhol had to confess that he liked Jerry, though he complained that she had intense "underarm body odor, like she hadn't taken a shower . . . so I guess Mick must like BO."

Keith Richards hated Hall. He saw the flashy blond Texan as animate proof of Jagger's sellout to glamor and artifice. The growing tension between the Glimmer Twins was eased somewhat that summer, when Canadian officials issued Richards a visa. While awaiting the outcome of his narcotics trial, Keith would be allowed to seek treatment for his heroin addiction in the U.S.

Since Richards was not permitted to travel more than thirty miles outside Philadelphia, where he and Anita Pallenberg were undergoing mild electroshock therapy, Jagger delivered the tapes of their *Love You Live* concerts to him. Mick pleaded with Keith to stay sober during their intense work session and, after downing a fifth of tequila, passed out himself. This turn of events struck both men as nothing short of hilarious, and served to repair the rift between them. They were a team again.

That October, Mick was packing to leave for Paris, where the Stones were scheduled to begin work on their new *Some Girls* album. Bianca, still trying to convince herself that his interest in Hall was fleeting, welcomed him back into her bed. This would be the last time Mick and Bianca had sex.

After months of diligent work on *Some Girls* the Stones took a break for the holidays. Mick returned to London, where he spent Christmas Eve with Jerry at the Savoy Hotel rather than with Bianca on Cheyne Walk. On December 27 Jagger and Hall flew to Barbados and checked into a hotel under the name "Beaton."

Fed up with the pursuing paparazzi, Jagger began taking a confrontational stance. In Barbados he threw a beer bottle at one photographer; when he lunged at another in Paris, Jagger was the one who ended up sprawled on the pavement.

Bianca now found it virtually impossible to keep up the facade of marital harmony. She was confiding to friends that she could not bring herself to sleep with Mick because she didn't think he was attractive.

Yet she still held out hope. "One day she's in a dream world, totally convinced Mick loves only her," said Halston. "The next she's in a panic, scared to death he'll leave her high and dry. Everyone knows it's over between them—everyone but Bianca."

By the time Mick returned to New York in March 1978, Bianca had accepted the inevitable and moved to protect her financial interests. Mick's total fortune was now conservatively estimated at $25 million, and though Bianca had been pressured into signing away any claim to the fortune in the minutes before their hectic Saint-Tropez wedding, she had no intention of walking away empty handed. She hired New York lawyer Roy Cohn and West Coast palimony expert Marvin Mitchelson to start divorce proceedings.

That spring Jerry, fed up with the pointed way in which the Pierre Hotel desk clerks called her "*Miss* Hall," preferred to stay with Mick at the staid Carlyle on Madison Avenue. Until then the Carlyle Hotel had been best known as the Kennedy family's New York headquarters.

Liz Derringer was visiting Jerry at the Carlyle when Mick was served with divorce papers. Bianca Rosa Jagger was suing her husband in London on grounds of adultery, naming

Jerry as corespondent. Mick appeared genuinely stunned. "Can you believe *she* served *me?*" he asked Derringer. "In all those years, have you ever seen me in the papers with another girl?"

Jagger wasted no time retaliating. He cut off Bianca's charge accounts and had all the furniture moved out of the Cheyne Walk house. According to Bianca he also made a flat take-it-or-leave-it offer of $100,000.

Mitchelson fought to have the case transferred from England to California, where community property statutes entitled her to half her husband's earnings during their marriage—regardless of French law. Thus Bianca demanded $12.5 million.

Mick, meantime, figured he would fare better on home turf and fought to keep the trial in London. While the matter was being ajudicated, Mitchelson asked the courts to order Jagger to fork over $13,400 a month to Bianca in temporary support.

Mick faced another crisis on the professional front. The Stones were set to tour again in the summer of 1978, and Keith—the threat of a life sentence still hanging over his head—was back on heroin.

Jagger wanted Richards off smack once and for all. His addiction jeopardized not only the upcoming tour but the band's very existence. The Stones picked Woodstock, New York, as the spot for their secret, closed-door tour rehearsals. There, according to Jerry Hall, she and Mick spent weeks nursing Richards. "Mick loves Keith, you know," said Jerry. "They're like a married couple. And it gave Mick a good feeling to be able to help Keith. . . . He got off heroin right on our couch."

In truth, Richards, still no fan of Hall, spent only three days with the couple before moving out. He spent most of his time being cared for by members of the Stones staff.

Some Girls was released on June 9, 1978, and, spawning such megahit singles as "Shattered," "Beast of Burden," and "Miss You," scored an instant critical and commercial bull's-eye. Once again the Stones were in drag on the album's Warhol-designed cover, juxtaposed with photos of various screen goddesses. Several of the famous women depicted, including Raquel Welch and Lauren Bacall, threatened lawsuits.

But the loudest protest came from black leaders objecting to the "Some Girls" lyric "Black girls just want to get fucked all night." Despite Jesse Jackson's condemnation of the album's racist tone, "Some Girls" went straight to No. 1, becoming the Stones biggest-selling to date.

Not everyone objected to the album's lyrics. Bianca was so touched by the romantic sentiments expressed in "Miss You" that she reportedly ordered her attorneys to slow down divorce proceedings. Unfortunately for the estranged Mrs. Jagger, the disco-driven "Miss You" was inspired by Mick's Studio 54 nights with Jerry Hall.

Before the 1978 tour began, Jagger hired longtime associate Keith Altham to replace Les Perrin as the Stones' publicist. Two years earlier Perrin had suffered a severe stroke from which he never completely recovered.

Altham was delighted to be offered the job, but asked what would happen to the much-admired Perrin. Jagger replied that he intended to fire him. When Altham suggested that Perrin be kept on in some capacity, Jagger refused. "I don't see any reason to keep two PRs," he shrugged.

"I told Mick that if he sacked Les he'd be hated by Fleet Street," said Altham. Unmoved, Jagger went ahead and announced that Altham was replacing Perrin.

"Jagger is completely, totally ruthless," observed Altham. "He doesn't have much loyalty. People come and go swiftly, and are decimated. Mick is also cowardly when it comes to personnel matters. He gets somebody else to fire you."

Altham claimed Jagger was equally charitable when asked to comment on the death of Decca chairman Sir Edward Lewis. "Tell them I said it was about time," sneered Mick. Altham asked if he would try to come up with something a little less hostile. "Yeah. Send some flowers," added Mick, "with the message 'Always behind the times.'"

As the Stones careened from one U.S. stadium to the next that summer, they resumed their on-the-road habits. "Drugs were *always* around," said Daniel Stewart, who helped supervise the Stones tour security. "There were literally mountains of dope, and Jagger wouldn't pass it up."

Stewart was also impressed with the mountains of cash that were lying about—allegedly $70,000 and up per night from the sale of T-shirts and souvenirs alone. "They kept it all in brown paper bags," recalled Stewart. "Everybody just dug in and pulled out handfuls of cash. Nobody said anything."

Backstage also teemed with groupies of both sexes. Keith's twenty-three-year-old assistant Tommy Edmonds claimed Jagger eased himself onto the couch next to the young man, put his hand on his thigh, and said, "You're doing a really good job. By the way, are you gay?"

"So I thought about it for a minute," admitted Edmonds. "You know, this *is* Mick Jagger. And I said, 'No, man. I'm not gay.'"

Fuming, Jagger leapt to his feet and blurted out, "Well, I'm not either!"

As for female companionship, the groupies that now threw themselves at the Stones seemed to be younger than ever and decidedly scruffier. "Punk was the thing then," said one tour member. "Some of the girls were straight out of *Sid and Nancy*—rubber bracelets, safety pins through the ears, the works."

Just a few weeks into the tour Jagger was dealt another legal blow by one of the important women in his life. Marsha Hunt, now on welfare in Los Angeles, had also enlisted the services of Marvin Mitchelson and was suing Jagger for a modest $2,190 in monthly child support. The previous winter Jagger and Hall had spent time with Karis in L.A. At the time, Hunt told him she was in desperate need of money and, she recalled, "he avoided the issue."

More important, Marsha wanted to establish Mick's paternity once and for all—for Karis's sake. "It's not like a normal child with an absent father," Hunt explained. "Mick's there every time you turn on the radio or see a magazine cover. If Karis has got to suffer that, I don't think she should also have to suffer being suddenly poverty-stricken." She added that it was difficult to keep Karis from feeling bitter and deserted "when he seems to give of his energy and money to other women but not to his daughter."

Jagger responded by ordering all twenty-five bodyguards in the Stones' employ to keep any and all process servers at bay. Several attempts at serving Jagger were foiled before a statuesque blonde named Leslie Spiller strolled toward Mick in the lobby of his Los Angeles hotel. A grinning Jagger waved his bodyguards aside, only to watch Spiller stuff a subpoena in his hand the minute she got close. Shocked, Jagger threw the papers to the ground and bolted for his waiting limo. But the intrepid Stiller tossed the subpoena through the open limo window as the car sped away. Mission accomplished.

Meantime, attorney Mitchelson made certain Jagger would not ignore Hunt's request this time. He obtained a court order restraining promoters from paying Jagger his share of the take from two concerts in Anaheim.

Jagger would eventually cave in, but not before bitterly attacking the mother of his eldest child. "She's a hustler," he said, "just out for publicity. She's an idiot; she won't take any fuckin' work. . . . She's a lazy bitch." When asked how many children he had, Mick shrugged, "I don't know. Not many."

In Tucson on July 21, hometown girl Linda Ronstadt joined Mick onstage to sing "Tumbling Dice," sparking more rumors about their intermittent romance. Gossip reached a fever pitch following the tour, when Jagger rented her Los Angeles mansion—despite the fact that Jerry moved in with him.

As if they did not have enough excitement in their lives, Jagger and Hall were awakened in the middle of the night by an intruder. Jagger switched on the lights and, according to his later testimony, "saw a leg sticking out of the closet—a shoe and sock on a brown leg."

Jagger got up and held the closet door tight so that he and Jerry could make their escape from the room. When the intruder made his getaway, it became clear that shoes and socks were all he was wearing. As he streaked past her and down the stairs, Jerry got a good look at the man "carrying a small khaki bundle—probably his trousers or something." Was he wearing underpants? "If they were black, maybe," Hall later testified, "but I didn't see any." Jerry identified the nude cat burglar, who made off with $15,000 worth of cash and jewelry, as former Jagger bodyguard James Harrington.

At thirty-five Jagger acknowledged that his years of nomadic carousing were finally beginning to catch up with him. "When I came here in 1964 I had a pink Cadillac and fourteen-year-old chicks," he told a reporter in Los Angeles. "Now I'm back with a black Cadillac and fifteen-year-olds."

How much longer did he plan to perform? "People like Bing Crosby go on forever—that's horrible. It's too awful to think about that," he said. "I don't want to play when I'm old. But right now I think I can cut almost everybody onstage."

On October 24, 1978, the Stones held their collective breath as Richards's drug case finally came to trial in Toronto. In exchange for his pleading guilty to possession, the trafficking charge was dropped. Keith was sentenced to one year's probation and ordered to give a concert to benefit the Canadian National Institute for the Blind.

Although "Mr. and Mrs. Phillips" (Mick and Jerry) usually stayed at the Carlyle when they were in New York, Jagger still stayed solo at the Plaza from time to time. The lobby at the Plaza was big enough for savvy groupies to wait for their idol without being too conspicuous.

Yet even an expert like Kevin, who trailed Jagger for years, found it difficult to go undetected. "I was always being picked up by hotel security, fingerprinted in the basement, and thrown out," he said.

In late 1978 a newcomer to the ranks of Jagger groupies began hanging out in the Plaza Hotel lobby. She had dark hair, chewed gum nonstop, and, like Kevin, had been a third-string dancer with the Alvin Ailey dance company.

"This girl was obnoxious, but also very friendly," recalled Kevin. "She'd walk up to you and say in a loud voice, 'I want to be a singer. I can sing anything. Wanna hear?' And then before you could tell her to shut up she'd start singing and everybody would turn and stare. I thought, *Get me away from this obnoxious girl. She's blowing my cover!*" Unfortunately, said Kevin, "there was no way to get away from this girl. She was there a *lot*, and she called herself a Jagger groupie. He was the only Stone she was interested in—and I got the feeling she thought he'd help her with her career."

Something about this irrepressible, twenty-year-old newcomer appealed to Jagger. On more than one occasion he invited her to join him upstairs. "They slept together back then," recalled Kevin. "She was wild, and that appealed to him." They would not meet again for years—though it was unlikely he would ever forget her name: Madonna.

"When she's older, I'll tell Jade to watch out for men like me."

"You can't keep it up with sixteen-year-old girls forever. They're very demanding."

Before a capacity crowd at the Oshawa Civic Auditorium, Keith Richards served part of his sentence by giving a benefit concert. The audience went wild when Jagger and the rest of the Stones joined him onstage for two shows. Hosting the event was comedian John Belushi, on whom the lesson of the evening was obviously lost; three years later Belushi died of a drug overdose at age thirty-four.

For Mick 1979 marked not only the end of a decade but the end of his turbulent, headline-grabbing marriage. Bianca's flamboyant lawyer, Marvin Mitchelson, continued his campaign to have the case moved from London to Los Angeles. When the case came before L.A. Superior Court Judge Harry T. Shafer, His Honor professed never to have heard of Mick Jagger. "I don't follow rock singers," said the judge. "I'm strictly a Lawrence Welk man."

Like the marriage they sought to end, the divorce proceedings quickly became a media sideshow. At one point Mitchelson ordered his client to hide in the ladies' room for two hours rather than be questioned by the opposition without Mick present.

Once she did take the stand in Los Angeles, Bianca wept as she told Judge Shafer that she hoped the couple would reconcile even after she filed for divorce. "There was always a possibility I would go back with my husband," she said, wiping away tears. "That was always in the back of my head, Your Honor."

To get the case tried in California, Bianca testified that her husband had resided and recorded in Los Angeles, but kept it a secret to avoid paying taxes. Describing himself as a "wandering minstrel," Jagger pointed out that he was in the process of building a lavish home on the island of Mustique in the West Indies. "I have every intention of spending a considerable part of my life when not performing abroad at my home in Mustique," he testified. "I consider it an ideal place for my daughter to visit, and she adores it."

The case ultimately shifted to the other side of the Atlantic, and after months of legal wrangling the divorce was finally granted by a London court. The property settlement was arrived at after an eighteen-minute hearing. Bianca was awarded $1.4 million, and custody of Jade. A year later she managed to get that settlement figure raised to $2.5 million.

"I think if I weren't so beautiful," Bianca once said, "maybe I'd have more character." Now she admitted, "It's time for me to grow up. I have always been a dreamer. For a while I almost lived in a fantasy world. But I have learned from the past that I should not be so trusting." Bianca nixed any thought of remarriage. "I expect too much out of it." As for sex: "I can spend years without anybody. Sex without emotion and tenderness and love is nothing. Sex for the sake of sex—I don't need that."

It was not a claim Mick was likely to make, though he had plenty to say about his ex-wife. "I think she just wanted the divorce to drag on so long so she could get her name in the papers," he speculated. "She has been so difficult and devious that I'll never be friends with her again."

In late July of 1979 the Divorce of the Year was shoved

off the front pages by a ghostly specter from the Stones' satanic past. While a drugged Anita Pallenberg dozed in the bedroom of her suburban Westchester County, New York home, a seventeen-year-old high-school dropout named Scott Cantrell loaded a pistol, put it to his head, and pulled the trigger. The gun Cantrell used to end his life was Pallenberg's unlicensed .38 revolver. (By this time Keith Richards was living with the stunning young American model Patti Hansen).

ROLLING STONES GIRL ANITA PALLENBERG HAS BEEN LINKED TO A WITCHES' COVEN IN WESTCHESTER blared the *New York Post*. Jagger could hardly believe how drugs and booze had transformed the once sleek Pallenberg into a bloated matron with eyes, as one writer put it, "like a demon night nurse." Once the rumors of black magic and covens died down, it was determined that Cantrell may have been playing Russian roulette. All charges against Pallenberg were dropped except for possession of an unlicensed handgun. For that, she was fined $1,000.

At about the same time the teenager killed himself in his onetime lover's bed, Jagger moved with Jerry into a town house at 135 Central Park West, just around the corner from the Dakota apartment of his old friend John Lennon.

During the time in the late 1970s when Lennon lived with May Pang, the Stone and the former Beatle spent quite a lot of time together in New York. "Mick would drop by at our apartment on East 52nd Street," said Pang, "and the two of them would talk about who was the hot new guitar player, or they'd just sit on the floor, eating Chinese food and watching television. Very normal." That changed when Lennon went back to Yoko Ono. Jagger would leave notes for John with the Dakota doorman that read *Mick was here*, and always sent Lennon postcards when he and Jerry traveled abroad.

"John Lennon—whatever happened to him?" asked Mick. "He lives like ten yards from me, but does he ever call me? Does he ever go out? No! Changes his phone number every ten minutes. I've given up. I like John really a lot, you know? He's just kowtowing to his bleedin' wife, probably. She's probably trying to screen him off. I know, I've seen it all before. He lives like a cloistered nun."

Lennon lashed back in a *Playboy* interview: "In the eighties they'll be asking 'Why are these guys still together? Can't they hack it on their own? Why do they have to be surrounded by a gang? Is the little leader afraid someone's going to knife him in the back?' . . . They'll be showing pictures of the guy with lipstick wriggling his ass and the four guys with the evil black makeup on their eyes trying to look raunch. That's gonna be the joke in the future."

Jagger was miffed at Lennon's comments, but chalked them up to jealousy. The Stones had, after all, managed to stay on top for an incredible seventeen years. Nor was Mick about to become another rock recluse—though he did appreciate the anonymity his new full beard accorded him. Bearing a faint resemblance to Czar Nicholas II, the bewhiskered Jagger was virtually unrecognizable that fall of 1979. He enjoyed the freedom his beard afforded him—until he walked up to the front door of Hurrah's disco in Manhattan and was denied admittance. That Christmas he shaved it off.

On New Year's Eve, Liz Derringer interviewed her long-time friend for *High Times* magazine over champagne at the New York town house. Most of the interview was predictably coarse and provocative. Among other things Jagger proclaimed himself "staunchly anti-Catholic," joked about performing fellatio on rocker Tom Petty, and labeled the entire population of one Middle Eastern nation gay.

In an uncharacteristically serious moment he also took the opportunity to slam the publication for promoting the drug culture. "I think it's disgusting," he told Derringer. "I think that you shouldn't encourage young people to take drugs anyway. I think that's just awful." Jagger was always outspoken in his opposition to heroin, but what did he think of cocaine? "I very rarely take drugs. I think cocaine is very bad, a habit-forming bore," he claimed. "I don't understand the fashion for it."

Such statements may have been what Jagger thought his aging baby boomer audience wanted to hear, but they had little bearing on the reality of his life. At private parties and in very public settings Jagger indulged in cocaine and smoked pot freely.

Celebrity photographer David McGough recalled sitting just a few feet away from Jagger and Hall in the balcony at Studio 54. "Mick and Jerry just sat there, smoking pot, snorting coke, taking drugs from anyone who came up to them," said McGough. "People just wanted to say they turned Mick Jagger on. But it was incredible that he would just take *anything* they handed him."

When a mutual friend dropped by unannounced with Jagger in tow, the stunned New Yorker offered him a drink. No, said Mick, but have you got any coke? His host sent him to the refrigerator to fetch his own soft drink when he suddenly realized what Mick really had in mind. "*Cocaine*," said the mutual friend. "Rock stars sprinkle it on their cereal, don't they?"

On March 1, 1980, Mick and Jerry joined Andy Warhol and writer Victor Bockris for dinner with *Naked Lunch* author William Burroughs. "It was terribly awkward," recalled Bockris. "Here were these great figures of the sixties who couldn't think of a thing to say to each other."

Since Warhol had once been shot by a disenchanted protégée and the heroin-addicted Burroughs had accidentally shot his wife between the eyes, Bockris got the ball rolling with the most provocative question he could think of.

"Well, Andy, you were shot by someone," said Bockris, "and Bill shot someone, and, Mick, did you ever shoot anyone?"

Jagger looked nonplused. "Bill, you shot someone?" said Jagger. "Who did you shoot?"

Bockris was stunned. He assumed that anyone with even

the slightest knowledge of Burroughs's life was aware of his wife's tragic death.

There was an interminable silence. Finally, Burroughs spoke. "I haven't shot anyone lately, Mick," he said. "I promise you that I have been on good behavior."

While he waited for the new album to be released in late June, Jagger added to his already impressive real estate holdings. To the New York town house, the empty Cheyne Walk mansion, and the new estate on Mustique, Jagger now added two new French properties—a chateau in the Loire Valley and an elegant Paris apartment on the Isle de la Cité, smack in the middle of the Seine.

Jagger paid $586,000 for La Fourchette, a spectacular seventeenth-century chateau previously owned by France's Richet family; Charles Richet won the Nobel Prize for Medicine in 1913. Designated an historic monument by the French government, the mansard-roofed chateau boasted twelve bedrooms, a private chapel (where Mick and Jerry slept during the three-year, $2 million renovation job), a nursery worthy of a dauphin, and its own vineyard. The most glowing endorsement of La Fourchette ("The Fork") had come two centuries earlier from the Duchesse de Choiseul: "You," she told a friend, "will love it madly."

On June 26, 1980, the Stones threw a party at New York's Danceteria to celebrate the release of their new album, *Emotional Rescue*. According to Victor Bockris, "Each band member was given a bodyguard; Jagger took his into the toilet and proceeded to snort half a gram of coke, smoke a big joint, and bolt half a bottle of whiskey in order to become "Mick Jagger" for forty-five minutes."

Jagger was not completely satisfied with *Emotional Rescue*; it clearly lacked the raw power of earlier efforts. But it had been two years since the Stones' last album, and their audience, larger than ever, quickly made *Emotional Rescue* a worldwide No. 1 hit. The album remained in the top spot for seven weeks in the U.S., and the "Emotional Rescue" single, featuring a disco beat and Mick's falsetto, climbed to No. 3.

Most significantly, *Emotional Rescue* was the group's first hit of the 1980s. Yet there were still those skeptics who took obvious pleasure in pointing out that Wood and Wyman were already over forty and the rest were about to be. They dubbed them "The Strolling Bones."

At about the time of *Emotional Rescue*'s release, Mick's friend Earl McGrath decided to resign as president of Rolling Stones Records and pursue his own business interests. He was replaced by Arthur Collins, a young Atlantic Records executive. Ironically, Collins would eventually become Marianne Faithfull's manager.

Collins, like all who preceded him, was frustrated by Mick's reluctance to sign new artists to the Rolling Stones label. They had the opportunity to sign the Stray Cats and the Neville Brothers, among other hot groups, but in each case Jagger vetoed the deal. The only artist they signed was reggae star Peter Tosh, and he soon complained bitterly that his career was being neglected by the Stones management.

"It was very frustrating," said Collins. "Mick was very pragmatic. He didn't want to take the risk." Yet Jagger remained a hands-on manager, conferring constantly with Prince Rupert Loewenstein, Ahmet Ertegun, and the handful of others at the core of his business empire.

Throughout his six-year tenure at Rolling Stones records, Collins was "amazed" at Jagger's business acumen. "He came in to the office to check on things often. *Too* often," conceded Collins. "He's a very global guy, and detail oriented. He was very concerned, for example, about Peter Tosh's record sales in Italy, and expected you to have those figures at your fingertips."

The fiercely competitive Jagger also wanted up-to-date intelligence on the financial dealings of other rock stars. Recalled Collins: "He always wanted specific details about other stars' deals—'What about Michael Jackson's deal?

How much is Madonna's deal *really* worth?' You had to be very precise, or he'd just walk away."

Collins recalled casually commenting to Jagger that Paul McCartney and Michael Jackson had a new hit with their "Say Say Say" duet.

"Is it a hit?" Mick inquired.

"It's a good song," replied Collins.

"But is it a *hit?*" Mick repeated.

"I thought he was joking at first," said Collins, "but Mick was dead serious. He felt very competitive toward McCartney and toward Jackson, for very different reasons, and it really mattered to him how well their song was really doing. Mick is very much a bottom-line guy."

As for Jagger's management style: "If he was displeased with something, he let me know," said Collins. "But he never yelled at me, never cursed at me. But if he was angry, everybody knew."

The other Glimmer Twin wanted desperately to tour that summer, but Jagger postponed his decision on the matter until he and Jerry left on a Moroccan holiday. From Fez he telexed the Stones' office in New York's Rockefeller Center that there would be no 1980 tour. Once again Jagger's innate fear of confrontation prevailed.

Richards, still no fan of Hall or the effect she seemed to have on Mick, was livid. "Mick waited until he was three thousand miles away and just sent a telex. I mean, he could have told me this, in person, two days earlier, before he flew away! During that period we almost came to blows— or worse."

The decision to forgo a tour that year was not arrived at arbitrarily. More than anyone, Jagger appreciated the fact that the group was more a business phenomenon than a musical one. Now that the Stones were all middle aged, a strategy was needed to preserve the group's priceless mystique. Jagger had already decided to pace the tours so they occurred no more frequently than every three years—long enough to let a new crop of record-buying and concert-going teens to mature, but not too long to keep old fans waiting for their fix.

On December 8, 1980, Mick's neighbor and friend was shot to death outside the Dakota by a deranged fan named Mark David Chapman. Mick made no official comment at the time, but the killing of Lennon left him shaken. Jagger, it was later learned, had been on Chapman's hit list. Mick began looking for an apartment on a less-traveled side-street, far from the site of his friend's gruesome murder. Meantime, he carried a gun.

That holiday season Jagger counted among his newest admirers another schoolgirl twenty years his junior: dark-haired Natasha Fraser, seventeen-year-old grandchild of Britain's Lord Longford and the daughter of best-selling bi-ographer Lady Antonia Fraser.

When news of their secret meetings in London hit the papers, Natasha's family was anything but incensed. They even invited him to attend the upcoming wedding of Lady Antonia to playwright Harold Pinter.

Jerry was less hospitable. She warned Natasha in no un-certain terms to stay away from her man. Not that Hall blamed Mick. "If a man didn't look at other girls he wouldn't be normal," she said. "I don't believe in monog-amy. I know because I was once in love with two men at the same time."

Knowing that Mick slavishly followed accounts of his life in the press, Hall fought back with flattery. "Mick's eter-nally young," she told one reporter. "He's still a kid at heart, but he's also one of the few men I know who can get into girl talk . . . about makeup and things like that. He's a genius, always ahead of everybody."

As for Jagger's prowess: "Mick is one of the sexiest men in the world and the best lover I've ever had." She even claimed to fantasize about him on the job. "I can't believe how weird and dirty he is," gushed Hall. "When I have to be sexy in front of the camera, I think of Mick and it al-ways does the trick."

That Christmas Eve, Jagger and Jerry invited Andy Warhol, Ahmet Ertegun, Earl McGrath, and the Hall family over to the town house on Central Park West for a holiday lunch. Jerry stood in the kitchen fussing over the turkey, the very picture of domestic bliss—until she unzipped her frilly apron and pulled out a cloth penis. She then went back to her duties, turkey baster in one hand and phallus in the other.

Jagger took the artistic depiction of male genitalia more seriously, investing thousands in graphic paintings of penises by Andy Warhol. Whenever her mother would come to visit from Texas, Jerry scrambled to take them down off the wall. For the new album *Tattoo You* Jagger even mentioned decorating the back cover with a photograph of a tattooed phallus. The Stones had come a long way since the *Beggars Banquet* bathroom-wall controversy. Or had they?

On its surface the true story of a man obsessed with building an opera house on a Peruvian mountaintop hardly seemed the perfect vehicle for Jagger. Yet Mick approached German director Werner Herzog for the lead role in *Fitzcarraldo*. Herzog cast Jason Robards in the part, but did offer Mick a supporting role as a simpleton actor who spends most of the film spouting Shakespearean soliloquies. Jagger grabbed it.

The day after Christmas Jagger departed for the Amazon jungle. No sooner did the cast and crew arrive and pitch their camp on the banks of the Amazon than tribal Indians in the region—supposedly headhunters—went on a rampage. Before long shooting resumed under conditions that Jagger quickly found intolerable. Everyone lived in tents, without electricity or direct contact with the outside world. Twice a week someone would venture into the nearest town to pick up whatever mail might have made it via the Peruvian postal system.

Midway through shooting Robards came down with a severe case of amoebic dysentery and quit the production, charging unsafe conditions on the set. According to Jagger mishaps during filming claimed five lives. Eventually the entire film was reshot with Klaus Kinski in the lead role.

Jagger seized upon this opportunity to bow out of *Fitzcarraldo*, citing his own commitment to tour with the Stones in 1981. In reality Jagger confided to friends that he was "cold, wet, tired, scared, and fed up" with conditions on the set. Herzog claimed to have been so impressed with Jagger's performance he couldn't bear to see anyone else in the role of the dim-witted actor. Thus Jagger's character was written out of the script entirely.

Mick's ordeal in the jungles of South America did not dampen his desire to become a movie star, however. He turned down a $2 million offer to play Rooster in Ray Stark's film version of *Annie*, but snapped up the movie rights to Gore Vidal's *Kalki* for $1.3 million. The 1979 best-seller dealt with a Vietnam veteran who claims to be the reincarnation of the Hindu god Vishnu. Jagger also screen-tested, without success, for the role of Mozart in *Amadeus*.

"Start me up, I'll never stop." Twenty years after Jagger and Richards first met on the train-station platform in Dartford, it seemed there could be no more fitting slogan for the Stones as they got ready to launch another history-making tour in the summer and fall of 1981.

Originally recorded in 1977 as a reggae tune, "Start Me Up" was dusted off, rerecorded, remixed, and released as a single in August. Propelled by Richards's throbbing opening chords, the song was not only an enormous hit for the Stones but their anthem for the new decade.

Tattoo You assumed the customary No. 1 position the week it was released, and critics hailed the new album as a sign that the Stones had at last stopped flirting with disco and reggae and returned to their rock roots. "On earlier albums," wrote Robert Palmer in *The New York Times*, "the Stones played the role of aging adolescents; they boasted, they swaggered, they portrayed themselves as down-and-out rebels even when they were living in luxury. On *Tattoo*

You they are playing themselves; they have grown up. But will the young people who make up the rock concert audience pay to see a bunch of grown-ups play rock and roll? One suspects that they will if those grown-ups are the Rolling Stones."

Jagger was determined not to appear *too* grown up. During six weeks at the Stones' rehearsal camp in rural North Brookfield, Massachusetts, Mick trained like a boxer preparing for a title bout. While Keith chain-smoked Marlboros and breakfasted on Stolichnaya over ice, Mick's daily regimen included a seven-mile run, weight-lifting, and the calisthenics Joe Jagger had drilled into him as a child. "Hours of torture every day," he said at the time. "Stretching, gymnastics, running. You can't do what I do onstage for two and a half hours without being in shape, and it's much harder as I get older." By the time the tour started, Mick weighed 125 pounds and had a twenty-seven-inch waist.

When he wasn't sweating, Jagger was in charge of every detail from set designs and costumes to publicity and finances. "No one else," Mick griped, "lifts a finger." Besides, Jagger insisted, he was only going ahead with the tour because "the others pleaded with me until I said yes. I mean a tour is great fun for a while, but it's like sex; you don't want to do it all the time. I have to stay sober, in training for ten weeks, and it tears the life out of me."

There was still obvious tension between the Glimmer Twins. Richards had let Jagger make all the plans for the tour, but when he discovered at the last minute that Jagger planned to be hoisted aloft on a cherry picker, Keith blew up at Mick for making the tour look like "a fucking sideshow." He also criticized his partner for spending $1.2 million of the group's money on staging, most of it designed to showcase Mick. Intent on creating a spectacle that the fans could not soon forget, Jagger prevailed.

Once Richards walked into the basement recreation room the Stones all shared to play pool and encountered several flamboyantly effeminate designers inspecting Mick's costumes. Keith promised to pummel them if they returned. "It's love-hate all the way with those two," admitted their assistant, Jane Rose. "Constant friction."

Meantime a whole new generation, persuaded that they had never really seen a rock concert if they hadn't seen the Rolling Stones, clamored for tickets. John Lennon's untimely death only a few months before was at least partly responsible for the tumultuous response—there was no telling how much longer Jagger and his hard-living brethren would be around.

In New York alone 3.5 million people vied for 100,000 available tickets, making the $15 seats worth $250 and up on the black market. The scene was repeated throughout the country. Once Mick mounted a cherry picker and showered carnations on the frenzied opening-day throng of 90,000 at Philadelphia's JFK Stadium, it was clear this would make the 1978 tour pale by comparison.

Again, it was carried out with military precision. Each night, as they struck up the third-from-last song, "Brown Sugar," the limousines and vans were lined up backstage, ready to whisk the Stones to the airport. "By the time the kids were streaming into the parking lot," said Rolling Stones Records' then-President Art Collins, "we were already five miles away."

In the wake of Lennon's assassination Jagger was a little edgier than usual—and he had every reason to be. In Seattle a woman who approached Jagger carrying a .38 handgun was disarmed by a bodyguard and later arrested. In New Orleans thirty handguns were confiscated from audience members.

Jagger was more adamant than ever about carrying his own pistol when the situation looked potentially dangerous. And he had no qualms about pulling the trigger. "There would be no point in carrying a gun," he said matter-of-factly, "if you wouldn't use it."

HBO taped the final concert in Hampton Roads, Virginia, for a prime-time cable special. Jerry, dragging her full-length purple mink behind her, watched from the wings. While Jagger belted out "Satisfaction," a fan leapt onto the stage, zigzagged past security, and headed straight for him. Richards managed to take off his guitar, slam it over the fan's head, and resume playing as if nothing had happened. Needless to say, footage of the incident was cut from the HBO special.

The ten-week, twenty-eight-city tour grossed $50 million, making it the richest in history. It also made clear that the music was almost incidental; the Stones and Jagger in particular were bona fide global institutions. The 1981 tour was an event that, as one observer put it, divided Americans into two camps: the two million people who saw one of their forty-six concerts and the 224 million who wished they had. As a reflection of the Stones' newfound respectability, the tour was sponsored by Jovan Musk cologne for men.

Counting his take from the tour and royalties from *Tattoo You*, Jagger's personal fortune now topped $40 million. In poignant contrast his look-alike younger brother, Chris, his wife, Kari-Ann, and their three sons were on welfare in England while Chris struggled to make it as an actor. "It sounds awful to say it," he said sadly, "but I really don't know my brother that well."

Once the U.S. tour was over, Jagger focused not on family matters, but on pumping life into his stillborn movie career. An important first step was bringing *Kalki* to the screen. Vidal delivered a polished script based on his novel, and Jagger used it to line up Alec Guinness as his costar and Hal Ashby as director (Ashby had already shot the Stones' 1981 concert film, *Let's Spend the Night Together*). But the projected budget was $15 million, and even with his impressive lineup of talent Mick could only manage to wring $8 million out of European investors. Jagger could easily have made up the difference, but it was a risk he was not willing to take. After a few months the entire project collapsed.

In need of a little consolation, Jagger made the rounds of Manhattan's nightlife sans Jerry. Around the release of the

hit single "Waiting on a Friend," Jagger's sentimental celebration of his friendship with Richards, Mick was waiting
on several young ladies while Jerry was out of town.

A typical conquest was Julia (not her real name), whom
Jagger spotted at the birthday party of a mutual friend.
"Mick was with [Warhol associate] Fred Hughes," she recalled, "and he told Fred to switch places with me," she
remembered. "He was witty, charming, amusing—and I was
flattered by the attention."

That night they returned to his apartment and began a
brief affair. "He told me Jerry had spies everywhere," said
Julia, "and that he had to be very careful." The fling was
short lived—"a night, a half day, a lunch, an afternoon"—
and took place at his apartment and at hers.

"Mick was very good in bed," said Julia, "a perfectly normal, red-blooded male. There was nothing kinky—no
whips, knives, or chains. But *great* sex? Yes!"

Later, Julia was invited by a friend of Hall's to attend a
surprise birthday party for Jerry at Mr. Chow's restaurant in
New York. Julia's presence was certainly a surprise for Mick.
"We were all introduced," she recalled, "and Mick was very
convincing. If Jerry knew about our little interlude, she
didn't let on." Julia was not the only woman Jagger flirted
with that night. "He was after every girl in the room," recalled dancer Erica Bell, "right under the nose of his pregnant girlfriend."

Hall had mentioned the previous year that she wanted
to bear Mick a child by March of 1982 at the latest. With
that deadline passed, it became increasingly obvious that
Mick was beginning to chafe under the weight of domestic
bliss.

In the press Jagger professed his love for Hall. But he also
condemned the institution of marriage while candidly discussing his need for a varied sex life. "As far as I'm concerned," he stated, "marriage is just legalistic, contractual
claptrap."

As for sex: "Sex is important to me. For an artist it's
another form of expression." How important was it in his

relationship with Hall? "A woman who doesn't have an orgasm is not going to be happy, no matter how stimulating the intellectual conversation. She isn't going to stay with that man for long." Jagger was none too subtle in his view of fidelity. "I think it's inevitable in a long relationship that one or both partner is unfaithful to each other," he said. "I'm not saying you should do it every weekend. That wouldn't help things. . . ."

If there was any doubt that 1982 would be as chaotic as any other year for Mick, it quickly evaporated. Mick was in Paris putting the finishing touches on their *Still Life* 1981 tour album when news ricocheted around the world that he had suffered a fatal heart attack in his sleep at two A.M.

"I've got to laugh," said Jagger, shaking his head. "Already this year I've been shot twice, had an earlier heart attack and now today I'm dead all over again."

As the Rolling Stones tore across Europe during the spring and summer of 1982, the rift between Jagger and Richards widened appreciably. Jagger tried to rush the pace along, while Richards intentionally dragged his feet. During "Time Is on My Side," an early hit of which Richards was particularly fond, Jagger camped it up outrageously. "Jagger donned an absurd outfit and minced around the stage, a purse hanging from an exaggeratedly limp wrist," wrote journalist Nick Kent. "Richards fixed him with a withering glare. . . ." Later, Keith commandeered Jagger's cherry picker and was hoisted aloft for a lengthy guitar solo while Jagger, fuming, watched helplessly from the stage.

All the Stones' families were on hand backstage to celebrate the group's triumphant homecoming at London's Wembley Stadium—and, Hall hastened to point out, her fifth year with Mick. "He's the greatest boyfriend in the world," gushed Jerry. "He's so *understanding*."

And, it seemed for a time, vice versa. The fourteen-year difference in their ages was causing a strain in their relationship. Apparently Jagger didn't think the difference was big enough. Now that he was facing the big 4-0, Mick sought the company of women younger than Hall.

A convenient supply of worshipful teenagers was to be found among the daughters of his contemporaries. Jagger had known the celebrated artist Larry Rivers ever since Rivers's daughter Gwynne was a toddler. Rivers actually introduced his daughter to Mick on a visit to Montauk. She was fifteen at the time. Now that she was seventeen and lushly beautiful, Mick was in hot pursuit. Jagger and Gwynne deftly outmaneuvered the paparazzi for weeks, until he showed up at Studio 54 in the predawn hours to help her celebrate her eighteenth birthday. When a photographer shot the couple kissing on the dance floor, Jagger beat a hasty retreat.

At the same time he was dating Gwynne Rivers, Mick was involved with blond "Deb of the Decade" Cornelia Guest, eighteen-year-old daughter of New York social lions Winston and C. Z. Guest. Even more beguiling to Mick, Cornelia was the duke of Windsor's goddaughter. While the two partied at clubs like Regine's and Xenon, Hall's friends took bets on how Jerry was going to react.

Young women were not Jagger's only indulgence. Even while he was publicly denouncing drug use in an apparent effort to revamp his image during the "Just Say No" 1980s, Jagger was still observed using cocaine. "He would be taken to an upstairs room at Xenon," said McGough, "where he was given free coke for *hours*."

McGough watched Guest leave one event at Xenon, and then trailed Jagger when he left an hour later. "Mick went to the Carlyle Hotel, and she was sitting in the lobby with a girlfriend, waiting for him at five-thirty in the morning. Mick had made her go to the Carlyle and wait for him!" Jagger kicked and shrieked at the waiting photographers, then grabbed Guest and escorted her upstairs.

A week later McGough and several other photographers were waiting to shoot Paul McCartney at New York's Kennedy Airport when he noticed Jagger step off a plane and head for his waiting Lincoln Town Car. Jagger was, said McGough, "completely drunk." As soon as he spotted

McGough, Jagger went after him. "What do you want?" Mick demanded.

"We had a tip Paul McCartney was on the plane," replied McGough.

"Well, *fuck* Paul McCartney," Jagger shouted back. "He's nothing but a fucking asshole." With that he kicked photographer Ron Galella in the groin, smashed his camera and staggered toward the waiting car.

When she read of Mick's flings with Rivers and Guest, Jerry was livid. She had tolerated much over their years together, not the least of which were his mood swings. "He covers the spectrum," observed Liz Derringer. "Mick can be so charming and loving and sweet you end up treating him like a teddy bear. Mick can also be snotty and nasty and venom-mouthed and snarl at you. You just shrivel. You shrink and you walk away."

Hall also endured some not-so-good-natured ribbing. "Mick would imitate Jerry's Texas accent sometimes," said a friend, "and you'd cringe out of embarrassment for her."

Jerry was even willing to tolerate Mick's infidelity as long as he exercised a modicum of discretion. But now she was convinced that he was flaunting his affairs with ever-younger women in a calculated effort to humiliate her.

Hall would often come home and find other women's rings or earrings on the nightstand by their bed. When she picked up the phone, there was invariably a strange woman on the line.

Jerry moved out, though she and Mick decided to keep dating. According to Hall, Jagger stood her up on three separate occasions, explaining each time that he was " 'out with some eighteen-year-old debutante'—you know," fumed Hall, "rubbing it in."

Hall's revenge was swift, and excruciatingly public. She abruptly ran off with another man—not a rock star or even a member of the tanned and moneyed Eurotrash set. Jerry galloped off into the sunset with stocky, married forty-six-year-old British-born horse breeder Robert Sangster.

Why Sangster? "Where could I go after Mick?" the British columnist Nigel Dempster quoted Hall as saying. "Robert can buy him out ten times over." Her calculations were not far off the mark. Boasting upwards of three hundred thoroughbreds in England, Ireland, and Australia, Sangster was regarded as the most powerful man in the world of horse racing. His personal fortune was estimated at some $400 million. Even though the 1981–1982 U.S. and European tours grossed a combined $75 million, Jagger lagged seriously behind his competition. "The guy," commented a friend of Jagger and Hall, "makes Mick look like he's on welfare."

It was not Sangster's first scandalous affair. He had left his first wife in 1976 to run off with Susan Peacock, the then-wife of Australian Foreign Minister Andrew Peacock. They left their respective spouses to live at the Nunnery, a renovated nineteenth-century convent on the Isle of Man.

While his wife, Susan, kept busy overseeing the redecorating of their $6 million mansion in Sydney, Sangster and Hall—both ostensibly in California on business—checked into adjoining suites at the Beverly Wilshire Hotel.

Not since Liz Taylor dumped Eddie Fisher for Richard Burton had anyone been so publicly cuckolded. MICK AND JERRY SPLIT blared the *People* magazine cover story, which went on to note that "Mick's curiously durable romance with supermodel Jerry Hall—a five-year union that has made them rock's First Couple—may have shattered."

Hall coyly insisted that she had "no hard feelings toward Mick at all. I am sorry what was intended as a private and possibly temporary parting has embarrassed him." She allowed that Jagger was "obviously upset. Who wouldn't be, with so much wild gossip flying about?"

The "wild gossip" in fact devastated Jagger. He phoned Jerry and, sobbing uncontrollably, begged her to come back to him. (Sangster, apparently privy to the call, said Jagger "cried like a big baby.") Hall agreed to rendezvous with Jagger in Paris. When Jerry got off her plane at Charles de Gaulle airport, Mick jumped out from behind a pillar to surprise her. "Where have you been, then?" he asked as she rushed into his arms.

The reunion was short lived; during the limousine ride from the airport to their Paris apartment, Jagger and Hall exchanged heated accusations. The next day she flew back to New York, vowing not to see Mick again.

Left behind in Paris, Jagger was consoled by his old friend Roman Polanski. The famed director was living in Paris as a fugitive from U.S. justice, charged with having had sex with a thirteen-year-old girl. Mick spent the next two nights prowling Paris's nightclubs, collecting women as he went along. After one all-night binge he stumbled home to his apartment with no fewer than nine French beauties. "The last thing I want to hear," he mumbled, "is English voices."

Jagger lured Hall back to Paris in time to celebrate Thanksgiving together. His bait: the promise that they could at last start a family of their own.

Not everyone, apparently, was pleased with their reconciliation. While Mick and Jerry holidayed in Barbados that December, someone scrawled insults and obscenities in red paint across the front of their new West Eighty-first Street town house in New York. The tamer messages: HOT HAG JERRY and JERRY HAG HALL.

That Christmas, Cornelia Guest went through her closet in search of a dazzling evening outfit to lend to a friend. Guest came upon a flashy, double-breasted black lamé jacket, and told the other girl to try it on. "It's spectacular," said Guest's friend, checking herself out in the mirror. "Oh, it should be," replied Cornelia. "It's Mick's."

It had been six weeks since his tearful reconciliation with Hall. Yet it seemed that precious little had changed in the private life of Mick Jagger. Tina Turner, the woman whose moves Mick coopted, gave a much-ballyhooed concert at the Ritz in New York. At the special table reserved for him upstairs, Jagger sat with a beautiful Oriental woman. "He's just sitting there with his dark glasses on," recalled photographer McGough, "and she's got her hands down his pants. Everybody in the room was staring at them." At that point the club's owner warned McGough, "If you take pictures, I'm going to bust your head."

In the predawn hours Jagger sneaked down a back staircase at the club, then led photographers on a high-speed chase to his apartment. When the pursuing paparazzi rushed past the doorman and up to Jagger's floor, he was startled. With memories of Lennon's death still fresh he thought for a moment that he might be attacked. Later Jagger told one of the photographers that he had come perilously close to being killed. "My bodyguard almost shot you. *Please*," Jagger pleaded, "don't do that again."

Mick was not, it turned out, entirely incapable of change. Jagger's contact with his eldest child had, to be sure, always been sporadic. Yet on her twelfth birthday Karis returned from a surprise party in her honor at the home of Sting to find three presents from Mick. The most important gift was a phone call from him. Hunt said she wanted to "jump up and down and cheer" when the call came through from New York because it signified that Jagger wanted to be a part of Karis's life. From that point on, he was.

At the end of 1982 the famed English publisher Lord Weidenfeld plunked down $5 million for the rights to Mick's memoirs—the largest advance for a book in British history. Eight years and several ghost writers later Jagger reluctantly paid the money back. One of Jagger's friends theorized that Jagger was congenitally incapable of telling the whole truth. Others theorized that drug use had clouded his memory, particularly when it came to the early years of his career. As the saying went, if you could remember the sixties, you weren't really there.

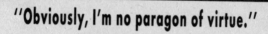

"Obviously, I'm no paragon of virtue."

It was the biggest-selling album of all time, spawning seven monster singles, spending thirty-seven weeks at No. 1 and selling 40 million copies. Jagger eyed the phenomenal success of Michael Jackson's *Thriller* with envy. As an artist he respected Jackson's work. As a businessman he knew that in the hands of the wrong record company *Thriller* would never have been the epic sensation it turned out to be, regardless of Jackson's talent.

While "Billy Jean" and "Beat It" blasted out of car radios everywhere, Jagger embarked on the daunting task of hammering out a new distribution deal for Rolling Stones Records. Mick dealt from a unique position of strength within the industry. He not only possessed all the charisma and allure of a pop superstar, but he was also widely respected by the record company "suits" as a sophisticated, no-nonsense negotiatior.

The Stones' last four albums had been global smash hits, and their headline-making tour had been the biggest ever. Jagger himself appeared to be at the zenith of his powers, simultaneously striking fear, love, loathing, and lust in the hearts of trembling teens as well as their baby boomer parents. More than anyone else on the planet Mick had made shock chic.

Jagger had long toyed with the notion of launching a solo career, and there seemed no better time to do it. In his own bid for freedom from the constraints of a group, Jackson had succeeded spectacularly. Jagger wanted to know the Gloved One's secret. "Mick became obsessed with Michael Jackson," said a colleague. "He wanted to know every detail about Jackson's life, his contract with Columbia, how the *Thriller* singles were selling, who was pulling the strings."

Certainly one of the main string-pullers was Columbia Records President Walter Yetnikoff. In sharp contrast to Atlantic Records' suave Ahmet Ertegun, Yetnikoff was bellicose, burly, and crude. Yet Jagger and Yetnikoff, who had also championed Bruce Springsteen, seemed oddly compatible.

In a bold move even for the high-flying Yetnikoff, he offered twice what Ertegun could afford to pay: a staggering $28 million for the Stones, including part of their backlist and Jagger's first two solo albums. Still basking in the glow of Jackson's solo career, Yetnikoff was confident that the rock god of *his* youth would pay off just as handsomely.

During the complex contract negotiations Jagger found Yetnikoff to be a worthy adversary. Yetnikoff recalled a meeting at the Ritz Hotel in Paris: "Mick is there on one side of the table, Keith is there, Prince Rupert—I don't know what he's prince *of*—the Stones' financial adviser, and we get to a point about the Stones having the right to select singles from their album product. We're disagreeing over the numbers. Suddenly Jagger explodes: 'You fat fucking record executives!' he screams. 'What do you know?' He jumps up. *I* jump up. 'Fuck you!' I scream back. I'm pretty sure I can take him, but I don't want to get into a real fistfight. He backs down. I think he has to try you—it's part of his personality—but *nobody* out-*geschreis* me." Once they finally hammered out the details, Jagger, Richards, and Yetnikoff signed what was then the richest record contract in history at three o'clock in the morning.

That March, a month after the Stones' concert documentary *Let's Spend the Night Together* was released to mixed reviews, there was talk of another contract—the one reportedly taken out on the life of Mick Jagger following the events at Altamont. Testifying before a U.S. Senate Judiciary Committee, a former Cleveland Hell's Angel identified only as "Butch" told stunned committee members that the Angels had vowed revenge on Jagger for not standing behind them when Meredith Hunter was stabbed to death at the free concert in 1969.

Butch claimed that there had already been two attempts at carrying out the contract. In 1975 a Hell's Angel carrying a gun equipped with a silencer staked out the Plaza Hotel and waited for the Stones. "He stalked them," said Butch, "but they never showed up."

The Angels apparently tried again in 1979, setting out in a rubber raft to plant plastic explosives under Jagger's Montauk house. "They was gonna put a bomb up underneath it," the former Angel testified. "They were gonna blow the whole band and everybody in the party up." The plan supposedly fell apart when the raft sprang a leak and sank with the explosives still on it.

"Whoever does it, well, it will be quite a trophy," Butch went on. "They swear they will do it. . . . This has been discussed many times. . . . Eventually it will happen."

Within a week Hell's Angels leaders held a press conference in New York to deny the allegations. The Angels, said a spokesman, just wanted to "lay to rest the rumors that for fourteen years there has been a contract out to kill Mick Jagger." In truth, they were embarrassed by stories that depicted them as bunglers. Mick, not entirely reassured, made sure his .38 was loaded when he wasn't being shadowed by bodyguards.

The furor over the alleged death plot did not dampen Mick's enthusiasm over his debut in a dramatic role on television. Coaxed by his longtime friend Shelley Duvall to act in an episode of her star-studded *Faerie Tale Theatre* series, Jagger assayed the role of the emperor in Hans Christian Andersen's *The Nightingale*. To sweeten the pot Jerry and another pal, Anjelica Huston, had bit parts in the classic fable.

"Anyone who wonders if forty-plus rock 'n' roll idols

have a future," wrote Bob Brewin in *The Village Voice*, "look no further than Mick Jagger's magical transformation from his usual hyperkinetic self into an autocratically reserved emperor of Cathay."

Buoyed by the response to his first acting role in years, Jagger offered a reported seven figures for the rights to portray Gregory McDonald's *Fletch* character on screen. "I'm a great admirer of Mick," conceded the author. "He's electrifying onstage. But he's certainly no one's idea of an American male!" With Chevy Chase in the title role *Fletch* and its sequel became box-office blockbusters.

As the summer approached, the world suddenly took note of a sobering fact: Mick Jagger was turning forty. Such staid publications as the *Times* of London, *The Washington Post*, and *The New York Times* devoted columns to contemplating the true meaning of this cultural milestone.

The most thought-provoking (if not altogether laudatory) of these commentaries was a lengthy birthday message from Mick's friend Pete Townshend published in the the *Times* of London under the headline JAGGER: A BUTTERFLY REACHES 40. Townshend, given to public displays of affection, surprised onlookers when the two emerged from the New York nightclub Trax and kissed good-night.

"Jagger and David Bowie," wrote Townshend, "are two of the few people in the mainstream of rock to whom I can talk in the knowledge that they understand precisely what I mean when I talk about pressure. . . . I am anxious, therefore, not to alienate Jagger."

That caveat aside, Townshend went on to admit that "Jagger wrote the blues before I did, made a million before I did . . . tried LSD, DMT, cocaine, marijuana, and so on before I did. He probably had a hundred groupies before I even poured one a polite drink back in the Holiday Inn."

Townshend went on to speculate that Jagger's beauty was "his own greatest joy," confessing "when I am with Jagger I do love to look at him. He is still very beautiful in my eyes; much has been said of his 'androgynous' attraction, and I suppose my response to his physical presence confirms all that." Townshend also worried whether Mick would "suffer (as Olivier is said to have suffered) if youthful beauty flees in late middle age."

Townshend asked rhetorically if Jagger was really a "ruthless, conniving, duplicitous, scheming evil-touched, money-greedy, sex-mad, cowardly, vain, power-hungry swine." He concluded by predicting that "Mick will still be beautiful when he's fifty. . . . His talent will be as strong at fifty as it is today."

The object of all this rumination hied off to a cozy Vermont inn with Hall. He checked out the next morning, said the innkeeper, "with a smile on his face."

Shortly after his birthday Jerry learned she was expecting. Years earlier Hall had become pregnant by Bryan Ferry and underwent an abortion procedure that left her traumatized. This time the blessed event was not entirely a surprise; she had been trying to conceive for over six months, and it was only after visits to medical experts in Paris, London, and Manhattan that she became pregnant. Hall's first official act as a mother-to-be was to contact Yves Saint Laurent. He did not have a line of maternity wear, but he agreed to whip up a few designs expressly for her.

Mick was thrilled at the prospect of becoming a father again, but not so thrilled that he would marry Jerry without a prenuptial agreement. Jagger did propose—he had hoped they would make it to the altar before the baby's arrival— but Hall steadfastly refused to sign away her claim to Jagger's massive fortune.

While Jagger reportedly pressured Hall in private to see his barristers and sign a prenuptial contract, the press was hearing a different story. Mick said he wanted to have a total of three children with Hall, but marriage? "Nah, definitely not. It gives me claustrophobia."

Unlike Bianca before her, Jerry at first stood her ground on the issue of marital property rights. But even after she capitulated to the demand several years later, Jagger balked at matrimony.

* * *

Undercover, the Stones' last original album for Atlantic, triggered the usual controversy upon its release in November 1983. Easily one of the group's most violence-laden offerings, the album featured songs like "Tie You Up," "Too Much Blood," and "Pretty Beat Up." Sample lyric: "He cut off her head, put her body in the refrigerator, and ate her piece by piece!"

Feminists were outraged by the blatantly misogynist lyrics. In the Julian Temple–directed "Undercover of the Night" video, Keith played the leader of a group of Latin American terrorists who kidnap Jagger. The bloody vignette was banned by the BBC for being exceedingly violent—a move Jagger blasted as censorship. (Another video based on the album, "She's So Hot," starred Anita Morris as a writhing nymphomaniac. One scene, in which Morris's undulations cause the buttons on one man's pants to burst, had to be recut after this video was banned by MTV).

Protests and bannings would normally be counted on to turn even a mediocre record into a hit. Not so this time. Public as well as critical reaction was lukewarm, and in the U.S. *Undercover* topped out at No. 4—the first time in fourteen years that a Stones album had not made it to the top of the charts.

Jagger's first solo album—which would feature Jeff Beck, Herbie Hancock, and Pete Townshend, among others—was still in its embryonic stages when Jerry gave birth to an eight-pound, two-ounce baby girl on March 2, 1984, at New York's Lenox Hill Hospital. Mick was on hand for the event—including a few tense moments when the obstetrician realized the umbilical cord had become wrapped around the infant's neck. After the baby let out her first healthy wail, Mom declared that little Elizabeth Scarlett had "the cutest lips, just like her daddy."

Four days later photographers were waiting to snap the first pictures of the littlest Jagger when she was spirited out a side entrance of the hospital by a nurse and whisked off to West Eighty-first Street. In the ensuing scuffle outside Jagger's town house bodyguards punched one photographer in the stomach and hurled another to the pavement, knocking him unconscious. All the while Mick dozed upstairs.

Jagger, in fact, turned out to be of little help in the nursery. He did not change diapers, and became agitated when Jerry brought Elizabeth Scarlett to the couple's bed in the middle of the night to be breast-fed. Jagger claimed he could not stand the smell of Jerry's breast milk.

Elizabeth Scarlett was barely six weeks old when her father went to New York's Foley Square and told a federal judge that he wanted Allen Klein "out of our future" once and for all. Jagger testified that Klein wanted "a hold on our careers," and that the Stones had been "trying to get rid of him since 1972 and still are."

Now that the Stones' pre-1970 hits still under Klein's control were being rereleased on compact disks, additional millions were at stake. A week after he testified, Jagger dropped the suit when he got what he really wanted—a promise from Klein to pay the Stones their royalties on time.

Jagger went straight from the courthouse to the Helmsley Palace hotel for a meeting with Michael Jackson. Having just taped Bette Midler's "Beast of Burden" video at L.A.'s Peppermint Lounge, Mick was now being courted by the music industry's top-grossing artist to record a duet.

Jackson had already forged a profitable relationship with Mick's contemporary, Paul McCartney. After they paired up to record two hits, "The Girl Is Mine" and "Say Say Say," Jackson paid $47.5 million for publishing rights to the Beatles' songs.

While Jackson admired McCartney as a composer but not as a singer, he owed many of his onstage moves to Jagger; Mick was grabbing his crotch years before Jackson and Madonna coopted the gesture in the late 1980s. He was also intrigued by the way in which Jagger had been able to combine androgyny with a certain raw animal power onstage. "Michael was very hurt by the cracks people made about his sexuality," said a friend of Jackson's. "He saw that Mick could wear lipstick, sashay around, and still be thought of as a macho rocker. Michael wanted to find out Mick's secret."

"You've got your family, you don't need me," Jagger told Michael when Jackson asked him to record "State of Shock." Jackson insisted, and after several pleading phone calls Jagger relented. "State of Shock" was actually a godsend for Mick. Now hard at work on his solo album, he was beginning to have doubts. Virtually guaranteed to be a hit, the duet with Jackson would be Mick's first tentative halfstep toward independence.

With the Jacksons singing backup, "State of Shock" was recorded at the A & R Studio in New York City. Both men walked away from the experience unimpressed. Jagger found Jackson limp and boring. "Michael's very lightweight," Jagger said. "He's like froth on beer."

Jackson complained that Mick's off-key singing made their duet practically unreleasable. "How did *he* ever get to be a star?" Jackson asked. "I just don't get it. He doesn't sell as many records as I do."

On June 29 the Stones' last album for Atlantic, a collection of their recent hits entitled *Rewind*, was released. The next day "State of Shock" hit the record stores and rocketed to No. 3. Bolstered by the single's success Mick went back to work on his solo album, which he recorded in London, Jamaica, and New York.

His fellow Stones were livid. By unilaterally deciding to devote six months to his own project, Jagger in effect held the other Stones hostage to his solo career. Richards refused to return Jagger's phone calls for weeks, and in July of 1984 Wyman publicly entered the fray.

Wyman had kept a detailed diary ever since the group got together in 1961. Unable to remember much of what happened to the Stones prior to the mid-1970s, Jagger called up the stone-faced guitarist and asked for a little help. Wyman's reply: "Get stuffed. If you really want to know what happened, wait and read *my* book."

Wyman accused Jagger of being "lost in his own image. I've lost touch with whoever Mick is now," he continued. "I'm sure he has as well."

With rumors of the group's imminent demise flying on both sides of the Atlantic, all the Stones convened in London to sort out their differences. Within minutes the crisis session had dissolved into a shouting match.

Two weeks later Charlie Watts was the only Stone present when Elizabeth Scarlett was christened at St. Mary Abbots Church in London. The event took on all the pomp of a royal baptism. Jerry wore a Chanel suit, pearls, and a wide-brimmed hat, Mick a gray suit, and the baby a gown created by the Emanuels, designers of the princess of Wales's wedding dress. In covering the ceremony the British press made a point of the fact that Elizabeth Scarlett's parents remained unmarried. "We are, after all, christening the baby," harrumphed the archdeacon of Middlesex, "not her mother and father."

Ever since Lennon's death Jagger had felt vulnerable— especially to the crazies who roamed New York City streets. Now that he had a baby to protect, he turned his five-story town house on West Eighty-first Street into a citadel.

Anyone who wanted to find the house in the first place had to have very specific directions, since there was no number on the front door. Television cameras scanned all the entrances, and three heavily armed, shaven-headed bodyguards were on duty around the clock. Visitors were allowed inside by invitation only ("If your name isn't on the list," said a friend, "you could wait outside all day").

Even people whose names did show up on the list were first escorted into a small vestibule where the guards checked their packages and scanned their bodies with metal detectors. Then they were escorted onto an elevator and led upstairs to a high-ceilinged Victorian rococo parlor with Carrara marble pilasters and MICK spelled out in blue letters on the white marble floor. Given all the security precautions it seemed strange that a Union Jack, hanging on the wall of another room, was clearly visible from the street.

If he was looking for enemies, Jagger could find them among the members of his own band. He lost his last ally—Charlie Watts—when the Stones got together in Amsterdam in late October to iron out their differences. With the powerful Yetnikoff as his champion at Columbia Records, Mick was now even more full of himself than usual. After a night of drinking with Richards, Jagger returned to their hotel, phoned Watts's room and woke him.

"Is that my drummer? Why don't you get your arse down here," commanded Mick. Watts calmly got dressed in a suit and tie, came down as Jagger had ordered—and sent Jagger flying with a left hook. "Don't ever call me 'your drummer' again," said Watts. "You're *my* fucking singer."

A week after the normally docile Watts had been driven by Mick's overweening ego to punch him in the face, Jagger told Charlie he was "forgiven" for his rash behavior. Watts had to be restrained from doing it again.

Just as he had always been with the Stones, Jagger was the ultimate hands-on manager when it came to recording his first solo album. From midafternoon until dawn he went over every nuance of every track with coproducers Bill Laswell and Nile Rodgers (the man behind Bowie's pivotal *Let's Dance* and Madonna's *Like a Virgin* album). If a scream was not bloodcurdling enough, he went back into the studio and spent hours perfecting it.

Jagger hired the photographer for the cover, then described exactly what he wanted: "A man and a woman. They've just made love, and now they're doing their thing. He's watching TV. She's exercising, or maybe she's on a weighing machine."

Mick also wrote the story for the video to accompany the LP, called the modeling agency to line up girls for it, and personally sifted through the candidates' eight-by-ten glossies ("She's got to have tits. She'll be in profile.")

This in addition to approving every detail of the publicity tour for the album, picking out the clothes to be worn in publicity shots, and holding the line on every aspect of the budget from entertainment to models to studio time. He even oversaw the purchase of airline tickets for the trip to Rio, where the video was to be shot ("You're pretty stupid if you pay the first price they quote you. Better shop around.")

At forty-one Jagger was still a fidgety, bouncing blur of nervous energy. "Jagger shifts in his chair and tugs at his ears, his nose, and his crotch," wrote Jay McInerney in *Esquire*. "He is a study in raving body language, exercising either a genuine sensuality or the license of a star to scratch himself whenever and wherever he itches. Or both."

The punishing work schedule did not seem to put a crimp in Jagger's social schedule. Several nights a week he still managed to troll such throbbing eighties nightspots as the Ritz, the Limelight, and the Palladium—seldom if ever with Jerry.

Jagger and Hall still did go out on the town periodically—usually to private soirees thrown by Studio 54 refugees. That November, Mick, Jerry, and two of her sisters were at a party in the chic but small Park Avenue apartment of Diane Von Furstenberg when Bianca walked in with her new boyfriend.

There were a few tense moments until Bianca walked over to her ex-husband and said "Mick, you've slept with everybody in this room!"

"Oh, yes, why look," replied Jagger, "there's Mark Shand and Andy Warhol! I've had them all." Then he turned to Bianca. "Well, you've fucked every man in the room." Later, Jagger claimed he had indeed slept with most of the women at the party, and his wife with several of the men.

The Stones began work on their *Dirty Work* album that December in Paris. Clearly distracted by the upcoming March release of his solo album, Mick, normally the creative engine that drove the Stones, merely seemed to be going through the motions.

Richards was, as he put it, so "pissed off" at Jagger for giving the Stones album short shrift that he, too, came close to physically attacking him. "But," Keith added, "there's no joy in punching a wimp."

In fact, during one recording session at the Pathé-Marconi studios in Paris, Richards grabbed Jagger by the throat and screamed, "I'll kill you! One day I'll wipe you clean away!" Most of the time Richards was content to simply needle his nemesis. Keith, who had once picked up a book by a "Brenda Jagger," now took to calling his friend "Brenda"; this new nickname infuriated Mick every time he heard it.

Ron Wood made his feelings known without confronting Mick directly. Ringo Starr, Peter Frampton, Rod Stewart, and all the Stones were invited to Wood's wedding in January—all the Stones except Mick Jagger. At the ceremony the reverend looked out at the crowd and remarked, "Some of you are considered rock idols. The Bible does not look too favorably upon idols."

On the home front Jagger once again reveled in his role as paterfamilias. He was photographed sitting in an armchair holding Elizabeth Scarlett, flanked by the baby's half sisters, Karis and Jade. Although Jade lived with Bianca and Karis with her mother in London, whenever the girls visited their father in New York he insisted on personally screening their boyfriends. He admitted that for a teenage boy, the experience of meeting Mick Jagger before taking out his daughter must have been "horrific." But Mick, once every parent's nightmare, was now very picky about the kinds of boys his own daughters dated.

"I think it's important to try and encourage the ones who are interesting and discourage the ones who are jerks," he explained with a perfectly straight face. "That doesn't mean that the girls don't go off with the ones who are jerks. But you've just got to check them out."

Jade was mortified by her father's comments about her in the press. She was already plotting her revenge, telling friends that she "couldn't wait" to have a baby to call Mick and Bianca Grandpa and Grandma.

Mick was surprised at how naturally Jerry took to motherhood, and relieved that she no longer badgered him about getting married. Hall's tolerance of Jagger's philandering was also remarkably high. "You can't have a stable relationship and go around and screw everything in sight," he said. "Yet I've told Jerry I also can't feel cut off from one half of the population. She's pretty good about it."

Still, Hall wanted desperately to marry Jagger. So much so that, whenever she traveled, Hall carried a plastic ring and an orange-blossom corsage in her suitcase—just in case.

On Christmas morning Hall ripped the wrapping off her gift from Jagger and stood in stunned disbelief. "Oh, Mick, wow!" she said, gazing at the present. "An electric iron, just what I need." Jagger suggested she look more closely, and when she did she found a magnificent sapphire bracelet clipped to the handle. (At about the same time, he told one interviewer that he found Jerry's love of jewelry and furs "a bit silly, passé, tacky, and . . . immature.")

She's the Boss was released in March of 1985 and promptly went platinum. A cut from the album, "Just Another Night" made it to No. 12 on the singles charts. A very respectable showing, though not the *Thriller*-sized event that had been widely predicted.

To promote the album and perhaps revive his long-dormant film career, Jagger hired *Undercover* director Julien Temple to make a ninety-minute video based on all the songs in *She's the Boss*. Filmed in Brazil, the video deals with a shallow, obscenely spoiled rock star whose world falls apart when he goes to Rio to make a video. As the rock star, Jagger stomps off the set with three women—all transvestites who beat him up and toss him onto a passing meat wagon.

At one point in the video Jagger, who concocted the story, could not resist camping it up in a wig and flaming red dress. In a small part as the rock star's girlfriend, Jerry wore skimpy bathing suits while Rae Dawn Chong wore very little or nothing at all. Jagger's friend Dennis Hopper, playing the director of the video-within-a-video, remained clothed.

Just as the debate had raged over the sex scenes in *Performance* fifteen years earlier, there were reports that Jagger and Chong weren't just acting. "Sex is the nature of both Mick's and my personalities," admitted Chong, "but we were never romantically or sexually involved."

Even Chong, who had appeared nude throughout the film *Quest for Fire*, was taken aback by the graphic nature of *She's the Boss* (later retitled *Running Out of Luck*). "Just sex scenes, pure and unadulterated," she said of the video. "I'm not at all against love scenes as long as they are tasteful. The scenes in this video are not tasteful." Chong breathed a sigh of relief when *Running Out of Luck* bypassed theaters and went straight to release on home video.

Live Aid more than compensated for these minor disappointments. After the Stones collectively did not even bother to respond to Bob Geldof's invitation ("I don't trust big charity events," said Richards), Jagger accepted as a solo act and turned his twenty-five-minute portion of the landmark event into a tour de force.

The concert took place at Philadelphia's JFK Stadium on July 11, 1985, before a live audience of 90,000 and a global television audience of 1.6 billion. Backed by Daryl Hall and John Oates, Jagger sang as he ripped off Tina Turner's skirt in front of a significant part of the world's population. Then Jagger and Turner bumped and ground their way through a sweatily lascivious rendition of "Honky Tonk Women." Jagger's Live Aid pièce de résistance: the world premiere of his eyebrow-raising "Dancing in the Streets" duet with David Bowie.

As much as Live Aid was a triumph for Jagger, it turned out to be a singular embarrassment for Keith Richards and Ron Wood. In a last-ditch effort to steal Jagger's thunder, Richards and Wood hastily agreed to back Bob Dylan for the show's much-ballyhooed grand finale. The result was shoddy and unprofessional; Stones fans around the world cringed in embarrassment as these two spindly-legged, vaguely pathetic outlaws from another era floundered without their leader. If anything, the sad spectacle proved that the Rolling Stones owed their longevity not to virtuoso guitar-playing but to Jagger's razzle-dazzle showmanship. "Nobody but Mick could front the Stones," said Richards's biographer Victor Bockris, "and every time Keith tried to find a replacement it was a disaster."

All pouty lips and pelvic thrust, Jagger still knew how to excite and provoke millions. Yet unlike Richards and Wood, he realized that the ravaged-rocker look was frowned upon by fitness-obsessed, button-down Yuppies. While they teetered on pointy boots and swilled Jack Daniel's, Mick wore knee-pads and drank bottled water onstage.

Jagger also sought to reshape his private image—something that his close friend David Bowie had undertaken with considerable success. Having shed his wife, Angela, in a messy divorce and made a marginally successful transition to stage (on Broadway in *The Elephant Man*) and film (*The Man Who Fell to Earth*), Bowie transformed himself from the King of Glitter Rock to a tastefully attired reflection of the Me Decade.

Seeking to make himself more acceptable to a conservative baby-boomer audience, Bowie now claimed that calling himself bisexual "was the biggest mistake I ever made." This startling reversal, accepted at face value, proved once again that the public's memory is exceedingly short.

If Bowie could pull off such blatant revisionism, there was no reason Jagger couldn't reinvent himself as well. In interview after interview he claimed that he had never really taken drugs or in any way promoted or advocated their use, that his songs were not misogynistic, that he had never really been a rebel, that there was no discord among the Stones, and that rumors concerning his bisexuality were just that—rumors.

Tall Tales, Jerry's autobiography, was published by Pocket Books that summer. The book made Jagger's transformation from rock's ultimate hell-raiser to wholesome family man complete. "Poor Mick," wrote Robert Hilburn in *The Los Angeles Times*. "There is a guy who has labored years to build a controversial mystique. His songs have been attacked as sexist by feminist groups and as corrupting by parental organizations. None of which hurt sales. But Hall bares all: Mick is really this softhearted sweetie-poo."

On August 28, 1985, the "softhearted sweetie-poo" was on hand when, after twelve hours of labor, Jerry gave birth to seven-pound James Leroy Augustin Jagger. Mick held Hall's hand, but turned so squeamish that he faced the wall rather than watch the delivery. When the doctor handed Jagger a pair of scissors to cut the umbilical cord, Mick, horrified, shoved them away. "Oh, no," Jagger protested. "You have more experience. That's what I hired you for."

"I love my daughters," declared Jagger. "But there's nothing like having a first son." Concurred Jerry: "He's crazy about his girls, but to be honest, a fourth daughter would have been a real disappointment. Mick's so English, you know." At his christening in England, James's presents would include a silver potty.

When it was announced—erroneously, it turned out—that Jagger would now marry Hall because she had borne him a son, feminists were once again up in arms. "He's betrayed the youth of a whole generation of women who grew up with his music," said one. "Jagger stood for rebellion. Now he stands for chauvinism, for patriarchy, for all that's worst about tyrannical, unthinking men."

Hall had, in fact, kicked aside the last hurdle to their marriage. For the first time she was now offering to sign a prenuptial agreement just as Bianca had done. But Jagger remained unconvinced, and there was little Hall could do but wait for him to take the initiative and propose. "I'm not unhappy about the way we are," she sighed. "It's just that I'd rather be married."

Mick, meantime, did not object when Hall fattened her personal coffers by posing for pinup calendar shots that wound up in the pages of *Playboy*. For one of the sexy photos Jerry stood in front of a Christmas tree wearing a red ribbon—and nothing else.

Deprived of Mick's total involvement in recording the *Dirty Work* album, Richards leaned heavily on Stones stalwart Ian Stewart for moral support. Stu was on the way to meet Richards at the studio in London when he stopped at a West London clinic complaining of shortness of breath. While he sat in the waiting room, Stewart suffered a fatal heart attack. He was forty-seven.

All the Stones were shaken by Stu's death. "With him went our conscience," said Wyman. "How could we ever forget his immortal words in hundreds of dressing rooms as we waited to go onstage: 'Come on, my little shower of shit—you're *on*.' "

At the funeral attended by all the Stones as well as Eric Clapton, Glyn Johns, and Jeff Beck, Keith turned to Ron Wood and muttered, "Who's gonna tell us off *now* when we misbehave?" On February 23, 1986, Pete Townshend, Simon Kirk, Beck, and Clapton joined the Stones in a musical tribute to Stewart at London's 100 Club. The tragedy brought the band back together, if only for the moment. Richards and Jagger walked out of the club red eyed, their arms around each other's shoulders.

Two days later, at three A.M. at London's Roof Garden Club, Clapton presented his friends with the most coveted Grammy of all—the Lifetime Achievement Award. The ceremony, fed back live to the U.S. via satellite, was long overdue; amazingly, in their twenty-four years together the Stones had never won a Grammy.

Jagger thought the Lifetime Achievement honor pegged them as senior citizens. Yet the event offered the perfect opportunity to debut the video of their new single, a remake of the 1969 Bob and Earl hit "Harlem Shuffle," before a huge prime-time audience. Jagger was proud of the video, which showed cartoon characters cavorting with the Stones onstage at the "Kool Kat Club."

"Harlem Shuffle" was a hit, and so was the album it came from—though by Stones standards *Dirty Work*, which peaked at No. 4, was another major disappointment. "Unfortunately," wrote Geoffrey Himes in *The Washington Post*, "Jagger's vocals often sound as if they were phoned in as an afterthought."

Jagger and Richards resumed sniping at each other from afar. Keith blamed Jagger for sabotaging their debut album for Columbia by refusing to go on tour to support it. "This is the first album in a new contract," said Richards. "We'd be *idiots* not to get behind it."

Jagger stood by his decision not to tour with the Stones in 1986. The band members were in such bad shape physically, said Mick, "they couldn't walk across the Champs-Elysées, much less go on the road." Besides, he admitted, the last thing he wanted to do was "spend another year with the same people. I just wanted to be out. . . . I'm not nineteen anymore," he added. "The Rolling Stones are not my only interest in life."

As for the rumors that Mick was planning a solo tour with another band as backup, Richards left no doubt as to where he stood. "If Mick tours without this band," said Keith, *"I'll slit his fuckin' throat."*

Getting together at London's Elstree Studio to film the video for "One Hit to the Body," Jagger and Richards engaged in an on-camera tussle—all in fun, they later explained. Not everyone was convinced.

Even without a solo tour, that summer Jagger had plenty to keep him occupied. His theme from the Bette Midler–Danny DeVito film *Ruthless People* was released as a single by Epic records. Three days later, on June 20, 1986, Mick and Bowie performed "Dancin' in the Streets" before Charles and Diana at the Prince's Trust concert in Wembley Arena.

Jagger's appearance represented a small victory for Diana in her war with the stuffy prince. At home alone she would don her Sony Walkman and bop around the palace to the music of her favorite group, Duran Duran. Diana was also an ardent Jagger fan, and shortly after her marriage had planned to invite Jagger to tea at Kensington Palace.

Charles, keenly aware of Jagger's lady-killer reputation and his preference for long-stemmed blondes in Diana's age bracket, demanded that she cancel the affair. After an angry exchange she grudgingly obeyed. Charles did not object to the less threatening Phil Collins, however, and he was invited instead.

Drawn together by the success of their "Dancin' in the Street" duet, Jagger and Bowie were once again a fixture on the club scene. There was an embarrassing moment at one London disco when the man at the door beckoned Bowie in but barred Mick, calling him a "fossil." Both superstars turned on their heels and left, along with several outraged patrons who had overheard the remark. Bowie and Jagger also caused a stir when they showed up together at Prince's opening at Madison Square Garden. Bowie and Jagger once again began kicking around movie ideas—most notably a remake of *Some Like It Hot* that would have allowed them both to do most of their parts in drag.

When Madonna rolled into Wembley, all of Britain was Madonna crazed, and Jagger was no exception. Mick had long since forgotten sleeping with the pushy brunette New York groupie, and she was not about to remind him. At a party after the concert the first person they saw was Madonna's then-husband, the vituperative Sean Penn. To divert Penn's attention away from his wife, Bowie cornered Penn while Jagger chatted with Madonna. "After about forty-five minutes we switched places: I talked to Sean and David chatted up Madonna. I don't think Sean ever noticed."

Jagger claimed to have walked away from that meeting liking Madonna, but most of his comments about her to friends were less than charitable. "I'm so bored with Madonna," Jagger said. "I wish she would just go away and then I might even get to like her. Someone said that Madonna was a thimbleful of talent thrown into a sea of ambition and I don't think I'd argue too much with that."

Jerry was not at all threatened by Jagger's strange friendship with Bowie; she far preferred it to his dalliances with teenage debutantes and the daughters of his middle-aged friends. Quite apart from Mick, Jerry and David got along splendidly. Bowie joined Tina Turner, Michael Caine, and Faye Dunaway in singing "Happy Birthday" to Mick and Jerry at their London town house. (Tina turned up at Mick's forty-third birthday bash three weeks later, joined by Sting and Eric Clapton.)

That summer Jagger and Hall were also invited to fellow château owner Malcom Forbes's annual hot air ballooning party, and later to Forbes's sixty-seventh birthday party aboard his yacht, *The Highlander*. The flamboyant magazine publisher was an incorrigible celebrity-hound, but Jagger's fame was apparently not the only thing that Forbes found appealing. The divorced father of five had always kept up the charade of a romance with Elizabeth Taylor, but in truth Forbes was a closet gay who routinely cruised New York's rougher leather bars. One of America's great collectors, Forbes owned more Fabergé eggs than the Kremlin, perhaps the greatest collection of American autograph material (including a rare signed copy of the Emancipation Proclamation)—and, for a time, a Cecil Beaton painting of Mick Jagger's derriere.

Undaunted by the less-than-spectacular success of *She's the Boss*, Jagger spent the early months of 1987 at the Blue Wave Studios in Barbados recording his second solo album, *Primitive Cool*. Jerry decided to soak in the island sun with Elizabeth Scarlett and James before jetting off to Paris on a modeling assignment.

On January 21 Hall started a chain of events that would deal a huge setback to Jagger's newly crafted image as a clean-living family man. She drove to the airport to pick up a canvas bag, filled with sweaters for the Paris trip, sent along from the Jaggers' Mustique hideaway. Instead, customs officials showed her a cardboard box marked G. HALL.

"I'm sure it's not my bag," she told them. "But, well, look, I'll open it and if my things aren't in it, then it's not mine." She opened the box, and inside were plastic bags containing twenty pounds of marijuana worth $60,000 on the open market.

Hall was arrested, and wound up spending the night in a tiny, windowless concrete cell that stank of urine and excrement. There was no bed, so she crouched in a corner and waited for morning. She put her hand on the concrete floor and felt something sticky; it was then she realized she was crouching in a pool of blood.

At four A.M. she was let out to walk the prison hallways in her flimsy summer dress. "They just wanted to look at me," she later said. "They wanted to look at the girl with the golden hair."

The next morning Chief Magistrate Frank King ordered that Hall be released on $5,000 bail, but held on to her passport so that she wouldn't leave the country. After her release Hall showered five times to wash off the prison filth.

Facing a $50,000 fine and two years in prison, Jerry fought back in the press. "You know, I've never even had a traffic ticket," she protested. "Everyone who knows me knows that I'm very antidrug. My friends say I'm the Nancy Reagan of the rock 'n' roll world. My only vice is Chanel."

While she waited to go on trial, Hall, whose annual income now hovered around $1.5 million, faced the cancellation of $100,000 in modeling fees—not to mention long-term damage to her reputation. For Jagger it was all a worrisome replay of the drug arrests that had plagued the Stones in the 1960s and '70s. He knew this had to affect his career, just as he was planning his first solo tour for the following year. "It's a matter of guilt by association," he complained. "There will be countries that won't let me in to work—all that crap. The attitude is that there is no smoke without fire."

After a week-long hearing the judge dropped the charges for lack of evidence. "They wanted to set me up," Hall lashed out, "because I am an American, female, famous, and rich. I want an apology. There is nothing more dangerous than stupid people in power." Hall vowed never to set foot in Barbados again.

*   *   *

Amid the persistent rumors that the Rolling Stones were
no more, Keith Richards signed a solo deal with Richard
Branson's Virgin label. Jagger, meanwhile, filmed videos for
"Let's Work" and "Throwaway," two of the singles from his
new album. "See," he told British journalist John Blake,
weighing his words carefully, "things have not been going
well with the Rolling Stones for over five years, so I have
been trying to keep it together through all the ups and
downs the band has had. But I now find it just impossible.
I have really lost patience with it, and I am tired of trying
to glue everyone together."

In his new album Jagger made a concerted effort to distance himself from the Stones musically. Turning his back
on the nihilism of the past, Jagger touted a peculiar kind of
cockeyed optimism in "Primitive Cool." "Let's Work" was
a giddy celebration of the Puritan work ethic, while
"Throwaway" praised fidelity. In "War Baby," he served up
a syrupy plea for world peace. In "Kow Tow" and "Shoot
Off Your Mouth" Jagger took thinly disguised potshots at
his estranged alter ego, Keith.

Walter Yetnikoff and the CBS brass were ecstatic over the
reviews for *Primitive Cool* when it was released in September.
USA Today credited coproducer Dave Stewart of the Egoryth-
mics for the album's "tight, shimmery texture," and praised
Jagger for being "as kinetic and clever as ever. As the Rolling
Stones simmer on the back burner, Mick Jagger is at full boil."
Rolling Stone called the album "Mick Jagger's long overdue re-
juvenation," while *Newsday* noted what a "stylish" vocalist
Jagger had become.

The public disagreed. *Primitive Cool* was an unalloyed disaster, struggling to No. 41 on the charts. Jagger took time to
regroup. Mick was disappointed by the album's failure, but he
still regarded the Stones as a "millstone" around his neck. Most
of all, he feared that the other members of the group might
alienate young audiences, and that if the Stones went down
they'd take his career along with them.

Jagger had a point. Of all the Stones, Mick was the only one who did not look every minute of his age—at least not from the neck down. The others were stooped, wrinkled, bony, haggard-looking, and gray. "I can't go on the stage with them," he said. "They look like a bunch of pensioners. I don't need this bunch of old farts."

To prove it Jagger decided he would become the first Stone to tour Japan. As he planned his one-man assault on the Far East, it was hard to imagine that Jagger had just been dealt one of the most serious setbacks of his career.

Liz Derringer dropped by at the New York town house and found twenty-month-old Jimmy Jagger sitting in the living room, transfixed by a Tarzan movie on television. Suddenly Cheetah came swinging out of the trees and began, in true chimpanzee fashion, mugging, scratching, screeching, and jumping about. Jimmy's eyes widened, and he pointed to the screen. "Dada," he said. "Dada!"

Derringer shook her head and laughed. "Perfect," she said. "Just perfect."

"I think on Mick's part, there is a little bit of a Peter Pan complex."
—Keith Richards

"I can't go on pretending to be eighteen much longer."

Behind a phalanx of bodyguards Jagger bolted from the limousine, then ran a gauntlet of screaming fans to the doors of the Federal Courthouse in lower Manhattan. It was 1988, and once again Mick found himself testifying in his own defense—this time against charges of plagiarism.

Patrick Alley, a Jamaican reggae singer living in The Bronx, had accused Jagger of stealing the chorus for his 1985 single "Just Another Night" from a tune—also called "Just Another Night"—written by Alley six years earlier. Alley also claimed the drummer on Jagger's "Just Another Night" had played on *his* "Just Another Night" in 1979. Alley sought $7 million in damages.

"My credibility is on the line," snapped Jagger, who told the jury that he had never heard of either Alley or his song prior to writing "Just Another Night." He played tapes of "Brown Sugar" and "Let's Spend the Night Together" to illustrate how his music had evolved. When he hummed a few bars of "Jumpin' Jack Flash," cheers went up from the courtroom packed with fans.

After two days of deliberation the jury ruled in favor of

Mick—but not before one juror ran screaming to the bathroom after hearing tapes of both songs played one too many times.

The Japanese had waited more than a quarter century to see the Rolling Stones in the flesh, and as it turned out they would have to wait even longer. But when Jagger came in April of 1988 to give eight solo performances, that was good enough; Japanese rock and roll fans hailed his arrival as the second coming.

It quickly became obvious what the 170,000-plus fans had come to see: Jagger cut three of his solo numbers so he could spend more time strutting to Stones classics like "Under My Thumb" and "Honky Tonk Women." He did not short-change Japanese audiences in the spectacle department either. Backed by forty dancing girls clad in black and pink, Jagger sang "Sympathy for the Devil" wearing a Japanese devil mask. For the grand finale production of "Satisfaction" Jagger was ringed by smoking volcanoes. For those millions of Japanese fans who were unable to buy tickets, the concert was filmed for a prime-time television special. Jagger's total take for his Japanese escapade: $8 million, or $1 million a show.

Numbers like that eased the pain of having to cancel his U.S. tour because of disappointing advance sales. Abroad, audiences viewed Jagger as the soul of the Stones, and were willing to pay accordingly. As soon as he returned to New York, Jagger accepted an offer to tour Australia, this time for a reported $20 million.

There were other business offers Jagger found decidedly less appetizing. The Trend Connection, a Vienna-based novelty company, wanted permission to market his ashes in hourglasses to be sold one month after Jagger's death at $1 million per hourglass.

"Mick Jagger is the best symbol for a whole generation of action and motion in music," said Trend Connection co-owner Guenter Roth. The company figured that Jagger's ashes would fill at the very least a hundred hourglasses.

Jagger's heirs would hardly need the money. Rock's original renegade was now easily worth $100 million. Yet no amount of money could keep Jagger from suffering the frustrations that vex all parents of teenagers. While Karis was a model student at the same London school attended by Princess Margaret's children, sixteen-year-old Jade was proving herself to be a handful.

"Jade was a very sweet girl and fairly well grounded," said Bianca's personal secretary at the time, Barbara Levine. "But she was not a shy child and she seemed kind of worldly. Very hip."

Three years earlier, when she was thirteen, Mick had yanked Jade out of New York's exclusive Spence School because he feared Manhattan offered too many "distractions" for his daughter. After a thorough search Jagger enrolled Jade at St. Mary's School in the hamlet of Calne, some ninety miles west of London. Regarded as one of the best girls schools in England, St. Mary's was both academically demanding and far removed from the temptations of the big city.

In the spring of 1988 Jade informed her parents she was leaving school to accept a $1 million modeling contract. Dad and Mom refused. "Bianca and Mick were both concerned parents," said Levine, "but he was more indulgent, less focused, than she was. There were great battles between Bianca and Jade over the phone—screaming matches. Then Mick and Bianca would confer about what to do with her. In the end Mick offered to buy Jade *anything* just to stay in school."

"Anything" apparently wasn't enough. By way of divine retribution the man who had once been every parent's nightmare watched helplessly as his daughter was expelled from school for climbing out her bedroom window at two A.M. to meet her twenty-one-year-old boyfriend, Josh Astor.

The son of raincoat manufacturer Lord Kagan, Astor had been kicked out of Eton at fifteen and now lived on his sizable inheritance. Apparently he had a fondness for

Stones offspring. During a drug bust six weeks earlier Astor had been rousted out of bed nude. His companion at the time was reportedly Charlie Watts's daughter Serafina.

Astor was out partying at a London nightclub with Jade's best friend, sixteen-year-old Emma Ridley, when Jade called and pleaded with him to rescue her. Astor and Ridley, dubbed "Wild Child" by the British press for running off to marry a man twice her age, headed straight for the school.

Caught in the act of escaping, both girls were thrown out of school. "My dad will kill me!" cried Jade. "What shall I do? I can't stand school—I love Josh and I want to live with him. Why can't Dad see I have my own life to lead?"

Fuming, Jagger dragged Jade to his château in the Loire for a stern lecture. Wild Child Emma Ridley was as defiant as ever. "What a hypocrite!" she said of her friend's famous father. "Here is the big sixties rebel acting just like any other overprotective parent."

Jagger faced domestic turmoil of another sort that summer. Hall had given him an ultimatum: Either marry her by 1988—their tenth anniversary as a couple—or else. The deadline passed, and Jerry began laying the financial groundwork for a life without Jagger. By way of asserting her financial independence Hall signed a $1 million contract to launch her own swimwear line and accepted a $500,000 fee from a British company to appear in television spots for beef bouillon.

Since her fling with Robert Sangster had worked so well at getting Mick's undivided attention, Jerry also began seeing other men. There were reportedly flings with Lord James Neidpath and Count Adam Zamoyski, but it was Hall's flirtation with Lord David Ogilvy that Mick found especially annoying. At thirty, Ogilvy was not only substantially younger and handsomer than Mick, but he was also something Mick could never be: a true English aristocrat.

"At a party the other night," a friend was quoted as saying of Hall and Ogilvy, "they were dancing so close you would have needed a blowtorch to separate them." In retaliation Jagger flew off on a Caribbean vacation with twenty-three-year-old British model Camilla Nickerson.

In the interest of the children Jagger and Hall still put on a united front. Mick urged her to take a small part in the movie *Batman* (as the Joker, Mick's old friend Jack Nicholson disfigured Jerry with acid) and helped her prepare for her stage debut as Cherie in a Montclair, New Jersey, production of *Bus Stop*.

Jagger was on hand opening night to cheer her on. It was also his forty-fifth birthday. As the lights went down, Jagger slid into his seat and turned to his friend Liz Derringer. "Liz, got a joint?"

"No," she replied.

"Any coke?"

Derringer shook her head.

Jagger paused for a moment. "How about a blowjob, then?"

Derringer nearly collapsed on the floor laughing. "It was vintage Mick," she said. "He was kind of bored, I think. But he wanted to be there for Jerry."

At the opening-night cast party there was a big cake that said CONGRATULATIONS, JERRY on one side and HAPPY BIRTHDAY, MICK on the other. Would they ever marry? someone had the temerity to ask. "The M word," moaned Hall. "Golly, I'm tryin'! Y'all quit rubbin' it in!"

Meanwhile, Mick's professional marriage was foundering. While Jagger toured Down Under, Keith's solo album, *Talk Is Cheap*, was released to rave reviews. One of the songs, "You Don't Move Me," was a full-frontal assault on Mick ("What makes you so greedy/Makes you so seedy"). Richards embarked on a tour of his own to support *Talk Is Cheap*, and after the last show five hundred people attended his forty-fifth birthday party. Mick was not among them.

It was announced that the Rolling Stones would be inducted into the Rock and Roll Hall of Fame on January 18,

1989. The time had come for a showdown—a face-off between Jagger and Richards that would decide once and for all the fate of the Rolling Stones. If the band was truly finished, the Rock and Roll Hall of Fame Awards seemed like the perfect forum for making the announcement.

Jagger and Richards agreed to meet in Barbados ("It's Jerry that won't go back there," claimed Mick, "not me. I like the place.") Before he left, Keith told his wife of five years, Patti Hansen, to expect him back in two days or, in the unlikely event things worked out, a few weeks.

Minutes after their meeting began, Keith and Mick were shouting at each other. By the end of the first day they were sharing a joint and a bottle of Jack Daniel's—and laughing uncontrollably over the terrible things they had said about each other in the press. Richards called home to tell his "old lady" that he would not be home for weeks.

Following their induction into the Hall of Fame, Mick and Keith summoned the rest of the band to Barbados to record their first album in three years. One of the first cuts, with Jagger on guitar, was "Mixed Emotions," a torchy number Jagger had penned in reply to Richards's wounding "You Don't Move Me."

It had been nearly twenty years since Brian Jones's death, and they wanted to do something special to mark the occasion. For the song "Continental Drift," they hopped a plane to Morocco and enlisted the aid of the same JouJouka pipe musicians who had recorded with Brian back in the sixties. From beginning to end the *Steel Wheels* album took only ten weeks to produce.

Bill Graham, who had also produced Mick's solo tour of Japan, assumed he would be handling the Stones' upcoming *Steel Wheels* tour. But he could not match the $70 million guarantee of Toronto promoter Michael Cohl—far and away the biggest tour deal ever. Always the businessman, Jagger found this offer impossible to refuse. Even if the promoters took a financial bath, the Stones would get their millions. "The element of risk," said Mick, "was completely taken out."

To sweeten the pot Jagger approved plans to market up-scale Stones souvenirs. T-shirts bearing the lapping-tongue logo would continue to be a staple. But this time Rolling Stones Rockwear—everything from five-dollar kerchiefs to skateboards, sweatshirts, tennis shoes, and $450 leather bomber jackets—would also be sold at concert sites. For those unable to make it to a concert, the items would also be available at Rolling Stones boutiques in Penney's, Macy's, Marshall Field's, and Bloomingdale's.

For Graham, who had been strung along by Jagger and then told by a functionary that the job was going to someone else, the loss of the Stones tour was shattering. Graham was plunged into a downward spiral of depression that left him unable to function for months.

Michael Jackson was also less than thrilled with Jagger's ambitious touring plans. When Jackson's lawyer, John Branca, told him he would be in Barbados to meet with "Mick" on a business matter, Jackson exploded. *"Mick? You mean Mick Jagger?"* When Branca confessed that he would be handling the *Steel Wheels* Tour, Jackson, who had just completed his *Bad* Tour, began his interrogation: "Well, is it a big tour? It's not going to be as big as mine, is it?"

Jackson was reportedly frantic at the possibility that Jagger—the man he had dismissed as an off-key no-talent—was about to eclipse him. Not long after, Jackson fired Branca.

For a brief time that June, Jagger found himself supplanted on the front pages of Britain's tabloids by the marriage of fifty-two-year-old Bill Wyman to Mandy Smith, eighteen. Wyman had met his Lolita five years earlier, and paid for her private schooling even as he courted her. To add to the scandal Wyman's twenty-seven-year-old son Stephen was reportedly dating Smith's divorced mother. The May–December romance would soon end in acrimony, but for the time being Jagger quipped that the nubile Mrs. Wyman was keeping her husband "in shape" for the tour.

* * *

In July of 1989 the Stones descended on the Norman Rockwell–perfect town of Washington in Connecticut's horsey Litchfield Hills. Appropriately enough, the site for their six weeks of rehearsal was Wykeham Rise, a defunct girls' boarding school.

The locals, who numbered Dustin Hoffman, James Taylor, Meryl Streep, Stephen Sondheim, and Michael J. Fox among their many famous neighbors, were unfazed by the arrival of the World's Greatest Rock and Roll Band in their midst. Not even the sight of Jagger jogging backwards—a technique he employed to intensify his aerobic workout—caused much of a stir among the townsfolk.

Still, each warm summer night between six P.M. and four A.M.—the band's working hours—the curious would park near the school and listen to the strains of "Satisfaction" and "Honky Tonk Women" wafting through the maples and sycamores. A security guard patrolling the grounds was listening to the band play "Brown Sugar" full-throttle when the music stopped abruptly. "The night sort of became silent," he recalled. "I kept waiting for them to pick it up again, but nothing happened. Finally I walked over to the window and looked in. They were all huddled around looking at the sheet music, trying to remember how the song went."

The Stones and their wives gathered at Washington's Mayflower Inn for Mick's forty-sixth birthday party. It turned out to be an uncharacteristically staid event—"The perfect cure," said one guest, "for insomnia."

More accurately, the quiet before the storm. To formally announce the tour the boys rolled into Grand Central Terminal aboard an antique caboose and confronted more than three hundred radio, print, and TV reporters. No, it would not be the Stones' last tour, Jagger insisted. As for the much-publicized bickering between Jagger and Richards, Mick hugged his Glimmer Twin and said, "We don't have fights. We just have disagreements." Muttered Richards, "We both gave up masochism." It was left to Jagger to bring down the curtain. "Just one more question," he said, "because my mascara is running."

A few nights after the Grand Central press conference, more than seven hundred people—many of them Yale students—paid three dollars apiece to attend a "Rock Party with the Cruiser" at a New Haven club called Toad's Place. Instead, they gasped when the Stones stepped onstage and launched into an eleven-song sampler from the tour.

The *Steel Wheels* album, released on August 31, 1989, went straight to No. 3 and remained on the charts for nearly six months. In his cover story on the Stones entitled "Roll Them Bones," *Time* magazine's Jay Cocks rhapsodized over the Stones' rebirth: "Just look at these guys. Giants. Golems. Geezers with a quarter-century history together. After all the band's public bickering and rheumatic concertizing, after all this time and all these damn years, the Rolling Stones can still rock the boat. They are back all right."

The day the album was released, *Steel Wheels* started rolling across the continent. Kicking off the four-month tour of thirty-three cities at Veterans Stadium in Philadelphia, the Stones would reach more than three million fans. Jagger, aware that the Stones' faces sported more grooves than their records, worried that he might look like a parody of himself. "I just hope," he confided to a friend, "people don't laugh when I get out there."

To everyone's surprise the audiences were younger than ever. The baby boomers were present in force, to be sure. But their numbers were surpassed by teenagers and college-aged fans. "They don't have all this baggage and its much easier to deal with them," said Mick. "I like them all ages but there's no doubt that the younger the audience, the greater the energy. And that helps *you*."

In terms of pure spectacle *Steel Wheels* was the Stones' most ambitious undertaking ever. A crew of 380 technicians had been hired to construct and operate the two three-hundred-foot-long, ten-story-high "industrial holocaust" stage sets—the biggest ever built for a rock show.

The Stones' four generators put out 2.4 million watts, sufficient power to light forty city blocks. For "Honky Tonk Women," two fifty-foot-high Brobdingnagian beauties were inflated on either side of the stage. There were also plenty of pulsing strobes, piercing lasers, a three-hundred-foot wall of flame, and the requisite blinding fireworks.

At the center of this hurricane of sight and sound was Jagger, barely breaking a sweat as he pranced, jumped, sprinted, bounced, and mugged his way through twenty-seven songs over three hours. Crowds ranging in size from 60,000 to 120,000 gazed openmouthed as images of that furrowed face and adolescent body flashed overhead on billboard-sized video screens.

The band's four-night stint at the Los Angeles Coliseum reportedly upset Michael Jackson. "The Coliseum! The Coliseum!" he yelled at John Branca after hearing the news. "That's bigger than the Sports Arena, where I played! How many dates? They're not playing as many dates as me and my brothers played at Dodger Stadium, are they?"

Hollywood's A-list crowd could not have been more delighted, however. Madonna, Bruce Springsteen, Barbra Streisand, Meryl Streep, Warren Beatty, Michelle Pfeiffer, Priscilla Presley, Michael Douglas, Jack Nicholson, and Anjelica Huston all turned out to pay homage to the Stones. Mick clearly reveled in the adulation; an amused Richards now took to referring to Jagger as "Her Majesty."

There were also several old standbys hovering around Mick in L.A.—Clapton, Bowie, even Jagger's old flame Cornelia Guest. Mistakenly barred from the opening night party at Morton's: Guns N' Roses, the Stones' opening act.

It might not have been a mistake. "Mick was incredibly jealous of Axl Rose," said one observer on the tour. "Rose was preening around in his little jogging shorts, and the girls were all going nuts. Mick is extremely sensitive about his age and how he looks, and here was a kid who was easily young enough to be his son stealing his thunder. You could see from the way Mick watched Axl out of the corner of his eye that he was burning up. In that respect Mick was sort of like a woman jealous of another woman."

Jagger also felt hamstrung by Jerry's presence at several stops during the tour. This time all the Stones' wives made a point of tagging along to keep an eye on their middle-age-crazy spouses. When Eric Clapton appeared backstage with an eighteen-year-old model, Jagger watched him enviously. "Mick was torn between Clapton playing around with this young chick," said a member of the Stones entourage, "and Jerry standing there in her Chanel suit with the two towheaded kids. As soon as Eric turned his back, Mick was flirting with the girl outrageously. Jerry just ignored it, but you couldn't help but feel sorry for her."

The Stones were on the road when a devastating earthquake struck San Francisco in October of 1989. They contacted Bill Graham, who had not yet recovered from losing the tour, and asked what they could do to help. Graham suggested they contribute between $100,000 and $750,000 to earthquake relief.

Jagger wrote out a check for $250,000 to aid homeless quake victims, and on behalf of the Stones donated the same amount to victims of Hurricane Hugo in South Carolina. To show his concern Mick then toured two of the towns hardest hit by the quake, Santa Cruz and Watsonville, aboard a schoolbus packed with reporters.

The tour swaggered on through December. Commercially, critically, artistically, *Steel Wheels* was an undiluted triumph for the Stones. The U.S. tour alone grossed around $140 million and similar raids on Japan and Europe were planned for early 1990. A pay-per-view television broadcast of the final stop in Atlantic City reached 13.5 million homes—the largest pay-per-view audience ever. The *Steel Wheels* album went double-platinum. Both critics and readers of *Rolling Stone* voted the Stones Artists of the Year (as well as Best Band of the Year and as having had the Best Tour of the Year). The magazine also proclaimed the Stones' "Satisfaction" as best rock record of all time.

Jagger could scarcely imagine a better way to welcome the new decade.

After pocketing $30 million for two weeks at Tokyo's Korakuen Dome, Jagger and the Stones took what was now called their "Urban Jungle Tour" to thirty-seven European cities from Rotterdam to London. In addition to the fifty-foot-high Honky Tonk Women, the set for the European Tour featured several mammoth, rabid-looking hellhounds. Jagger punched and pummeled the genitals of one of these inflatable beasts to the tune of "Street Fighting Man."

Before the Urban Jungle Tour got under way, Angela Bowie told Joan Rivers before a nationwide television audience that she had once caught her then-husband David in bed with Mick. Jagger was furious; there was a whole new generation of fans that knew nothing of the Glitter Rock Era and his ambiguous sexual past.

Frantic, Jagger called Bowie and asked him to deny the story. Bowie declined. In the end both men decided denials would only prolong the controversy.

None of this bothered Jerry. But when Jagger was photographed at Munich's P1 Club with twenty-four-year-old beauty Christina Hack, Hall broke down in tears. Hack claimed that, after they left the nightclub, she took Jagger home to her apartment.

A worried Jagger sent Jerry a $350 arrangement of orchids—as he had done when he was rumored to be seeing women in Tokyo and Paris—and issued a press statement. "I only spoke to this girl for a few minutes in a nightclub," he insisted, "and she is obviously making the most of this brief time with me."

In a ham-fisted attempt at damage control one of Jagger's publicists claimed to have set the whole thing up to counter Angela Bowie's disclosure that she had caught her husband and Mick in bed. "I think it worked well," said publicist Bernard Doherty. "I think it has restored Mick's reputation as a lady-killer."

That scenario was disavowed by another Jagger spokesman. "It's absolutely absurd to think Mick would get involved," said Tony King, "in any stunt likely to affect his lover and family."

The high point of the European Tour came on August 19, 1990, when the Stones arrived in Prague to play before a stadium full of newly liberated Czechs. The band had once been denounced by the old Communist government as a corrupting capitalist tool. THE TANKS ARE ROLLING OUT, read posters advertising the concert, AND THE STONES ARE ROLLING IN!

"I used to listen to their music often," said President Vaclav Havel, who had personally extended an invitation to the Stones to perform. "Songs like 'Satisfaction' can hardly be forgotten. If their concerts are half as good as people write and talk about them, I can't wait to see them live with my very own eyes." The show went on in a drenching storm, though that didn't seem to bother Havel or any of the other 110,000 fans. Quipped Mick: "What's a little acid rain between friends?"

That summer Jagger, who had been apart from Jerry for most of the previous eighteen months, marked their twelfth year together by building a $100,000 heart-shaped swimming pool for her Texas ranch. "Every time Mick buys me a present for no reason," said a wary Hall, "I think I'm sure he must have done something. . . . I'm a jealous maniac. I've heard all the rumors about him and other women and I want a commitment."

Again, Hall issued an ultimatum. "That's the last time," she declared, referring to his on-the-road philandering. "You're not a teenager anymore, and neither am I. Either you marry me or I don't want to see you again."

This time Jagger agreed. With what was now a $200-million fortune to protect (he had pocketed $25 million in the previous eighteen months alone), Jagger instructed his lawyers to draw up a new prenuptial agreement. Jerry, a multimillionaire in her own right, signed away any claim to Mick's millions.

Then it was off on an exotic six-week vacation that took Jagger, Hall, their children, Mick's assistant Alan Dunn, a tutor, and a nanny to India, Nepal, Bhutan, Thailand, and finally the fabled island of Bali in Indonesia.

On November 21, 1990, at six P.M., Jagger and Hall were married in a ceremony steeped in Hindu ritual. The wedding took place on the patio of a hilltop home owned by Jagger's friend, wood-carver Amir Rabik. But before they could set foot inside, a small black chicken had to be sacrificed and its blood sprinkled around the house to purify it.

Once they arrived, the bride and groom bathed together in scented water, and afterward donned multicolored sarongs with silver brocade tops called *kebaya*s. Then, with offerings of fruits and flowers heaped in front of them, they stood before a Hindu priest who read prayers in Sanskrit and dabbed a yellow mark on each of their foreheads.

Jerry placed a small mat on the floor. Then Mick pulled a dagger with a jagged blade called a kriss out of his waistband and pierced the mat—an act symbolizing their union. Jagger concluded the festivities by "beating" his new wife with a banana. The wedding was not without its Western touches: Dunn was best man, Elizabeth Scarlett a bridesmaid, and son James a pageboy.

Jagger and Hall spent their first night as a married couple at Rabik's. While his bride got ready for bed, Jagger allegedly made a play for his host's mate. "He *jumped me*, can you believe it?" the woman later confided to a friend. "Mick tried to make love to me on his wedding night!"

After a thirty-six-hour honeymoon the Jaggers went their separate ways—Mick to New York and Jerry to their London town house. "Apart from signing the marriage certificate and having a priest there, the situation remains the same," said Eva Jagger. "We're very fond of her. To me she has always been a daughter anyway."

The situation may have indeed remained the same, for within days of their departure questions arose as to the legitimacy of their marriage. The Hindu leader who married them later renounced the wedding, apparently on grounds that he was unsure of the Jaggers' commitment to the Hindu faith.

Nearly two years later Jagger himself could only shrug when asked if he was legally married: "Depends what you call . . . I *think* so. Next question?"

If there was considerable doubt as to the legality of their marriage, Hall preferred to ignore it. She never removed the enormous diamond ring and wedding band on her left hand, and referred to Mick as "my husband" with annoying regularity.

The Jaggers spent January of 1991 at their sprawling compound in Mustique (from *moustique*, French for mosquito). Part of the Grenadines, the island was acquired in 1958 by British developer Colin Tennant (now Lord Glenconner). Tennant built a scaled-down model of the Taj Mahal, and gave his friend Princess Margaret property on which to build her own hideaway.

Princess Margaret invited her friend Mick to visit the island in 1970, and the following year he and his then-wife Bianca bought a modest cottage on L'Ansecoy Beach. By the early 1990s Stargroves, named after the castle he had bought twenty-five years earlier for Marianne Faithfull, included a series of adjoining Japanese pavilions: a children's cottage, a game room (boasting a floor inlaid with thousands of tiny Contac capsules), guest rooms, a bathhouse with hot tub, a sun deck, moon deck, and teahouse—all connected by burnished teak walkways. Even though they were directly on the beach, the house also boasted a grottolike swimming pool and a huge croquet lawn.

Like the other seventy-odd homeowners on Mustique (including Princess Margaret's son Lord Linley, Lord Litchfield, and American advertising mogul Mary Wells Lawrence), Jagger fought to keep Mustique an enclave for the chosen few. Only three miles long and a mile wide, the island boasted one restaurant, Basil's Bar, and a single small hotel, the Cotton House. A member of the Mustique Company, Jagger led the fight to keep cruise ships from dropping anchor off Mustique, and thwarted plans to build a golf course on the island.

Jagger also donated $500,000 to build a three-room schoolhouse for the children of native Mustiquans, many of whom work as servants for the wealthy landowners; Jagger's staff in Mustique includes a butler, a cook, a maid, two gardeners (Rocky and Pebbles), a nanny, and a tutor.

With outsiders kept to a minimum (the island's airstrip wasn't long enough even for a small private jet, and there were no lights for night landings), Jagger and Hall felt free to picnic with the locals on Macaroni Beach, romp with their barefoot children in the surf, and go to the Wednesday steel band "jump-ups" at Basil's Bar.

At a beach party thrown by Jagger that January, Mick's guests—including race-car legend Jackie Stewart and Lord Litchfield—watched their host wail the suggestive lyrics of a reggae song while bouncing off the back of every young woman seated at a picnic table. Just a few feet away Jerry watched with cool detachment.

"Jagger flirts outrageously," observed writer Stephanie Mansfield, who observed Mick and Jerry in their Mustique habitat on assignment for *Vogue*. "It's embarrassing, but Jerry is obviously willing to put up with it."

Jagger was also holding on to other vices. Mick was capable of consuming significant quantities of champagne and—despite his claims to the contrary—he was not altogether abstemious when it came to drugs. "He still smokes dope," said Mansfield, "but maybe he doesn't regard it as a drug."

The Jaggers certainly qualified as Mustique's flashiest inhabitants, though in the 1990s they received some stiff competition with the arrival of David Bowie. Amid all the rumors regarding his past relationship with Mick, Bowie moved into his own Indonesian-style hilltop estate not far from Jagger's Stargroves. (Jagger was strangely absent when Bowie married the African-born model and actress Iman in 1992.)

In March more than a hundred celebrities, including

Kevin Costner, Meryl Streep, and Richard Gere, banded together to record a morale-boosting single for GIs fighting in the Persian Gulf War. At the same time the Stones released "High Wire," a single that took a swipe at the West for having sold arms to Saddam Hussein in the first place. "We got no pride, don't care whose boots we lick," Jagger sang. "We act greedy, makes me sick, sick, sick."

Public reaction was overwhelmingly negative, particularly in England, where "High Wire" was banned by the BBC. "The song only expresses the ambivalent feelings," Jagger tried to explain, "many people have about the war."

The tour album, *Flashpoint*, was released to critical raves, despite the fact that "Highwire" had been clumsily tacked on to it. "Now, with concerts packaged as lip-synching stunts and MTV pantomimes," mused *Rolling Stone*, "it's startling to hear rock and roll so craftily passionate—and from players whose ages hover near fifty and who come trailing chains of history, myth, and cash."

While talk-show hosts and members of Parliament were busily denouncing Jagger's "High Wire" lyrics, he was in Atlanta working on his first feature film in twenty years. After Jagger and Bowie lost *Dirty Rotten Scoundrels* to Michael Caine and Steve Martin, and (thankfully) *Ishtar* to Warren Beatty and Dustin Hoffman, Jagger campaigned for the role of the sleazy British tabloid reporter in *Bonfire of the Vanities*. (The character was rewritten for an American and went to Bruce Willis instead.) It was then that Jagger was cast in the unlikely role of a villainous bounty hunter stalking Emilio Estevez in the futuristic thriller *Freejack*.

That March, Hall was worried that Mick might be making his own play for freedom with twenty-two-year-old, sable-haired model Carla Bruni, an heir to the Pirelli tire fortune. In Jagger tradition he had lured the sultry Italian away from his old pal Eric Clapton during the Urban Jungle Tour.

At first Hall chalked up the Bruni affair as just another of Mick's many peccadilloes. But after it dragged on for over a year, Jerry felt threatened. When a gossip columnist hinted at the affair, Jerry flew into a jealous rage. Mick stormed out, and Hall, terrified that she had driven him out of her life forever, sat down to pen him a tearful apology.

A few days later vacationer David Lake happened to be relaxing in the bar of the Crane Beach Hotel on Barbados when he spotted Jagger and Hall kissing at a nearby table. After the couple left to take a stroll on the beach, Lake noticed they had left an envelope behind. Out of curiosity he picked it up and read the letter inside.

"Oh, my darling Mick," the note read, "The thought of losing you breaks my heart in two. I'm truly sorry I was jealous.

"I tried to punish you and was unsympathetic a few times. Mick, you're all that matters to me in the world. I love you with all my heart. Please don't take your love away.

"I want you to have your freedom and I won't mind if you fuck other girls," the letter continued. "I'll do it with other girls and you too. I'll be good to you and give you all my love.

"I respect, admire, trust, need, and love you all through my being. I think you're a genious [sic], and I love the way you are. I love to fuck you. I don't want to change you at all. I just want to be your #1 girl. I LOVE YOU. Your Baby, Jerry."

The shocking missive, reportedly authenticated by a leading New York handwriting authority, may have had the desired effect. Within a month Hall was pregnant with Jagger's child for the third time. And in May he rewarded Jerry with Downe House, a $4 million white Georgian mansion high atop a hill overlooking the Thames in the London suburb of Richmond—the same town where the Rolling Stones had first rocked the roof off the Crawdaddy Club three decades earlier. Among their neighbors: Ron Wood and Prince Rupert Loewenstein.

By this time Bruni (who had also ended an affair with Crown Prince Dimitri of Yugoslavia) was already hot on the heels of another high-profile womanizer: New York real estate mogul Donald Trump. Bruni told Trump that if he agreed to break up with his then-fiancée, Marla Maples, she would dump Mick—"a man," Trump later said, "she was desperately stuck on."

Things returned to normal that summer as Jagger and Hall hosted the annual round of weekend house parties in France. For these affairs Jagger would dispatch his private jet to fly in twenty of his upper-class English friends, along with their nannies and children. His charmed circle of moneyed aristocrats had changed little over the years. There were the Guinnesses, of course, as well as Christopher Gibbs, Prince Rupert, Lady Ann Lampton, the duchess of Beaufort, and the marquess and marchioness of Worcester. (Jagger's hobnobbing with titled folk did not prevent him from committing a royal faux pas at the Prince's Trust Dinner at Windsor Castle that June of 1991. While shaking hands with Prince Charles, Mick kept his other hand in his pocket—a breach of etiquette that one paper blasted as "especially insulting to the Royal Family.")

At La Fourchette there were hot air balloon rides over the Loire, languid lunches under the chestnut trees, and— most important of all—lots of games: backgammon, charades, Scrabble. The consummate party-giver, Hall came up with a few games of her own. One was a competition between guests to see how far they could carry a coin between their buttocks. Another game involved leaving the room with a partner, returning twenty minutes later, and challenging guests to determine what was different about them. In Jerry's case no one guessed that she had removed all her underwear.

The game Jagger's highborn British pals most enjoyed was cross-dressing. "Everyone comes down to dinner in drag, and it's just huge fun," said one guest. "Masses of people sort of screaming, running in and out of each other's bedrooms, applying makeup on the boys." Once, Jagger allegedly dressed up as Madonna in cone-shaped bullet bra, blond wig, and black mesh stockings; he even sported a beauty mark. Another evening Mick was waving around a long cigarette holder as Coco Chanel, clad in a tight black shift, silver fox wrap, and pearls.

Jerry and Mick tossed the last of their wild parties at La Fourchette in September. Hall returned to London with the children and Mick flew back to New York to work on his third solo album. Unbeknownst to Jerry, Jagger would return to their château in late October to play games of another sort—with the persistent Carla Bruni.

Jagger had high hopes that his performance in *Freejack* might jump-start his movie career. But his biggest screen success—literally—came with the October release of the IMAX film of the world tour. Shot with high-tech cameras at concerts in London, Turin, Italy, and Berlin, the eighty-minute film presented the Stones larger than life—*much* larger—on screens sixty feet high and one hundred feet wide.

Appropriately, the next month the group signed the biggest record deal of their career—and one of the biggest in history—with Richard Branson's Virgin label. In a deal masterminded by Mick and Prince Rupert, Branson paid them a $45 million advance for just three albums and the rights to all Stones records going back to *Sticky Fingers* in 1971.

The Virgin deal helped to offset the embarrassing failure of *Freejack* in January of 1992. So did the arrival on January 12 in London of seven-pound, thirteen-ounce Georgia May Ayeesha Jagger.

For Jagger this was apparently not enough. The day after Georgia May's birth he flew off to Thailand and, under the Thai name Someching, booked himself and Bruni into Villa 15 at the luxurious Amanpuri Hotel in the aptly named resort of Phuket. There they lounged by the villa's private pool and, during one night on the town, were spotted at a local disco "drinking beer, hugging, and kissing on the lips."

Bruni denied reports that she was the "dark-haired beauty" spotted cavorting with Jagger in Thailand. "I hardly know this man," she insisted. "I'm fed up with the rumors." But privately Bruni called Jagger "my boyfriend" and gushed to friends about his sexual prowess. "Mick is incredible in bed," she said. "He is a wonderful lover—for an old man."

Jerry, caring for their newborn baby in London, was devastated. She confronted Mick about the rumors when he returned, and he flatly denied them. She then phoned Bruni and told her point-black to "leave my man alone." Bruni hung up on Hall, but later, when Hall was vacationing with Elizabeth Scarlett, James, and Georgia May on Mustique, Carla called back. "There's a family here," said Hall, who was breast-feeding Georgia May at the time, "and there are three children involved."

Hall then launched a counterattack in the press. Without telling Mick, Hall invited the British women's magazine *Hello* to photograph her and the children on Mustique. Jagger turned up unexpectedly and refused to pose for even a single family photograph. "Jerry put on a brave front," said *Hello*'s reporter, "not letting a trace of the strain she was under show through. She wanted the world to know her life was perfect when she knew it wasn't."

Readers of the French magazine *Voici* were served up vintage Jerry when she told the magazine that she hoped Jagger would still be making love to her when she was ninety. "Making love is by far the best way for me to keep my figure," she said. "That is why I hate those times when Mick is far from me. But when we are back together, we make up for lost time, believe me."

Meantime, at Jerry's insistence, the couple visited a marriage counselor. "I didn't want our marriage to end without any attempts to save it," she would later say. "I was determined to fight this and support Mick. I was absolutely heartbroken but I was the loving wife."

Hall put on a brave face on May 25, 1992, when she and Mick joined Marsha Hunt in New Haven to attend Karis's graduation from Yale. Although New York Governor Mario Cuomo and actress Mia Farrow were among the other proud parents on hand, Jagger, armed with a video camera like scores of other fathers, turned the most heads.

Six weeks later, on Jerry's thirty-sixth birthday, Mick had yet another reason to celebrate: Jade, then living with her twenty-two-year-old artist boyfriend Piers Jackson on a farm in Dorset, gave birth to a girl at home. Her name: Assisi. Great-grandmother Eva Jagger claimed her son was not at all depressed at becoming a grandfather. "You're only as old as you feel," she shrugged.

Perhaps, but as he faced his forty-ninth birthday, Granddad Mick once again seemed intent on proving his virility. In Los Angeles to continue work on his solo album, he was photographed with another stunning twenty-two-year-old model, this time a blond American named Kathy Latham. A few days later a statuesque brunette was photographed stepping out of the pool at Jagger's rented Beverly Hills villa. Once again speculation in the press focused on Bruni.

The marriage counseling had clearly not worked out. "Mick's never going to change," Jerry decided. "Those remedies don't work unless both of you are absolutely committed."

Both Hall and Bruni were in Paris on modeling assignments when they ran into each other in the lobby of the Ritz Hotel. According to one witness a "a catfight" ensued when Hall called Bruni a tramp. "Why can't you leave my husband alone, you bitch?" Jerry yelled at Carla.

"Tell your husband," Bruni shouted back, "to leave *me* alone."

At the showing of the Thierry Mugler collection that afternoon, Hall felt "humiliated" as the other runway models stared and whispered behind her back. When a reporter from London's *Daily Mail* walked up to her at the fashion show and asked her to comment on the rumors, she cracked. "How did you find out," she asked, "about me and Mick?"

Hall then poured out her heart to *Daily Mail* columnist Baz Bamigoboye. "Yes, it's true," she said, "we are separated, and I suppose we'll get a divorce. I'm in too much pain for this to go on any longer. . . . It's unforgivable what happened, and I don't think there's any hope for us anymore."

AIDS topped Hall's list of concerns. "Fidelity is very important," she told *McCall's* for an article plugging her new line of sexy lingerie. "Especially these days, when there's a venereal disease around that *kills* people, which should make you think a lot harder.

"We've tried very hard," she went on, "although there's nothing more humiliating than loving him so much that you forgive the infidelities. But I've always hoped that one day he'll outgrow these things and it won't happen again. You know, we always live in hope. And time always heals."

Hall's concerns may not have been ill founded. "The word around Los Angeles," said Jagger's former lover Bebe Buell, "is that Mick was sleeping with all these girls without condoms. These guys in their forties and fifties feel AIDS won't affect them because the girls they sleep with are too classy for that. And *boom*, that's it."

Bruni agreed. "I've had lovers before who think that just because I look fresh and pretty they don't have to wear a condom with me, and I think that's such a big mistake. It's ridiculous."

At the Los Angeles club Saturday Night Fever, Jagger snatched the camera away from a photographer after he had snapped Mick kissing Kathy Latham. The photographer then chased Jagger to his black Lincoln Continental and banged on the tinted passenger window, asked for his camera. Jagger allegedly told his bodyguard to run the photographer down if he didn't get out of the way.

That August, Jagger was still on the prowl, attending a wild party at the Los Angeles home of record producer Rick Rubin. When police were called in at three A.M. to break up the rowdy affair, they found Mick surrounded by a dozen young women.

Afterward, he and fellow aging rock idol Rod Stewart got together to compare notes. "They had a heart-to-heart about their marital affairs," said a female acquaintance, "and agreed that women age differently from men. They decided when a woman turns forty, it's over."

The breakup of rock's longest and arguably most celebrated union was trumpeted in front-page headlines around the world. Hall found an unlikely ally in Keith Richards, now supposedly a stable family man. "I think it will be a real shame if Mick and Jerry do split up," said Richards. "I hope the man comes to his senses—you know, the old black book bit. Kicking fifty, it's a bit much, a bit manic."

But questions concerning the marriage's legality remained. Apparently the necessary paperwork had not been filed, in that case making the marriage invalid in the U.S. and Great Britain.

If Hall and Jagger were indeed legally married, was the prenuptial agreement enforceable? Divorce attorneys everywhere were salivating at the prospect of dividing up Jagger's $200 million fortune—prenuptial agreement or no.

Certainly such monetary considerations played a part in Jagger's decision to call Hall immediately and beg her to reconsider. After two frantic calls from California, Jerry agreed to meet Mick in Dallas. Three days later they were sharing a romantic lunch at one of the most visible spots in Dallas—the restaurant of the Mansion at Turtle Creek.

Bruni remained behind in Paris, licking her wounds. Although she never admitted to having had an affair with Jagger, she left little doubt that she was shattered by his decision to return to Hall. "I thought I would never get over it," she said. "I used to wake up every morning in despair. I thought I would never fall in love with someone else. When your heart is broken you think the pain is never going to stop." As for sleeping with married men: "Don't do it. It's terrible, awful. It's a ticket to pain and it leaves you very bitter."

With his personal life tentatively back under control, Jagger once more turned his attention to his solo career. Mick's next album, for which he returned to Ahmet Ertegun at Atlantic, was to have been released in November. But when both Ron Wood and Keith Richards decided to release their solo projects in the very same month, Jagger wisely chose to wait until February of 1993 rather than add to the glut of loose Stones on the market. The album's planned title gave Hall some cause for concern: *Wandering Spirit*.

At the nationally televised MTV Awards in Los Angeles, a shaggy-maned, velour-jacketed Jagger offered the most trenchant comment of the evening before presenting the top prize for best video to Van Halen. "On a serious note," said Jagger, "I want to thank Woody Allen and Mia Farrow for making our rock and roll marriages seem so blissful."

Had Jagger truly mended his ways? One had only to check his Christmas list for the answer. Mick ordered up twenty crates of a fifty-dollar coffee-table book to send to all his friends: Madonna's raunchy bestseller *Sex*.

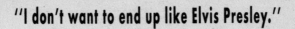

"I don't want to end up like Elvis Presley."

Epilogue

He is by any definition an original, and one of the dominant cultural figures of our time. A swaggering, strutting, sometimes sinister clown prince of rock, his career spans four decades—from the turbulent sixties and sybaritic seventies through the whoring eighties to the cautious nineties.

Mick Jagger's is the story of a generation. With Elvis and John Lennon gone he is really the last of the rock titans. Even during their lifetimes neither Presley nor Lennon—for all their genius—could match his mesmeric power as a performer.

Yet Mick Jagger remains such an enigmatic figure that even he appears incapable of laying bare the truths of his life—even when a British publisher paid him $5 million to do so. Is he a Street Fighting Man? The Midnight Rambler? A Man of Wealth and Taste? All these, it turns out, and considerably more.

Like one other pop giant of the late twentieth century—Madonna—Jagger has endured by continually reinventing himself. And like Madonna's, his chameleonlike changes stem from fundamental unresolved contradictions in his character.

Jagger is the pale, middle-class English schoolboy who burst on the music scene sounding as black as any Mississippi Delta blues singer; the well-read London School of Economics history major who talks like a cockney chimney sweep; the fitness-obsessed PE teacher's son identified in the public mind with every mood-altering substance known to man; a leather-jacketed, ill-mannered teddy-boy tough with the refined tastes of an English gentleman; the Satanic Majesty who dutifully christens his children in the Church of England; the irredeemable misogynist who gossips and shares makeup tips with his gal-pals; the androgynous dabbler in bisexual love with boundless heterosexual appetites, and—most intriguing—the flagrant social-climber who rose to global fame as an enemy of the Establishment.

Jagger is the quintessential quick-change artist, moving too fast ever to be labeled, categorized, defined. That is what both fascinates and infuriates us about the man.

In that sense Jagger has always slavishly reflected what was happening in the lives of his contemporaries. For a generation that grew up after World War II, he symbolized every movement, trend, fad, and phase. The Beatles made growing one's hair over the shirt collar a small act of rebellion; the Stones bragged that theirs was matted and dirty. When the Vietnam War led to student riots in the streets, Jagger provided protestors with rage-filled anthems.

As the occult came into vogue, Mick wrapped himself in the crimson cloak of Beelzebub. During disco mania he donned satin jumpsuits, sprinkled himself with glitter, and indulged in the chic (and supposedly nonaddictive) drug of the time, cocaine. The arrival of the button-down, money-mad, "Just Say No" 1980s brought another transformation—this time to an antidrug, politically conservative family man. Jagger's new line: "I never really did any of those things."

Yes, he did. And then some. If anyone embodied the "Sex, Drugs, and Rock and Roll" ethos, it was Mick Jagger. Others who might have vied for the title did not survive trying to live up to it: Jimi Hendrix, Janis Joplin, and Jim Morrison, to name but a few.

Closer to home, death never seemed far from Jagger. Among the bodies left beind: Brian Jones, Ian Stewart, Gram Parsons, Keith Moon, Michael Cooper, Tara

Browne, Tara Richards, Andy Warhol, and, of course, Meredith Hunter and the victims of Altamont. Sadly, soul mate Eric Clapton's four-year-old son, Conor, died in 1991 after falling from a window of his mother's Manhattan apartment. That same year his erstwhile promoter Bill Graham was killed when his helicopter struck a transmission tower.

Yet Jagger endured.

The video for his new falsetto-laced single "Sweet Thing" became a major hit on both MTV and its sister music network, VH-1. The video, which featured Jagger prancing about as seminude couples writhed in mud, helped propel "Sweet Thing" onto the charts. Jagger celebrated by watching an X-rated video at the Manhattan club USA with his guitarist Jimmy Ripp and two female backup singers.

To promote *Wandering Spirit*, Jagger appeared on NBC's *Saturday Night Live* in February 1993. In one skit he donned pointed boots, shades, and a bandanna, then mumbled his way through a memorable impersonation of Keith Richards. Several days later Jagger gave a rare, VIP-packed solo concert at New York's Webster Hall. Afterward, he celebrated with Jerry and fan Robert De Niro at the Manhattan nightclub Tatou.

The commercial and critical success of *Wandering Spirit* blunted the trauma of reaching the half-century mark—as did the induction of Jagger and Richards into the Songwriters' Hall of Fame that June. Still, it was pointed out repeatedly that Mick Jagger was now older (by three years) than the President of the United States. "But younger," Jagger replied, "than the secretary of state!"

The Rolling Stones showed no signs of gathering moss in the 1990s. Their feud resolved for the time being, Jagger and Richards planned another blockbuster album and world-rattling tour for early 1994—despite Bill Wyman's decision, at age fifty-six, to leave the group. In searching for Wyman's replacement Jagger seemed to favor more mature-looking musicians who would not make him and the other aging Stones suffer by comparison.

In the end it is that singular, galvanic force called Jagger—a phenomenally charismatic creature who clearly would have achieved stardom with or without the Rolling Stones—who continues to mesmerize after thirty years.

As Jagger turned fifty in 1993, baby boomers and their children seemed unfazed by the fact that the penultimate antihero had become the First Grandfather of Rock. Did Jagger, an ancient head atop a teenager's body, intend to keep taunting and tantalizing stadiums full of fans even into his next half-century?

"I suppose I can imagine myself doing it at fifty," said Mick, "though it seems a crazy thing to say." Given the evidence of three tumultuous decades, it seems crazier *not* to say it.

Acknowledgments

A tremendous amount of research is necessary for any comprehensive biography, and this was especially true in the case of *Jagger Unauthorized*. Even more time was spent tracking down sources: friends, former teachers, classmates, coworkers, family members, neighbors, acquaintances, employers, employees, mentors, protégés, an ex-wife, and multitudes of lovers. Some of the sources asked not to be identified in the book. I respected their wishes.

On several occasions I attempted to contact Mick Jagger for an interview, but he remained unavailable. A number of people close to Jagger—Atlantic Records founder Ahmet Ertugen, for example—seemed willing to talk until they contacted Mick directly and were instructed not to. Fortunately, many who claimed they were ordered not to speak to me did so anyway. Hundreds of others talked candidly, without ever bothering to seek Jagger's approval.

I am especially grateful to my editor, Leslie Schnur, for her passionate commitment to *Jagger Unauthorized*, and to the entire Dell Publishing family—particularly Kathy Trager, Evan Boorstyn, Sibylle Kazeroid, Phil Rose, and Craig Schneider. For her advice and friendship, I thank Ellen Levine. I also thank her talented associates Diana Finch and Anne Dubuisson in New York and Lisa Eveleigh of AP Watt Ltd. in London. My thanks as well to Martin Fletcher, my editor at Simon & Schuster Ltd. in Great

Britain, to his associate Daphne Bien and copyeditor Jenny Parrott.

Hazel Southam was my intrepid and resourceful researcher in Britain. Hazel, along with fellow researchers Leni and Peter Gillman, played an important role in helping to unearth never-before-revealed facts about Mick's life in England.

For their encouragement and loving patience, I am grateful—as always—to my wife, Valerie, and our daughters, Kate and Kelly.

Additional thanks to: Chrissie Shrimpton Messenger, Andrew Oldham, Gered Mankowitz, John Dunbar, Bebe Buell, Liz Derringer, Angela Bowie, Christopher Gibbs, Keith Altham, Barry Miles ("Miles"), Peter Jones, Bianca Jagger, Earl McGrath, Dick Taylor, Phil May, May Pang, Marianne Faithfull, Paul Jones, Geoff Bradford, Brian Knight, Dick Cavett, Rodney Bingenheimer, Leee Black Childers, Steve Turner, Victor Bockris, Carlo Little, Harold Pendleton, Tom McGuinness, John Michell, Nicolas Roeg, Sandy Lieberson, Arthur Collins, Trevor Churchill, Christopher Makos, Pat Hackett, David McGough, Chris O'Donnell, Patricia Lawford Stewart, Daniel Stewart, Marvin Mitchelson, Kevin Kahn, Valerie Watson Dunn, Walter Murphy, Norah Darwen, Wayne Darwen, Fred Hauptfuhrer, Tony Brenna, Fred Hughes, Stephanie Mansfield, Rita Jenrette, Victoria Balfour, Jouet Moreau, Elena Brenna, Lance Loud, Michael Gross, Brian Morris, Ruby Mazur, Chuckie Starr, Kenny Valente, Gael Love, Joyce Wansley, Peter Frame, Wendy Leigh, Steven Karten, William Wilkinson, Dick Allen, Walter Bennett, Arthur Page, John Wilkinson, David Herrington, Tony Smith, Allie Willis, Greg Fillenganes, Russell Turiak, Vinnie Zuffante, Lee Wohlfert, Mary Boone, Robert Littman, Erica Bell, Jeanette Andersen, the late Truman Capote, Halston, Steve Rubell, Roy Cohn, Malcolm Forbes and Bill Graham, Donna Miller, Gore Vidal, Bobby Zarem, Susan Crimp, Valerie Wimmer, Baird Jones, Barbara Levine, Michael Horovitz, April Todd, Stephanie Bluestone, Rosemary McClure, Wendi Rothman, Mary Vespa, Peter Newcomb, Lindzee Smith, Anne Di Pasquale; the staffs of Dartford Grammar School in Dartford, Kent, and the London School of Economics; the Lincoln Center Library for the Performing Arts; the New York Public Library; the Hartford, Woodbury, Southbury, Watertown, New Milford, Middlebury, and Danbury, Connecticut, public libraries; the Silas Bronson Library, Graphictype, Cindy Amaro, Rex Features, Syndication International, the Image Works, the Bettmann Archive, Wide World, the Associated Press, Gamma Liaison, Movie Star News, Photoreporters, Retna Ltd., Globe, Archive Photos, Sygma, and DMI.

Sources and Chapter Notes

The following chapter notes are designed to give a general view of the sources drawn upon in preparing *Jagger Unauthorized*, but they are by no means all-inclusive. The author has respected the wishes of many interview subjects to remain anonymous and accordingly has not listed them either here or elsewhere in the text.

CHAPTER 1

The author covered the events before, during, and after Altamont for *Time* magazine, and therefore, much of the information included here is based on personal observation and scores of interviews conducted at the time with organizers, fans, roadies, groupies, law enforcement officers, Hell's Angels, state, county, and city officials, overdose victims, medical and first-aid personnel, neighboring ranchers, and the people of Livermore, California. Among the most important of these were Sam Cutler, Melvin Belli, Grace Slick, Gram Parsons, Dick Carter, Bill Graham, and Rosemary McClure.

Accounts of Altamont also appeared in numerous newspapers and magazines, including *The New York Times*, *Rolling Stone*, the *Los Angeles Times*, *Newsweek*, the *San Francisco Chronicle*, and the *San Francisco Examiner*.

"Mick kept saying . . .": Pamela Des Barres, *I'm with the Band* (William Morrow, 1987), p. 159.

CHAPTER 2

Interviews include Dick Taylor, William Wilkinson, Dick Allen, Walter Bennett, Arthur Page, John Wilkinson, David Herrington, Tony Smith, Phil May, and Victor Bockris.

Among articles consulted were: Henrietta Knight, "Mick Jagger's Mum Shares Their Secrets," *TV Times* (July 7, 1990); "Everyone Has to Be Tied Down to Something . . . ," *Radio Times* (April 5, 1973); Sally Brompton, "I'm an Ordinary Mum, Says Mrs. Jagger," *The London Sunday Express*, May 16, 1971; John Salmon, "Mick Jagger as a Schoolboy Rebel?," *Today* (May 8, 1992); Roy Carr, "Mick Jagger," *Vox* (1979). Books include Danny Danziger, *Eton Voices* (Viking Penguin Ltd., 1988), and by Georgia Holt and Phyllis Quinn with Sue Russell, *Star Mothers* (Simon and Schuster, 1988).

CHAPTER 3

The author drew on conversations with Dick Taylor, Phil May, Paul Jones, Geoff Bradford, Brian Knight, Peter Jones, Harold Pendleton, Tom McGuinness, John Mayall, and Steve Turner.

Articles include Robert Greenfield, "The Rolling Stone Interview: Keith Richard," *Rolling Stone* (August 19, 1971); "Introducing the Rolling Stones," *Rave* (July 1964); G. R., "Can Rolling Stones Crush the Beatles?," *Chronicle* (November 29, 1963); John Carpenter, "Mick Jagger Raps," *Eye* (November 1968).

CHAPTER 4

Interview subjects included Chrissie Shrimpton, Peter Jones, Andrew Oldham, Keith Altham, Phil May, Carlo Little, Brian Morris, Valerie Watson Dunn, and Chris O'Donnell.

Among the articles consulted: Denna Allen and Matthew Norman, "Darling Cleo," *The Mail on Sunday*, August 16, 1992; Mike Ianchhetta, "They Wouldn't Dare!," *The Sunday News*, January 5, 1969; Unity Hall, "What Makes Mick Tick," *The Sun*, March 11, 1970; Anthony Carthew, "Shaggy Englishman Story," *The New York Times*, September 6, 1964. Books include David Dalton, *The Rolling Stones: The First 20 Years* (Thames and Hudson, 1981) and Bill Wyman with Ray Coleman, *Stone Alone* (Viking Penguin, 1991).

CHAPTER 5

Interview subjects for this period included John Dunbar, Chrissie Shrimpton, Andrew Oldham, Barry Miles, Victor Bockris, Michael Horovitz, Brian Morris, Peter Jones, and Earl McGrath.

Articles include Ian Dickson, "Marianne Faithfull," *Vox* (1974); Al Aronowitz, "Brian Jones," the *New York Post*, July 10, 1969; various pieces on the Stones' American invasion in *The New York Times*, the *Los Angeles Times*, *Time*, *Look*, *Newsweek*, *The Washington Post*, and other periodicals. The author also screened early performance footage of the Stones, including *The Hollywood Palace*, all *The Ed Sullivan Shows* on which the group appeared, and several BBC programs (as well as transcripts of BBC interviews with Jagger and Richards).

CHAPTERS 6 AND 7

For these chapters, the author drew on conversations with, among others, Chrissie Shrimpton, Marianne Faithfull, Gered Mankowitz, Christopher Gibbs, John Dunbar, Keith Altham, Brian Morris, Earl McGrath, Rodney Bingenheimer, Allie Willis, Greg Fillenganes, Barry Miles, and Stephanie Bluestone.

Articles and books included: Anthony Haden-Guest, "She Devil," *The Sunday Correspondent*, February 11, 1990; Mandy Aftel, *Death of a Rolling Stone* (Sidgwick & Jackson, 1982); A. E. Hotchner, *Blown Away* (Simon and Schuster, 1990); Tina Turner and Kurt Loder, *I, Tina*, (William Morrow, 1986). The Redlands Scandal ranks as one of the most widely covered drug cases in history, covered in every major news publication from *The Times* (London), *The Guardian*, *Time*, *Newsweek*, and *The New York Times* to *Paris-Match*, *Der Spiegel*, and even *Pravda*. The author also consulted the trial transcripts. In addition, the diaries of Cecil Beaton were a major source for accounts of Jagger's escapade in Morocco.

CHAPTER 8

Interview subjects include Barry Miles, Paul Jones, John Michell, Chrissie Shrimpton, John Dunbar, Andrew Oldham, Gered Mankowitz, Peter Jones, Chris O'Donnell, and Pete Frame.

Published sources include: Nik Cohn, "A Briton Blasts the Beatles," *The New York Times*, December 15, 1968; Martin Elliott, *Rolling Stones: The Complete Recording Sessions* (Blandford, 1990); "No, the Rolling Stones Are Not Fascists," *The New York Times*, December 28, 1969.

CHAPTERS 9 AND 10

Information for these chapters was based in part on conversations with Nicolas Roeg, Sandy Lieberson, John Dunbar, Bebe Buell, Victor

Bockris, Lindzee Smith, Melvin Belli, Stephanie Bluestone, Robert Littman, Sam Cutler, Keith Altham, Earl McGrath, and Bill Graham.

Published sources include: "Mick Jagger and the Future of Rock," *Newsweek* (January 4, 1971); "Prince Rupert Loewenstein Is the Man . . . ," *The Independent on Sunday*, August 23, 1992; Tony Sanchez, "Mick Jagger, MP!," *Sunday People* (November 26, 1978). *Rolling Stone* magazine, *The Rolling Stone Interviews 1967–1980* (Rolling Stone Press, 1981); Marsha Hunt, *Real Life* (Chatto & Windus, 1986). The author also screened the never-before-aired *Rock and Roll Circus* and behind-the-scenes documentary footage of the Hyde Park concert.

CHAPTER 11

The author drew on conversations with Trevor Churchill, Ruby Mazur, Bebe Buell, Lindzee Smith, Victor Bockris, Michael Gross, Sandy Lieberson, Christopher Makos, Lance Loud, Barry Miles, John Marion, Pat Hackett, Mary Boone, Gael Love, Fred Hughes, and Wendy Leigh.

Among articles and other published sources used: Ronald Maxwell, "Marianne Faithfull," *Sunday Mirror*, December 5, 1971; Barry Norman, "Mick Jagger Talking as Never Before," *The Daily Mail*, August 19, 1970; *Ramparts* (April 1970); "Eclectic, Reminiscent, Amused, Fickle, Perverse," *The New Yorker* (May 29, 1978); James Fox, "Madame Sex," *Vanity Fair* (May 1987); Robert Greenfield, "Prodigal Sons Tour Mother Country," *Rolling Stone* (April 15, 1971); Martha Smilgis, "Bianca Is Tired of Playing Zelda to Jagger's Scott," *People* (May 2, 1977); Fredric Dannen, *Hit Men* (Random House, 1990); Tony Scadutto, *Everybody's Lucifer*, the *New York Post*, August 1, 1974; Pamela Des Barres, *I'm with the Band* (William Morrow, 1987). Carey Schofield, *Jagger* (Beaufort Books, 1985); *Rolling Stones File* (Panther Books, 1968). Detailed accounts of the Saint-Tropez wedding of Mick Jagger and Bianca Perez Morena de Macias appeared in scores of newspapers and magazines around the world, including *The Times* (London), *The Daily Mail*, *The Evening Standard*, *The Daily Telegraph*, *The Daily Mirror* and *The Express*, *The Washington Post*, *Rolling Stone*, the *New Musical Express*, *The New York Times*, the New York *Daily News* and the *New York Post*, *Women's Wear Daily*, *Newsweek*, *Life*, and *Time*.

CHAPTER 12

Interview subjects include Liz Derringer, Dick Cavett, Truman Capote, Earl McGrath, Bebe Buell, Marvin Mitchelson, Keith Altham, and Victoria Balfour.

Articles include: Thomas Thompson, "The Stones Blast Through the Land," *Life* (July 14, 1972); Robert Greenfield, "Stones Tour: Rock & Roll on the Road Again," *Rolling Stone* (July 6, 1972); Don Heckman, "Feeling . . . ," *The New York Times Magazine*, July 16, 1972; Robert Greenfield, "In Chicago . . . ," *Rolling Stone* (August 3, 1972); Jack Lewis, "Mick Jagger Shocks Lady X on Jumbo Jet," *The Daily Mirror*, December 1, 1971; Grace Lichtenstein, "Jagger and Stones Whip 20,000 into Frenzy at Garden," *The New York Times*, July 25, 1972, and "Mick Jagger, 29, Gets a Put On, Turned On Send-off," *The New York Times*, July 29, 1972; Harriet Van Horne, "The Rolling Stones Party," the *New York Post*, July 29, 1972. The author reviewed more than 130 legal documents, including divorce papers filed in Los Angeles Superior Court (Case No. D 985 336). Also screened: the unreleased documentary film *Cocksucker Blues* and miscellaneous concert footage.

CHAPTER 13

The author drew on conversations with Angela Bowie, May Pang, Leee Black Childers, Chuckie Starr, Kenny Valente, Bebe Buell, Liz Derringer, Kevin Kahn, Christopher Makos, Walter Murphy, Rodney Bingenheimer, and Keith Altham.

Articles include: Kenneth Eastaugh, "Ask a Silly Question," *The Sun*, January 23, 1971; Don Short, "When I'm 33—That's When I'll Quit!," *The Daily Mirror*, August 5, 1972; Judith Martin, "Jagger Stones 'Em in D.C.," *The Washington Post*, May 3, 1973; David Wigg, "Jagger: A Stone Rolls Home," *The Daily Express*, August 23, 1973; Anthea Disney, "There's a Certain Singer I'd Like to Tear into Pieces," *The Daily Mail*, November 1973; Rosemary Kent, Bianca Jagger interview, *Viva* magazine (November 1973); "I Don't Know Mick Now, Says Bianca Jagger," *The Evening News*, January 29, 1974; David Wigg, "Baby, That's the Way It's Going to Be," *The Daily Express*, August 24, 1973.

CHAPTER 14

Interview subjects include Dick Cavett, Earl McGrath, May Pang, Liz Derringer, Bebe Buell, Angela Bowie, Chrissie Shrimpton, Pat Hackett, Christopher Makos, Kenny Valente, Halston, Vinnie Zuffante, Truman Capote, Keith Altham, Steve Rubell, and Patricia Lawford.

The 1975–76 Rolling Stones tour generated hundreds of stories worldwide. Among these and other articles covering Jagger during this period: Mary Campbell, "Jagger Talks of Latest Tour," Associated Press, May 29, 1975; John Rockwell, "The Pragmatic Jagger: Planning Stones Onslaught," *The New York Times*, May 15, 1975; Steve Lawrence, "Moving Mick Jagger," the *New York Post*, June 7, 1975; Marian McEvoy, "Mick Rolls On," *Women's Wear Daily*, June 24, 1975; Bill Hagerty, "Diamond Studded Stone," *The Daily Mirror*, April 27, 1976; Roderick Gilchrist, "Mick and Marsha End Baby Row," *The Daily Mail*, February 12, 1975; "Mick Jagger 'Had Drug Overdose,' " *The Evening Standard*, February 27, 1976; Bob Hart, "Jaggernauts!," *The Sun*, April 29, 1976.

CHAPTER 15

Among interview subjects: Liz Derringer, Keith Altham, Earl McGrath, Halston, Roy Cohn, Marvin Mitchelson, Victor Bockris, Bobby Zarem, Pat Hackett, Daniel Stewart, Kenny Valente, Lee Wohlfert, and Russell Turiak.

Articles include: Ian Ball, "Canada Agog over Stones and Mrs. Trudeau," *The Daily Telegraph*, March 10, 1977; James Johnson, " 'Mrs. Trudeau? I Wouldn't Go Near Her with a Barge Pole,' " *The Evening Standard*, September 14, 1977; David Wigg, "Jagger: Putting the Record Straight," *The Daily Express*, September 14, 1977; Robin Denselow, "People Like Bing Crosby . . . ," *The Guardian*, October 10, 1977; David Felton, "Absolute, Ultimate Fantasy," *The Washington Post*, June 16, 1978; Gordon Burn, "Mick Jagger Holds Court in New York," *The Sunday Times* (London), June 25, 1978; Pauline McLeod, "Money, Women and Me!," *The Daily Mirror*, August 29, 1978; Jonathan Cott, "Mick Jagger: The King Bee Talks About Rock's Longest Running Soap Opera," *Rolling Stone* (June 29, 1978); "Jaggers Divorced," *The New York Times*, November 3, 1979; Marsha Hunt, "Mick Made Me Beg for Money," *The London Star*, October 14, 1986; Mick Jagger, "Bianca and Me!," *The Sun*, June 23, 1980; Marsha Hunt, "Mick, Money and Our Child," *The Daily Mirror*, October 24, 1986. Again, court documents generated in Los Angeles and in London pertaining to the divorce of Mick and Bianca were used as background material for this chapter.

CHAPTER 16

Among those interviewed: Liz Derringer, Bebe Buell, Earl McGrath, May Pang, Trevor Churchill, David McGough, Russell Turiak, Arthur Collins, Gore Vidal, Joanne Bobrowicz, Erica Bell, Baird Jones, Victor Bockris, Marvin Mitchelson, and Wendy Leigh.

Articles and other published materials include: Liz Derringer, "Mick Jagger: The Man Behind the Mascara," *High Times* (June 1980); "Mick Jagger Is Rolling Again as the Stones 'Tattoo' the U.S.," *People* (October 12, 1981); Maureen Cleave, "Confessions of a Dilettante Englishman," *The Observer*, August 30, 1981; Robert Palmer, "The Rolling Stones: Once Adolescent, They've Grown Up," *The New York Times* August 26, 1981; "Never Too Old to Rock and Roll: Mick and the Stones Storm Again," *Life* (November 1981); Carl Arrington, "Mr. Rolling Stone Finds Sweet Satisfaction with Rock's Richest Tour Ever," *People* (Decmeber 28, 1981); "Mick Jagger: Cocktails with Jerry Hall, Charlie Watts, Bob Colacello & Andy Warhol," *Interview* (August 1981); "What I Want from a Woman by Mick Jagger," as told to Rick Sky, *The London Daily Star*, June 16, 1982; "Mick Jagger and Model Jerry Hall Call It Quits," *People* (November 22, 1982). Court transcripts and affidavits regarding the divorce case of Bianca and Michael Philip Jagger (Case No. D 985 336).

CHAPTERS 17 AND 18

Interviews include: Angela Bowie, Kevin Kahn, Malcolm Forbes, Rita Jenrette, Barbara Levine, Susan Crimp, Bobby Zarem, Jouet Moreau, Stephanie Mansfield, Patricia Lawford, Fred Hauptfuhrer, Bebe Buell, Liz Derringer, and April Todd.

Among articles consulted: Vincent Coppola with Nancy Cooper, "Rock Grows Up," *Newsweek* (December 19, 1983); "Why I Want Babies with Jerry—by Jagger," *The Sun*, July 3, 1983; Pete Townshend, "Jagger: A Butterfly Reaches 40," *The Times* (of London) July 25, 1983; Lisa Robinson, "Mick Jagger," *Interview* (February 1985); Jay McInerney, "Jagger-Watching," *Esquire* (May 1985); Christopher Connelly, "Stepping Out," *Rolling Stone* (February 14, 1985); Bill Flanagan, "Mick Musically," *Musician Magazine* (April 1985); Susan Toepfer, "Mick Jagger Fumes," *People* (June 13, 1985); Jay Cocks, "Roll Them Bones," *Time* (September 4, 1989); David Gates, "The Stones Start It Up," *Newsweek* (September 11, 1989); Peter Newcomb, "Satisfaction Guaranteed," *Forbes* (October 2, 1989); Robin Eggar, "Not Fade Away," *Us* (November 27, 1989); Anthony De-

Curtis, "The Rolling Stones: Artists of the Year," *Rolling Stone* (March 8, 1990); Stephanie Mansfield, "The Jagger Mystique," *Vogue* (May 1991); Stephen Schiff, "Mick's Moves," *Vanity Fair* (February 1992); "Hey Mick Get Offa Her Cloud!," *People* (August 17, 1992); Edna Gundersen, "Jagger's Hard Rock Life," *USA Today*, February 9, 1993.

Bibliography

Aftel, Mandy. *Death of a Rolling Stone*. Sidgwick & Jackson, 1982.

Aldridge, John. *Satisfaction*. Proteus Publishing, 1984.

Balfour, Victoria. *Rock Wives*. William Morrow, 1986.

Bockris, Victor. *Keith Richards*. Poseidon Press, 1992.

————. *The Life and Death of Andy Warhol*. Bantam, 1989.

Booth. Stanley. *The True Adventures of the Rolling Stones*. Sphere Books Ltd., 1985.

Bowie, Angela, with Patrick Carr. *Backstage Passes*. G. P. Putnam's Sons, 1993.

Cohn, Nik. *Rock: From the Beginning*. Stein and Day, 1969.

Coleman, Ray. *Clapton!* Warner, 1985.

Cooper, Michael. *Blinds and Shutters*. Genesis, 1990.

Dalton, David. *The Rolling Stones*. Rogner & Bernhard, 1981.

Dannen, Fredric. *Hit Men*. Random House, 1990.

Danziger, Danny. *Eton Voices*. Viking, 1988.

Des Barres, Pamela. *I'm with the Band*. William Morrow, 1987.

Edwards, Henry, and Tony Zanetta. *Stardust: The David Bowie Story*. McGraw-Hill, 1986.

Elliott, Martin. *The Rolling Stones: The Complete Recording Sessions*. Blandford, 1990.

Flippo, Chet. *On the Road with the Rolling Stones*. Doubleday, 1985.

Frame, Pete. *Rock Family Trees*. Omnibus Press, 1980.

Goodman, Pete. *Our Own Story by The Rolling Stones*. Bantam, 1965.

Graham, Bill, and Robert Greenfield. *Bill Graham Presents*. Doubleday, 1992.

Greenfield, Robert. *S.T.P.: A Journey Through America with the Rolling Stones*. Dutton, 1974.

Hackett, Pat, ed. *The Andy Warhol Diaries*. Warner, 1989.

Hall, Jerry, and Christopher Hemphill. *Jerry Hall's Tall Tales*. Pocket Books, 1985.

Hoffman, Dezo. *The Rolling Stones*. Vermillion, 1984.

Holt, Georgia, and Phyllis Quinn with Sue Russell. *Star Mothers*. Simon and Schuster, 1988.

Hotchner, A. E. *Blown Away: The Rolling Stones and the Death of the Sixties*. Simon and Schuster, 1990.

Hunt, Marsha. *Real Life*. Chatto & Windus, 1986.

Kamin, Philip, and James Karnbach. *The Rolling Stones in Europe*. Beaufort Books, 1983.

Mankowitz, Gered. *Satisfaction*. St. Martin's Press, 1984.

Miles, Barry. *Mick Jagger in His Own Words*. Omnibus, 1982.

Norman, Philip. *Symphony for the Devil: The Rolling Stones Story*. Linden Press, 1984.

Pang, May, and Henry Edwards. *Loving John*. Warner, 1983.

Phillips, Julia. *You'll Never Eat Lunch in This Town Again*. Signet, 1992.

Rivera, Geraldo, with Daniel Paisner. *Exposing Myself*. Bantam, 1991.

Rolling Stone magazine, *The Rolling Stones*. Straight Arrow, 1975.

———. *The Rolling Stone Interviews*. Rolling Stone Press, 1981.

Sanchez, Tony. *Up and Down with the Rolling Stones*. William Morrow, 1979.

Scaduto, Tony. *Mick Jagger: Everybody's Lucifer*. David McKay, 1974.

Schofield, Carey. *Jagger*. Beaufort Books, 1985.

Taraborrelli, J. Randy. *Michael Jackson: The Magic and the Madness*. Carol Publishing, 1991.

Turner, Tina, and Kurt Loder. *I, Tina*. William Morrow, 1986.

Wheen, Francis. *Tom Driberg: His Life and Indiscretions*. Pan, 1990.

Wyman, Bill, with Ray Coleman. *Stone Alone*. Viking Penguin, 1991.

Photo Credits

1. © Rex Features Ltd.
2. © Christopher Andersen
3. © Christopher Andersen
4. © Rex Features Ltd.
5. © Archive Photos
6. Gered Mankowitz © Bowstir Ltd.
7. Gered Mankowitz © Bowstir Ltd.
8. Fred Bauman © Globe Photos
9. © Rex Features Ltd.
10. Gered Mankowitz © Bowstir Ltd.
11. © Topham/The Image Works
12. © Cecil Beaton/Camera Press London
13. Liaison Agency Inc.
14. © Syndication International Ltd.
15. © Rex Features Ltd.
16. © Syndication International Ltd.
17. © Popperfoto
18. © Rex Features Ltd.
19. © Topham/The Image Works
20. © AP/Wide World Photos
21. © Rex Features Ltd.
22. © United Artists Corporation
23. © Beth Sunflower
24. Jens Glargard © Rex Features Syndicate
25. G. Sipahioglu © Liaison Agency
26. Gamma
27. © Rex Features Ltd.
28. © Archive Photos
29. © Pictorial Press
30. © Retna Ltd.
31. © Syndication International Ltd.
32. © Rex Features Ltd.
33. © Michael Putland/Retna Ltd.
34. © Michael Putland/Retna Ltd.
35. Alan Davidson © Globe Photos
36. © Rex Features Ltd.
37. © Michael Putland/Retna Ltd.
38. © Rex Features Ltd.
39. © Rex Features Ltd.

40. © Michael Putland/Retna Ltd.
41. © Martin Benjamin/The Image Works
42. © Ann Clifford/DMI
43. © David McGough/DMI
44. © David McGough/DMI
45. © David McGough/DMI
46. © AP/Wide World Photos
47. © Syndication International Ltd.
48. © David McGough/DMI
49. © David McGough/DMI
50. © Syndication International Ltd.
51. © Malcolm Heywood/Retna Ltd.
52. © Rex Features Ltd.
53. David Parker/© Alpha
54. Richard Young/© Rex Features Ltd.
55. © Rex Features Ltd.
56. © David McGough/DMI
57. ©Albert Ferreira/DMI
58. David Gerrard/Spooner/Gamma
59. © Michael Putland/Retna Ltd.
60. © Russell C. Turiak
61. © Kopel/Stills/Retna Ltd.
62. © Movie Star News
63. © David McGough/DMI
64. © Syndication International Ltd.

Chapter number 1. © Joseph Modica
Chapter numbers 2, 3, 4, 5, 6, 7, 8, 9, 0. Photofest

Index